DREAM STATES

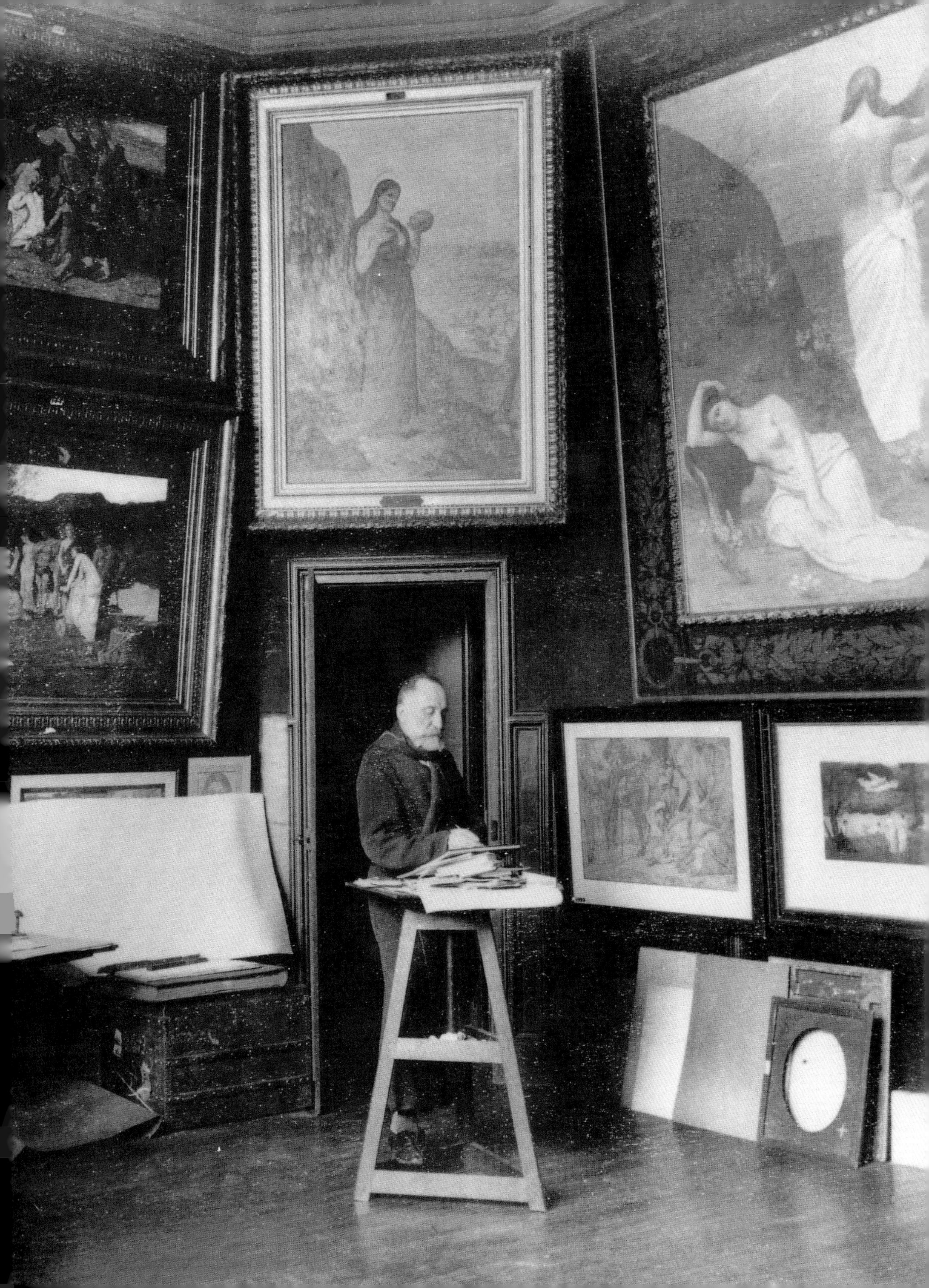

DREAM STATES

Puvis de Chavannes, Modernism, and the Fantasy of France

Jennifer L. Shaw

YALE UNIVERSITY PRESS | NEW HAVEN AND LONDON

Frontispiece: Pierre Puvis de Chavannes in his Place Pigalle studio, ca. 1884–87

Publication of this book has been aided by a grant from the Millard Meiss Publication Fund of the College Art Association.

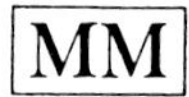

Designed by Daphne Geismar
Set in Electra and Franklin Gothic type by Amy Storm
Printed in China through World Print

Library of Congress Cataloging-in-Publication Data
Shaw, Jennifer Laurie.
Dream states: Puvis de Chavannes, modernism, and the fantasy of France / Jennifer L. Shaw.
p. cm.
Includes bibliographical references and index.
ISBN 0-300-08382-3 (alk. paper)
1. Puvis de Chavannes, Pierre, 1824–1898—Criticism and interpretation.
2. Symbolism in art. 3. National identity in art. I. Title.
ND553.P9 S53 2002
759.4—dc21
2001003130

A catalogue record for this book is available from the British Library.

The paper in this book meets the guidelines for permanence and durability of the Committee on Production Guidelines for Book Longevity of the Council on Library Resources.

10 9 8 7 6 5 4 3 2 1

For John, Emily, and William

CONTENTS

ACKNOWLEDGMENTS

This book began as a doctoral dissertation written at the University of California at Berkeley. The research and writing of that dissertation were supported by grants from the Mellon Foundation, the Georges Lurcy Trust, and the University of California at Berkeley. The transformation of the dissertation into a book was supported by an Andrew W. Mellon Postdoctoral Fellowship in the Humanities at Stanford University. I am grateful to the members of the Department of Art at Stanford University for their support and feedback while I held this fellowship. The College Art Association provided a generous grant to help with the production of the book. The School of Arts and Humanities, Sonoma State University, helped cover costs of the black and white illustrations. Thanks are due to William Babula, Dean.

Portions of this book have appeared in preliminary form. A part of Chapter 2 appeared as "The Wandering Gaze: Modernism, Subjectivity and the Art of Pierre Puvis de Chavannes," in Barbara Cooper and Mary Donaldson-Evans, eds., *Moving Forward, Holding Fast: The Dynamics of Nineteenth-Century French Culture* (Amsterdam: Rodopi: 1997). A portion of Chapter 5 and portions of the introduction and conclusion were published in "Imagining the Motherland: Puvis de Chavannes, Modernism, and the Fantasy of France," *Art Bulletin* (December 1997).

While I was in France, members of the Puvis de Chavannes family offered to share material from the Puvis de Chavannes estate with me. I am also grateful for the help I received during my research in France from the staffs of the Bibliothèque Nationale, the Bibliothèque Historique de la Ville de Paris, the Service de la Documentation at the Musée d'Orsay, the Hôtel de Ville de Paris, and the Service de la Documentation at the Musée des Beaux-Arts, Lyons. The Department of European Paintings and the Department of Drawings at the Metropolitan Museum of Art in New York, the Boston Public Library, and the Fogg Museum of Art allowed me to consult their archives and to look at works that were not on public view. Teri Hensick at the Fogg Museum of Art was particularly helpful. I would also like to thank Aimée Brown Price for sharing some of her vast knowledge of

Puvis de Chavannes with me, and Margaret Werth for allowing me to read her work on Puvis de Chavannes when we were both at the dissertation-writing stage.

Thanks are due to the editors at Yale University Press: Judy Metro, who so enthusiastically took this project on, and Patricia Fidler, who saw it through to completion. Mary Pasti edited the manuscript, and John Long helped secure the images reproduced here.

Many who read and discussed my work at various stages gave me valuable feedback. They include Svetlana Alpers, Caroline Arscott, Susanna Barrows, Paula Birnbaum, Brigid Doherty, Jacques De Caso, Charlotte Eyerman, Stacy Garfinkel, John House, Melissa Hyde, Christina Kiaer, Antony Lee, Steven Z. Levine, Evelyn Lincoln, Amy Lyford, Richard Meyer, Jeannene Przyblyski, Christopher Riding, Nancy Troy, Kathryn Tuma, and Marcus Verhagen. Amy Lyford and Paula Birnbaum undertook the monstrous task of reading the manuscript in its entirety at a late stage, for which I am extremely grateful.

Special thanks are due to Anne Wagner, Carol Armstrong, and T. J. Clark. Anne Wagner's insightful feedback on the conceptualization of this project and her attention to my career more generally have been invaluable. Carol Armstrong has supported my academic career as an art historian from my undergraduate days until now and continues to offer not only helpful criticism but inspiration and friendship, for which I will be forever grateful. This project was conceived while I was working as a graduate student instructor for Timothy J. Clark. He has enthusiastically and painstakingly seen it through from beginning to end. For his constant encouragement, our many discussions, the close readings he gave to this manuscript at the dissertation stage, and his brilliant scholarship, which provided the foundation for my own work, I cannot thank him enough.

Finally, I want to thank those who have nurtured the project from other vantage points: the many close friends and family members who have provided moral support as I birthed not only this book but my beloved Emily and William; my mother and father, who have each in their own way made it possible to write this book; and, most of all, John Arnold, who has been a constant source of encouragement, enablement, strength, and love throughout the ten years of this project, and Emily Margaret and William Francis Arnold, who are my inspiration and my joy.

INTRODUCTION

What Rembrandt is to Holland, Puvis de Chavannes will be to France—he is OURS. Thanks to his "thusness," our art will become national again. ALPHONSE GERMAIN

Pierre Puvis de Chavannes occupied a remarkable place in the culture of late nineteenth-century France. The epigraphs in this book give some sense of both the admiration he elicited and the political and aesthetic context into which his art must be set if we are fully to understand its significance. His murals decorated public buildings throughout France—museums in Amiens, Rouen, and Lyons, as well as the Sorbonne University and the city hall in Paris. More than the work of any other public painter, Puvis's murals were imagined to embody a vision of France and to impart a sense of Frenchness—through images of characteristic regions, allegories of the French heritage, or evocations of the nation as an embracing motherland.

Picturing France to itself was a particularly difficult task at the end of the nineteenth century, when new forms of political and cultural polarization marked French culture. Syndicalism emerged on the Left, and extreme forms of exclusionary nationalism on the Right. The consolidation of trade unionism in the form of the Conféderation Générale du Travail was counterbalanced by the codification of the racist and anti-Semitic nationalism that would become Action Française. Anarchist bombs exploded in Paris, and the Dreyfus Affair began. When the extreme Right and Left both returned to parliamentary political power in the mid-1880s, the division in society was not just a matter of political factions disagreeing on matters of policy.[1] It went much deeper. Along with opposing positions went very different conceptions of what Frenchness was. There was disagreement about which regions best represented France and which historical moments were authentically French. Those on the Right, for example, believed that the French Revolution of 1789 was an aberration and had put the country on the wrong course. Republicanism seemed to them to be a form of government at war with the true nature of France. Others saw the establishment of the Republic as the founding moment of the nation, the beginning of a tradition of democracy that defined Frenchness itself. During this period, the republican government did its best to instill its own version of Frenchness in the citizens of France. The centennial celebration of the French Revolution (which coincided with the Paris International

Exposition in 1889) and the reconstruction and decoration of the Hôtel de Ville in Paris were among the grand gestures of this ideological strategy. The state commissioned work by Puvis de Chavannes on both occasions.[2]

In this climate of disagreement and uncertainty the need for a national idiom was stronger than ever before. Yet at this very moment the tradition of cultural production, which was so central to France's identity, was also in a state of upheaval. The visual and literary arts were polarized in ways that had complex and often contradictory relations to the politics of the time. There was little agreement, even within self-consciously "advanced" artistic circles, about the direction that painting should take. Naturalism was out of fashion, but so, too, were the old academic paradigms of idealization and transcendence. The French tradition of high art based in classicism, a tradition heretofore dominated by the Academy, seemed to have been lost along with old certainties about France's identity. These paradigms were still promoted, however, by a legion of conservative critics with legitimist leanings. Modernist avant-gardes were moving from the margins to the center of the cultural scene. The development of a dealer-critic system, combined with a relaxation of publishing laws, led to the proliferation of avant-garde practices and the promotion of individual artists and styles by critics.[3] Artists and critics had strong opinions about the proper direction for art and the proper relation between culture and politics, but even within particular avant-garde circles there were few simple correspondences between aesthetic and political positions. Critics who championed Symbolist form, for instance, could hail either from the extreme Left or from the neo-Christian Right.[4]

What is particularly striking about this moment for our purposes, however, is that virtually all of the artists and critics of the day had great admiration for Pierre Puvis de Chavannes. His admirers hailed from the political Right, Left, and Center, from the avant-garde, the Academy, and the state. Almost everyone agreed that Puvis de Chavannes was France's greatest national painter. In a letter to Paul Gauguin, the dramatist August Strindberg described Puvis's status among the avant-garde in the mid-1880s: "People did not want to hear any more talk about schools and tendencies. Liberty was now the rallying cry. . . . However, . . . one name was pronounced with admiration by all: that of Puvis de Chavannes."[5]

Puvis came to this position of prominence slowly. It was not until 1879 that the artist, who had already been exhibiting his work for more than twenty years, drew widespread attention at the Salon. At that time, critical reaction to such easel paintings as *Young Girls by the Seashore* (1879) and *Poor Fisherman* (1881) and such murals as *Ludus pro Patria* (1882) was characterized by a combination of fascination and dumbfoundedness. His paintings were often deemed to be incomprehensible. They claimed status as high art in size and subject matter, yet flouted academic convention. Puvis's drawing seemed to distort rather than idealize his figures. His canvases were dominated by large expanses of color and had a rough, plastery look. Correct drawing, careful modeling, distinctions between figure and ground, respect for perspective—he put all of these under pressure in murals and easel paintings alike. Puvis had not been trained at the Ecole des Beaux-Arts. For some, the lack of academic correctness in his work added up to a naive incompetence. For others, it was the sign of a valuable poeticism. By the 1890s, only the most conservative critics dismissed his work as incompetent, however. Almost everyone was willing to agree that Puvis's work was both strange and powerful and that his pictorial mode brought something to the province of high art that promised an alternative to outworn academic conventions even as it aimed to occupy the place of the ideal.

Puvis painted his most important murals during a time when critics regularly complained that the grand French tradition of public decoration, which aimed to edify and educate the collectivity, was dying out. Alphonse Germain was among a legion of critics who feared the death of a national idiom and what that might mean for French culture as a whole, but who saw a glimmer of hope in the work of Puvis de Chavannes. In speaking of Puvis's "thusness" (*ipséisme*), Germain was referring to Puvis's style—to its particularity, its power, and its absolute difference from anything else on offer in the 1890s. Puvis's unique pictorial mode, Germain suggested, would reinvigorate the tradition and in doing so would give France back its sense of itself. The republican critic André Michel concurred with Germain, saying that Puvis had "brought to French art, at a critical hour in its history, the eloquence for which it had the greatest need."[6] Puvis's pictorial mode injected new life into the tradition of "idealism" in public decoration, which was, by the late nineteenth century, dominated by predictable and sometimes even crass academicism. With his uniquely modern form of high art Puvis had, in the words of Michel, "saved idealism, which had fallen into disrepute, less as a result of attacks from its enemies, than by the unintelligent and sterile formalism of its followers and official representatives."[7] Both Puvis's painterly style and his ambition to reclaim and rejuvenate the terrain of high art made his approach quite distinct from the avant-garde practices (such as Impressionism and Neoimpressionism) that had come to prominence in the 1880s and 1890s. Still, even the most advanced members of the avant-garde—Denis, Gauguin, Seurat, Toulouse-Lautrec, and, later, Matisse and Picasso—admired and drew from his work.[8]

Puvis de Chavannes's murals restored eloquence to French public painting. However—and this is the key to understanding the artist's oeuvre—the roots of this eloquence lay in its silences. Rather than specifying France at the risk of annulling one or another conception of France, Puvis's murals left the work of completing those pictures to their viewers. In his murals the formal qualities we now usually associate with the avant-garde—large flat areas of color and generalized, disjunctive forms that defied the conventional academic languages of high art—were put to the task of picturing France. No other artist of the period brought together these two elements—the tradition of grand public art and modernist form. In this book I elucidate the structures of beholding provoked by Puvis's painterly mode by combining close attention to the murals themselves with analysis of descriptions of them by contemporary critics. Examining Puvis's work provides new insight into debates about modernism and tradition in art by setting those debates in an overtly political context.

PUVIS DE CHAVANNES AND MODERNISM

When Maurice Denis famously proclaimed, "Before it is a battlehorse, a nude woman, or an anecdote, a painting is a flat surface covered with colors arranged in a certain order," he had Puvis de Chavannes's work in mind. This statement appeared in "Definition of Neotraditionism," an essay in which Denis attempted to describe the ways that modern painterly form might rejuvenate the tradition of French art. Denis's dictum was followed by a parody of an audience straining to see Puvis's easel painting *Poor Fisherman* (1881) as trompe l'oeil: "I have known young men who devote themselves to exhausting gymnastics of the optic nerve in order to see trompe l'oeil in *Poor Fisherman*" (fig. 1). Denis's parody was meant to be both scathing and ironic. How strange it would be, he suggested, if the world actually looked like this: the landscape a surface in shades of muddy bluish gray, patterned by alternating triangles of land and water; the bodies that inhabit it grotesquely distorted and generalized, cut to pieces by shadows, stretched into contortions by line. And how myopic an audience who, despite Puvis's extreme emphasis on painterly materiality and painterly form, attempted to look past the paint as through a window onto "the real." Instead of showing us a scene that could be confused with a slice of life, Denis implied, the message of the painting, and its power, derived from the suggestiveness of its visual form.[9] Denis might have joked just as easily about another of Puvis's easel paintings, *Young Girls by the Seashore* (1879), or about any of the murals we will discuss in later chapters (fig. 2).

That Denis could mock Puvis's audience in this way indicates that by 1890, when Denis wrote his essay, the characteristics of Puvis's style were well known and had already begun to be associated with certain kinds of modernism in painting—despite the differences between Puvis's work and (to use T. J. Clark's phrase)

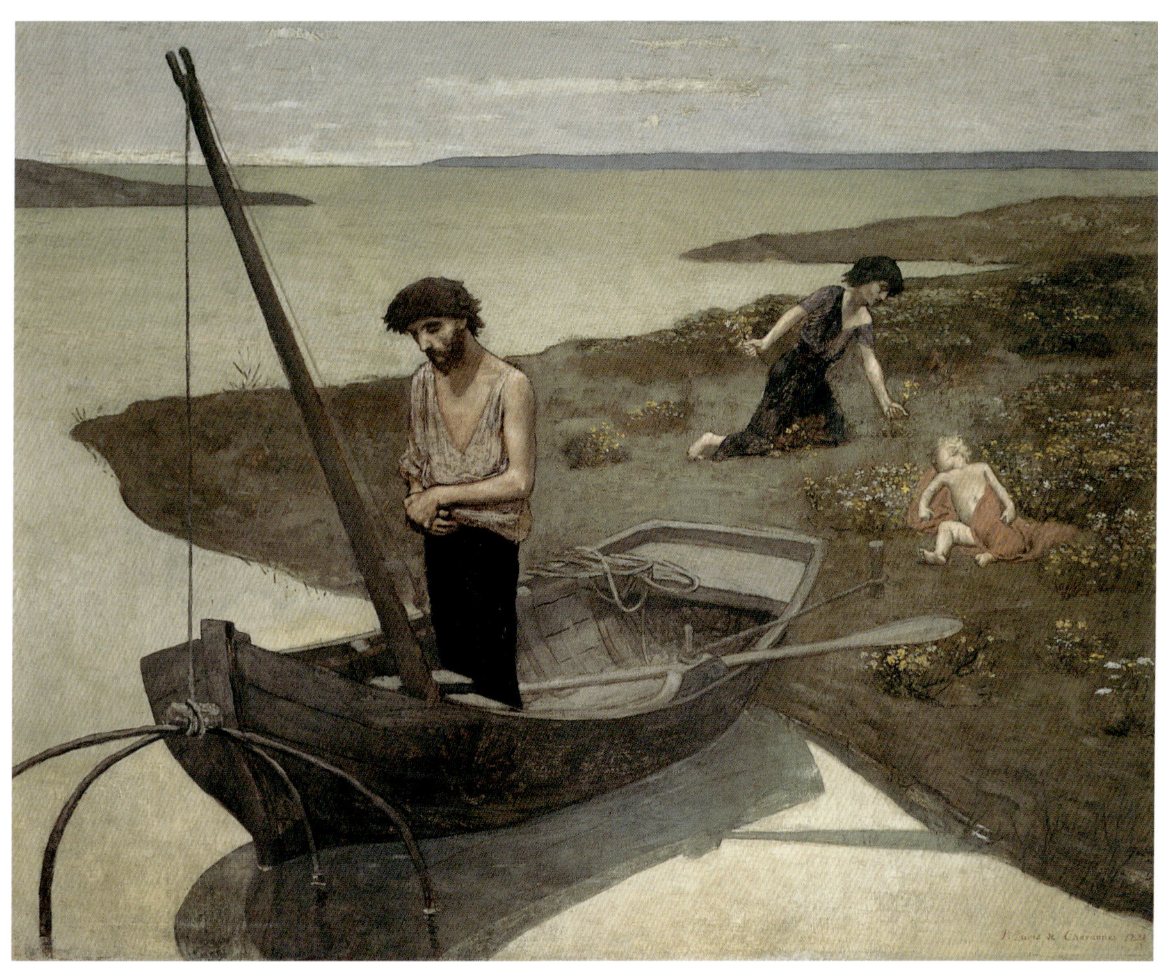

1
Pierre Puvis de Chavannes,
Poor Fisherman, 1881.
Oil on canvas, 61 1/2 x 76 in.
(156 x 193 cm).
Musée d'Orsay, Paris

2
Pierre Puvis de Chavannes,
Young Girls by the Seashore, 1879.
Oil on canvas, 80¾ x 60½ in. (205 x 154 cm). Musée d'Orsay, Paris

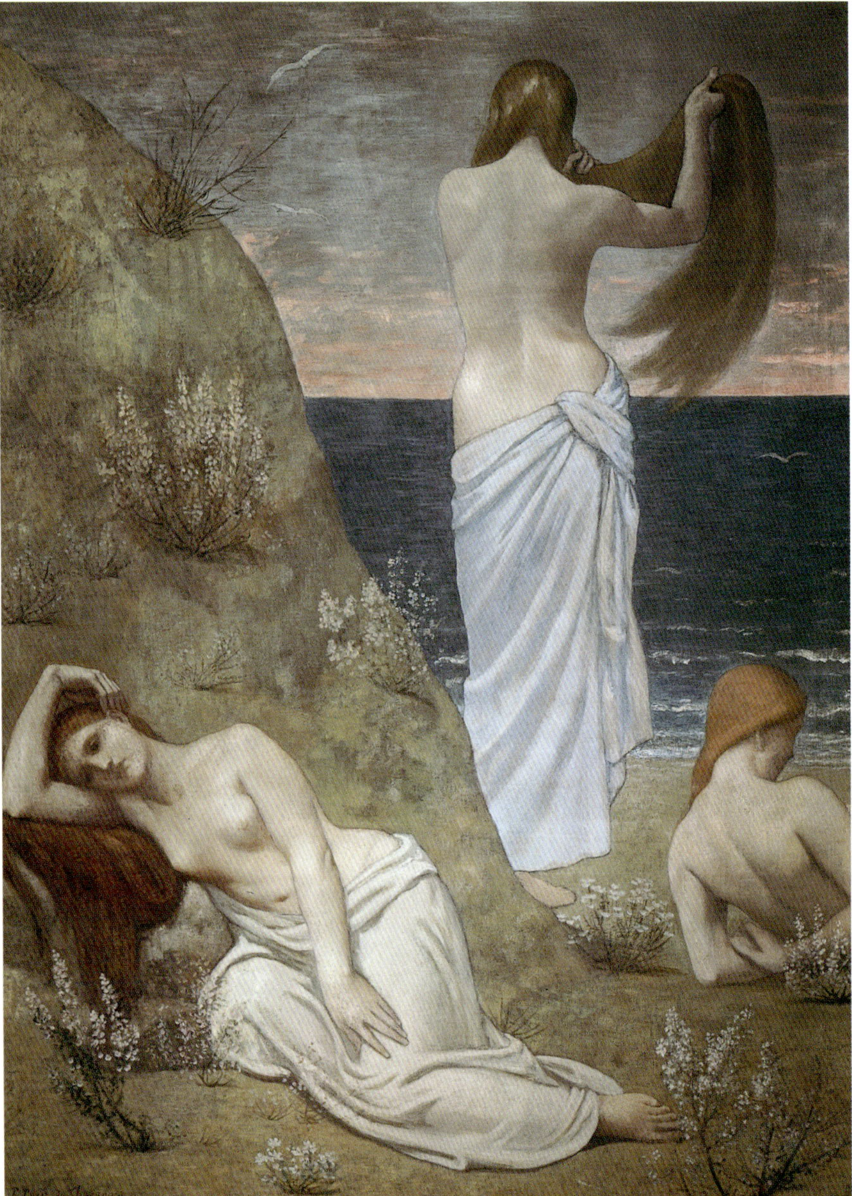

the "painting of modern life," Impressionism. Indeed, many young artists whom we now associate with the most advanced modernist practices—Gauguin, Matisse, Seurat, Picasso—looked directly to Puvis for their inspiration.[10] One salient example is Picasso's blue-period painting *Poor People on the Seashore (The Tragedy)* (1903; fig. 3). The simplified landscape clearly draws on *Young Girls by the Seashore*. The pose of the man is drawn directly from *Poor Fisherman*. Picasso seems to be looking, too, at Puvis's expressive use of line and his limited palette. What he learned from Puvis influenced aspects of Picasso's painting that dominated his blue and rose periods and remained important throughout his oeuvre. Puvis seems to have provided Picasso with the most important example of how an artist could make an emphasis on painterly form to elicit an emotional response from viewers.

Puvis de Chavannes's work was central to nineteenth-century theorizations of modern painting that later gave legitimacy to modernist formalism, specifically, the art historical approach to painting most famously elaborated by Clement Greenberg in the mid-twentieth century. For the late Greenberg and his followers, exploration of the procedures of painterly practice by members of the avant-garde

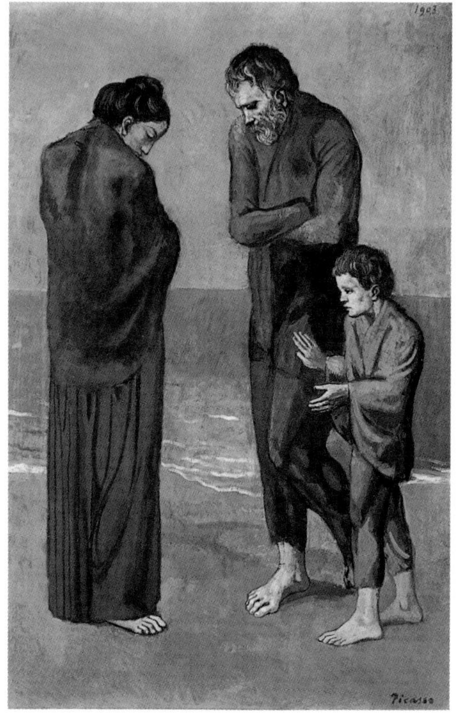

3
Pablo Picasso, *Poor People on the Seashore (The Tragedy)*, 1903. Oil on panel, 41 1/2 x 27 1/4 in. (105.4 x 69 cm). Chester Dale Collection, National Gallery of Art, Washington, D.C.

led to abstraction and "flatness." Painting's true subject matter was painting itself.[11] Maurice Denis's essay "Definition of Neotraditionism" (1890) seems to support the notion that modernism encompassed a body of avant-garde practice that used increasingly abstract form and in doing so brought to the fore the particular qualities of the chosen medium. What is often not acknowledged is that his essay was an attempt to describe the ways "modern" painterly form might rejuvenate the tradition of French art—an attempt, that is, to describe exactly what many thought Puvis de Chavannes's painting was doing.

When we look at Puvis's work in its original context, we see that the characteristics of his painting that Denis was addressing had meaning far beyond the meanings often attributed to formalist abstraction. If we are to understand the origins of what we now call modernism in the practices of painting considered modern by Denis and his contemporaries in the late nineteenth century, our account of modernism is greatly enriched. Rather than implying that a focus on the formal means of making paintings involved the rejection of history, culture, and politics, Puvis's contemporaries saw that the qualities of this abstraction—sensuousness, materiality, indefiniteness of rendering, suggestiveness—themselves had cultural, even political, significance. Puvis's contemporaries described these qualities as modern rather than modernist. Throughout this book, however, I shall refer to them as constituting Puvis's "modernism" because I believe that they are an early example of the kinds of experiments in painting that have, from the early twentieth century on, been referred to as modernist. It is a central claim of mine in this book that close scrutiny of Puvis's work and its place within the wider cultural milieu allows us to enlarge our understanding of modernism while maintaining an interest in its characteristic formalism.[12]

MODERNISM AND THE UNCONSCIOUS

Puvis's paintings were part of a general cultural trend in which the classical goals of order, clarity, unity, hierarchy, and idealization long associated with both literary and visual academicism and tradition were replaced by modes of representation that focused instead on the sensuousness and materiality of the work. Indeed, aesthetics in the 1880s and 1890s were the subject of a widespread debate over the proper direction for representation, a debate that revolved around these terms and encompassed both literary and visual production. The stress in Symbolist poetry on repeated sounds and rhythms, Mallarmé's use of the blank page as a medium, the experiments in increased abstraction carried out by painters of the avant-garde—all of these can be characterized as modernist. They were seen to be modern by Puvis's contemporaries not just because of their self-referentiality but also because of their emphasis on sensuousness and materiality and the tendency of these qualities to generate fantasy in their audiences' minds. The very writers and poets who battled over these terms in the literary realm also wrote and spoke about Puvis's work.[13]

It is true that associating academic practice with order, clarity, idealization, and modernism with sensuousness, materiality, indeterminacy, and fantasy involves an oversimplification of a complex history of representation in which the terms on each side of the opposition often intermix. It would be impossible to trace that entire history here. What is important for our purposes is that in the last decades of the century the dissolution of the Academy, the increased privatization of artistic production, and the developing interest in new psychological paradigms meant that the artistic and literary field was polarized around such oppositions. Looking at the way they played themselves out in the discourse surrounding Puvis's work helps us to understand how modernism itself was conceived at the very moment when its most basic terms were being formulated by people like Maurice Denis.

It is not enough, therefore, to correct the outworn formulas of modernist art history by turning our attention back to the subject matter that formalists have ignored. We must also ask about the social meanings of the formal properties themselves. The ambiguity, materiality, and sensuousness of modernist form and the absence of precise, clear meanings were seen by Puvis's contemporaries to present a particularly powerful challenge to old paradigms of representation that valued idealization and clarity.[14] The problems that modernist form posed for classical paradigms of representation corresponded with, reinforced, indeed were part and parcel of, broader challenges to the notion of the autonomous human subject—a male subject for whom thought and representation had the potential to be transparent to one another. Modernist form was itself intimately linked with a general reconceptualization of human subjectivity that took place with the "discovery of the unconscious," to use Henri Ellenberger's phrase.[15] Along with the discovery of the unconscious came a wholesale reconsideration of structures of human subjectivity—a reconsideration that had profound consequences for contemporary politics and aesthetics and was integral to the development of modernism.[16]

One salient example of this theorization of the unconscious and consequent questioning of the nature of subjectivity is to be found in the popular fascination with hysteria, hypnosis, and "suggestion." The power of suggestion was thought to be especially strong when the subject of suggestion had a weak or nervous personality or was in a state of openness, as in the somnambular state induced by hypnosis. Women were thought to be particularly susceptible owing to their weaker nervous constitutions. There was much debate over whether "normal" men with strong personalities were also subject to the suggestion of others.[17] Although the psychologist Jean-Martin Charcot emphasized that visual receptivity was a characteristic of abnormal or pathological patients—particularly women—that assumption was contested in the 1880s by scholars at the Ecole de Nancy, led by Hippolyte Bernheim. Bernheim's experimentation with hypnosis led to the controversial conclusion that the mental openness often attributed to women and hysterics was characteristic of normal male subjects as well. Bernheim's contention was so hotly contested because it opened up the possibility that the subjectivity of normal males was less autonomous than generally imagined. It opened up, that is to say, a space for the influence of the unconscious in everyday life. By the late 1880s the importance of the unconscious was widely acknowledged. In 1889, Jules Héricourt stated in *Revue Scientifique*: "The unconscious activity of the mind is a scientific truth established beyond any doubt. . . . Even in daily life, our conscious mind remains under the direction of the unconscious."[18] In 1891, Alfred Fouillée summed up the consequences of recent psychological discoveries by asserting that "contemporary psychology has wrested from us the illusion of a bounded, impenetrable, and absolutely autonomous ego."[19]

These new conceptualizations of subjectivity had important consequences for the practice of art. The notion that subjectivity was determined by unconscious forces raised particular questions for those interpreting the increasingly abstract work of modernist painting. To what extent was the understanding of a painting caused by the sensual appeal of forms and colors rather than the intellectual appeal of conventional tropes? To what degree was a viewer's belief in a painting's message the product of an address to unconscious desires and fantasies rather than the result of an address to the rational mind? At least some theoreticians thought they had the answer. As the republican social philosopher and poet Jean-Marie Guyau put it, "There is no aesthetic emotion that does not awaken in us a multitude of desires and needs that are more or less unconscious."[20] The philosopher Henri Bergson argued that art and hypnosis depended on analogous psychological mechanisms for their power. These are just two examples of the widespread intermixing of contemporary aesthetics with emerging theories of the unconscious. New understandings of subjectivity brought with them reconceptualizations of the relationship between the viewing subject and the work of art that were integral to the formulation of the aesthetics of both visual and literary modernism.

This emphasis on the unconscious was most clearly signaled in relation to Puvis de Chavannes's murals by critics' repeated claims that the artist's paintings were like dreams. But why would the French state want to put indistinct and sensuous "dreams" on the walls of its public buildings rather than straightforward, legible allegories?[21] Why would the solution to the stagnation of public art in the hands of academic practitioners be found in an artist whose work replaced the clarity and transcendence of the academic mode with a peculiar form of modernism that drew on the unconscious?

Ironically, fears about the end of public art in France (like those expressed by Germain and Michel) emerged most strongly at the very moment when the state was commissioning more public decoration than ever before. Much republican-sponsored public art, however, seemed to relinquish the traditional task of education in favor of offering pure decorative pleasure.[22] Puvis de Chavannes's murals stand apart from those large-scale public decorations that imitated the styles of market-oriented easel paintings, as well as from murals that held to the rules of academic correctness. Because his murals combined the goal of education with a formal mode that straddled modernism and high, public, educational art, they provided a site where the social consequences of the address to the unconscious found in modernist abstraction could be explicitly theorized and debated. The enthusiasm for Puvis's work—the belief that his murals provided the best hope for a continuing tradition of high art in public decoration—derived from the ways his paintings mobilized individual subjectivity and personal fantasy for the purpose of public edification. In his murals Puvis de Chavannes used large flat areas of color, rhythmic composition, and suggestive subject matter to appeal as if in a dream to the individual subjectivities and feelings of viewers. He attempted to teach by appealing to the unconscious—to the deepest levels of subjectivity—rather than to convince on an intellectual level using the language of conventional tropes. By commissioning work from Puvis de Chavannes, the state attempted to forge a new aesthetic for public decoration that would instill, through individual fantasy, a sense of collective identity in the viewing public—an aesthetic that would draw people together by encouraging simultaneous dreams of France.

What, then, were the structure and the content of the dreams that Puvis offered to his viewers? Such questions lie at the heart of this book.

Throughout this book, we are met with critical reactions to Puvis's murals in which femininity is interwoven with modernism and national fantasy. These interconnections were part of a wider sense that subjectivity itself was significantly determined by unconscious processes of mind. Thus, structures that had associations with the feminine were now attributed to male subjects. Ironically, despite Puvis's status as one of the *grands hommes* of France, his work ultimately contributed to a destabilization of traditional notions of French masculinity. This was perhaps the aspect of Puvis's modernism that was most threatening to conservative critics. Furthermore, the fantasies of nation conjured up by Puvis de Chavannes's work drew upon individual fantasies of maternal origins. If the power of Puvis's work came, at least in part, from its invocation of maternal fantasy, this suggests that his murals participated in a more general shift away from the alignment of Frenchness and male fraternity, which had characterized France since the Revolution of 1789, in favor of imagining France as mother.[23]

The artist and his murals were written about incessantly in the last decades of the nineteenth century, and the rhetoric that surrounded his work was always overdetermined. To write about Puvis de Chavannes's painting was also to write about much more than an individual artist or work. It was to explore larger questions of modernism and tradition; it was to examine the relations between fantasy, human subjectivity, and gender; and it was to attempt to define Frenchness itself.

1

HIGH ART'S OTHER BODY

In the 1880s, when Puvis de Chavanne's two most famous easel paintings were exhibited, the art world was only beginning to be acquainted with his mature style. What exactly were the characteristics of Puvis's paintings? And why were they associated with modernity? Looking at Puvis's two best-known easel paintings, *Young Girls by the Seashore* (see fig. 2) and *Poor Fisherman* (see fig. 1), will help us understand both what distinguished his work and why it was associated with modernity despite the seemingly traditional subject matter and despite Puvis's clear bid to offer a form of high art. Emile Cardon's description of *Poor Fisherman* is representative of many of the responses that these paintings elicited when they were first displayed at the Salon: "It has, as always, the privilege of leaving no one indifferent; it has an enigmatic side that escapes most people, something strange that surprises. . . . All that I know is that it is imprinted with an irresistible and poignant poetry to which one submits and which escapes all analysis and reason. Try, if you will, to explain the sensation it elicits; I, for my part, give up and content myself with declaring that the impression has been deeply felt. For me, it is quite a poem."[1] This passage is characterized by the kind of rhetoric that is found over and over again in response to Puvis's work.[2] The painting is "enigmatic," it "surprises," it "escapes all analysis and reason" and cannot be explained; yet despite its inscrutability it is "irresistible and poignant," a matter of "sensation," offering a "deeply felt" impression. The strangeness of the painting both bemuses and attracts this critic. He is drawn to it, but knows not why. "Poetry" is the only word in this passage that begins to describe the painting. But even "poetry" signals the allusiveness of the painting, the fact that the most important aspects of *Poor Fisherman* are to be found in what it does not say. The rest of the passage is centered on the way Puvis's work makes Cardon feel, the lack of control he has over that feeling, and the impossibility of understanding concretely what is causing it.

Poor Fisherman was not the first of Puvis's paintings to provoke such a response. Cardon had a similar experience two years earlier when he saw *Young Girls by the Seashore*. He called it "a vague and untranslatable melody, which penetrates the soul and escapes brutal analysis."[3] Here again the sensation given could not quite be translated using the tools of art criticism. It was better described in the language of synethesia—as something like a visual melody that evoked an emotional response. Here was what a picture would feel like if its visual rhythms were translated into sound. Something about Puvis's style caused critics to turn again and again to the language of emotion and sensation.

Sensation had already been associated with modernity through the critical language of Impressionism.[4] In positivist accounts of Impressionism, sensation was a matter of perception. Its ultimate aim was the analysis of nature. In response to Puvis, however, sensation was aligned with feeling and divorced from analysis. The language of modernity was being shifted from the artist's transcription of the external world to the viewer's sensations before the painting. Nor was it only the positivist rhetoric of Impressionism that was being shifted in Cardon's descriptions of Puvis's paintings. The language of academic criticism was also on Cardon's mind.

If *Poor Fisherman* and *Young Girls by the Seashore* were thought to "defy all critical analysis," it was because they did not fit easily into the categories that the critics had at hand. The old tropes of the typical academic vocabulary—the balance of line and color, idealization—did not describe them any better than did the developing vocabulary for Impressionism. These paintings challenged academic and avant-garde forms and the languages developed to describe them. The body lived at the center of this challenge. It was the place where Puvis's pictorial mode took on its most poignant form. And it was the space from which Puvis's audience spoke of the power of his work. Puvis's work demanded that critics replace a vocabulary centered on reason and analysis with one centered on emotional affect and the play of desire. It makes sense, then, to begin by looking at the painting that raises the specter of the body in its most explicit form, the painting that more than any other challenged the genre of the nude: *Young Girls by the Seashore*.[5]

YOUNG GIRLS BY THE SEASHORE

When the republican critic Georges Lafenestre described *Young Girls by the Seashore* in his review of the Salon of 1879, nothing less seemed to be at stake than the future of French painting. The continuing superiority of the French School was, of course, a matter of national pride. Critics had been searching for some time for the artist who would rejuvenate high art in France. Lafenestre, who was part of the state arts administration, thought Puvis de Chavannes was the answer.[6] To make this point Lafenestre compared *Young Girls by the Seashore* to another work displayed at the Salon that year, William Bouguereau's *Birth of Venus* (1879; fig. 4). *The Birth of Venus* was the quintessential nude—a work in the genre that had once been the representative of high art but was now a liability to the French tradition.[7] The study of the body was the basis of the academic training that was meant to serve as the foundation of the practice of high art. The male nude was the staple of training at the Ecole des Beaux-Arts, which prepared young artists to submit history paintings to the Prix de Rome competition.[8] However, the nude as a genre had long meant a depiction of the female body.[9] In academic theory, the female nude was supposed to epitomize the transcendence of high art.

Charles Blanc's aesthetic handbook *Grammaire des Arts du Dessin* helpfully summarizes viewing art as a transcendent experience and makes clear why the female nude was the most important genre for male artistic idealization. Blanc began the *Grammaire* with a narrative of the origins of high art from which he derived the general principles of academic practice. He imagined man in the Garden of Eden, surrounded only by beauty, which, in this case, was quintessentially represented by woman. If woman was initially the representative of beauty, she was

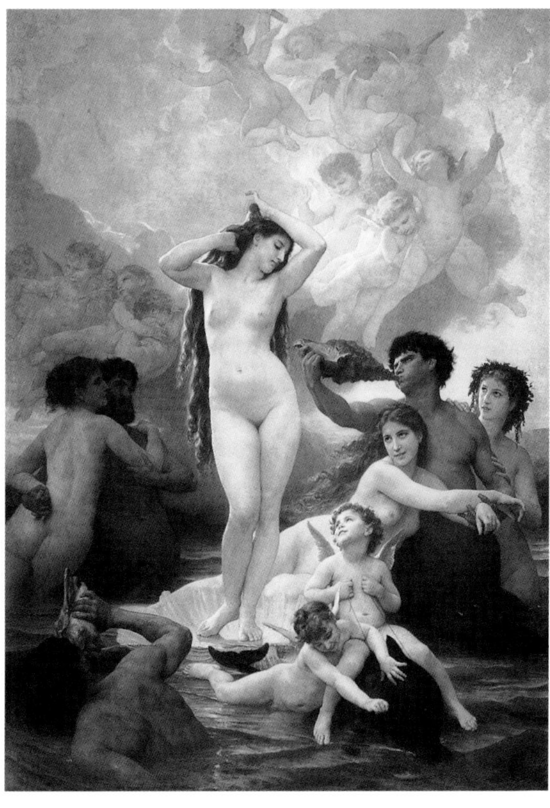

4
William Bouguereau, *The Birth of Venus*, 1879. Oil on canvas, 118 x 85¾ in. (3 x 2.18 m). Musée d'Orsay, Paris

also the cause of its disappearance. By tasting the apple she "pour[ed] catastrophes onto the earth" and caused the "beautiful" to "obscure itself." Thus, woman's original sin, as described by Blanc, was the source of all that is ugly and foul. By eating the apple, she gave rise to the need for art, compelling man to transform what she had defiled back into "the beautiful." Although woman caused the beautiful to disappear, there was still hope that man might regain access to beauty. According to Blanc, "Nature still shows, here and there, beneath the somber veil that covers her, a few traces of her original beauty." This "secret intuition of 'the beautiful,'" said Blanc, is the source of "the ideal." However, only men of genius carried an intuition of beauty, "in an illuminated state." These artists took the transformation of tainted nature back into the beautiful as their life's work. Women, on the other hand, were themselves part of the veiled nature that had to be transformed. In fact, because her uncontrolled act caused the need for art in the first place, woman was the most important site for the transformation of nature back to its original state of grace. This is why, in late nineteenth-century academic theory, the female nude epitomized high art.[10]

In a successful nude, the ideal was to be secured by the artist's transformative elevation of the individual body from its material state to a representation of universal beauty through the perfect balance of drawing and color. The critical language of academic criticism was organized around these gendered tropes. This division was part and parcel of an artist's education at the Ecole des Beaux-Arts, where training was first and foremost based in drawing. The values underlying the terms that the language of academic art criticism employed are again best illustrated by Blanc. Just as the artist was necessarily male in Blanc's schema, "drawing"—"the masculine sex of art"—was his tool for idealization. For painting to carry out its idealizing mission, Blanc stressed, drawing had to be prior to and dominant over color—"the feminine sex" of art: "The union of drawing and color is necessary for engendering painting, just as the union between man and woman is for engendering humanity; but it is necessary that drawing keep its domination over color. If it is otherwise, painting courts its ruin: it will be lost by color just as humanity was lost by Eve."[11]

The dominance of drawing over color was imagined as a kind of sublimation. Color had to be "subdued by drawing just as sentiment must be subdued by reason." Only through this sublimation of the feminine qualities of color and sentiment (which were related to desire) by the masculine powers of drawing and reason (which were thought to be disinterested and transcendent) could painting transcend its own materiality, break its ties to the physical body of the woman being depicted, and deliver the message of beauty—or so went the long-held academic paradigm.

For conservative academic critics at least, the very status of French painting was thought to be secured by the relative elevation of its nudes. Writing for the *Journal des Débats* on the Salon of 1879, the conservative critic Charles Clément stressed the importance of the nude: "We have said it very often and cannot repeat it enough: the nude is the only solid basis of high art, and in-depth study of the human form is the necessary point of departure of all serious artistic education."[12] But for years critics had complained that instead of providing a vehicle for transcendent thought, the nude was a forum for overt sexual provocation. Even Clément found that his exhortations were falling on deaf ears. The paintings on display that year did not represent ideal beauty. Instead, he lamented, "the nudes are in general very weak, and several of them are nothing more than pinups."[13] The presence of so many unsuccessful nudes at the Salon indicated that artists were catering to the debased bourgeois taste for the titillating display of the female body. The use of conventional poses and mythological subject matter was seen to serve as a thin veil for such display.

Furthermore, by 1879 drawing and color were explicitly acknowledged to signify more than themselves, even in the least intelligent criticism. The partisan of drawing was supposed to pursue an act of mind, to elevate the superficial forms of nature to a higher ideal, whereas the partisan of color reveled in its quotidian vulgarity. Drawing remained the academic standard. A painter was a partisan of drawing if he "possesse[d] a style in the special eloquent language; this is the universal language of beauty, of inspired forms and figures invented for education and aesthetic edification."[14] In contrast, the colorist emphasized not only color itself but the facture of paint and the touch of the brush. He remained too tied to the physical world. He employed "various vulgar languages" and represented only that which was available to the "eyes of the profane."[15] Academic critics held onto an idealist formula to promote the superiority of drawing and to rail against the threat posed to French painting by the vulgarities of both academic colorists and the even less academically correct Impressionists.[16]

However, even the proponents of drawing seemed by this point to be engaging in the vulgarities of the quotidian. Bouguereau had become the best-known proponent of line, and he continued to be praised by the most conservative critics. Yet it was generally acknowledged that his work, with its all-too-contemporary-looking nymphs and satyrs, represented a a stultified adherence to academic convention combined with a pandering to the lowest common denominator of public opinion. His *Birth of Venus* was the perfect example. This painting proved that the academic nude, whether it depended on line or color, had come to offer not an imagined transcendent grasp of beauty but an imagined sexual possession of the bodies on display. Indeed, it seemed as if the academic categories themselves had lost their relevance. As a result, many critics were searching for something new that would dismantle such categories and save French painting from disaster.

Lafenestre thought Bouguereau's Venus showed "the triumph of traditional education" but was "not great art, . . . even less living art." He considered that Puvis's *Young Girls by the Seashore* showed a way forward for high art. But here is the surprising part of the story. When Lafenestre described *Young Girls by the Seashore*, he called attention to Puvis's "fearful insufficiencies," "summary drawing," and "hazardous modeling." Bouguereau's Venus, on the other hand, exhibited the "dexterity of his brush."[17] If Puvis's work was full of faults, how could it allay the critics' worries? The answer is to be found in the ways Puvis's paintings revised long-held understandings of the body in high art.

Young Girls by the Seashore proposed a completely different relation between the body and painting from the one entrenched in the academic paradigm of idealization and transcendence. With *Young Girls by the Seashore*, Puvis posed a visual challenge to the academic nude. The subject matter of Puvis's painting was close enough to an academic nude to make that challenge clear. Puvis offered semidraped female figures standing and reclining, seen from front and back, inviting the viewer to imagine all sides of the body. Referring to the standing figure in the painting, the republican critic Louis de Fourcaud identified an iconography of Venus that had been established over decades of academic practice: "Venus Astarte . . . twisting her hair."[18] This was the same pose Bouguereau chose for his Venus. But Bouguereau's Venus takes the typical position, seen from the front, eyes averted, body laid out in a careful *contrapposto* that made visible her breasts and just enough of her genitals, whereas Puvis reverses it. His Venus turns away from the viewer, denying the expected access to the body. Bouguereau's Venus is given skin that is delicately smooth, hair that falls gently in ringlets over her back, and a hand that touches the hair in a caress. Bouguereau uses drawing and modeling to correct the imperfections of a natural body but leaves enough detail in the nipples and a hint of pubic hair to allow for the viewer's titillation.

Puvis, on the other hand, leaves out these details. Yet he does not idealize in the traditional way. His canvas has a rough texture that calls attention to its materiality without making specific brush strokes visible. In Puvis's central Venus figure there is little differentiation in texture between skin and hair. Neither his drawing nor his facture give us much help in imagining an idealized woman who is nonetheless available to us. Instead, they call attention to the distortions embedded in the process of getting a three-dimensional object down in two dimensions using the medium of paint—they call attention, that is, to processes of painting. In the central figure, for example, the viewer's eye moves from the absolute flatness of her cutout foot, through statuesque drapery, and up the heavily contoured hip and side to the more strongly modeled musculature of the arm and hand gripping her hair. The arm looks more like the arm of an athlete than that of a Venus. Puvis's drawing exaggerates the harshness of the figure, becoming more pronounced where the hands grip the hair. Thus, in the place where in Bouguereau's *Venus* a self-reflexive gesture prompts a fantasy of touch and asks us to imagine flesh upon hair, Puvis emphasizes the distorting qualities of line. Rather than correcting the female form, Puvis's heavily drawn contours seem to have their own logic, which stretches and pulls at the body. Puvis calls attention to the problem of color by muting it and dissociating it from painterly touch. He calls attention to drawing by overemphasizing it. Yet, I would claim, he also prevents drawing from serving to idealize the figure in any conventional way.

The allegiances and aims of an academic master like Bouguereau were easy to tell from his paintings. Critics had no trouble classifying Bouguereau as part of a "school of drawing" which has its roots in Raphael: "Drawing with unending accuracy; marvel of composition; perpetual softness, unsurpassed morbidezza. . . . As for facture, do not look for it anywhere." Bouguereau's *Birth of Venus* demonstrated "the qualities of drawing, the taste for composition and the science of the human body." But Bouguereau—"a man who knows his Raphael by heart and shows it far too much"—was too tied to tradition. He lacked personal inspiration; his manner was "facile" and "agreeable" and "owe[d] everything to the past." Bouguereau had transformed this Renaissance style into a glossy and seductive illusionism that transmitted its message to the viewer all too quickly and easily.[19]

Whereas "everyone—the ignorant and the initiated—[could] equally well appreciate M. Bouguereau," even the critics had trouble placing Puvis's work in the existing framework. Puvis was clearly not a colorist. Critics compared *Young Girls* to a cameo and described it as "coloring hidden behind a fog."[20] Neither did Puvis seem to have allegiance to Bouguereau and the school of drawing. In fact, Bouguereau and Puvis were "diametrically opposed." Where Bouguereau idealized the female body in an attempt to give the most seductive and lifelike illusion of the body—to make that body seem available to, even desirous of, the viewer—Puvis did just the opposite. In *Young Girls by the Seashore* the female body was "frankly ugly." "No pretty woman would be tempted to commission her portrait from the author of this bizarre and disobliging painting," said Messire-Jean.[21] Where Bouguereau's Venus was characterized by "dazzling color," "ravishing modeling," and "perfect *morbidezza*," Puvis's drawing was incorrect, and the coloring was "milky," "dull" and "pale." In fact, Bouguereau's manner demonstrated absolute control and mastery of his medium, but Puvis's was tentative, inquiring, and ignorant, "like that of a child" or a primitive.[22] Despite Bouguereau's mastery, he "offered nothing that could be new, not one suggestive form."

Georges Lafenestre, who had hailed Puvis as a potential savior of French painting, thought that Puvis had intentionally taken on the task of reforming high art and, in order to be heard, had "insisted beyond all reason on his principles." If Puvis's desire to reform high art helped to explain the extremity of the artist's painterly means, the strategy was ultimately successful. In the end, Lafenestre's assessment of *Young Girls by the Seashore* focused on the effect the painting had on its viewers. As the critic moved from an assessment of Puvis's purposes to a description of the painting, his language shifted to a poetic evocation of the feeling he was given by the painting, a painting made of "fragments so sweet to the eyes in which a tranquil color harmony so simply allows the expressive contours of the figures to develop themselves."[23] Once someone had experienced Puvis's spare simplicity, he suggested, that person would meet a work like Bouguereau's with revulsion. It was Puvis who offered a future for high art in France, concurred another critic: "We prefer to find this gauge in the asceticism of M. Puvis de Chavannes."[24]

What did it mean to describe Puvis's "asceticism"? On one level, this description points to the way the typical pleasures of the nude are obfuscated by the bodies in Puvis's painting. But it also suggests the power of Puvis's style derived less from what it showed than from what it withheld. The woman on the left reclines, leaning on a rock, in the pose of an odalisque. The sense of easy possession normally promoted by such a figure's self-absorption is quickly denied, however. To begin with, the viewer is not given much to see. The breasts are barely formed by undeveloped shadows, the pubic region is covered, the form of the body is not clearly legible under lumpy drapery. The viewer is teased with the signs of the academic nude, which are given in incomplete form. In fact, the more one looks at the figure on the left, the more one has to strain merely to keep her body whole. Rather than caressing the side of her head, her right hand hangs like the dead portion of a dismembered limb. This sense is amplified by the shadowy area where the arm should attach to the body. The definite contours of the hand and fingers contrast sharply with the shadowy face, whose eyes look like empty sockets and whose expression is vague and unreadable. It is impossible to tell where the neck ends and the body begins, and yet the shadows below the chin also allow the head to appear severed. The hair that drapes down the rock seems to have little to do with the hair that falls behind the figure's head. Rather than being given a sense of solidity by the play of light and shadow, as in academically correct modeling, the viewer is given a body disintegrating into pieces.

The figure on the right, with her strange and emaciated arms and shoulders and undifferentiated face, affords even less in the way of viewing ease. She is cut off such that not only her breasts but her buttocks are hidden. The figure seems to oscillate between flatness and solidity. Her head is almost completely abstract, her facial features rubbed out by shadow, giving the face a cutout flatness (fig. 5). Yet the contour of the hairline and the delicate modeling of the hair as it falls around the head achieve a sense of solidity. The arm upon which she is leaning seems to bend too far where it meets the body and appears inordinately thin until we realize that the shadow at its pit forms a part of it, giving it bulk. Her back, too, with its strongly indicated spine looks thin and ungainly and appears to end where it meets her right arm. But looking over the heavily contoured right shoulder, the viewer suddenly notices what appears to be another patch of flesh, perhaps the indication of a breast. Read this way, the torso is suddenly excessively weighty.

Again and again, the viewer is asked to work hard to give the figures a pleasing wholeness. In this painting Puvis gives us ample signs of femininity, casts them in the recognizable conventions of the female nude, then denies the fantasy of access to the body that the Salon audience had come to expect through the popularization of the nude by painters like Bouguereau. If academic vocabularies are invoked in *Young Girls by the Seashore*, they are quickly revoked. Drawing does not aim for mastery, color refuses a sense of lifelikeness and beauty, touch does not metaphorize ease of access, poses circumvent visual possession of bodily wholeness. Puvis's treatment of the nude suggests a knowledge of academic trope and convention not because it confirms them but because, with shrewdness, they are negated, reversed, or avoided.

A caricature by Stop for the parodic paper *Journal Amusant* reinforces this reading (fig. 6). The figure on the right echoes in a more ungainly form the fragmentary nature of Puvis's woman. The head and torso of the figure on the left are cut off, leaving only a dismembered arm on a lump of drapery from which feet awkwardly protrude. The standing figure's body becomes excessively long and emaciated. The joke of the caricature centers on this figure, who (as the caption reads), "attacked by two gulls . . . defends herself against this unspeakable aggression." The almost imperceptible white birds drawn in the gray sky at the center of Puvis's canvas are turned into menacing predators in the caricature. These take the position vis-à-vis the female body that would normally be occupied by Salon viewers looking at a painting of Venus. The caricaturist is playing on the resistances to the viewer's access to the female body that Puvis incorporated into his painting.

Although this caricaturist made a joke of Puvis's portrayal of the body, the critic Edmond About thought *Young Girls by the Seashore* was no laughing matter. His response to the painting evinces a discomfort with Puvis's negation of academic convention mixed with criticism of his depiction of the body. In one of his diatribes against the painting, which (legend has it) ended his friendship with Puvis, he wrote: "Here one notices only his faults, and these faults are pushed to the extreme. His figures are nothing more than larvae without form and without color, dry and dislocated shadows. I do not want to enter into the details of these errors, which detract from the rest, but to signal a leg that is lacking or an excessive breast. It is the system that is bad, the point of view that is false, the route that must be surveyed in the opposite sense."[25]

Despite the vitriolic rhetoric, About's description of Puvis's painting contains many of the elements also found in more favorable reviews. First, we have a language of exaggeration. The "faults" of the painting are "pushed to the extreme." Paradoxically, however, what is exaggerated is deficiency itself. Both form and color are wanting to such an extent that we are given not bodies but "larvae"—undifferentiated potential bodies, "shadows" that are insufficient even as shadows. About's

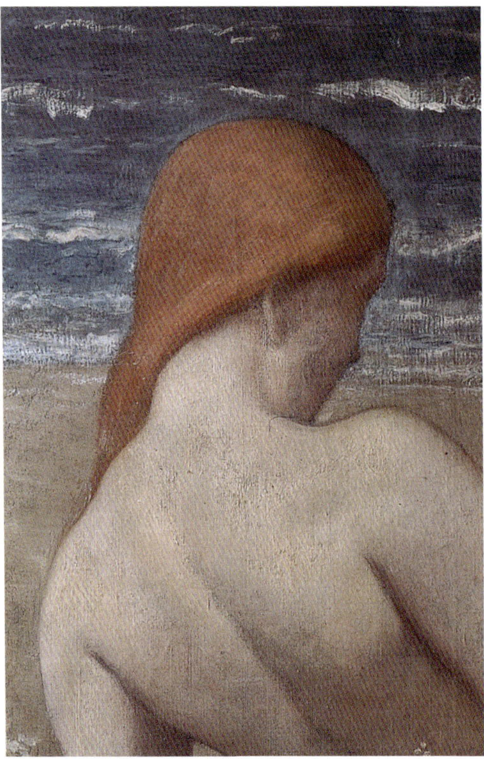

5
Pierre Puvis de Chavannes, *Young Girls by the Seashore* (detail of fig. 2; head of figure on right)

description of Puvis's work is important because although it is negative, it points us to the very same qualities that other critics thought defined the poeticism of Puvis's painting: incompletion and potentiality. Puvis seems to offer not bodies themselves but the potential for corporeality or signs of a corporeality somewhere beyond the viewer's purview, bodies unseen but intimated by a shadowy presence. The body is not full and whole but dry and ungainly. The general vocabulary is not one of plenitude and pleasure but of incompletion and lack. This is emphasized rhetorically in the French by About's repeated use of *sans* (without)—"sans forme et sans couleur"—which is applied to the critical tropes of academic vocabulary.

In addition to critiquing academic paradigms for art, *Young Girls by the Seashore* offered an alternative to market-oriented easel painting. The painting was, said Paul Mantz, anything but a typical Salon painting: "painting, as we understand it today, pleasant painting that one frames with gold and hangs in the living room among mundane trinkets."[26] Instead, "assiduously rising up against fashion," Puvis "dreams of gentle and austere decorations for large wall surfaces," searching for "decorative effect" in both his mural and his easel paintings.[27] Although Mantz felt that decorative use gave license to Puvis's distortions, he did not think that they should be overlooked. Rather, they were integral to the attraction of Puvis's paintings, which found their power in the difficulty of the detail and the pleasure in a whole permeated by repeated forms and rhythms. His description of *Young Girls by the Seashore* is perceptive and deserves to be quoted at length:

> M. Puvis de Chavannes remains completely indifferent to details of embellished form. When, on Judgment Day, we take stock of his virtues and his deeds, we will see that he drew many barbarous feet, many adventurous hands. In *Young Girls by the Seashore* . . . the disdain for beauty does not attempt to disguise itself. One of the women has the thinnest shoulders in the world. What is surprising is that after remarking on the author's inelegances, you forget them. The perfect harmony of the ensemble, the appropriateness of the impression, the sobriety of colors, which speak so softly that they seem to want to silence themselves, and, above all, a certain strangeness in the final accent, in the incomplete or paltry detail—that is at least our current impression. It wasn't formulated in a day. With M. Puvis de Chavannes we began with resistance, and it took us some time to appreciate his slightly morbid charm.[28]

Besides identifying significant aspects of Puvis's style, Mantz described what looking at his paintings felt like. The simplification of form led, he rightly pointed out, to distortions of the body, such as the thin shoulders of the reclining figure. These distortions are often in the parts of the body that are normally the most expressive:

the hands and feet, which, as the bearers of gesture and bodily stance, normally help to focus meaning. In another evocation of an aspect of the painting that hinges on potentialities rather than givens, Mantz described the colors, which "speak so softly that they seem to want to silence themselves." Mantz claimed that bodily "inelegances" are soon forgotten when one takes in the overall harmony of the ensemble. By the end of the passage, however, he was alluding again to those distortions of the body. The most powerful element of the decorative effect, he said, was the "strangeness in the final accent, in the incomplete and paltry detail." These aspects of the body have come back to haunt him. Apparently he himself continually resupplied the "perfect harmony of the ensemble" to the painting, and that harmony was perpetually reachieved as the painting demanded compensatory reverie from its viewers.

Louis de Fourcaud also attempted to explain what the experience of viewing *Young Girls by the Seashore* offered. Fourcaud describes *Young Girls by the Seashore* as a rewriting of the traditional relationship between viewer and nude. Unlike Bouguereau's canvas, which spoke in detail, says Fourcaud, it was "summary and quiet." Rather than being enticed by Puvis's figures, Fourcaud was struck by their disengagement from the viewer—one figure with her back turned, another lost in contemplation, and a third who "surprises passersby with her silent melancholy." Even more than the subject matter, Puvis's painterly means are the key to understanding the work. First, Fourcaud points to the mutedness of color: "The sea is a pale blue, the rocks are of gray tints, and the young girls veil themselves uniformly in white drapery." But the cultivation of potentialities goes even further. Says Fourcaud, "M. Puvis de Chavannes's facture is, however, not as simple as one thinks at first glance. The contours are ringed with black strokes; the painting looks as if it has been made with a scraper."[29] Fourcaud was one of the few critics perceptive enough to note that although touch was never metaphorized in paint, *Young Girls* still had an insistent materiality that derived from the overemphasis of contour and the all-over roughness of surface (see fig. 5). What we are given is neither the plastic quality resulting from a sensual piling on of paint nor the absolute lack of facture found in the sleek surface of a Bouguereau, but a painting that declares its materiality through absence where paint is scraped away. We are given traces of potential facture, just as we are given shadows of potential bodies.

Let us take stock, then, of the range of descriptions we have seen so far. Even Lafenestre, who believed that Puvis's painting showed the way forward for the French School, admitted that *Young Girls by the Seashore* was replete with "fearful insufficiencies," "summary drawing," and "hazardous modeling." Whereas About saw in this incompletion "larvae without form and without color," Lafen-

6
Stop, caricature of *Young Girls by the Seashore*, "Attaquée par deux mouettes . . ." *Journal Amusant*, May 31, 1879, p. 5

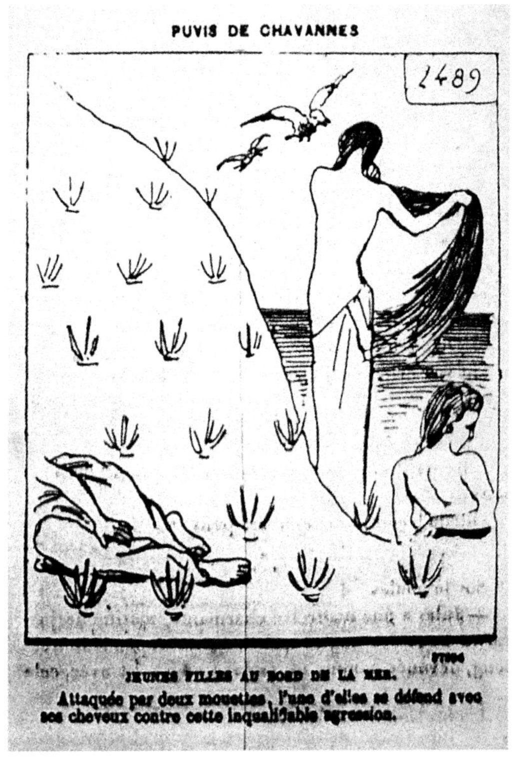

estre was struck by "tranquil color harmony" and "expressive contour." Fourcaud attributed the expressiveness of the painting to Puvis's unconventional handling of color, line, and surface. All of these critics were attempting to make sense of Puvis's painterly mode, and all put their fingers on its important elements. The power of *Young Girls by the Seashore* lay in the ways it deviated from academic correctness to portray potentialities rather than givens. This is the sense in which Puvis's art was "poetic." As in a poem, the figures portrayed in form and rhythm have their own import, and the ultimate meaning of the work issues from the resonances they generated as their allusive power encouraged viewers to transform the bodies on display from a larval state to wholeness in the mind's eye.

When the critics described his paintings as poetic, they were trying to find words for work that did not lend itself easily to exegesis. Puvis's work was untranslatable, and to attempt to detail its meanings was to lose hold of its most powerful elements. One critic tried to make a joke of this aspect of Puvis's work. "I won't even try to describe his . . . *Young Girls by the Seashore*," he said. "Useless to explain Chinese to those who do not want to learn it. Besides, it would take a long time to translate; and I have neither the strength to play the pedant nor the need to be boring."[30] Yet when he spoke seriously of the painting, he called Puvis a "poet" and emphasized how much *Young Girls by the Seashore* depended on that aspect of response that can never be directly translated—on emotion and on the visceral reactions of the body: "He is a poet who feels deeply and who knows how to express his depth of feeling."[31]

Because Puvis's painting did not claim to master its subject, the critics themselves felt powerless. Yet they also were drawn in by the inscrutabilities of the painting. Over and over again they likened viewing Puvis's paintings to a submission of will, although many could not yet describe the operation of the painting in any but the most general terms. Attempts to analyze *Young Girls by the Seashore* soon gave way to evocations of the way the painting made them feel. According to Fourcaud, "One begins by being troubled; one finishes by submitting to its charm."[32] "Protest if you like against the penetrating charm of his manner!" said another critic. "Me, I admit that I submit to it in the most absolute fashion and won't even try to escape."[33]

The most explicit account of the fantasmatic power of the painting was given by the poet Théodore de Banville:

> The paintings of M. Puvis de Chavannes respond to a need, to a very current modern feeling. There are moments when, disgusted with . . . the enormous crazy noises, with theories of the picturesque and of the importance continually claimed for itself by the riffraff in turbulent circumstances, one would like to take refuge in something naked, something infinite, in a nothing-at-all that at least is calm and silent. Such are the *Girls by the Seashore*, who, reduced to their most abstract forms, let down their hair and dream, naked before the immobile waves, where nothing will ever stir, under an unchangeable sky, in an atmosphere without movement or life. Despite being as pure as azure—at least I like to believe it so—they seem desperate, like Baudelaire's Damned Women; they want to go even further away, to an even more tranquil sea, where neither the flight of white birds nor the gaze of human eyes will glide over them. Ah! I understand![34]

This passage is beautiful and complicated. Its meanings are multiple. In the first phrases an evocation of Baudelairean ennui—that boredom with and disgust for modernity that the poet of *The Flowers of Evil* so often wrote about—goes hand in hand with loathing for the art critical enterprise itself. On one level, Banville's enthusiasm for the painting seems to come from the lack of purchase it offers to the critics' "enormous crazy noises" and "theories of the picturesque." But

Banville is attracted by its visual form and describes it quite eloquently. "Naked," "infinite," "calm," and "silent"—all these adjectives are meant, I think, to describe the tendency toward abstraction. The very form of *Young Girls by the Seashore,* Banville suggests, provides an escape from the everyday aspects of modernity and the art world. The women are "reduced to their most abstract forms," the waves are "immobile," the painting seems to be receding into total blankness, a process that will ultimately end in "nothing-at-all." Banville has done an excellent job of capturing the way Puvis's painting works visually and the degree to which, if one wants truly to understand it, traditional forms of criticism are beside the point.

Banville's is also an emotional response to the visual form of the painting. The passage, which is filled with longing, captures the feeling evoked by *Young Girls by the Seashore* better than any other writing I know. The language used by the poet and the forms portrayed by Puvis point the viewer toward something that can never be represented adequately. With his "ah, I understand," Banville simultaneously describes his feelings about the painting and the feelings he imagines the women depicted must themselves have as, gazing at an "immobile sea where nothing will ever stir," they dream desperately toward the infinite. The abstraction of their bodies, he suggests, provides the same kind of open field for the viewer. Banville makes explicit his identification with the female figures, suggesting that the painting causes him, too, to dream and that the dream is all about desire.

The women represent for him a perpetual state of desire. Their desperation leads him to compare them to Baudelaire's "Damned Women," and with this reference their struggle—for a stillness, a silence, a loss of self approaching death—is inextricably linked to sexual fantasy, as is the viewer's. There are two versions of Baudelaire's poem, one that appeared in *Fleurs du Mal* and another, subtitled "Delphine et Hippolyte," which was excised by censors from the 1857 version of *Fleurs du Mal* and not published until 1866, along with other "condemned works," collected under the title *Les Epaves*. Both versions take as their theme the search for the infinite through sexuality. Using lesbianism as the metaphor for the impossibility of fulfilled desire, the poems describe a never-ending search whose real purpose seems (for the poet at least) to be desire's eternal perpetuation.[35]

The less controversial version of the poem has a more direct iconographic relation to the painting:

> Pensive as cattle resting on the beach,
> they are staring out to sea; their hands and feet
> creep towards each other imperceptibly
> and touch at last, hesitant then fierce.[36]

In this stanza the stare out to sea has parallels with the incommunicativeness of Puvis's women. In addition, the imperceptible creeping of limbs, which implies the impending impact of touch, resonates with the bodily distortions of *Young Girls by the Seashore*. In the poem, the initial furtive touch that takes place as the women contemplate the sea is followed by an evocation of tortures endured in the name of desire. The poem ends with the poet's identification with the women.

> you whom my soul has followed into your hell,
>
> Sisters! I love you as I pity you
> for your bleak sorrows, for your unslaked thirsts,
> and for the love that gorges your great hearts![37]

It is tempting to think that Banville also had the censored "Damned Women: Delphine and Hippolyte" in mind when he compared Baudelaire's poem to the figures in Puvis's painting. This poem, which narrates the seduction of the virgin Hippolyta by Delphine, thematizes a rejection of a male sexual aggressor by a woman. Says Delphine to Hippolyta,

> My kisses are as light as those May-flies
> which graze the great transparent lakes at sunset;
> *his* would trace their furrows on your flesh
> like the tongue of some lacerating plough—
>
> as if you had been trampled by a team of oxen with inexorable hooves.[38]

Delphine encourages Hippolyta to forsake heterosexual love and stay with her: "You will drift to sleep in my arms dreaming an endless dream." This description has direct parallels not only to the dreamy and self-sufficient sense we are given by Puvis's *Young Girls by the Seashore* but also to the resistance that Puvis's painting offered to conventional male viewers.

Although Hippolyta is haunted by turmoil and fear, she decides to remain with Delphine. The cost is an inner emptiness, an abyss, "searing as lava, deeper than the Void!" Again lesbianism is linked to an inner emptiness and a perpetual state of desire. Here the voice of the poet is less sympathetic than in the previous example. He no longer explicitly identifies his own plight with that of his "poor sisters." Instead, the desperate tone of his description of the women's "descent" into the depths belies his identification with them:

Downward, wretched victims!

. . .

Down, frantic shades, and fall to your desires
where passion never slakes its raging thirst
. . . and flee
the infinite you bear within yourselves![39]

There is much more than a hint of misogyny in Baudelaire's characterization of lesbian desire, a sentiment to which Banville is also party. Yet the point of both versions of "Damned Women" is the despairing identification with the women's perpetual state of desire and their unfulfillable "void." This relinquishment of consciousness to the unending wandering of fantasy and the tyranny of desires and drives is, Baudelaire ultimately suggests, the truth about modern subjectivity.

Banville's allusion to the poem tells us much about the way *Young Girls by the Seashore* made him feel. He suggests that the painter's constitution of a world in paint does not, as academic convention would have it, provide vicarious possession of the ideal. Instead, he implies, viewing the painting is a process of giving oneself up to desire, as Baudelaire's women do. By providing the spur to such relinquishment of consciously controlled subjectivity, Banville claims, Puvis fulfills a need that is "very current, and very modern." And as we have seen, he does so using painterly means that are themselves "modernist."

By connecting Puvis to Baudelaire, Banville was articulating a modernist interpretation of Puvis that surely would have pleased the Symbolist poets. Baudelaire was one of their heroes. And the challenges that their poetry posed to classical verse were analogous, in many ways, to the challenges that Puvis's paintings posed to traditional paradigms of high art. If we look at the cultural debates about Symbolism that took place in the following decade, we see that they centered on the sensuousness of Symbolist verse and the way it threatened to cause a proliferation of fantasy in readers. In fact, the very writers and poets who battled over these terms in the literary realm also wrote and spoke about Puvis's work.[40]

Perhaps the most outspoken critic of Symbolist allusiveness was Ferdinand Brunetière, an academician and editor of the *Revue des Deux Mondes*, who attacked Baudelaire and the Symbolists in a campaign of articles. Brunetière complained that Symbolism, rather than using verse to "express," "idealize," "generalize," or "reveal a secret meaning," was "the art of sensing an object and abandoning oneself to the suggestions provoked, until finally, having taken on the inconsistency of dreams, the poem conveys sensations that imitate their floating, unreal, and bizarre character."[41] Despite his conservatism, Brunetière conceived of signification as an arbitrary process.[42] This was why there was so much at stake in promoting an appropriate use of language. The lack of a fixed relation between sign and signified necessitated a stable, convention-bound, and idealizing definition of art: "In general, art must correct, rectify, modify, continue, and prolong that which it imitates."[43] Brunetière's definition of the proper role of art is quite similar to the conservative academic description of high art. According to Brunetière, "We want to tear the veil; and we want ultimately to reach the essence whose evidence frolics on the surface of things." This aesthetic model is diametrically opposed to what Brunetière describes as the Symbolist cult of the "the vague and the imprecise, the floating and the fugitive, the celestial and the imponderable."[44] Already Brunetière's description of Symbolism sounds much like the criticisms of Puvis's painting. But the parallel becomes even clearer when we look at Brunetière's specific criticisms of Baudelaire.

According to Brunetière, Baudelaire's verse took the evocation of sensation to an extreme, using language to make his readers imagine not only color, form, and sound but also smell, "the most 'animal'" of all the senses, "the sense whose impressions exchange most easily with those of the others."[45] Brunetière argued that while color and form "limit the freedom of dream by drawing their contours with some precision, smells on the contrary, emancipate it, facilitate it, magnify it."[46] The allusiveness of Baudelaire's descriptions, their multivalency, and their tendency to evoke the senses in ways that promoted the proliferation of fantasy were what made Brunetière uncomfortable with Baudelaire's poetry. Symbolism was, Brunetière argued, an amplification of Baudelaire's cult of sensuality and dream, which threatened to lead to "disorder, incoherence, even madness."[47] This has many parallels to the kinds of comments that were made about Puvis's work. Puvis was, it is true, limited by his very medium to color and form—the descriptive elements that Brunetière claimed have the potential to control the freedom of dream. But, as we have seen, Puvis did not use color and form to draw precise contours. Instead, they themselves became the sites of suggestibility. What Brunetière saw as the problem with Baudelaire's poetry—the field that it left open for fantasy—was, for Banville, the most powerful aspect of Puvis's work.[48]

What needs to be understood is that Brunetière was never simply addressing a problem in Baudelaire's poetry. He believed Baudelaire to be symptomatic of a general crisis in French cultural production, a crisis brought on by the modernist threat to tradition. Baudelaire now had a "school" of followers, the Symbolists, and Brunetière worried that not only language, but human subjectivity itself, was under threat from the Symbolist cult of allusion. "Instead of tyrannizing the freedom of the imagination and of dream," said Brunetière, the Symbolists "demand that poetry make them take flight. . ."[49] He believed this promotion of fantasy had dire consequences for writers and readers. The ultimate goal of Symbolist poetry was "to dissolve the unity of the self in a diversity of successive states . . . to return it to the wandering voluptuousness of dream."[50] Symbolism thus threatened to unseat both stable signification and the conception of subjectivity implicit in it—one in which the *moi* was whole, autonomous, and free from the influence of desire and the unconscious.

According to Brunetière, Symbolist allusiveness and Symbolist egoism went hand in hand. Allusiveness led to fantasy, and this led to an inward-turning egoism in both writers and readers: "One of the worst consequences that can possibly follow is the isolation of art, the isolation of the artist, and the transformation of him into an idol, closing him up in the sanctuary of the self. . . . There is no longer anything that he respects or that he spares . . . the true definition of immorality. . . . It is the glorification of egoism and by consequence the negation of solidarity."[51] Brunetière worried enough about the influence of Symbolism and other forms of modernism to write a series of articles railing against them. His battle against Symbolism derived from his belief that art should be "a place of common consent."[52] The danger of Symbolism, he thought, was that it would encourage the atomization of its public, a promotion of the kind of egoism that would finally end in anarchy. As we will see when we turn to the banquet for Puvis de Chavannes held in 1895, Brunetière would ultimately attempt to show that Puvis was more allied with tradition than with modernism.

Despite Brunetière's attempt to describe Puvis's work as unified classicism, the majority of viewers seem to have felt that Puvis's pictorial mode was much closer to the play of fantasy and imagination celebrated by the Symbolist mode than to the traditional idealizing version of art that Brunetière professed. Yet it would be wrong to suggest that Puvis saw himself as a Symbolist. Puvis de Chavannes initially produced his characteristic style—large, rough, relatively undifferentiated areas of color, distorting line, and echoing rhythms of form—as he struggled to make large decorative works. When he transmuted the techniques he had used for large decorations onto smaller canvases and exaggerated them even further, the reactions he elicited were striking. Neither did any of the critics I have quoted (with perhaps the exception of Banville) believe that Puvis was trying to paint as Baudelaire or the generation of writers who followed him wrote (although in the 1890s Symbolist poets would themselves make such a claim). What they did find in Puvis's work was a replacement of traditional forms of representation and the values associated with them by a simplification of form and rhythmic patterning that had its own peculiar kind of sensuous allusiveness—an allusiveness that conjured desire and evoked dream.

In *Young Girls by the Seashore*, Puvis addressed viewers through incompletion. They came to the painting expecting to find something that fit with the conventions of the nude. But habits of viewing were quickly disrupted as the contrast between what was expected and what was given became apparent. Viewers were faced with disturbing insufficiencies in the bodies on display and enticing potentialities in muted color. Desire was perpetuated when the inconsistencies of the painting prevented closure. The space was opened for individual fantasies. Thus, the subject matter of the nude, the drawing and modeling of the body, were made to operate differently. This was far from the academic paradigm. And yet few of the critics denied that *Young Girls by the Seashore* was high art.

POOR FISHERMAN

The status of *Poor Fisherman* was not as easy for critics to discern (see fig. 1). When Puvis exhibited *Poor Fisherman* at the Salon of 1881, he again employed the exaggerated and understated style that had so baffled the critics. While it was clear in 1879 that Puvis was presenting his audience with a nude, no one knew quite what to make of the subject matter of the 1881 painting. In *Poor Fisherman*, Puvis flouted the academic hierarchy of genres. Was *Poor Fisherman* a genre scene or a work of religious symbolism? The critics were not sure. The fisherman is Christ-like in his emaciation. He bows his head in contemplation and folds one hand over the other in an approximation of the gesture of prayer found in medieval books of hours. From this perspective, the painting looks like a religious scene. However, it is also a depiction of work undertaken by a person whose dress and demeanor speak of indigence and marginality. Many critics returned to the theme that dominated responses to *Young Girls by the Seashore*—Puvis's rejection of academic paradigms of painting and conventional languages of description—and called the painting a mistake,[53] a "rebus,"[54] and "a challenge to the public by a painter of talent."[55] What is perhaps most striking about *Poor Fisherman* is the way the body, the element of high art that had conventionally provided the most information to the viewer through gesture, comportment, and clothing, refuses to signify unambiguously. Instead of using the body to portray a legible narrative, Puvis offered bodies parceled up by repeating forms and echoing meanings.

As with *Young Girls by the Seashore*, Puvis chose a muted palette, limiting himself almost exclusively to grays, greens, and blues. Furthermore, he dissociated color from painterly touch and refused to make variations in touch fit with the objects he was depicting. The silhouette of the fisherman is slight, suggesting emaciation, but no clear details of that emaciation are visible. The folds of his clothing blend and meld and tell us nothing about the body underneath. What we see of the fisherman's face from a distance—downturned eyes, chin, mouth—soon dissolves. The beard and shadow become two triangles that echo the neck of his shirt. His hair seems to be stuck onto rather than growing from his head.

The female figure on the bank is similarly undefined, aside from her hands, which grasp at flowers. She serves as a pivotal point of the painting, pointing with one arm to the fisherman and with the other to the baby on the shore. Yet her age, her relationship to the fisherman and baby, and even her gender seem insecure. The fleshy tones of her neck are scumbled down onto the front of her tunic and dress, preventing the definition of her body's form. It is impossible to tell whether she has breasts—an element that might clarify her relationship to the other figures in the composition. Critics sometimes identified her as the fisherman's wife and other times as his daughter. The flowers growing between her legs as she kneels divide the dress in two, making it look like the fisherman's pants. Once we notice this, her head begins to resemble the fisherman's, but without the beard and seen from the other side. From this perspective, she looks like a younger version of the fisherman. Thus, at the point in the composition where Puvis could have supplied his audience with narrative clarity, he instead opted for lack of definition, which led to narrative confusion.

The artist's use of line was similarly unconventional. This element of painting whose purpose was to idealize the body does anything but that. The head of the baby lying naked on the ground on a brightly colored blanket is out of proportion to its body. The baby seems to writhe inexplicably on the bank. Its face is nothing more than an ill-defined blob. Its arms are tiny and thin, and its right leg is huge—wider than the fisherman's arm, which is closer to the foreground. The leg looks like a dismembered body part arranged on its blanket. Here, more than anywhere in this painting, we are given the sense of a body in pieces. Puvis emphasizes the contours of the fisherman's body, outlining it with a dark gray line. However, this line does not idealize the body or make it readable. A heavily contoured bare arm and hand perform a gesture that at first seems to signify resignation and prayer. But when we look at it more closely, we see that the bare arm and hand press against the fisherman's body with a force that is inexplicable. A pose that initially appears calm is unsettled by the heavily outlined emphasis on the limbs.

The conservative critic for the Catholic journal *Le Moniteur Universel* berated Puvis for ignoring academic conventions. He thought the transformatory power of line lent itself more to caricature than to idealization. "By dint of wishing to transfigure his Poor Fisherman," said the critic, "the artist has not so much spiritualized him as turned him into an unsavory fellow."[56] Puvis wanted to use the fisherman to allude to the suffering of Christ, but his fisherman showed a lack of respect "approach[ing] parody": "What is this lamentable Ecce Homo, this false, half-nude Christ with hands joined in front of him, an old rag around his head in the guise of a crown of thorns, in sad contemplation before his mast as before the instrument of his passion?" the critic asked.[57] Similarly, Edmond About thought the high seriousness of Puvis's painting was undercut by "laborious error[s]" that "made a serious and convinced caricaturist of him."[58] The fisherman was "praying for himself (*ora pro nobis piscatoribus*)" rather than for humankind "and demanding a fish from the sea the way a beggar demands a sou from us."[59] The painting seemed to About to parody both priest and beggar, religious painting and genre scene. The figure of Christ, whose role it was to sacrifice himself for humanity, was praying only for himself. Both critics associated Puvis's generalization of the figures and landscape with an attempt to move painting from the material to the spiritual, to create high art, and both found it to be a failure.

Louis de Fourcaud agreed with more conservative critics that "one can reproach M. de Chavannes for everything, the placement of his figures and their naive construction, the drawing, the color, the impression." However, Fourcaud thought Puvis's "faults" were his greatest asset. The power of his work derived from the ways it deviated from a superficial adherence to the traditional tenets of high art. To explain this, Fourcaud made a distinction between two kinds of painterly address—each of which centered on the artist's (and thus ultimately the viewer's) bodily relation to painting. On the one hand, there were *peintres d'oeil*, "painters of the eye," who took it as their task to fix on the canvas "lively appearances" and surfaces of things. On the other hand, were *peintres de cerveau*, "painters of the mind" or "brain"—painters like Puvis de Chavannes—who gave material form to intellectual struggles. The painters of the eye were preoccupied with extracting pleasure from the visual surfaces of things. Rather than being challenging, their work put forth a vision of life that was "intellectually easy and pleasant." This sense of ease with the world they portrayed was passed on in their painterly style, which bore no hint of struggle: "They realize their furtive vision with the most adroit hand" and make "the sweetness of their pleasure radiate around them."[60] The painters of the eye were best represented at this Salon, Fourcaud suggested, by *Glorification of the Law*, a ceiling decoration by the academician Paul Baudry commissioned by the government for the Cour de Cassation (Supreme Court; fig. 7). This was, he thought, a prime example the debasement of public decoration by academy practitioners.

Unlike Bouguereau, the representative of the school of line, Baudry's almost rococo brushwork placed him in the academic school of color. The problems with his painting were basically the same as Bouguereau's: too much (and too superficial) reliance on tradition, overeroticization of his female figures, lack of innovation in form and technique. Baudry's painterly touch created the opposite of Bouguereau's smooth glossy surfaces. But in the end a similar relationship between viewer and work was achieved. Baudry's brushwork metaphorized an intimate, erotic engagement with the figures. Through his sensual strokes, the viewer was granted a fantasy of their accessibility.

Nothing was further from this than Puvis's "austere" canvas, in which "the charm does not come from the palette itself" but "comes despite the palette." "Puvis's painting," said Fourcaud, was not visually dazzling but "flat and almost dull." Requirements for correct use of the artist's métier—perspective, modeling, correct drawing—had no purchase here. The distortions of Puvis's style were testi-

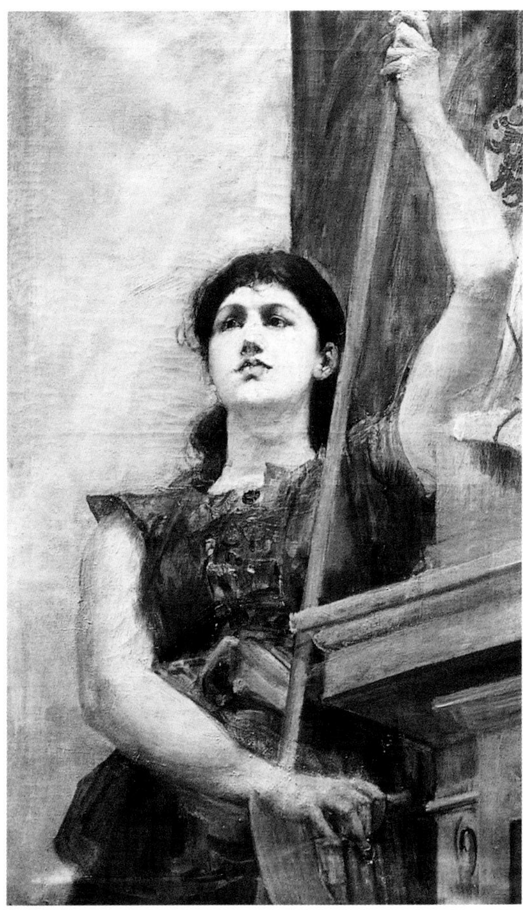

7
Paul Baudry, *Authority*, detail of figure from *Glorification of the Law*, 1882. Oil on canvas, 43 1/4 x 28 1/3 in. (110 x 72 cm). Musée Municipal de La Roche-sur-Yon, France

mony to a process of making in which ideas, themselves furtive and difficult to grasp, were transmuted, however partially, into the materiality of paint and canvas, into line and color, into visual form. This struggle to give inner thoughts and feelings material form was characteristic, Fourcaud said, of painters of the mind: "They never judge themselves to be penetrating enough, never advanced enough in the intimacy of being, never master enough of their conceptions. Their art is truly, following a celebrated phrase, the exteriorization of their ideas. If they dominate the tools of their craft, they despise all artifice; in any case, they arrive at concentrations that are so grand, at syntheses that are so powerful, that one holds them above the métier, and all is permitted to them."[61] Puvis's "researches [were] incessant and his pursuits painful." Not only was the initial conception fraught with difficulty, but the materialization of ideas through the means of representation left him "persecuted by the bitter desire to exteriorize the lofty images that haunt him." The painters of the mind, said Fourcaud, always ended in failure. Their attempts to "exteriorize their ideas" in paint ended in works whose awkwardness was testimony to the strangeness and difficulty of representation.[62]

Fourcaud was willing to admit that the "faults" of *Poor Fisherman* initially caused "irritation" in viewers looking for correct drawing, modeling, and the like. But this initial discomfort was only the first stage of the address to feeling. Ultimately, said Fourcaud, the painting "ends by moving us. It has escaped from the depth of a human dream; it has a profound humanity."[63] In attempting to capture the pursuits of such an artist, Fourcaud chose a language of immanence rather than transcendence. The painter of the mind struggles to "penetrate" the material world, to understand the "intimacy of beings," rather than to rise above them or to transform them into some more perfect state. It is important that Fourcaud characterizes this as a struggle, for it is an attempt to capture the feelings that ensue from Puvis's painterly process. The painter's struggle, like the viewer's irritation, are discomforts that have an emotional component; they are sensed in the depths of one's being and felt in the body.

In this reformulation of high art, Fourcaud described the opposite of academic idealism. If the academic artist aimed to transcend the material world through an act of intellectual genius and mastery of materials, the painter of the mind instead dwelled on the connections between thought and sensation or, rather, imagined the two to be completely intertwined. Fourcaud summed up *Poor Fisherman* by calling it "the emotion of a child translated by a primitive." With this phrase Fourcaud made clear that he saw Puvis not as a searcher after "truth" or "ideal beauty" but as an artist attempting to give some kind of material form to the inner life of feeling. *Poor Fisherman* was an attempt, Fourcaud suggested, to see the world as if it were new—with the same wonder experienced by a child—and to translate that feeling into two dimensions as if one knew nothing about drawing, perspective, or color. In *Poor Fisherman* the raw experience exchanged between the artist, his subject matter, and the inherent qualities of the medium seemed to dictate much of the result. This exploration of the medium of painting in the pursuit of emotional affect was what made Puvis's work seem so modern to his peers and to the younger artists like Matisse and Picasso who drew from his work.

Fourcaud seems to have been looking for another way to describe high art—for something other than the transcendent idealism still preached by the Academy (even if none of its representatives seemed capable of practicing it). The attempt of the artist to materialize his subjective response to his subject matter and ultimately to elicit an emotional response from viewers led to a distortion of nature rather than an idealization of it. Art remained "the externalized worship of . . . ideas," but these "ideas" no longer coincided with a universal truth of beauty. Fourcaud was not a Symbolist critic. But in his description of Puvis he took up a vocabulary that has many similarities to that employed, a few years later, by promoters of Symbolism.[64] Fourcaud's aim was to align Puvis de Chavannes's address to feeling with modernity itself.

Fourcaud characterized the situation as a battle between tradition and the new, a battle being fought out not only in painting but also in literature and in music. Whereas traditionalists produced "thoughtful, spiritual works of skillful analysis," those who "embrac[ed] and spur[red] on the torment of novelty" produced works that were "uneven and sometimes incorrect, but . . . profound, synthetic, and have the value of symbols."[65] Fourcaud characterized the exhortations to young artists likely to come from each side: "Do not forget the past!" he imagined Baudry and his ilk to say. "Make the experience of the old masters from whom you descend a part of your works; be true to their methods." Fourcaud imagined the opposite advice from Puvis and his followers: "Engage yourself on your own road . . . ; probe life, probe your own soul, yield yourself to your own sensations, follow your own desires, succor your own obsessions, go straight to the future and never turn your head."[66] To look to the future, suggested Fourcaud, is to look inward. Central to the new high art, then, would be an address to feeling rather than reason and convention. With this address to feeling came an acknowledgment of the unconscious component of aesthetic experience. Obsession, desire, sensation—all of these are aspects of the self associated with unconscious drives and desires rather than with reason. All of them call to mind the terms we saw Brunetière denigratingly use to describe Symbolist egoism when he worried about the challenges posed to traditional modes of signification by modern, suggestive form.

Puvis's easel paintings emphasize the elements of painting traditionally associated with activities of mind—elevated subject matter, an emphasis on drawing, a de-emphasis on color—to such a degree that Fourcaud identified the artist as a painter of the mind. However, as we have seen, Puvis's works ultimately approached their viewers through an address to feeling. Puvis de Chavannes's paintings thus asked their viewers to focus on the connections between thought and sensation and to reconceptualize the possible connections between mind and body. The discovery of the unconscious posed an analogous challenge to the Cartesian subject, a challenge that in psychology, as in aesthetics, was associated with modernity.

Although Fourcaud saw Puvis's challenge to traditional modes of representation and evocation of feeling as assets, some critics worried that Puvis's summary execution in *Poor Fisherman* leaned so far to the side of suggestion that it ended with a denial of the material world. Puvis's painting was compared with the philosophy of Schopenhauer, which enjoyed a vogue in France in the 1880s, particularly among the Symbolist poets. In *The World as Will and Representation*, Schopenhauer argued that empirical reality was always dependent on individual consciousness; it was "mark[ed] with the stamp of ideality, and therefore of mere *phenomenal appearance*. Thus on one side at least the world must be recognized as akin to dreams, and indeed to be classified along with them."[67] Some critics thought that with easel paintings like *Poor Fisherman*, Puvis had retreated into the self-regarding egoism of a mystical dream: "The more he moves forward in this work," said Philippe Burty, "the more he plays the fakir, pursuing that contemplation of the navel which takes as troubling everything that faints under the sun, whispers in the leaves, pulses in the veins, perpetuates this image or this dream that we call 'the world.'"[68]

These descriptions of Puvis's dematerialization of his subject matter in favor of dream may seem to contradict both Fourcaud's description of Puvis's opposition to idealism and my claim that Puvis's work is about immanence rather than transcendence. Significantly, however, when critics attempted to evoke Puvis's idealism, the body always sneaked back into their rhetoric, like the return of the repressed. Much of the negative criticism and caricature of *Poor Fisherman* centered on bodies in their material states, bodies so ill or so thin that they call undue attention to their material natures. For example, a mocking critique from the caricatural *Journal Amusant* drew on traditional associations between painterly facture, color, and the body and set them in opposition to the traditional associations between line, drawing, and mind. Puvis's art, the writer suggested, was on the side of line and thus should evoke transcendence:

> Lord of Lords! . . . Righteous sky! . . .
> His poor fisherman, grisailles illuminated with patches of color [*plaques*], is an affront to common sense.
> Chlorotic epinal.
> No color on the canvas. No flesh on the bones. No creature in the clothing. No . . .
> Total: zero.[69]

The invocation of God and the sky parody the allusions in the painting to spirituality. As About had done with *Young Girls by the Seashore*, the writer lists what is lacking from the painting with his repeated refrain of *pas de* (no) and offers a final tally of what is there: zero. The elements that are lacking are conventionally associated with materiality in academic painting. It is as if "no color" is equated with "no flesh on the bones." And when the signs of body and materiality have vacated the canvas, the result is zero. We are met, the critic suggests, not with transcendent idealization but with the body's disappearance. Significantly, this emptiness opens up a space for the fantasmatic body. In this particular case, the reference to chlorosis and color patches likened to eczema links Puvis's distortions to the body with bodily illness. Thus, even as the conventional body of high art was erased from the picture, the body as a material entity returned and elicited a much stronger (bodily) reaction in this viewer—one of revulsion and disgust.[70]

Caricatures in *La Caricature* and *Le Charivari* depict the fisherman with a completely naked torso, supporting the view that Puvis's depiction called special attention to this male body (figs. 8–9). In a drawing for *La Caricature*, A. Robida emphasizes the fisherman's emaciation, indicating the ribs and chest bones, which are absent from the painting. In addition, he rolls up the fisherman's pants to reveal skinny legs and knobby knees. The return to the body was perhaps most evocatively represented in a caricature by Stop for *Journal Amusant* (fig. 10). Here the baby has turned into an overinflated frog, and the passage reads, "A dead toad gives cholera to a poor fisherman; his wife cuts fragrant flowers in order to neutralize the miasma." The body is evoked both morbidly and scatologically. The fisherman crouches slightly, holding his half-pulled-up trousers, physically consumed by the effects of cholera. The miasmas in question are indicated by the cloudlike forms hovering in the boat behind him. The responses to *Poor Fisherman* are thus marked by a to-and-fro between the dematerialization of the body in paint and the return of the fantasmatic body in its most material state.

We could dismiss these invocations of death and disease as the product of parody, meant to degrade the painting rather than to speak to the true sentiments it invoked. But to do so would be to miss what *Poor Fisherman* has in common with

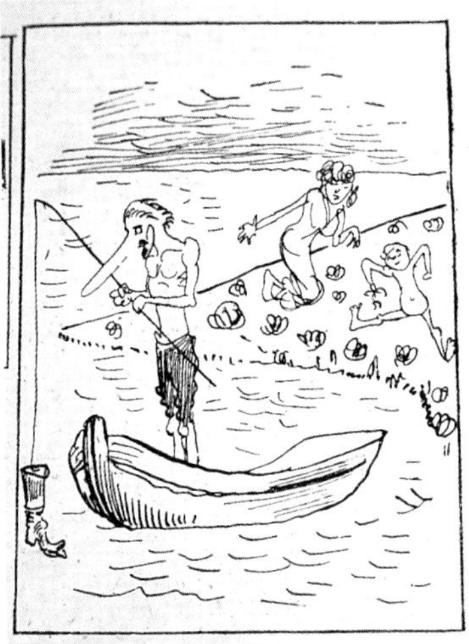

PUVIS DE CHAVANNES. — PAUVRE PÊCHEUR.
Friture et matelotte.
Ça ne mord pas ! Rien que des bottes et des vieux chapeaux ! .

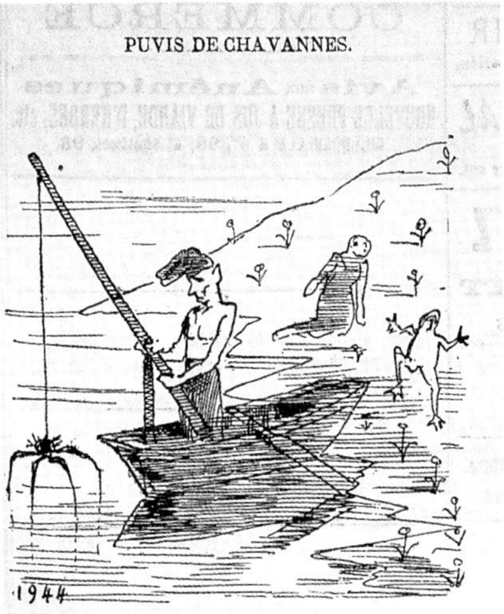

LE PAUVRE PÊCHEUR.
Pas de chance, en effet... pêcher une araignée !

Young Girls by the Seashore and what, as will become clear in the following chapters, I take to be the most important element of Puvis's work, murals and easel paintings alike: his rejection of conventional modes of painting leads to a particular kind of address to fantasy and desire that centers on the body. I am not only speaking here of the bodies depicted but of the feeling that Puvis's strangely sensuous abstraction gives to the viewer and of the fantasies of the body that ensue.

So far we have seen only general descriptions of *Poor Fisherman*. What happened, we might ask, when viewers tried, in good faith, to make sense of the painting? What kinds of feelings did it conjure up? What specific fantasies? Louis de Fourcaud was one of the only critics to make an earnest attempt to provide the painting with a narrative. The scene, said Fourcaud, was a specific site, near "the mouth of the Seine, in the area of Honfleur." He described the fisherman's appearance: "thin, wan, clothed in a rose shirt and tattered pants; ensheathed in his clothing; short beard, disheveled hair, deep sunken eyes." The fisherman's position expressed "eternal resignation, mute and eternal sadness," for his task was doomed to failure: "He may raise his net: never a single fish will he find." Fourcaud identified the "sickly young woman [who] cuts flowers feverishly" as the fisherman's daughter, and the infant as "a very young boy [who] rolls on a pinkish fabric that will serve as his shroud." Fourcaud was one of the few to try to explain the relationship between the three figures: "The fisherman is a widower; he brings his chil-

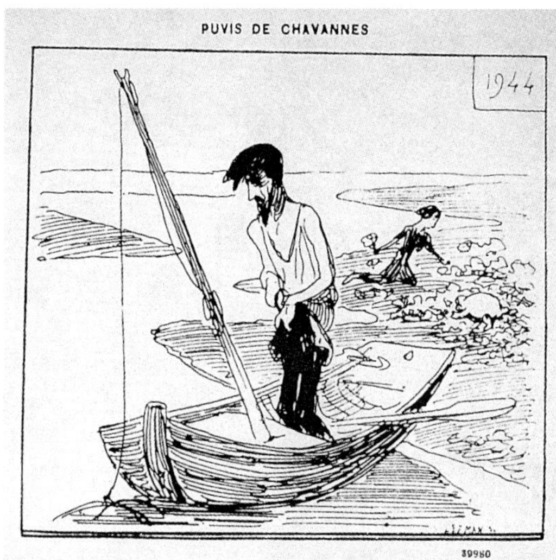

8
A. Robida, caricature of *Poor Fisherman*, "Friture et matelotte . . ." *La Caricature*, May 28, 1881, p. 169

9
Caricature of *Poor Fisherman*, "Pas de chance, en effet . . ." *Le Charivari*, May 19, 1881, p. 3

10
Stop, caricature of *Poor Fisherman*, "Un crapaud crevé . . ." *Journal Amusant*, May 28, 1881, p. 5

dren with him, not knowing where to leave them. He is annihilated by his solitude. He is crushed by the grandeur of nature. The water stretches before him, gloomy and solemn, to the infinite."[71] Here Fourcaud provides both a visual description and a narrative explanation of a picture. Yet what begins as a precise narrative about a family in distress ends with the loss of self, the "annihilation" by nature's "infinite" that Banville described when viewing *Young Girls by the Seashore*.

As in *Young Girls by the Seashore*, the suggestiveness of the figures and the ambivalence of their relationships to one another opened up the space for individual fantasy. In Fourcaud's particular case, it provoked fantasies of death and inertia that were linked to the absent wife and mother. The mother is dead, Fourcaud suggested, and the fruit of her womb would soon be also. Nature's refusal to provide sustenance to the fisherman was conflated with the dead mother's inability to nourish her children. Fourcaud's fantasy of death was a fantasy of the absence of the maternal. It was a fantasy of what it would be like if woman and nature no longer fulfilled the role of mother. In this sense it was not so very far from Banville's characterization of *Young Girls by the Seashore* as "damned women," who refused to make themselves available to the male viewer and refused their maternal roles.

On the most general level, the reticent and even threatening aspects of woman/nature/matter were implied by Puvis's own means of representation. In contrast to what I have characterized as the confidence in academic painting that representation offered a metaphorical possession of nature, we see in Puvis's employment of painterly means the difficulty and struggle in representing the material world, a means that doomed that struggle to end in failure. But the struggle was also the site of creativity. From it emerged a space passed on to the viewer where dream and desire became part of representation. In this process two aspects of subjectivity conventionally associated with the feminine—materiality and the body—reentered the scene of representation via feeling and fantasy.

Fourcaud's interpretation of *Poor Fisherman* kept both the struggle to possess the world in representation and the impossibility of doing so in play. The story he created was born out of the ambiguities encoded in Puvis's painting. When he described the effect that the painting should have on its viewers, the terms he chose suggested quite eloquently the painting's call to fantasy. Rather than a typical genre scene, we are given "an extraordinary country, strange, surprising, disconcerting, but sublime and with such a special magic that one forgets oneself in order to meditate on this poem, and one cannot dream of scrutinizing its execution. M. Puvis de Chavannes makes us enter into his painting, into his vision."[72] With these last words, Fourcaud displayed a certain confidence that the artist both promoted a state of creative openness in his audience and filled that space with a general message.

Fourcaud had confidence that the narrative he had spun about Puvis's painting, its message about the maternal, would somehow be shared among viewers. But here is the crux of the problem presented by Puvis's painting. How much could the allusiveness of Puvis's style—a style that throws each viewer into a dream state of his or her own —communicate a common message to all viewers? Another way of asking this question would be to ask about the relation between individual and cultural fantasy. Or, to put it slightly differently: What is the relation between individual desires and sensations and collective understanding? Although Fourcaud believed that this intense focus on individual sensation and desire produced the best work, others thought it threatened the future of cultural production.

The question that taunts us in Puvis's easel paintings and becomes even more pressing in his murals is this: Might the works offer the viewer the possibility of engaging in a process of viewing more akin to contemplation of the navel than to the reception of a grand moral message? Does the address to individual sensation and desire necessarily promote egoism? Or does it have the potential for a more powerful kind of address to the collectivity than traditional forms of high art have? By disturbing the academic schema, Puvis opened the space for fantasy. But he also opened a debate about the function of fantasy in his public paintings, a debate that became more pronounced in the following years. High art's other body was brought into being by Puvis. Its location was not in the picture but in the viewer.

2

DREAM'S BODY

The Sacred Grove Dear to the Arts and Muses

In August 1883, Puvis de Chavannes received the commission to decorate the new staircase of the Museum of Fine Arts, Lyons. The first installment of this decoration, *The Sacred Grove Dear to the Arts and Muses*, was exhibited without an accompanying text at the Salon of 1884 (fig. 11). Like all of Puvis's murals, it was painted on canvas in his studio before it was shown. The large canvas was mounted in the entry staircase of the museum in August of that year. An expansive idyllic landscape peopled by nearly life-sized Muses, *The Sacred Grove* was an allegory appropriate to an art museum. In a pamphlet provided to museum visitors, Puvis described its subject matter: "The Arts and Muses, in effect, symbolize and give birth to all the creations included in a museum consecrated to art."[1] On the face of it, then, *The Sacred Grove* was an allegory of the origins of creativity.

By the time of this commission, Puvis de Chavannes was already a well-respected public artist. His paintings graced the walls of the Panthéon in Paris as well as the entry halls of museums and city halls in Poitiers, Marseilles, and Amiens. These large-scale decorative works had followed the traditional strategies of depicting specific moments in French history or topographically identifiable sites.[2] None of them employed the extreme stylistic means that the critics had complained about with respect to easel paintings like *Young Girls by the Seashore* and *Poor Fisherman*. *The Sacred Grove* was different: here Puvis used the same provocative style he had been developing in his easel paintings. Nor was an explanatory text provided when *The Sacred Grove* was exhibited at the Salon before its installation in the museum. Not surprisingly, many Salon critics had trouble deciphering the allegory.

The allegorical mode was considered to be particularly appropriate to public decoration. Decorations for public buildings were generally required to serve an educational function. From the early eighteenth century, the allegorical mode had been associated with knowledge and reason. In traditional allegory, "following a well-known code, metaphors were shaped from objects that could attract the imagination and the eyes of viewers and express the values and virtues held up as slogans

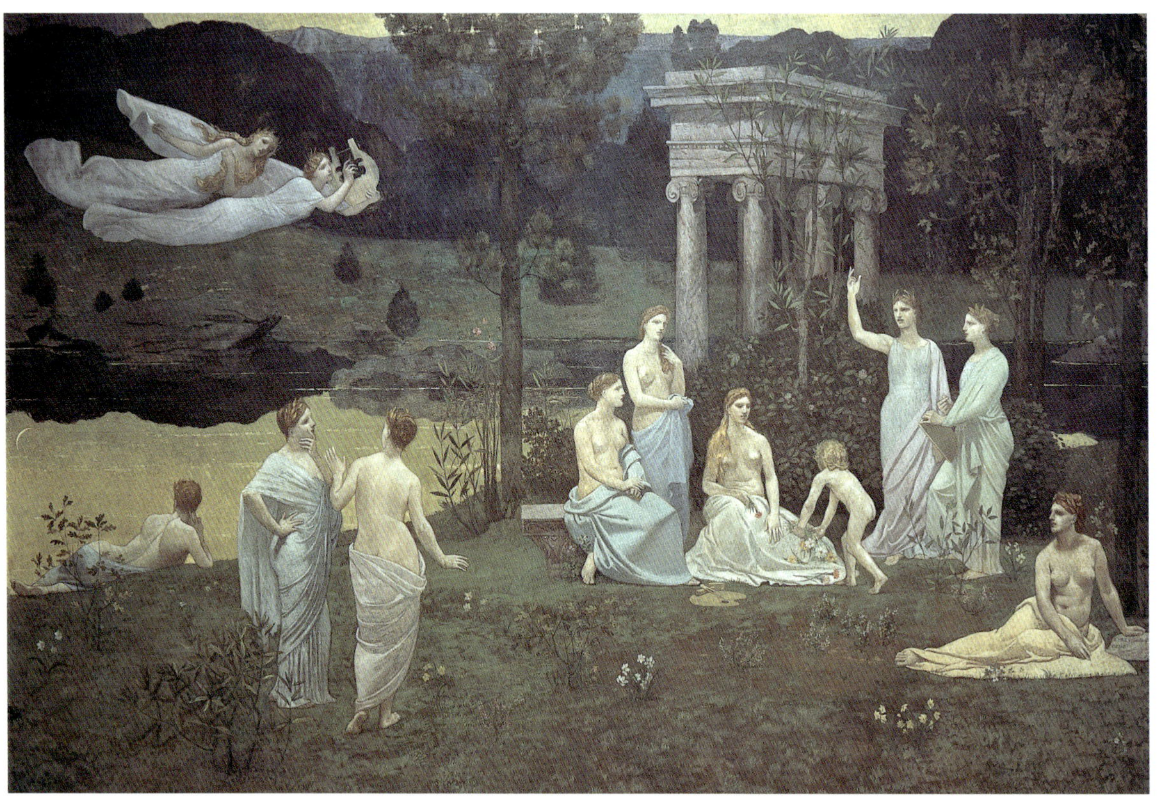

11
Pierre Puvis de Chavannes, *The Sacred Grove Dear to the Arts and Muses* (detail), 1884. Oil on canvas affixed to wall, 181 x 409 1/2 in. (4.6 x 10.4 m). Musée des Beaux-Arts, Lyons

of a regime."[3] To be successful, allegory required that its two main terms—"a figure: an idea"—be transparent and legible to each other. As Antoine de Baecque argues in his history of French allegory: "The power of allegory . . . resides in its ability, better than [that of] any other mode of representation, to link narrative and understanding, meaning and knowledge. . . . Saying and knowing, therefore, are intimately linked in allegorical representation."[4] When allegory was used in public art at the end of the nineteenth century, it was most often employed in decorative commissions. These had several identifiable characteristics. In general, compositions were hierarchical, with an allegorical figure seated or rising above surrounding figures and holding a legible attribute—a torch for Truth, a scale for Justice, tablets for Law (fig. 12). The allegorical body was usually female, often nude, and always idealized following the academic paradigm so that attention was focused on the signified allegory (Truth, Justice, Law) rather than on the body portrayed.

Although *The Sacred Grove Dear to the Arts and Muses* was clearly meant as an allegory, in it Puvis flouted many of these conventions. The subject matter appeared to be conventional, but the manner in which Puvis attempted to educate his audience most definitely was not. Indeed, Puvis's transformation of the allegorical mode was understood by many critics to be a subversion of rational attempts to decipher the mural in favor of other mental processes more closely aligned with the unconscious. Instead of following the allegorical paradigm—a figure: an idea—the mural provoked a much less directed form of viewing that was described by virtually all the critics as being like a dream.

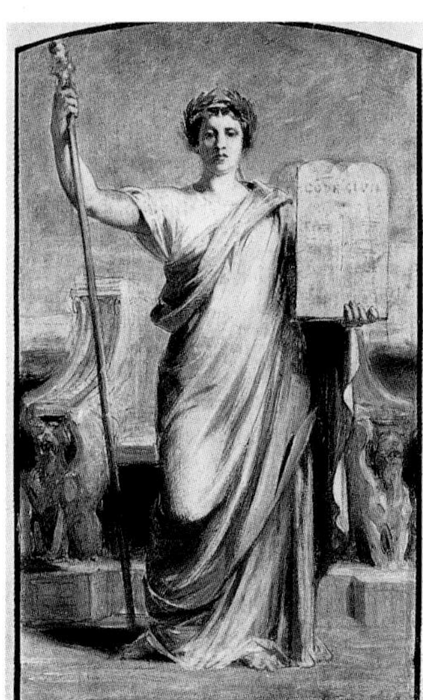

12
Achille Sirouy, *Allegory of the Law*, 1875. Sketch for Mairie du IIIe arrondissement, Paris. Oil on canvas, 12 1/2 x 9 1/2 in. (32 x 24 cm). Musée du Petit Palais, Paris

THE SACRED GROVE

When the critics described *The Sacred Grove* as a dream, they pointed to the unreality of the scene portrayed, to its distance from everyday life. But they also intended something more. Nineteenth-century psychologists generally conceived of dream as an associational chain of image fragments drawn from memory, driven by desire, and not subject to free will.[5] This mural called on each of these elements of the dream state. The combination of an open and inviting foreground and an encompassing and protective background made the landscape feel like a dream—"at once immense and familiar." Because it was "bounded by high black rocks that close off the horizon," the landscape offered "the deep peace of serene solitude."[6] Another critic suggested that it was here in this benevolent space, with the "calm" sensuousness of a "perfumed wood" and the protection of mountains, that creativity could take place as the Muses came "to dream and sing."[7] Another noted that in the foreground "a clearing amenable to walking" invited viewers to imagine entering this landscape and partaking in the reverie.[8]

Puvis's careful ordering of the canvas through both color and composition helped to create the sense of protective calm. One critic attributed this feeling to "the almost exclusive use of verticals and horizontals, the choice of a gray and dull tonality."[9] The landscape is divided into four main horizontal planes that alternate and are tied together with color: a green-banked foreground occupied by Muses, with a few flowers and shrubs scattered here and there; a middle ground with a golden river; another plane of verdant green; and purplish gray mountains. The color of the mountains is repeated in the middle ground by reflections in the golden water. These predominate toward the right of the canvas, and are in turn accented with golden highlights. The canvas, then, is divided into relatively simplified bands of color, each highlighted with elements from the others to give a sense of cohesive design. Their simplicity and opacity combine with the high horizon line to limit the sense of depth behind the figures.

Not only the compositional structure of the landscape but the disposition of the pictured bodies made the mural seem like a dream. Peopled with classically draped Muses, *The Sacred Grove* was meant to be an allegory of French creative genius. Puvis did not, however, portray a centralized, hierarchical composition filled with easily legible allegorical figures. If we compare his composition to another public decoration from the same period, Emile Bin's *Allegory of the Arts* (1879), we see that Bin attempted to "modernize" his allegory by including artists in contemporary dress (fig. 13). Yet the allegorical mode remains wedded to academic tradition. The composition is hierarchically arranged around a central allegorical group of Truth, holding up a mirror, and Renown, blowing on a trumpet.

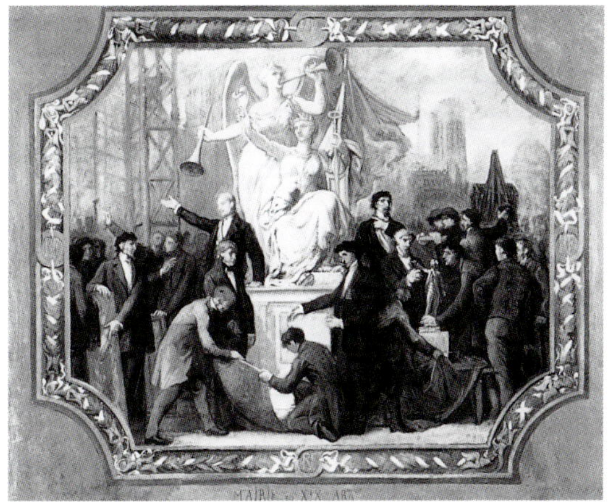

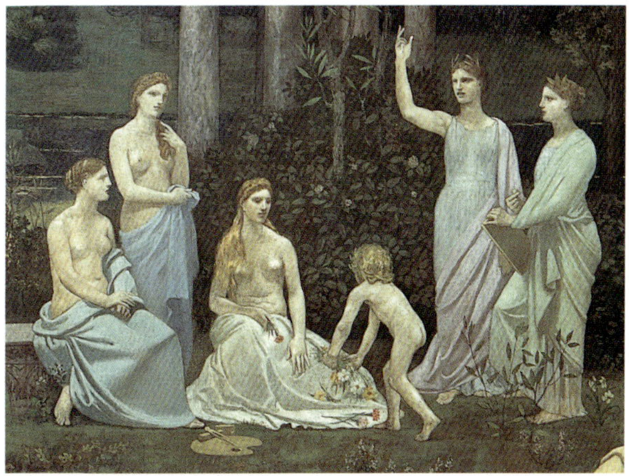

13
Emile Bin, *Allegory of the Arts*, 1879. Sketch for mural in Mairie du XIXe arrondissement, Paris. Oil on canvas, 44 1/2 x 52 3/4 in. (113 x 134 cm). Musée du Pétit Palais, Paris

14
Pierre Puvis de Chavannes, *The Sacred Grove Dear to the Arts and Muses* (detail of fig. 11; central group)

In contrast, the figures of the Arts and Muses in Puvis's mural are dispersed in loose groups across the canvas. Although the female figures seem intended to allegorize specific arts, the structure of the work prevents the associations from being easily decipherable. We are teased with allegorical attributes and gestures, but these are stripped of any precise meaning. For example, on the ground in front of the group of seminude figures before the temple, we see what appears to be a painter's palette (fig. 14). Close examination shows that piled on top of the palette are a sculptor's hammer and a compass. The figures are not holding the attributes; indeed, they seem completely uninterested in them. We are thus given the general notion that these figures represent the plastic arts, but it is difficult to assign a specific art to an individual figure. And the figures themselves distract our attention from the allegory being portrayed. Only a few critics discussed the identities of the figures and the meanings of their attributes, which suggests that even those well versed in academic iconography could not easily decipher allegorized meaning.[10] In fact, the figures themselves were thought to be one of the main sources of the dreamlike nature of the painting. When we look closely at them, it is not hard to see why the critics had trouble pinning down their meanings, for virtually all of them have generalized faces. This is not to say that the figures are all the same. The differences are vivid but issue from their bodies, from the varied positions, gestures, and states of dress or undress, and from the way, as in *Young Girls by the Seashore*, bodily distortion seems to give them an uncommon presence and materiality despite their obvious unreality.

The decorative effect of line distorts the bodies as in *Young Girls by the Seashore*. In *The Sacred Grove*, the sense that the outlines of the bodies are determined at least partly by the need to bring them in accordance with the decorative patterning of the landscape is even more pronounced. Puvis's figures are integrated into the landscape rather than set off from it. The seated figure on the left echoes the shape of the tree and helps it frame the composition. The floating figures hover above to the riverbank, the lower edge of their drapery echoing the reflection of the rocks in the water. The reclining figure also parallels the bank. Two standing figures are framed at the tops of their heads by the reflections in the water. The hand of the figure with her back to us forms a line that can be traced to the ground-line of the central group. In this central group, the raised arm of the standing figure and the upright postures of the others are continued in the columns and in the trees that extend to the right-hand side.

This decorative distortion combines with narrative ambiguity. In the central group, a seated female figure is approached by an adolescent male figure who, in a strange gesture, puts down (or dips into?) a bunch of flowers on her lap. Her left hand seems to block his access while her right hand offers (or receives?) a flower. The nakedness of the ephebe together with the discomfort of his position gives the viewer a heightened awareness of the material presence of his body. His left arm looks as if it is being wrenched from its socket and appears to be excessively long. Although we know from Puvis's explanatory text that this couplet was meant to represent the Lyons tradition of flower painting, few of the critics at the Salon were able to identify the allegory. Instead, the Muse's lack of definition and the difficulty of defining the boy's gesture make this group open to a range of fantasy, especially because flowers were traditionally associated with fertility and female sexuality.

The figures that round out the group also seem to aim at general evocation rather than precise definition. The two semidraped women to the left of the central woman-youth couplet echo and contrast with the two fully draped women to the right of the couplet. The standing figures immediately adjacent to the central couplet beg to be compared with each other. The semidraped figure at the left raises an arm and extends a finger toward her chin. She is both naked and self-absorbed. Her gesture, however, tentatively echoes the bold gesture of the standing figure to the right. This woman is, by contrast, fully clothed and extends her arm as if to speak. The seated figure at the far left of the group plays a similar role in relation to the tablet-holding figure at the far right. Their poses echo and contrast. Faces are seen in profile. Arms extend out from torsos—one naked, the other clothed, one self-absorbed, the other seemingly communicative. These figural pairs play off of each other to emphasize contrasts between the left and right sides of the group—between naked and clothed, between bodily absorption and intellectual projection. In doing so, they echo the viewer's own movement from attempts at conscious decipherment to experiences of unconscious desire. These allegorical bodies and attributes, which should help to fix meaning, instead undermine any certainty about meaning. Puvis sets up an expectation that allegory will work according to convention, but then substitutes imprecision and lack of definition for the identifiable allegory, hierarchical composition, and determinate message usually aimed for in public painting.

Puvis gives us even fewer clues as to the meanings of other figures in the mural. The two figures standing in the left foreground, for example, hold no allegorical attributes at all (see fig. 11). And their gestures are equally equivocal. Puvis has accentuated the thrust of hand on hip and emphasized the solidity of the hip with the drapery falling behind it. The gesture is reversed where her hand meets her chin. But rather than looking solid, the chin seems to disintegrate in shadow, leaving the hand strangely outlined and emphasized. And what of the interaction between the two figures? Is the semidraped figure walking forward, is she reaching out to touch that elusive chin, or is she simply taking up an unreadable pose, a pose that accentuates the nakedness of her arms, the curve of her hip and spine? Puvis's juxtaposition of naked and clothed draws attention to her body, in particular the way her drapery seems to be falling away from, rather than hanging from, her hips. It slips slightly too far down, revealing the tops of her buttocks and just a hint of the cleft between them. Focusing on this figure leads us to see the Muse reclining on the shore as a kind of alter-body, framing the draped figure with nakedness from the other side. The curve of this figure's spine, the view from behind, echoes the pose of the standing figure. Her drapery, too, sits just a bit farther down her frame than we would expect. And her body is paralleled in fully clothed form in the two figures who hover above her.

In a review of the Salon, written as if the writer were "on the wings of a bird," the critic for *Le Français* suggested that *The Sacred Grove* encouraged viewing more akin to the wandering process of a dream than to the concentration and directed meaning expected of high art: "We can stroll at ease in these large canvases; we fly to the left and the right without fear of crashing. We meet, at rare intervals, a pensive and solitary figure, who we can even fly into without great danger, so diaphanous is she. One might say that it is for us, the people of the birds, that M. de Chavannes paints."[11] This passage tells us not only about the type of viewing encouraged by the composition but also about the degree to which the bodies of the Muses contributed to the indeterminacy of the painting. In fact, "diaphanous" seems a rather strange description for any of the bodies on view, given their weightiness and the opacity with which they are rendered. The disjunction between the description of the bodies and what one actually sees when viewing the painting speaks, I think, to the expectation that the body will be dematerialized and idealized through the magic of paint—an expectation that is left unmet.

In another sense, "diaphanous" does seem to tell us something about the figures. It is meant to describe their indefiniteness—the way that precision of contour and detail of structure are lost in the hazy application of paint. It also points to the lack of precision with which we interpret their gestures and relationships. Here is another account of them, this time from the critic Gustave Geffroy: "No precise action, no definite occupation. These figures whose gestures and steps are like a rhythm, whose physiognomy speaks of a rest that nothing can disturb, appear in this silent wood like visions in a dream."[12] "Imprecision," "indefiniteness," "rhythm"—this is a description of Puvis's decorative abstraction. It is a description, that is to say, of what I have been calling Puvis's modernism. In this statement, the difficulty of determining the meaning of gesture, comportment, and physiognomy is connected to the formal qualities of the mural. If, as Geffroy suggests, this wood is silent, so, too, is the painting itself. It does not speak to the viewer—or not in a language whose grammar and lexicon are readily recognizable.[13]

The power of *The Sacred Grove* to captivate its viewers and engage them in a waking dream came not only from the color and design of the landscape but also from the way it provoked them to participate in imagining the body. The painting offered bodies that were just that much too hazy or amorphous—fields of undifferentiated paint bounded by strong bodily outlines, limbs, and features that equivocated rather than portrayed. "Puvis de Chavannes's willed abbreviations are not drawing errors," said Geffroy, "but voluntary and necessary sacrifices. Nothing has been precisely indicated in the bodies and clothing of these noble young women who live only in our imaginations."[14] Henri Fouquier, like Gustave Geffroy, saw the indefiniteness of Puvis's figures as a deliberate strategy to engage the viewer's imaginative participation in the work. He recognized that the power of Puvis's style derived from the way it shifted the burden of idealization from the artist to the viewer. "Instead of searching for an ideal that is impossible to attain," said Fouquier, Puvis de Chavannes "contents himself with evoking the notion in our minds. He leaves us, in sum, to make three-quarters of the painting."[15] This enticement of viewers into their own fantasy making was a threatening departure from the controlled intellectual engagement usually demanded by allegory.

The worry that *The Sacred Grove* replaced the idealizing transcendence of academic allegory with an emphasis on the body and fantasy took its most extreme form in the invective of Edmond About. About was particularly disturbed by Puvis's refusal to adequately describe and idealize the body. He sarcastically described *The Sacred Grove* as "pure negation." His criticism of the mural follows, to some extent, the formula for the denigration of Puvis's paintings that he had already established with reference to easel paintings like *Poor Fisherman* and *Young Girls by the Seashore*. This time About's language emphasized materiality—both the materiality of paint itself and the materiality of the bodies pictured. He criticized, for example, the vagueness of the general atmosphere, where "it is not day . . . and neither is it night," where "an absent moon reflects its crescent in something yellow that is nevertheless not water." The "something yellow," About mockingly suggests, was not identifiable as anything but paint itself. Furthermore, the painting was flat, like "a signboard" above which rise "badly formed trees" that "only have [the] intention" of being oaks, willows, pines, and laurels."[16] Later in the passage, About again links Puvis's willed incompletion to the materiality of the Muses' bodies. He describes the airborne Muses as "two flying sacs of plaster," referencing again the surface of canvas. About begins by talking about negation, about pure absence, and ends up with an account of the materiality of painting. He thus indirectly points to Puvis's modernism as the source of his anxiety.

About's account does not stop there. The materiality he describes also has to do with the bodies themselves. The wood is peopled, he says, with dead things—"formless mannequins"—and with things not yet fully alive—"pale, flaccid, and dislocated larvae that only recall the human figure very distantly." Perhaps most striking is that About centers his description of the figures on the body at its most material and least controllable—the body diseased, dislocated, dead. In general, he describes the figures as not yet fully formed, drained of life, or even wrenched to pieces. In particular, he mentions the materiality of the body as evoked in the Muses, whose limbs are said to swell painfully from cold. The distortion of the body is dramatized by the central boy, "who has arms that are palpably longer than his legs [and] contemplates the enormous hand of his mother with astonishment and asks her naively if her ailment might not be elephantiasis." About also brings the viewer's body into the equation by referencing sensual appetites. He describes one of the pubescent male figures as an "ephebe made of gingerbread." The architecture is "an Ionic portico in the style designed by candy or chocolate makers." About's language is as hallucinatory as it is derogatory. All of his descriptions suggest that he was supplementing the amorphousness of depiction with his own imagination. The kind of understanding the painting solicited was not transcendent and intellectualized but visceral and contingent. The faculties at play in viewing were connected to the appetites, and the response, for About at least, was a mixture of desire and disgust.[17]

We see this juxtaposition of the visceral and contingent with the ideal in another form in a parody of *The Sacred Grove* painted by Henri de Toulouse-

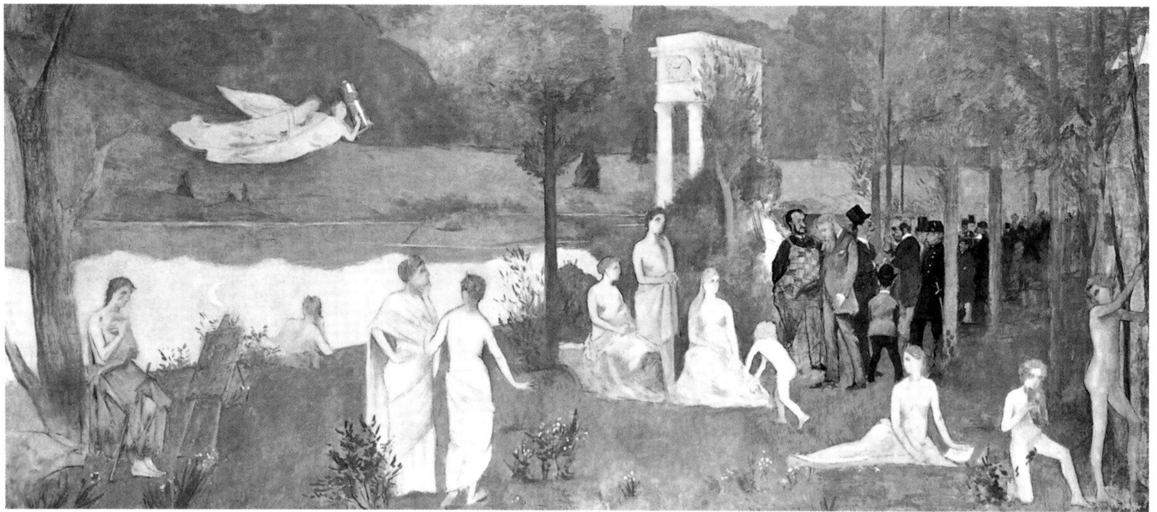

15
Henri de Toulouse-Lautrec and fellow students in Cormon's studio, *Parody of the Sacred Grove*, 1884. Oil on canvas, 67 3/4 x 149 1/2 in. (172 x 380 cm). The Art Museum, Princeton University. Lent by the Henry and Rose Perlman Foundation, Inc.

Lautrec and his fellow students in the studio of the painter Fernand Cormon (fig. 15). This work was both an homage to Puvis de Chavannes and a criticism of his abbreviated style. Looking at this attempt to make the figures "even more 'Chavannesque' than those of Puvis himself" reinforces the notion that incompletion was the key to the initial reception of Puvis's work. In the parody, the female figures are made even flatter and less differentiated. Only outlines and shadows are emphasized. The landscape, too, is even further simplified into flat bands of color. This simplification of means and its association with fantasy as opposed to reality are made to appear even more extreme by the insertion of realist details into the scene. The timelessness of the overall composition comes into jarring contrast with the clock on the Ionic portico (which designates the moment as five minutes past nine) and the equally contemporary figures inserted into the landscape at the right. These figures would have been identifiable to Toulouse-Lautrec and his contemporaries. In particular, just above the shoulder of the seated figure in the right foreground we see an image of Toulouse-Lautrec himself. Seen from the back, the artist stands in a posture which suggests that he may be pissing on the ground of the sacred grove. Here the visceral returns with a vengeance to haunt Puvis's image of the ideal, just as it did in About's diatribe.[18]

Not everyone had such a negative reaction to Puvis's incompletion. The anonymous critic for *Le Gaulois* thought that Puvis's painterly means had "a particular magic," derived from the combination of indeterminacy and sensual pleasure. Like a memory, the figures were too hazy and imprecise to be satisfying.

Despite his dissatisfaction, however, he described how, as he gazed at *The Sacred Grove*, his faculties of critical judgment gave way to the enjoyment of sensual pleasures offered by the work: "This general harmony where the blue dominates with the yellow is delicious; . . . I have before me a tapestry; it is impossible for me to take it as a work of truth, but my eye submits to ravishment. M. Puvis de Chavannes has never been further from the real, but his poetic fantasy imposes itself on me despite myself."[19] This unequivocal celebration of *The Sacred Grove* was the exception rather than the rule. Even those who supported Puvis's general project had their doubts about it.

The conservative critic Charles Clément hoped that Puvis's painting would encourage the viewer to take on the artist's vision and the elevated thought that went along with it. Yet he was also anxious about this prospect. He warned viewers to "take his [Puvis's] part in order to see what he includes." The viewer, Clément said, "must not insist on finding there what is not there." Puvis's paintings offered, he said, "the incompletely formulated dream of a very sincere artist with an elevated, distinguished, and poetic mind." Clément wanted to ensure that the dreamlike state induced by the painting remained bounded by an elevated message. Still, Puvis's painterly technique left him anxious. The artist, he said, "does not know how to give the painting the technical expression that is perfectly satisfactory to his thought." Because the dream that Puvis offered was only "incompletely formulated," the painting ran the risk of setting off a process of fantasy that was not limited by its message. Something about the material quality of the painting, something imprecise "from the point of view of technique," risked muddying the clarity of the high message that Clément deemed Puvis to be presenting.[20] The composition did not give the viewer enough direction, either. Clément complained that the figures were "too detached, too dispersed," and the whole had "too great a lack of focus and cohesion," even taking into account the exigencies of decorating a large surface. That is why Clément cautioned the viewer not to insist on finding in the painting "that which is not there to be found."[21]

A similar worry was expressed by Henri Fouquier—the critic who thought Puvis left his viewers to "make three-quarters of his paintings." Puvis, said Fouquier, was a "dangerous master" who should not be "enjoyed too much by everyone. He must remain in our school as a singular and charming exception."[22] Both critics cautioned their readers not to let their own dreams or fantasies infiltrate the process of viewing. They admonished them instead to take on Puvis's point of view, which was "sincere," "elevated," "distinguished," and "poetic." The risks of viewing Puvis's murals would be avoided, Clément hoped, if viewers followed his prescriptions. But what did Clément imagine would be an inappropriate response? I would suggest that the critics worried that the controlled and concentrated sublimation of desire into the ideal might slip over into the unleashing of unconscious will and sexual desire, that the imagination of transcendent beauty might fall instead into the fantasization of the sensual body, and that the high message of the painting might be lost. After mulling the situation over a bit, Clément concluded that Puvis said "enough, even so, to make himself understood and to lead the viewer after him to the high regions of art."[23] Following the extended concerns about the mural, this conclusion is hardly convincing.

More was at stake for Clément than the possibility that the painting would sexually arouse its viewers. Clément was hostile to all forms of modernity in painting. As the opening section of his Salon review makes clear, he espoused a version of academic classicism that saw art as an act of purely intellectual transcendence. He feared that this tradition was under threat from Naturalism, "in which the notion . . . of aesthetic transformation . . . exists little or not at all" and "gives pride of place to the qualities of material execution." For him, this threat was no small matter; it could, he feared, lead to the disintegration of high art and threaten the cultural identity of France. "These narrow, vulgar, materialist preoccupations," he said, had "diminished and tarnished" the "old and glorious artistic flag." In typically overblown antimaterialist rhetoric, Clément located Naturalism in psychological illness—in "rude and sick minds where the stupidest aberrations take root and grow." Implicit in the fulminations of this conservative critic was an attack on the republican administration whose support of natural and psychological science, Naturalism in art, and democracy in politics constituted its materialism. All of this Clement defined as essentially anti-French. The true path for the artist was set forth by the classical tradition running from Poussin through David, Proud'hon, and Géricault. Clément called for a return to a classical idealism in which the artist strives to "tear the veil" away from the material world in order to find some higher truth, to "pick the golden fruit." This call was best answered—though not as well as he would have liked—by Puvis de Chavannes. However, because Puvis's art gained its very power from incompletion—because, in Clément's terms, Puvis's technique was inadequate to express this thought—Clément was not sure Puvis could fulfill this role. He was not sure, that is to say, whether the processes of creativity that the painting encouraged the viewer to engage in would have results that would live up to his notion of Frenchness.[24]

In contrast to conservative critics like About and Clément, writers espousing republicanism embraced the sensuous materiality of Puvis's work in the course of praising him. In addition to writing extensive criticism for the republican press and several works of art history, Marius Vachon was a member of several arts administrations and *missionaire* of the Ministry of Fine Arts from 1882 to 1888.[25] Writing for *La France,* Vachon claimed Puvis for republican Naturalism. This involved both refuting academic appropriations of Puvis such as Clément's and quelling realist criticisms of Puvis's "ethereal idealism" and "aesthetic asceticism." Puvis, Vachon said, was "a true *naturalist*" who knew "how to join ampleness of style, originality, and imagination to a profound sentiment of realism." Even though Puvis's subject matter was not characteristic of Naturalism, said Vachon, the general feeling of the work was rooted in the material world. Vachon noted that the details of the landscape—flowers, shrubs, and rocks—were painted with "the research of realist exactitude." Puvis's confidence as a landscapist was demonstrated, said Vachon, by his willingness "to envelop [the landscape] in a sensation of poetry."[26] Yet in his description of Puvis's Naturalism Vachon avoided mention of the human body. When Vachon did discuss Puvis's handling of the body, he emphasized simplification, linking Puvis's technique to "the simplicity of ancient works." The "synthetic character" of Puvis's work was, Vachon said, like ancient poetry.

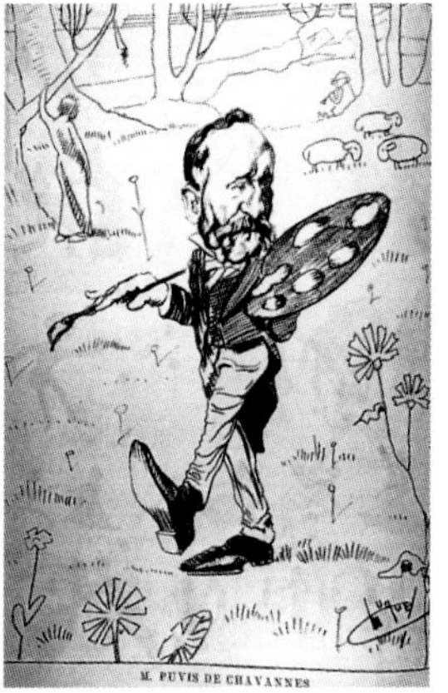

16
Lucque, caricature of Puvis de Chavannes, "Les Hommes du Jour—M. Puvis de Chavannes." *La Caricature*, May 8, 1886, p. 156

Puvis's paintings were achieved, Vachon claimed, not through idealization but through synthesis. They aimed not to move away from the material world toward a more ideal one but to bring out characteristics immanent in the world and thus picture the possibilities it offered. By treating Puvis's incompletion as unproblematic synthesis, Vachon aligned his painting with republican materialism while avoiding the problems raised by the issue of desire. The characterization of Puvis's work as synthesis was a strategy typical of republican and Left-leaning critics who, even when they used the notion of idealism to describe Puvis's work, attempted to redefine the ideal as something that was not transcendent and universal but immanent in humanity.

In a sense, then, Vachon, in describing *The Sacred Grove*, was as blinded by his own aesthetic and political agenda as Clément was. Neither critic was able to admit that the power of Puvis's work arose from the desires instilled by his indeterminate mode and the resultant calls to fantasy. A full-page caricature by Lucque published in *La Caricature* in the same year *The Sacred Grove* was exhibited suggests another model for the reception of Puvis's murals (fig. 16). The artist is shown wandering aimlessly through one of his own fantasy landscapes. This caricature makes explicit what lay behind the criticism of Puvis de Chavannes by About and Clément. What the critics failed to see was that the source of their anxiety was the most powerful aspect of Puvis's work: the address to individual fantasy. Or perhaps they did see this but were afraid to face what this power implied about Frenchness, about representation, about human subjectivity.

Others were not so short-sighted. In an article on Puvis written for the series "Notes on Art" that appeared in *La France* after the Salon closed, Octave Mirbeau stressed the roots of Puvis's painting in fantasy.[27] Good art, claimed Mirbeau, had either to be completely rooted in the real, as in the painting of Manet, or completely outside it. The "intermediary categories" in which art attempted to transform nature into the ideal, said Mirbeau, were "the great modern mediocrity." Mirbeau was referring to the academic discourse on the ideal. His discussion of Puvis began by negating academic conceptions of art like those espoused by Clément, and proposing instead an aesthetics tied to individual response. He criticized the notion that "Beauty can be taught like grammar, as if there existed a Beauty that was more Beautiful, a Beauty more true, a unique Beauty; as if Beauty were not a completely personal faculty."[28] For Mirbeau, whose later anarchism sprang from an extreme cult of individualism, this academic aesthetic straitjacket—in which "it is not permitted to us to break these forms and to fold these lines under the pressure of a personal idea or a particular vision"—had to be resisted. Mirbeau believed that Puvis was responding to his own personal vision. This, more than anything else, attracted him to the painter.

Puvis de Chavannes was Mirbeau's example of an artist who understood that art's power to move people came from its ability to provoke them to imagine: "It is necessary to create it in our imagination and to live in a pure dream." Puvis's murals, he said, depicted "the abstract and charming dream where humanity changes color and transforms itself."[29] For Mirbeau, this transformation came from an enmeshing of memory and fantasy that replaced both academic convention and Naturalism: "What moves me deeply in Puvis de Chavannes is that this great artist, who is also a great poet, is not from any time, from any school, from any clique or any habit. He seems to me to be a belated one [*attardé*] in this era of full-speed civilization and persistent prejudice: belated or reminiscent, I do not know for certain; belated by his latent and unrevealed poetry or reminiscent of lost paradises?"[30] With the question that ends this passage Mirbeau struggled to define the character of Puvis's art and pointed his readers to the crux of its power—the way it drew on individual memory and fantasy for its meaning.

Puvis seemed to Mirbeau to have a continuing contact with something concrete and primordial that was lost to most people and overlooked by those relying on academic conventions of beauty. He imagined that latent meanings and lost paradises were accessible to Puvis. If Puvis was a "belated one," suggested Mirbeau, he must be living in memory, dwelling in the possibilities of plenitude that his paintings encourage us to imagine. Here Mirbeau's description is close to Vachon's, to Vachon's confidence that Puvis has achieved a synthesis of the truths latent in the

Real. If Puvis was reminiscing, however, then he had only a memory of what was irretrievably lost. Although Mirbeau wanted to believe that the power of Puvis's art derived from something authentic and uncorrupted by modernity, his question suggests that what Puvis sought to picture might be lost even to the artist—might be less a product of contact and perceptiveness than of melancholy fantasy.

As the passage continues, Mirbeau suggests more strongly that Puvis's route to "lost paradise" lies in fantasy. While the century "runs, roars, hurries, and pants" around him, Puvis "neither looks nor listens." Instead, says Mirbeau, he closes himself up "in a magnificent dream." Mirbeau's description of Puvis's dream tells us a great deal about the way his painting functioned. The dream was "dominated by the ideal." However, it did not claim to offer the ideal wholesale as academic painting pretended to. Into the dream offered by Puvis "human sensibility nevertheless passes and shudders sadly, like a large and slow palpitation of wings in the azure." Evoking Mallarmé's poem "L'Azur," Mirbeau attempts to capture that struggle toward the forever inaccessible. The "sad shudder," the "slow palpitation of wings in the azure," the futile beating back and forth that never renders up its object but only flies toward it—all of that, suggests Mirbeau, was part of the process that brought forth the work, all of that lay at the origins of creativity pictured in *The Sacred Grove*. "The ideal" thus depended on, and was rooted in, human sensibility. When Mirbeau summed up the process of artistic creation, he chose three simple words: "He sees inside."[31] With these words, Mirbeau signaled once again the rootedness of Puvis de Chavannes's work in fantasy. And this returns us to the questions that hang about Puvis's public murals. If Puvis de Chavannes's creative process required an inward-turning "see[ing] inside," what chance of fulfilling an educational goal did his paintings have?

HYSTERIA, HYPNOSIS, AND THE LANGUAGE OF DREAM

Beyond the general questions that *The Sacred Grove* raised about the relation between modernism and human subjectivity were more specific questions having to do with the mission of the Lyons cycle. What, we might ask, could it mean to describe a work of public art as a dream? If painting was a dream, what was the content of the hallucination? Could it be controlled? If it could not, how could the painting educate its viewers?

The worries that haunted the descriptions of *The Sacred Grove*—worries about the power of its invocation of fantasy—are perhaps best expressed in responses that explicitly linked the mural to theorizations of the unconscious in contemporary psychology. The new language for bodily description—the peculiar conjunction of evocativeness and materialization—that characterized *The Sacred Grove* specifically

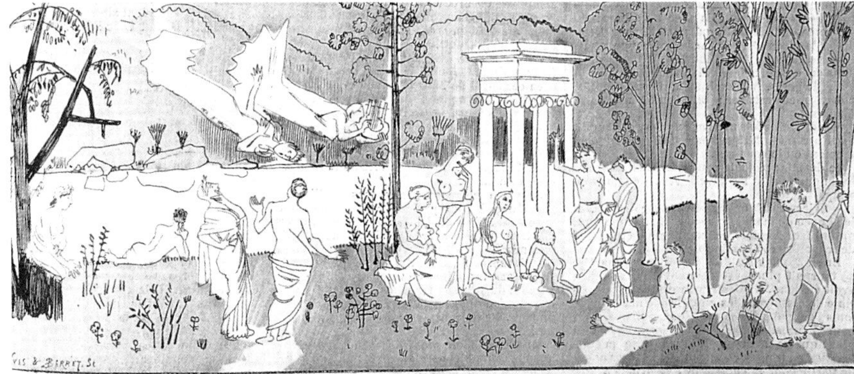

17
A. Robida, caricature of *The Sacred Grove Dear to the Arts and Muses*, "Antiquisme." *La Caricature*, May 17, 1884, p. 161

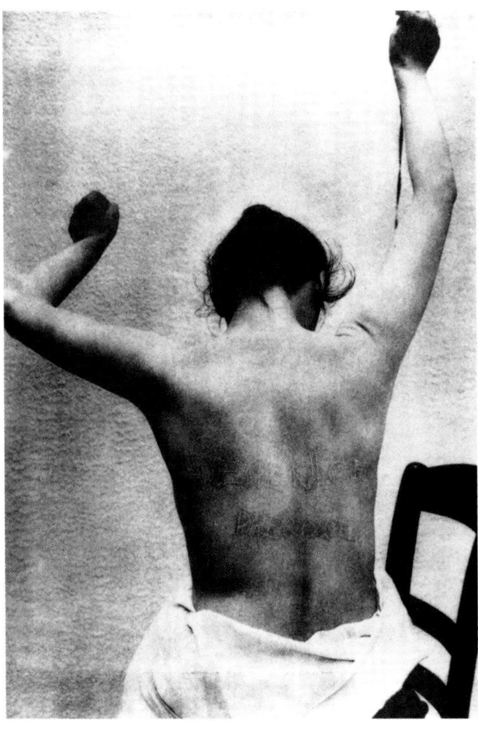

18
"Synoptic table of the grand hysterical attack"

19
A dermographic woman made to bear the imprint of her own diagnosis: dementia praecox

and Puvis's modernism more generally was parodied in a large color lithograph in *La Caricature* (fig. 17).[32] Much of the humor revolves around the tensions produced where bodies come into contact with themselves or are made to echo each other and the landscape. Puvis's subtle bodily distortions are greatly exaggerated here. The standing Muse at the left of the composition now seems to hit her chin and throw her entire upper body backward. Her torso now parallels the flying figures, who dive toward the shore. In the central group, the arm of the seated figure is even more elongated, and her hand is made clawlike. The self-reflexive gestures of the two figures on the left are more extreme (now finger is thrust into mouth) and paired with facial expressions that suggest mental disturbance. The figures are thus made over into images of hysteria.

The artist and model Suzanne Valadon posed for all of the figures. With this in mind, we can read the figures not as separate women but as the same figure repeated over and over, reminding us even more of contemporary psychology experiments in which women were recorded at different moments in a hysterical fit, in different *attitudes passionelles* (figs. 18, 19).[33] Janet Beizer has eloquently described the hysteric's body as a "ventriloquized body," a "narrative screen" upon which cultural myths are projected and contained—particularly those myths that equate femininity with disorder, duplicity, alterity, fluidity, unboundedness, responsibility for social upheaval.[34]

This caricature suggests, I believe, that Puvis's configuration of the female body invoked the potential for a similar process of inscription. What raised particular problems was the concern that only the blank page was showing, that Puvis had not adequately spoken for the bodies on view. They were thus left open to ventriloquization by individual viewers. And the fear was that Puvis's modernist mode of address might encourage the wrong stories to be told by the wrong narrators. I mean by this that the bodily address of Puvis's paintings was thought to provoke a relationship between viewer and work that had less to do with intellectual decipherment or critical judgment than with processes in which conscious control was diminished.

The sense that *The Sacred Grove* asked its viewers to give up conscious control of the self was perhaps best described by Firmin Javel, who exclaimed: "An involuntary respect seizes you, an unexplained charm pins you to the spot."[35] Involuntary immobilization, captivation by an outside force, submission to its will—this description borrows more from a popular fascination with hypnosis (to which hysterics, women, children, and anyone with diminished faculties were thought to be particularly susceptible) than from the language of high art criticism. By the end of the century an analogy between hypnosis and the aesthetic experience would be explicit. In a book dedicated to the relation between art and the hypnotic trance, Paul Souriau wrote:

> In the contemplation of beauty, in the effect a work of art can produce in us, there is something strange, something that we cannot yet explain very well. It is completely normal that we should look at beautiful things with pleasure. But don't we sometimes end up, after contemplating them for a while, falling into a sort of ecstasy that prolongs itself indefinitely unless some outside event calls us back to ourselves? In the illusions produced by painting, aren't there some aspects of hallucination? . . . Between the hypnotic state and the ecstasy of the beautiful, between the effects of suggestion and those of art, there is a singular resemblance, which makes one think. Even though they are evidently different in degree, aren't they at bottom of the same nature?[36]

We should hear in Souriau's troubled passage a reconceptualization of the aesthetic experience that is integrally related to the development of modernism. The key terms are "pleasure," "ecstasy," and "hallucination," and they establish a movement from sensual pleasure to unconscious processes of mind. The dreamlike nature of Puvis's style and his ability to infiltrate the unconscious of his viewers were central to the questions raised by some critics about the implications of his public art. There was a great deal of cultural anxiety about the potentially dangerous aspects of hypnosis and suggestion, and these, too, were linked to the question of human subjectivity and the degree to which it could be directed and controlled either by the self or by others.[37] At issue in hypnosis and suggestion was the degree of control the hypnotist or artist had over the subject's unconscious. The tone of the passage from Souriau suggests a concern about painting akin to Brunetière's fears that Symbolist poetry would entice readers and writers into their own egoistic worlds of fantasy.

Souriau's description, like Brunetière's attack on Symbolism, was written in the 1890s, at a moment when modernisms had begun to be explicitly associated with the unconscious—thanks in part to the work of Puvis de Chavannes. As early as the mid-1880s, however, when *The Sacred Grove* was exhibited, others more sympathetic to modernism and less wedded to traditional conceptions of subjectivity were giving the links between aesthetics and the unconscious a positive cast. The philosopher Henri Bergson, for example, in comparing aesthetic experience and hypnosis, wrote: "The object of art is to put to sleep the active or resistant strengths of our personality and to bring us thus to a state of perfect docility in which we experience the idea that [the artist] suggests to us, in which we sympathize with the expressed sentiment."[38] The methods of art are an "attenuated," "refined," and "somewhat spiritualized" form of the methods used to attain a state of hypnosis. For Bergson, the similarity between art and hypnosis was unproblematic. He confidently asserted the artist's power to control the responses of viewers.[39]

Bergson's description gives us a good sense of one way public art might have been imagined to capitalize on the unconscious. On this model, Puvis's murals would educate viewers by offering them the possibility of participating in *his* dreams. The dream state, like a hypnotic trance, was thought to offer a kind of semiconsciousness where the subject was open to the effect of suggestion on the unconscious mind. If the language of dreams gave critics a way of describing Puvis's murals, the language of suggestion enabled them to give that experience a constructive dimension. Indeed, many of Puvis's supporters seem to have felt that his murals successfully offered their viewers a noble and elevated dream. A portrait of the artist by Marcellin Desboutin shows Puvis in an armchair, imagining the figures and the landscape of *The Sacred Grove* and, with a gesture, directing his viewers to do the same (fig. 20). Another portrait of Puvis, by Georges Jean (fig. 21), also places him in a chair among the figures of *The Sacred Grove*,

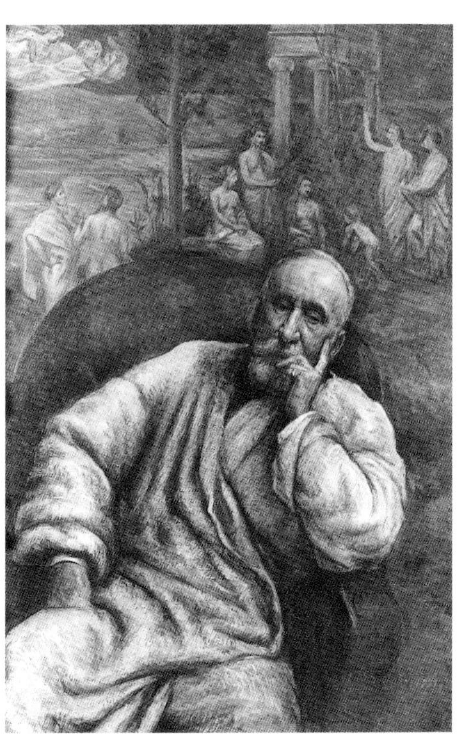

20
Marcellin Desboutin, *Portrait of Pierre Puvis de Chavannes*, 1895. Oil on canvas, $47^{1}/_{4}$ x $31^{1}/_{2}$ in. (120 x 80 cm). Musée de Picardie, Amiens

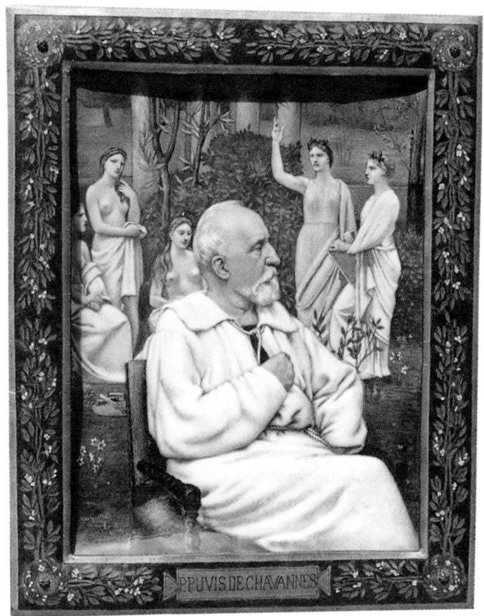

21
Georges Jean, *Portrait of Pierre Puvis de Chavannes*, 1895. Painted enamel. Private collection, France

but here the bathrobe he wore in Desboutins's image has been transformed into a monk's habit, as if to guarantee the virtuousness of his vision. In addition, he is shown in profile, as if to emphasize the strength of his French features. In fact, almost no one disputed Puvis's character or the aim of his dream. Puvis was held up as a model of the upright French citizen who embodied only the healthiest qualities.[40] His dreams, these two images suggest, were free from degraded forms of fantasy.

AESTHETICS, FEELING, AND COLLECTIVE DESIRE

During the same period that *The Sacred Grove* was criticized for its modern call to individual fantasy and feeling, some writers were attempting to theorize a positive role for the unconscious in representation. The republican social philosophers Jean-Marie Guyau and Alfred Fouillée recognized that if aesthetics were to continue to have any place in the experience of modernity, the role of desire would have to be taken into account. Their social theory was aimed not only at describing the experience of modern art but also at helping art to promote republican solidarity.[41] They proposed that art was a tool that could be used to transform desire from a source of anxiety into a source of political power.

Guyau contested the notion that aesthetic contemplation was disinterested and consciously controlled, and transcended the body. Such a view, he believed, turned art into an intellectual game, abstracted it from the material world, and thus trivialized it. Rather than conceiving of art as an attempt to grasp and make a moral example of transcendent and absolute forms of beauty, Guyau located aesthetics in that which "serves life" or maximizes the life force common to all people. In his book *Problems in Contemporary Aesthetics*, Guyau began his account of aesthetics by examining its origin in bodily functions, needs, and desires. "Need," "desire," and "the pleasurable," said Guyau, were "the primitive and most basic foundation of the aesthetic."[42]

Guyau challenged the notion dominating current aesthetic theory, that high art provided an aesthetically disinterested intellectual experience. Guyau pitted his argument against philosophical theories that posited an absolute and transcendent form of beauty. These theories underpinned nineteenth-century academic aesthetic theories of the kind that critics like Clément championed.[43] Guyau offered instead a version of aesthetics that recognized pleasure and desire as integral to the experience of art: "In sum, nothing is more inexact than the complete opposition . . . between the feeling of the beautiful and desire: that which is beautiful is desirable *by the same criteria*. . . . There is no aesthetic emotion that does not awaken in us a multitude of desires and needs that are more or less unconscious. . . . There is pleasure in desire itself, and the period of desire often leaves us with a state of mind that is more delicious than sexual pleasure [*la jouissance*]."[44]

What I want to highlight here is Guyau's focus on the unconscious components of aesthetic reception, as well as the links he makes between the unconscious and sexual instincts, drives, and desires. These form the unconscious base of a continuum of feelings of pleasure, which may be evoked, he suggests, by the experience of works of art.

As the aesthetic experience becomes more refined, desire increases to the point of being positively painful. The pleasures (*jouissances*) the poet takes in his work, for example, "imply a suffering," and this pain demonstrates the seriousness of the work: "The artist's despair and the thing that leads him easily to pessimism is to desire immeasurably and to be able to satisfy his desires only in small measure."[45] Indeed, Guyau suggested that there is even a sexual component in the desire through which works are created and received. Only in a superficial account of aesthetic feeling, said Guyau, could it be separated from sexual instinct.[46]

Guyau was well aware of the problem that his reintegration of desire into aesthetics would cause for many of his contemporaries. If the aesthetic experience was not about disinterested contemplation, what would prevent it from being nothing more than a spur to individual fantasy with the potential to release unconscious forces beyond anyone's power to control? Introducing desire as a component of intellectual processes seemed to threaten a total dissolution of the structures of civilization. Turning the tables on critics like Brunetière for whom egoism and desire went hand in hand, Guyau dismissed the notion that desire and pleasure were necessarily egoistic and divided human beings. Instead, Guyau imagined that desire was the force that could most profoundly bond viewers together.[47] Art's powerful address to the unconscious should be used for political purposes, Guyau suggested—to unite viewers "in the same pleasure" (*la même jouissance*).

Guyau believed that desire was not a force that threatened to unravel the social fabric but was instead a powerful tool for the promotion of national solidarity. Instilling solidarity would require the manipulation of the popular will. And this could be achieved if all members of the public could be made to desire the same things. Achieving this concordance of desire would require a manipulation, not of conscious reason, but of "sensations" and "sentiments." Guyau's student Alfred Fouillée summed up this view of the socializing potential of desire in an introduction to Guyau's *Art from the Sociological Point of View*.[48] According to Fouillée and Guyau, the common tools of social concord—metaphysics, morality, and the science of education—had thus far only been able to establish "a community of ideas and wills." What remained to be established was "an actual community of sensations and feeling." The role of great art was to "socialize" the sensations and feelings that initially seemed to operate on an individual level. Art could do this by "rendering them identical . . . from individual to individual": "From the incoherent and discordant depths of individual sensations and feelings, art disengages an ensemble of sensations and sentiments that can be held in common by everyone at once . . . and that can give rise to a *concordance* of pleasures [*jouissances*]. And the characteristic of these pleasures is that they do not exclude one another, in the manner of egoistic pleasures [*plaisirs égoïstes*], but are, on the contrary, in essential 'solidarity.'"[49]

At the heart of Guyau's theory, then, was the problem of how to integrate individual will into collective will, how to bridge that gap between individual sensations, feelings, and needs, on the one hand, and collective necessity, on the other. Art's unique potential to influence on the level of feeling is what seemed to provide the solution: "All art is a means of social concord, which is more profound than any other; because to *think* [*penser*] in the same manner is already a lot to achieve, but it is not yet enough to make us *desire* [*vouloir*] in the same manner: the great secret is to make us *feel* [*sentir*] in the same manner, and that is the marvel that art accomplishes."[50] Fouillée thus implied that the French state should make use of the new understandings of subjectivity that were the result of the psychological research it had fostered. Fouillée believed that the discovery of the unconscious showed that the *moi* (the self) was not autonomous and that the intellect was always structured by desire.[51] But if the subject was decentered by desire, Fouillée suggested, why not capitalize on this fact? Why not use works of art to instill a concordance of feelings and desires? Art's powerful address to unconscious desires through the senses could be used, he and Guyau maintained, to instill a sense of solidarity at the deepest levels of the psyche by making viewers "feel in the same manner." Embedded in Fouillée's rhetoric is a movement from conscious intellect to sensation and desire. The passage from intellect to feeling is also the defining feature of Puvis's revision of academic definitions of the aesthetic that had previously dominated public painting.

3

DREAMING THE FRENCH PATRIMONY

"If one takes note of the dreams that men have during a determined period," said Hegel to his disciple Heinrich Heine, "one sees emerge . . . a completely true image of the spirit of the period. . . ." Puvis de Chavannes's painted reveries express, with varied nuances of beauty and in different fashions, some of our habitual ways of dreaming or of longing for happiness, and this is why [this master] who has never reproduced . . . the formal appearances of contemporary life [is] nonetheless the most truly modern of our school. ANDRÉ MICHEL

When Puvis de Chavannes exhibited the last installment of his murals for the Museum of Fine Arts, Lyons, at the Salon of 1886, he entered into a group of intersecting debates about high art, creativity, and the French sensibility. *Ancient Vision* (1885) and *Christian Inspiration* (1886) showed two extremes of creative endeavor in settings that evoked the two major strands of the French heritage. In *Ancient Vision* a lone sculptor pursues his art in a vaguely Greek setting dominated by languorous women (fig. 22). In *Christian Inspiration* artist-monks undertake a spiritual engagement with transcendent form in a fraternal sanctuary (fig. 23). *Ancient Vision* exudes sensual plenitude and encourages open-ended fantasy. *Christian Inspiration*, on the other hand, both pictures and promotes a controlled and transcendent engagement closer to the masculine academic paradigm of idealization discussed in Chapter 1. The cycle as a whole suggested that each scene showed an aspect of the French heritage, and each kind of endeavor contributed to producing creative work that was quintessentially French.

A glance at these paintings makes clear that the approaches to creativity imagined in them and the models of subjectivity that each presupposed were conceived in gendered terms: sensuality was aligned with femininity, transcendence with masculinity. This impression is reinforced when we recall the way the paintings were originally displayed at the Salon. *Ancient Vision* occupied the left side of a triptych. *Christian Inspiration* was placed on the right. In between them were *The Rhône and the Saône* (1886)—allegories in a river landscape representing the two rivers of Lyons, with a doorway separating them (fig. 24). The left side of the space

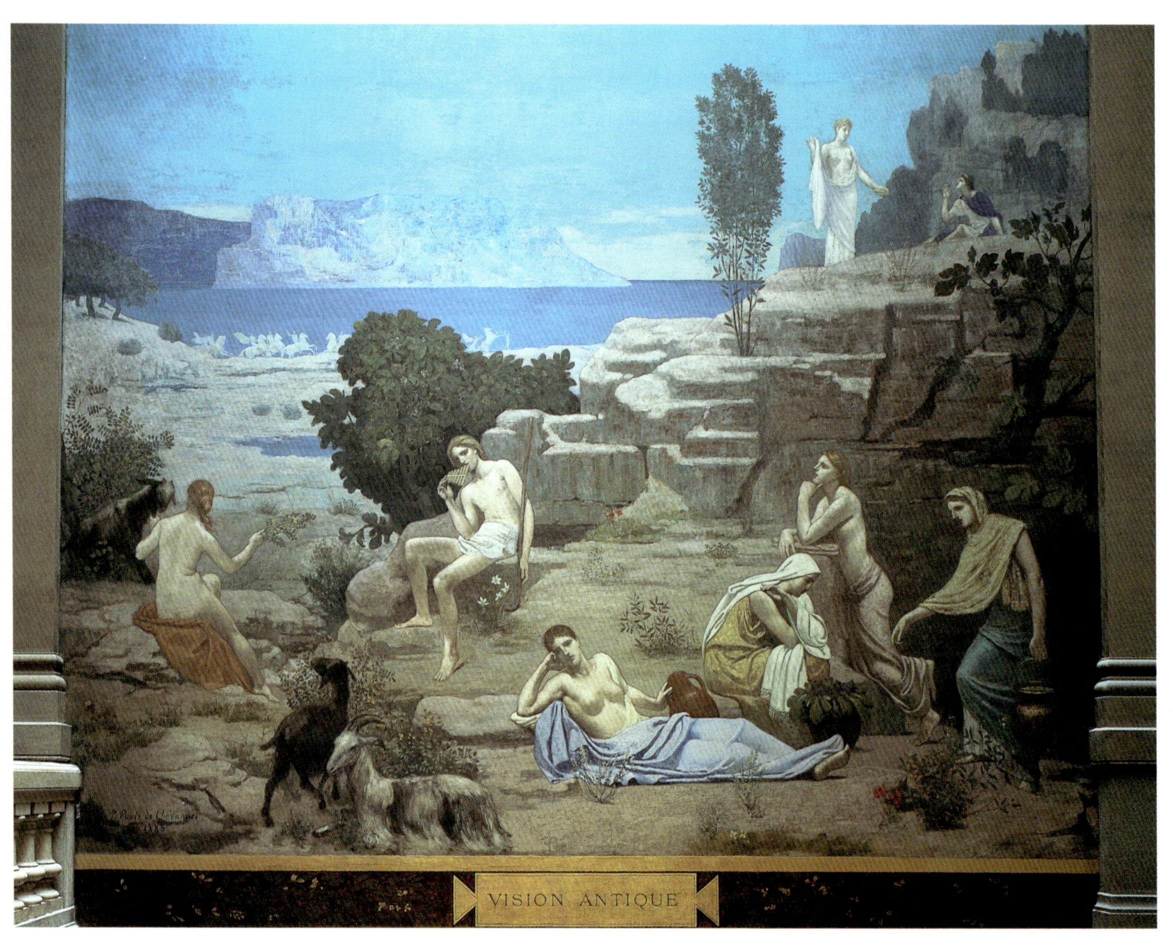

22
Pierre Puvis de Chavannes,
Ancient Vision, 1885.
Oil on canvas affixed to wall,
181 x 227 1/2 in. (460 x 578 cm).
Musée des Beaux-Arts, Lyons

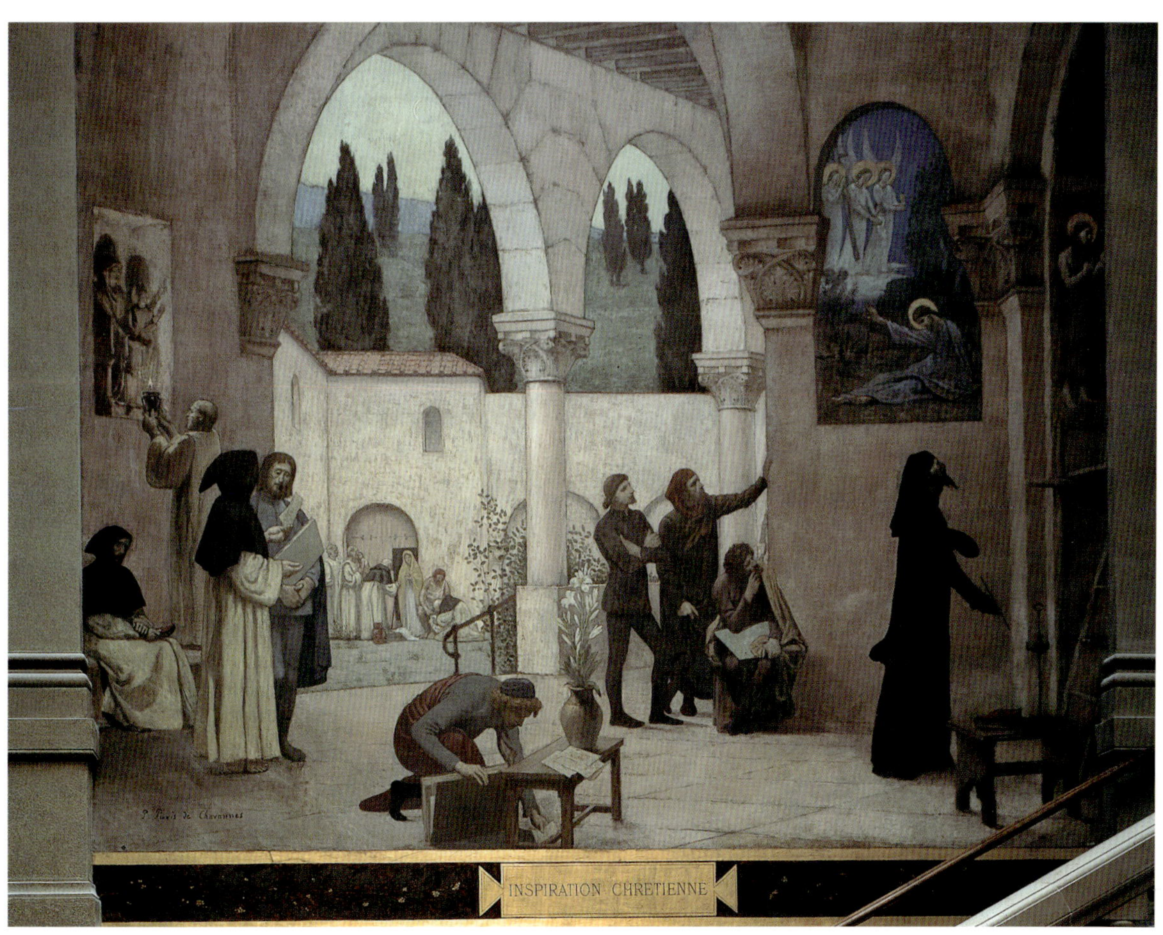

23
Pierre Puvis de Chavannes,
Christian Inspiration, 1886.
Oil on canvas affixed to wall,
181 x 227½ in. (460 x 578 cm).
Musée des Beaux-Arts, Lyons

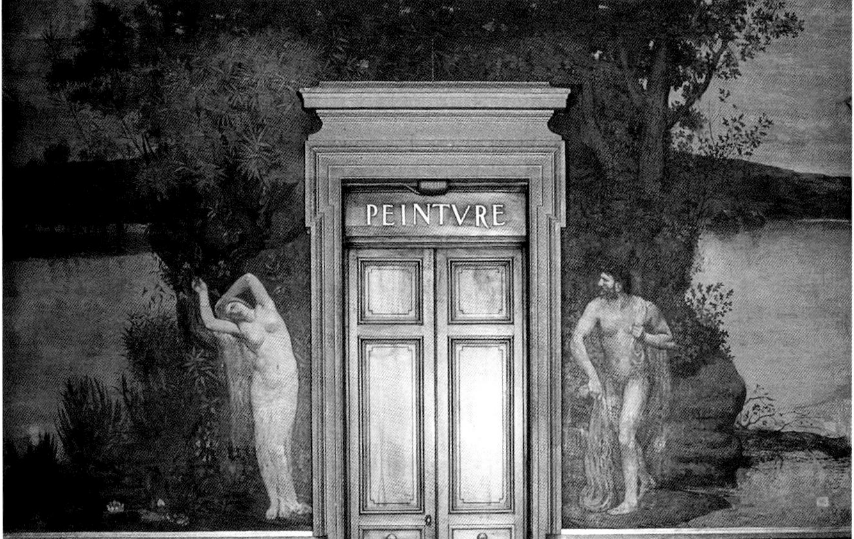

24
Pierre Puvis de Chavannes, *The Rhône and the Saône*, 1886. Oil on canvas affixed to wall, 181 x 409½ in. (460 x 1,040 cm). Musée des Beaux-Arts, Lyons

was peopled predominately by female figures—both those pictured in *Ancient Vision* and the one that allegorized the Saône. To the right of the doorway stood a male allegory for the Rhône flanked by the male figures of *Christian Inspiration*.[1]

To say that Puvis imagined *Ancient Vision* and *Christian Inspiration* to depict the origins of the French heritage is not to say that the artist gave each mural equal weight. When he exhibited the murals in the Salon of 1886, he included a text in the catalogue that not only identified the murals but referred his viewers back to the largest mural of the cycle, *The Sacred Grove Dear to the Arts and Muses*, which he had exhibited in the Salon of 1884. *The Sacred Grove*, said the catalogue entry, was the "primordial and generative composition" that had given rise to these other two "complementary subjects."[2] If *Ancient Vision* and *Christian Inspiration* taught about particular aspects of French creativity, *The Sacred Grove* represented a synthesis of them. It was meant to be an encompassing image of modern French creativity. As we saw in Chapter 2, *The Sacred Grove* offered a general allegory of creative inspiration. In it Puvis pictured Muses in a variety of postures scattered across an idyllic pastoral setting. It seems, then, that despite its earlier exhibition, *The Sacred Grove* was Puvis de Chavannes's final word on the truth about modern French creativity. Indeed, if we look at the cycle, we see that both *Ancient Vision* and *The Sacred Grove* are dominated by compositional structures at odds with the hierarchy, order, and transcendence pictured in *Christian Inspiration*. Instead, both *The Sacred Grove* and *Ancient Vision* encourage creative interaction dependent on those aspects of subjectivity aligned with the unconscious—with sensuality, dream, and fantasy.

What should we make of the fact that in the vision of Frenchness evoked by the cycle, Puvis emphasizes aspects of subjectivity at odds with the autonomy of the human subject and more aligned, in the discourse of the nineteenth century, with the feminine? What does the critical response to the virtual elision of transcendent idealism in *Ancient Vision* and *The Sacred Grove* tell us about contemporary understandings of Frenchness? What were the political implications of this rejection of autonomous subjectivity and traditional forms of creativity and this alignment of Frenchness and femininity? And what, finally, is the relation between these questions and modernism?

Puvis de Chavannes's murals for the Museum of Fine Arts, Lyons, had the aim of educating citizens about Lyons. But they also promoted a more general notion of Frenchness. By making his murals appropriate to the site for which they were destined, Puvis also portrayed French patrimony as a whole.[3] The city of Lyons was built on both ancient and medieval architectural remains and thus encapsulated the national patrimony. In choosing to picture ancient and medieval artists in the process of creation, Puvis drew on a notion of the French heritage that had its origins in republicanism. The project of defining a patrimony that was the property of all citizens was integral to republican national self-definition. It began with the French Revolution, and was explicitly mandated in 1837, when the Commission des Monuments Historiques created three primary categories of preservation—ancient ruins, religious edifices from the Middle Ages, and châteaux—thus formally defining the ancient Greco-Roman and medieval Christian heritages as the main strands of the patrimony.[4] The patrimony was neither fixed nor neutral. Rather, it was, from the beginning, the site of a battle over the definition of France, over who truly belonged to France, over whose traditions its riches embodied.[5] So, for example, whereas Catholics and royalists often emphasized the predominance of the medieval Christian heritage, republicans tended to locate the origins of France in the classical tradition of ancient democracies.

Like other municipal museums, the Museum of Fine Arts, Lyons, had the double role of promoting the national heritage and emphasizing the contribution of the region to *la patrie*.[6] The museum housed one of the prime collections of antiquities in France, as well as works by famous Lyons religious painters. It also participated in the *envoi* system, whereby works by contemporary artists exhibited in the Paris Salon were sent to provincial museums to educate those in the provinces about contemporary French art. The importance that the French state placed on formalizing the dissemination of the patrimony across the nation via the Commission des Monuments Historiques, the building of provincial museums, and the *envoi* system, together with the pride taken by the French in the notion that Paris was the center of the art world, suggests that their understanding of Frenchness was dependent on the patrimony.

The cultural artifacts that made up the patrimony were valued as signs of wealth and power. They were also thought to contain the material in which Frenchness inhered, for Frenchness was seen to be intimately tied to the processes of creativity that produced the artifacts of the patrimony. When Puvis de Chavannes painted the patrimony, he did not merely depict the objects that constituted it. He also evoked the processes of creativity that gave rise to those objects by picturing ancient and medieval figures pursuing their art. As we shall see when we look carefully at responses to the paintings, Puvis structured the murals to prompt viewers to engage in imaginative acts analogous to those undertaken by the figures portrayed. Furthermore, because creativity was thought to be at the core of the French sensibility, Puvis's murals ultimately asked their viewers to participate actively in Frenchness itself. The power of Puvis's murals came from the ways that they encouraged their viewers to enact the imaginative processes that, it was thought, were integral to Frenchness.

GENDER, CREATIVITY, FRENCHNESS: *ANCIENT VISION* AND *CHRISTIAN INSPIRATION*

What kinds of creativity and Frenchness were pictured in the Lyons cycle? In *Ancient Vision*, creativity is linked to sensuousness and desire. The mural has a calm and voluptuous opulence. The visual field is divided across a diagonal by rocks that climb from the lower left to the upper right of the painting. At the left, the landscape extends back to a completely flat and intensely saturated blue sea, cliffs, and sky. Toward the right a hill is topped by a grove of trees. The columns of a temple rise in the background. The palette that Puvis employs is much brighter and more intense here than in *Christian Inspiration*, which is dominated by beiges, browns, and grays. *Ancient Vision* thus pleasurably fills the viewer's senses on the level of abstract design and color. This sensuality is also thematized in the subject matter of the painting. Despite a somewhat arid appearance, the landscape gives the impression of bounteousness, which contrasts starkly with the asceticism of *Christian Inspiration*, a scene of a medieval monastery. Sustenance is offered in the basket of fruit next to the seated woman and in the jug of drink carried by another female figure. Most of the seminude figures lounge languorously in the rocky foreground, giving an impression of warmth and lassitude.

In *Ancient Vision*, inspiration is rooted not in immaterial contemplation but in sensory "vision." Puvis de Chavannes's entry in the Salon brochure explained that the painting was meant to give "the idea of form." By this the artist meant not transcendent Platonic form but visual form—the formal design of the landscape and, above all, the form of the bodies that occupy the foreground—the kind of form based in visual pleasure. In fact, in the upper right-hand corner of the mural on top of the cliffs, Puvis included the most common trope for art as vision—the image of an artist inspired by the sight of his muse's body (fig. 25). A half-draped female figure stands with her torso exposed to a seated man in a white toga and blue cape. In her right hand she holds the drapery she has just removed; with her left she offers the man a sculptor's hammer.

Linking vision and desire for the female body to artistic creation was nothing new. Puvis's innovation comes from the relation that this invocation of an old paradigm has to the overall structure of his composition. To understand this point, let us compare *Ancient Vision* to *The Poet and His Muse* (1888), by Jean-Léon Gérôme, which provides an example of how this trope was typically deployed in academic practice (fig. 26). In Gérôme's painting, the gestures and positions of the figures suggest a clear, legible narrative reminiscent of the academic paradigm for painting discussed in Chapter 1. A muse touches the poet, inspiring in him an elevated vision, represented by the figure of Venus rising from the sea. She is an idealized version of the bodies that writhe around her—bodies whose explicit positions and gestures suggest that they are products of a more degraded form of

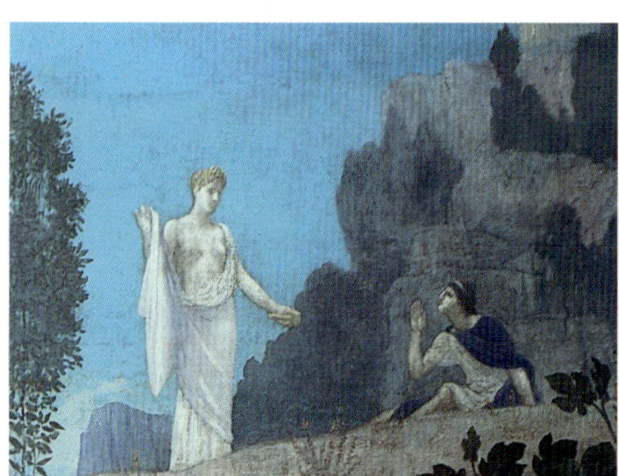

25
Pierre Puvis de Chavannes, *Ancient Vision* (detail of fig. 22; sculptor and muse)

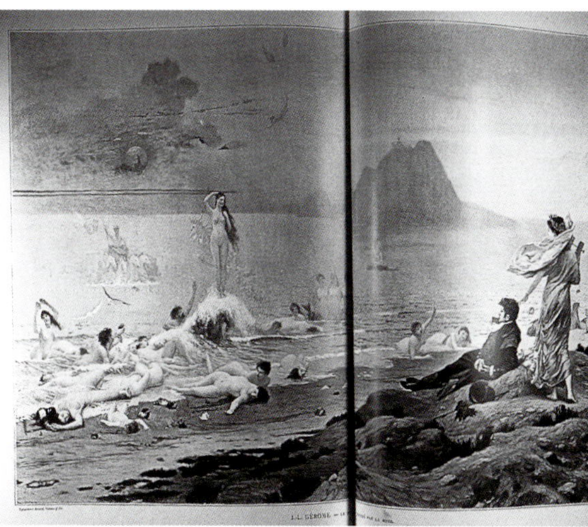

26
Jean-Léon Gérôme, *The Poet and His Muse*, 1888. Location unknown. Photolithograph. *Figaro-Salon*, 1888, p. 28

fantasy. In addition, a compositional trajectory is established from the muse's gesture to the poet's aesthetically disinterested gaze at Venus and beyond to the location where his creative precursor, the lyric poet of antiquity, hovers over the distant waves. The painting thus suggests that Gérôme's poet has mastered the sexual and material aspects of the female body and his desire for it. He has sublimated them in his prose, and they have been synthesized into the transcendent Platonic ideal that hovers seaward in the form of Venus.

Puvis's painting, on the other hand, offers no such clear message of mastery and sublimation. In *Ancient Vision*, as in *The Sacred Grove*, it is difficult to decipher the meanings of particular figures. Although some kind of narrative relationship is implied, the composition refuses to direct the viewer's decoding of it in the way Gérôme's does. Instead, Puvis's composition encourages the eye to circulate through the landscape and from figure to figure. Unlike Gérôme, Puvis does not make the artist and his muse the central focus of his composition or the force that determines the action taking place in the rest of the scene. He places them off in the upper right corner and leaves the relationship between them unclear. The role they play vis-à-vis the other figures in the composition is even harder to discern. The bodies in *Ancient Vision* fail to direct meaning through their gestures, positions, or attributes. Relationships between figures are established by echoes of pose that serve no obvious narrative purpose. For example, the only interactions between the three figures on the right are the formal echoes and responses among their bodies (fig. 27). These move the eye around the composition, from the outstretched arm of the water carrier, up along the torso of the pensive figure who leans against the rock, and down her limp hand and elbow to the head of the crouching woman with figs. The three do not acknowledge each other or the viewer. They are absent. And the viewer is left to fill in the blanks.

This enticement of the viewer into close scrutiny of the bodies on view leads to further disruptions of common conventions of viewing, disruptions akin to those in *Young Girls by the Seashore* and *The Sacred Grove*. In all of the women's bodies, firm and somewhat distorting outlines bound undifferentiated areas of paint that refer to the female body without transforming the paint into an illusion of delicately modeled flesh. Although the women seem to promise viewing pleasure, they, like many of the figures we have seen in Puvis's other compositions, ultimately refuse easy engagement. One of them, the woman with the figs, rather than laying herself bare to the viewer, crouches next to her fruit, her arms wrapped in a self-embrace, her head lowered. Her self-absorption is given a physical counterpart in her gesture, in particular by the way she touches thumb to fingers in the hand that rests on her shoulder. Her body has a sentient presence, but the viewer's

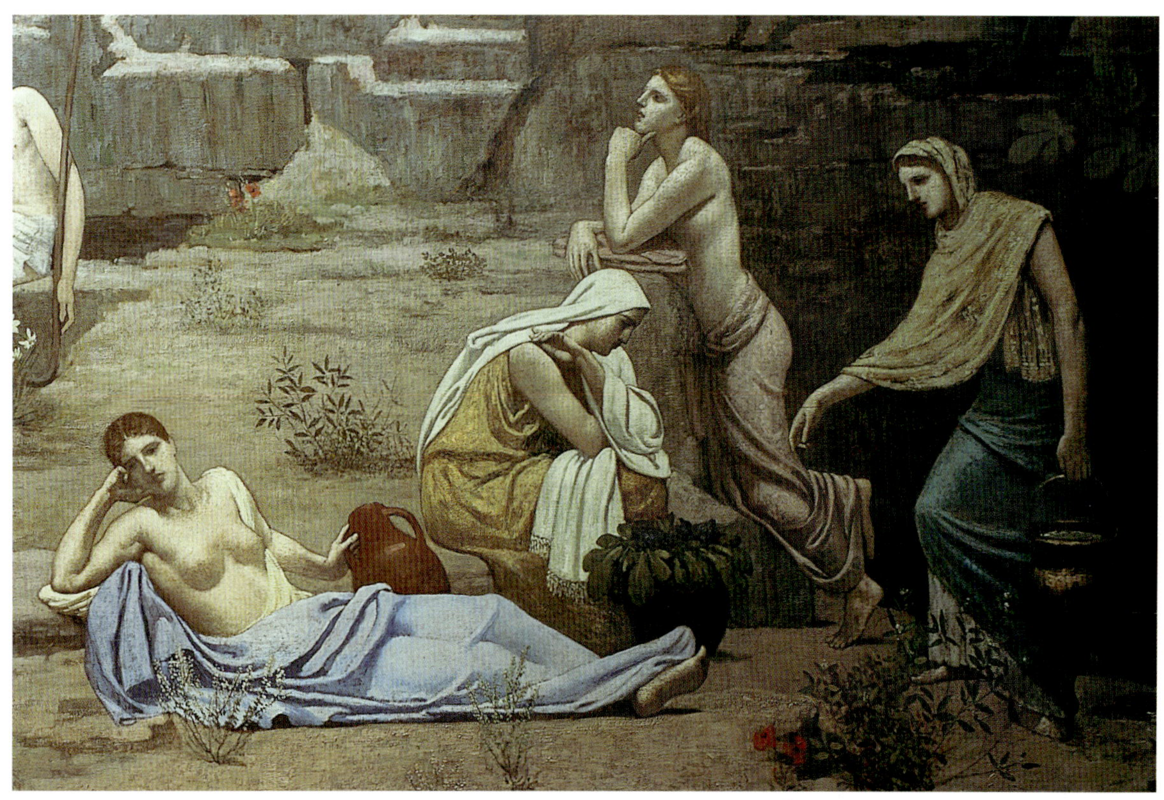

27
Pierre Puvis de Chavannes, *Ancient Vision* (detail of fig. 22; three women at right and reclining figure)

access to it is denied by her position. Her abandoned figs, attributes that would normally metaphorize the offering of her body, sit in open contrast to her self-enclosed posture. Similarly the nude torso of the reclining figure is carefully arranged for display (see fig. 27). Yet her body is disturbing. Her arm is excessively thick. Her chest is wide. Her breasts are strange shadowy cones, which look pasted on. In her left hand she holds a jug. However, she does not offer its open mouth to the viewer, but turns it away. Her eyes and the entire left side of her face are in shadow and seem almost to disintegrate under the viewer's gaze.

As one continues to look, attributions of gender that at first seem obvious are undermined. On the left side of the mural, we initially think we see a woman with a goat and a shepherd boy (see fig. 22). They occupy the same plane and are linked to each other on a narrative level. The woman's proximity to the goat associates her with the role of herding while the boy's pipes and staff identify him as the shepherd. Yet their exact relationship is unclear, and soon the connections between them surpass mere narrative. Their bodies tilt at a similar angle; each has an elbow bent and an arm raised. Their hair is the same color, and the shepherd's hair looks as though it could be falling long down his back, just as the woman's does. What appeared to be male and female figures now seem to be two views of the same figure—one seen from the front and the other from behind. But the indeterminacies go beyond these two figures. The shepherd's face and the woman's hair are so similar to those of the pensive woman leaning on the rocks (who occupies the same middle plane at the right side of the canvas) that the three figures are almost interchangeable. This pensive figure is strategically positioned so that her breasts are not visible. As one looks more and more closely at the relationships between figures it becomes harder and harder to determine who is male and who female. This effect is amplified when we compare these figures to the woman who reclines in the foreground, for surely her body is more conventionally masculine than the shepherd's. Her arms appear to be muscular, and her chest is wide. When the two are seen together, the shepherd appears even more feminized. Gender seems to be floating here, not easily securable to single bodies, but produced by the way bodies are juxtaposed; the structure of the painting encourages the viewer to play with comparisons between them.

This destabilization of gender was registered in the responses to the paintings. Some critics either did not notice that there were any male figures at all in *Ancient Vision* or chose to edit out their masculinity. In a statement meant to derogate the painting as a whole, the academic critic Meurville referred to the shepherd as a "hermaphrodite."[7] Edmond Jacques, on the other hand, praised the painting. But he, too, failed to make the appropriate gender distinctions. Clearly reveling in the sensuous appeal of the painting, he described all the figures in the foreground (including the shepherd) as women: "Below the women dream, rest, or work. One plays the pipes; the other lifts her calm eyes to the beauty of the site."[8] In addition to identifying the shepherd as a woman, Jacques also labeled the figures upon the cliffs—one male and one female—as "two Muses with slender forms." In Jacques's response to *Ancient Vision*, all signs of masculinity were erased from the scene, and the feminine was collapsed into the pleasures of flesh, food, music, warmth, and the landscape. In this account, the most important aspect of the painting, the theme of artistic creation, was virtually erased from the painting along with the signs of a male artist.

Like *The Sacred Grove*, *Ancient Vision* leaves its viewers to "make three-quarters of the painting." It encourages them to complete the idealization of the bodies and to imagine possible narratives rather than telling them what to think. Not surprisingly, then, critics steeped in the conventions of academic painting were not at all certain what they should make of the composition. "What absence of modeling, what negligence of details, what disregard for form and color in this Ancient Vision," the royalist critic Meurville complained.[9] Although some identified the figures on top of the cliffs as an artist or poet and his muse, others gave less explicit descriptions. The conservative critic Saint-Ange could say only that the two seemed to be discussing something. Others thought the artist and his muse were a pair of lovers but missed the relationship between vision and creativity.[10] Still others linked the figures to a dream. One critic suggested that the figures in the upper register were not truly present in the landscape at all. Instead, they were figments of a dream visualized by the women in the foreground as they listened to the shepherd's song of lovers.[11]

Unlike conservative critics who either failed to understand the painting or refused to acknowledge its theme because they were angered by its veering away from academic conventions, more adventurous critics were able to identify the theme of creativity and acknowledge that it was intimately linked to sensuality and dream. The republican critic André Michel and the individualist-anarchist critic Octave Mirbeau thought that the women in the foreground were themselves the unreal products of dream, materials from the mind's eye of the artist on the hill. In this scenario only the artist and his muse were "real," and the women in the foreground were mere figments imagined by the artist in response to seeing the naked torso of his muse. The mural, Mirbeau suggested, not only thematized dream in its subject matter but connected dream and creativity. He described the female figure on the cliffs as a muse waking the sculptor from his sleep: "With a noble and inspired gesture that embraces the landscape of the earth, the sea, and the sky, she seems to say to the wakened man: 'Look, fill your eyes with this vision, and work to make us gods!' . . . The artist continues to contemplate the spectacle that unfolds before him."[12] As the muse unveils her body to the artist, her embrace of the landscape begs a comparison between the scene portrayed—the earth, sea, and sky—and her now naked flesh. The spectacle that unfolds before the artist, the vision inspired by the muse's unveiling of her body, is pictured in the rest of the mural. The figures and landscape there, Mirbeau implied, are a product of the sculptor's fantasy as he gazes upon his muse's form.

Ancient Vision did not picture perfectly portrayed bodies in an easily decipherable narrative structure. Instead, it combined a pleasurable overall design with strangely equivocal bodies in order to provoke fantasies of physical pleasure—pleasure experienced in reverie by these critics and attributed by them to the artist on the cliff. According to Mirbeau, it is these fantasies, ignited by the vision of the muse's body, that the artist in the mural should use to "create gods." Pleasure, sensuality, desire, and fantasy were thus imagined to be the impetus for high art and the forces behind French creativity—creativity in which the audience was asked, through the solicitation of dream, to participate.

Most of the critics seem to have found Puvis de Chavannes's dreamlike mode of address in *Ancient Vision* to be both powerfully seductive and disturbing. Saint-Ange complained that in *Ancient Vision*, figures were "disseminated rather than placed," and this subversion of hierarchical structures made him feel uncomfortable: "We feel disoriented [*depaysée*], and that is enough to make us give in to the imaginativeness of the evocation."[13] The socialist critic Gustave Geffroy remarked that Puvis created a general atmosphere in which "the gaze circulates freely, goes, comes, stops, and loses itself."[14] This description suggests that to view the mural was to submit oneself to an increasingly unstructured process of viewing—a transformation from the moment when the gaze "circulates freely" to the end of vision, when the undirected gaze "loses itself," and the mind's eye turns inward in a process of individual fantasy.

This call to fantasy was made even more explicit in the response of another critic, Alexandre Georget. Georget found the mural to be both "troubling" and "poignant." The mural asked him to suspend rational controlled thought, to occupy himself with feeling, and to give himself over to dream: "emotion, that supreme quality of the artist, wins the spectator over and makes him think, daydream, dream despite himself."[15] Georget began with self-conscious and willed processes of thought and shifted to freer forms of imagination and fantasy—from thought (*penser*) to daydream (*songer*) to dream (*rêver*). Notice, too, Georget's sense that this process was initiated in "emotion" and took place against his will—

"despite himself." Like *The Sacred Grove*, then, *Ancient Vision* thwarted the intellectual attempt to determine a precise set of meanings. It addressed its viewers on the level of feeling and transformed looking from an intellectual pursuit of knowledge into an emotional, even bodily, engagement with desire and fantasy.

If we look closely at Mirbeau's description of *Ancient Vision*, it becomes clear that he was not only describing what the artist pictured in the upper right corner was supposed to envision in the dream evoked by his muse but also narrating his own experience of the painting and his own fantasmatic relation to it. Mirbeau's language is lush, eroticized, and a bit melancholy as he describes this vision of the origins of France—a vision that is provided to any viewer of Puvis's canvas. "From the immense, deep, and fluid sky falls a magnificent peace," said Mirbeau, "a peace made of laziness and voluptuousness."[16] With this rhetoric, Mirbeau surely meant to call to mind the luxury, calm, and voluptuousness of the land evoked in Baudelaire's "Invitation to the Voyage": "Là, tout n'est qu'ordre et beauté/Luxe, calme, et volupté." In Baudelaire's poem, the opulence of the natural landscape combines with an evocation of material plenitude to become a metaphor for the female body. Speaking to his "child" and "sister," Baudelaire evokes the land that resembles her, the land to which he dreams of flying ("Au pays qui te resemble"). Mirbeau, too, evokes such a dream. The landscape with its cliffs "flooded in a light dusty with lapis and opal," "rocks all blue and rose," glistens, as if adorned with jewels. Its features provide sensual pleasures: "the azure sea, which is not disturbed by a single ripple," "has a caressing softness." In contrast to what Mirbeau termed "the conventional group and the banality of academic allegories" usually found in official painting, *Ancient Vision* offered a space where, in Mirbeau's words, "daydream can wander to the infinite."[17]

Many critics seem to have recounted not what they actually saw in the mural but the way the experience of its radiant color and indeterminate composition made them feel, and the ensuing fantasies. Judith Gautier connected the fantasies encouraged by the painting with pleasurable feelings, smells, and tastes—"warm" (*tiede*), "balmy" (*embaumé*), and "sweet/soft" (*doux*) were the adjectives she used to describe the general atmosphere.[18] In her summation of the feeling evoked by the mural, Gautier metaphorically likened this sensuous plenitude to infantile satisfactions, evoking the safety and comfort of a child rocked in its mother's arms: "Everything in this canvas breathes the happiness and peace of the soul cradled in the beauty of things."[19]

Like Mirbeau and Gautier, André Michel described the landscape in terms of sensual plenitude reminiscent of Baudelaire's "Invitation to the Voyage." According to Michel, the cliffs in the background were not harsh, but soft like a "velvety rug" made in the jewel-like colors of "amethyst and lapis lazuli," the azure sky "caresse[d]" the scene, and—he used language that was surely meant to have a double meaning—the *mer* (sea)/*mère* (mother) reached out with loving arms.

All of these critics, then, thought the landscape presented a dream of plenitude in which all physical needs were pleasurably fulfilled. And all of them linked that plenitude to the female body. Although the connection was most explicit in the responses of Gautier and Michel, each suggested that the painting linked the origins of creativity and Frenchness to the fantasized plenitude of a time in infancy when all needs were met by a warm, voluptuous female body—a time when distinctions between the self and the maternal body had not yet been fully established.[20]

Sensation, desire, fantasy, the body—these were the terms used to describe both the subject matter of *Ancient Vision* and the experience of viewing the mural. They were also the aspects of human subjectivity commonly associated with femininity in the discourse of the nineteenth century. For Judith Gautier, the embrace of sensuality and materiality in the processes of creativity offered by *Ancient Vision* seems to have made room for a conceptualization of creativity available to women, who had long been described as unable to participate in the transcendent acts of mind required by high art because they were so tied to their bodies. The claims that *Ancient Vision* promoted an understanding tied to the body that exceeded intellectual thought, an understanding based in imagination and enthusiasm rather than "reality," were in a sense, claims that the painting also demanded a response that was "feminine." In *Ancient Vision*, where everything "breathes the happiness and peace of the soul cradled in the beauty of things," the "soul" excluded neither women nor the sensual experience of beauty.

In contrast to *Ancient Vision*, *Christian Inspiration* located the origins of France in a Christian heritage and pictured the making of art as a masculine transcendent activity (see fig. 23). Furthermore, whereas *Christian Inspiration* maintained certain aspects of Puvis's style, its overall visual structure mimicked the message of transcendence depicted in its subject matter. Thus, both the subject and the form of *Christian Inspiration* reinforced acceptable, even traditional, notions about art and creativity—notions that associated Frenchness, creativity, and masculinity. The message of the painting could easily be made to correspond with the traditional academic understanding of high art, making it more open to common conventions of viewing. First of all, the narrative structure is relatively clear, and the composition is hierarchical. All of the figures pictured undertake purposeful and directed activities of one kind or another. The central action of the scene revolves around the figure at the right of the canvas, an artist-monk who takes a moment to stand back and contemplate a work in progress. Although this painting lies mostly beyond the frame of the mural, a nearby mural of Christ in the garden visited by angels helps the viewer imagine its style and subject matter. Behind the painter, three students look on, watching their master at work. The rest of the scene inside the building presents details of the activity of the studio. At the center a figure looks through prints; to the left a monk shows a drawing to another artist. In a courtyard in the background succor is given to the hungry and the ill.

In contrast to *Ancient Vision*, with its association between femininity, creativity, sensuality, and dream, *Christian Inspiration* posits both the making and the viewing of art as a masculine, transcendent activity. The critic for *Le Radical* described how in looking at their master's work the student artists "elevate themselves from looking to contemplation and from contemplation to ecstasy."[21] The description moves away from an engagement between the senses and the physical world. "Looking," which depends on the presence of the physical world, turns into "contemplation," and contemplation transforms into "ecstasy" by direct contact with a "higher" spiritual life. Artistic practice is thus a vehicle for transcendent thought.

Other critics also made clear the association between the artistic process and transcendent thought. According to one critic, the image of the master revealed the "contemplativeness of his art and the inspiration of his thought," while his disciples "follow[ed] him in their minds." The monastery was a sanctuary for "the progress of ideas." Furthermore, the "severity" of the landscape—its failure to address the pleasure of the senses through form and color—was thought to be appropriate to this account of art making as an operation of the mind and not the body.[22] At first, we might suspect that, as with the *Poor Fisherman*, the emaciation of the monks' bodies would pose some difficulties for the critics. However, although the bodies are thinned out to the point of flatness in some areas of the canvas, their gestures are easily readable, and their features are detailed enough to suggest individual minds. The emaciated bodies of the artists and monks seemed only to amplify the notion that the mind, not the body, was the wellspring of art.

If the structures of creativity presented by *Christian Inspiration* called on associations between art making and masculinity, so, too, did the overall subject matter, for Puvis had depicted a fraternal space for the making of art. Even Octave Mirbeau, who had taken such pleasure in describing the sensual dream of origins in *Ancient Vision*, saw in *Christian Inspiration* "an idea of calm, of serene peace, of silence, of mysterious charm, and of contemplation." In this mural, the individual and unbridled desire invoked in *Ancient Vision*—what Mirbeau celebrated as an "egoistic fearlessness of pagan hearts"—was given a collective, spiritual aim as the monk-artists "turn[ed] toward an ideal of fraternity."[23] Indeed, in depicting young male artists following an older master, the mural evoked the homosocial setting of the artist's studio. Although the bonds between men were set in the context of an Italian cloister, the evocation of an artistic retreat populated exclusively by men was probably meant to conjure up other fraternal studio settings that had emerged after the French Revolution, such as Jacques-Louis David's studio or the retreat of the Primitifs.[24]

Perhaps better than any other account of the murals, Judith Gautier's descriptions of *Christian Inspiration* shows how clearly the cycle seemed to signify through a gendered discourse. To the warmth, beauty, and peace of *Ancient Vision*, Gautier juxtaposed a description of *Christian Inspiration* that conjured notions of emptiness and death. She described the walls of the cloister as "naked" and "cold." Outside them, the trees evoked not the plenitude of nature but "mark[ed] tombs." Gautier thought the rejection of sensual pleasure could be seen in the very bodies of the monks. The monks, she said, were "ugly, thin, and pale." Their "cowls play[ed] the role of shrouds." The celebration of life manifest in *Ancient Vision*—with its celebration of the flesh, in the bodies of the women and the sensual address of the landscape—was utterly negated in *Christian Inspiration*, with its depiction of "the saddening death of life, the torment of the heart emaciating the flesh, the disdain of present joys for the hope and the terror of a future

28
Pierre Puvis de Chavannes,
Christian Inspiration
(detail of fig. 23; monastery gates)

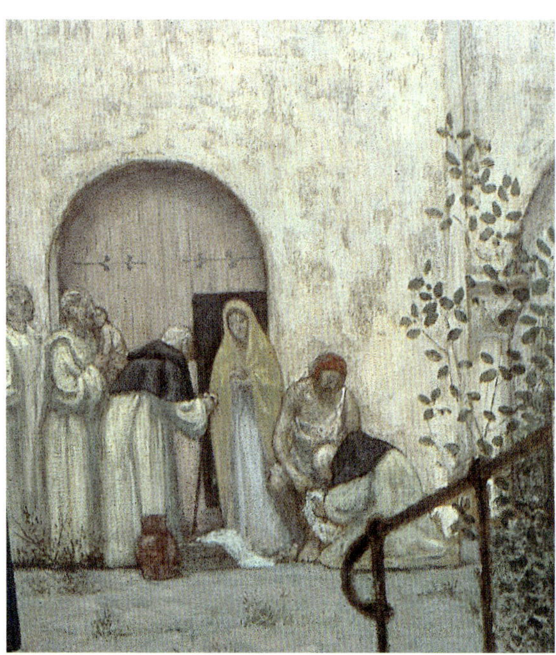

existence." Gautier lamented that the experiences of "miracle and ecstasy" pictured in *Christian Inspiration* had replaced "the marvels of nature and drunkenness of the senses" depicted in *Ancient Vision*. For this female critic, the associations between creativity and transcendence, Frenchness and fraternity, that permeated *Christian Inspiration* were also alienating. The painting, she said, pictured a "retreat from which women [were] excluded and love banished."[25] This comment was partly precipitated by the only women on view in *Christian Inspiration*: beggars outside the monastery gates (fig. 28). Still, it is tempting to read the exclusion she identified as more than just a refusal to give asylum. Here the cultural exclusion of woman from the realm of spiritual creativity and thus from one aspect of French identity seems to be at issue.

GENDER AND THE POLITICS OF FRENCH PATRIMONY

Overlapping the general question of whether French creativity should be imagined as masculine or feminine were more specific debates about the political implications of each strand of the French patrimony. Most critics interpreted *Christian Inspiration* as an evocation of the medieval Christian heritage. The intersection of Christianity and fraternity was problematic for republican critics who wished to maintain the association between secular republicanism and fraternity—an association that had its origins in the French Revolution. By contrast, the mural was especially pleasing to Catholic critics because it allowed them to locate the origins of Frenchness in a religious past that had been intermittently renounced by the state since the Revolution. Royalist critics also preferred *Christian Inspiration* to the other paintings in the cycle. In France in the nineteenth century royalism and Catholicism often went hand in hand. Critics for royalist papers were inevitably ardent supporters of Catholicism because the notion of the divine right of kings helped them to legitimate their call for the return of the monarchy.

It was not just the subject matter of *Christian Inspiration* that pleased conservative critics, however; it was also the way the composition reinforced the spirituality of the mural. The Catholic critic Saint-Ange described the painting thus: "A monk, a sort of Fra Angelico, is occupied with painting; he is completely absorbed in his work, the artist of an immaterial art, a pious worker for whom to paint is to pray."[26] The royalist critic Meurville also found *Christian Inspiration* to be "by far the best" painting in the cycle because of its "calm and contemplativeness." Said Meurville: "It is the peace of our Father reigning over the world of thought."[27]

Although Catholic and royalist critics praised *Christian Inspiration* wholeheartedly, they had little positive to say about *Ancient Vision*. Meurville's disdain for *Ancient Vision* was partly due to its subject matter. In contrast to *Christian Inspira-*

tion, with its depiction of a Christian heritage, *Ancient Vision* suggested that the origins of Frenchness lay in a classical past, embraced by republicans as a model of the secular democratic state. The mural also emphasized the pleasures of the senses and gave no evidence of interest in the Christian renunciation of the flesh.

In contrast to Catholic or royalist critics, who inevitably preferred *Christian Inspiration*, critics on the Left thought *Ancient Vision* the more powerful painting. Those who had the greatest stake in locating the origins of France in the world of ancient democracies also had the greatest need to promote *Ancient Vision* as the truer image of France's origins. Their reactions were often extremely conflicted, however. Their responses to *Ancient Vision* centered on the question of whether a mural that encouraged a "feminine" response, in which "the gaze circulates freely, goes, comes, stops, and loses itself," was a desirable form of public painting. What, after all, would such a painting be able to teach its viewers about collective origins if it evoked individual fantasy? And how could a form of creativity so rooted in individual fantasy approximate the fraternal ideal usually associated with republicanism?

29
Pierre Puvis de Chavannes, *Ancient Vision* (detail of fig. 22; horses in background)

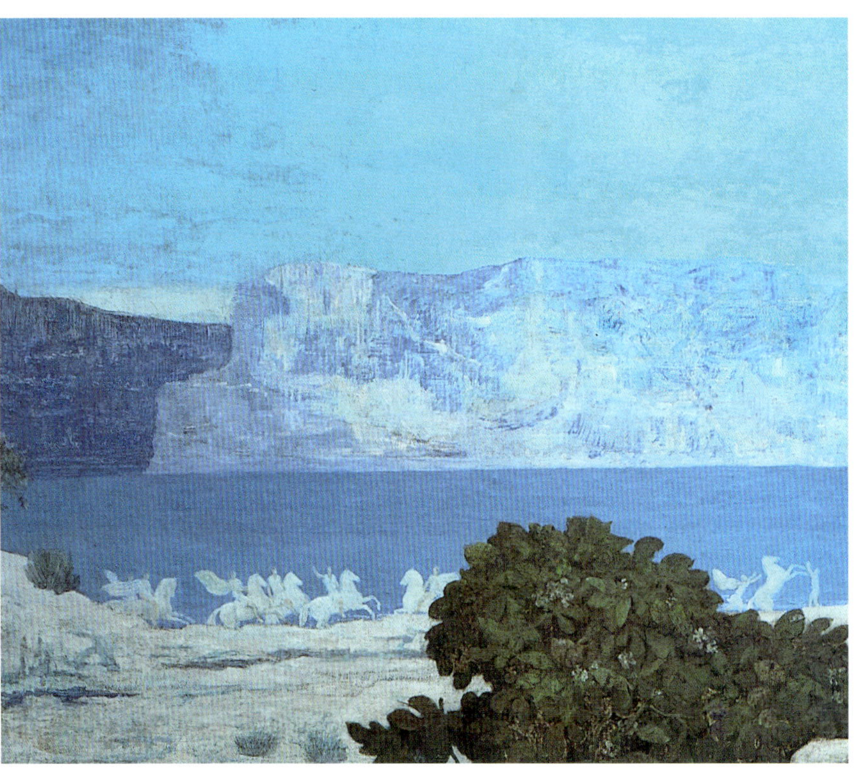

The republican critic André Michel hoped that *Ancient Vision* would provide the more convincing image of Frenchness. Indeed, he found *Ancient Vision* to be both more beautiful and more powerful than *Christian Inspiration* in its evocation of France's origins. As we saw, Michel described the painting using a language of plenitude that metaphorized the female body. But Michel was also left with a deep sense of longing. *Ancient Vision*, Michel said, was a "distant vision" that held both the "gentle magic" and melancholy of dream. And we sense, upon reading Michel's evocation of the landscape, that there was much more at stake than what Puvis actually pictured. It is as if the painting had touched something in Michel, a wellspring of deep desire for plenitude of the kind implicit in Baudelaire's poem. Just as Baudelaire's land of voluptuousness is not present, but "there" (*Là*), beyond reach, except by the imagination, Michel's evocation of plenitude surely outstripped the mural itself. It was more a product of fantasies inspired by the mural than a mere reaction to what was there in paint. Michel admitted as much when he described the women pictured in *Ancient Vision* as "creatures of dream . . . whose slow gestures seem enveloped in sweetness."[28]

At the same time, Michel was made uncomfortable by the mural, and that discomfort came both from the subject matter and the structure of the painting. Michel quite explicitly connected the dreamlike nature of the mural to Puvis's painterly style: "In the gentle unfolding of synthesized and slightly stiff lines and the subdued notes of blue, tan, pink, and silvered or blued green and pale yellows, above which vibrate the intense blue of the sea, one has the sensation of the flight of this ancient dream, heretofore unattainable."[29] As he viewed the mural, then, Michel had the feeling that the plenitude it was asking him to imagine was slipping away. Thus, Michel suggested, the painting both showed its viewers what plenitude might be like and denied them the possibility of ever participating in it. It did this phenomenologically and symbolically. Experiencing the "radiant" color harmonies, viewers were enticed into fantasies of plenitude. Yet the composition of the painting was disorienting, and many of the figures were disturbing. The general composition promoted an oscillation between pleasure and disturbance. This was the phenomenological level.

The withdrawal of harmony was expressed symbolically in particular figures. The meaning of the mural, Michel suggested, hinged on the contrast between the cavaliers in the background (fig. 29) and the shepherd in the foreground. "Among the figures evoked by the artist," said Michel, "suffering beings slip themselves in without [Puvis's] knowing it." Significantly, the most central male figure in the composition, the shepherd, was Michel's prime example of a figure whom Puvis had unconsciously imbued with the mark of modernity. In a remarkable passage,

Michel linked the loss of plenitude that the painting asked him to acknowledge with representation itself. "Look at him," said Michel of the shepherd. "He wears on his impoverished limbs the ineffaceable imprint of the Fall and of original sin. He appears incongruous among these pagan visions." Michel thus established a contrast between the plenitude offered by the landscape and the female bodies that dominated it, on the one hand, and, on the other, the impoverished representation of the shepherd's body, tainted by "the Fall and original sin." As in Charles Blanc's account of artistic idealization (which we saw in Chapter 1), the desire that Michel associated with the failure of representation was a desire provoked by the Fall. However, as we saw in Blanc's account of the nude, the female body was usually the object of idealization, all the way back to the original state of grace. By linking the shepherd's body to this discourse of the female nude, Michel implied that the shepherd's body had been both sexualized and feminized.

For Michel, the longing for original harmony was both quintessentially modern and inextricably linked to representation. According to him, the shepherd "comes to signify that the modern artist no longer really knows how to be an artisan of noble and voluptuous beauty, that the secret of the antique eurythmia is forever lost." In this passage a fullness of being in the world is explicitly linked to an impossible fantasy of representation in complete harmony with the world, representation that does not, by its very nature, signal division and distance from the beauty represented but itself *is* that beauty and is therefore not representation at all. If the wan body of the shepherd symbolized the lack of harmony that so disturbed Michel, the charging cavaliers in the distance were the visualization of the flight of the kind of virile, fraternal masculinity that he imagined still had access to plenitude and fullness of representation. The cavaliers in the background, said Michel, embodied harmony—a "joie de vivre" that was all but lost under the conditions of modernity. When such plenitude was "reflected in a modern soul"—as it necessarily had to be when painted by a modern artist for a modern audience—it could only be shown as inaccessible. This explained why the charging cavaliers were such a tiny, almost illegible element of the landscape. Michel suggested that the modern soul had to strain to imagine what ancient plenitude might have been like.

In the end, despite the fantasy of plenitude, the painting proffered "some sort of unexpressed lamentation [that was] mixed with this serenity and [that rose] from the saddened earth toward the radiant sky." Michel, then, offered an extremely conflicted and melancholy account of *Ancient Vision*—one that associated the origins of France with the fantasized plenitude of the ancient world but also acknowledged the distance between the world pictured and the modern world he, the viewer, inhabited; one that described the original plenitude through a fantasy of maternal origins but also expressed a desire for a masculinity that could have access to the plenitude of the maternal while maintaining its autonomy; one in which it is realized that the mode of address in the painting asked him to give up the position of a controlling subject in favor of an experience of subjectivity rooted in sensuality and the unconscious; one that made it impossible for him to identify with anything but the feminized figure of the shepherd.

Another critic who struggled with his interpretation of the murals was the socialist critic Gustave Geffroy. Geffroy, like Michel, contrasted the tiny cavaliers in the background with the large female figures in the foreground. For Geffroy, the cavaliers represented harmonious order and placed that harmony in the ancient world. They "obey[ed] a rhythm," and like the horses of the Parthenon Frieze, they seemed to move forward in a unified "active will." Thus, for Geffroy, the distant vision of the tiny cavaliers on the shore represented the kind of purposeful and harmonious fraternal activity that he nostalgically imagined to characterize both ancient democracies and French republicanism. The tiny cavaliers, then, embodied the only section of Puvis's cycle in which fraternal activity was pictured in a potentially democratic setting. In contrast to the image of fraternity in *Christian Inspiration*, the one represented by the cavaliers in *Ancient Vision* did not rely on notions of transcendence or Christianity.

Geffroy could not ignore the female figures' domination of *Ancient Vision*. Nor was anything further from the image of active harmony represented by the cavaliers in the distance than the atomized dreaminess of the women who filled the visual field. Geffroy commented: "The women in the foreground do not present such obvious proof of the comprehension of antiquity; they have, from Greece, the attitudes and stiff gestures of statues, but they seem to bring to this joyous land isolated and uneasy existences. They rest on an elbow, they lie on the ground; a lassitude invades them; their sad gazes wander in dream."[30] Implicit in this description is the notion that ancient Greece was in truth characterized by collective harmony. The "isolation" and "uneasy existences" that marked the women in the foreground signaled their distance from antiquity and associated them instead with more modern times. The vision of the solidarity in motion and "active will" represented by the cavaliers was put so far in the distance, suggested Geffroy, because it was inaccessible to the modern viewer. The women in the foreground, by contrast, were closer to the viewer both compositionally and thematically. Their languorous bodies and dreamy faces suggested an emptiness that was wrenching to him.

This feeling of discomfort was conditioned, I would claim, by Geffroy's own relationship to women and to the mural as a whole. When we compare Geffroy's description of the "sad" and "wandering" gazes of the women to his account of what it felt like to view the mural ("the gaze circulates freely, goes, comes, stops, and loses itself"), we see that the two are very similar. It is as if the landscape, which made the cavaliers so small and distant, withheld access to the feeling of fraternity that Geffroy desired, and forced him instead to identify with the female figures. The lack of control implied by the wandering gaze was clearly aligned, by Geffroy, with the feminine. Thus, *Ancient Vision*, in its very structure, seems to have encouraged Geffroy, like Michel, to participate in an experience he saw as feminine, even as he glimpsed the image of fraternal harmony in the background. The melancholy that permeates Geffroy's description of the women's wandering gazes implies his own feeling that he no more participates in the plenitude represented by the charging horses than could the women in the foreground.

Yet Geffroy still wanted to offer the cavaliers as the proper ones for viewers to identify with. He wanted the viewers of Puvis's murals to believe that France's true origins lay in the ancient world and were, despite the women in the foreground of *Ancient Vision*, truly characterized by fraternal harmony. Geffroy's desire was complicated by the fact that the most prominent image of fraternity in the Lyons cycle seemed to be pictured by Puvis in *Christian Inspiration*, which located it not in an ancient democracy but in a medieval Christian setting. Geffroy was therefore forced to explain why *Christian Inspiration* was an inappropriate image of the origins of France.

Although he praised the compositional unity of *Christian Inspiration*, in which "the harmony between the site, the figures, and their occupations is absolute," his description of the mural was not unconditionally positive. Even though they initially appeared to present an image of fraternity, said Geffroy, the monk-artists were not appropriate figures for viewers to identify with. The master had "the fixed eye of an ecstatic" (*l'oeil fixe d'un extatique*). The artists who followed him were "absorbed by a fixed thought" (*absorbé par une pensée fixe*). Geffroy thus described them in terms that call to mind the "ecstasies" and "idées fixes" of hysteria.[31] By associating the monks' spirituality with mysticism and ultimately with obsessiveness and hysteria, Geffroy attempted to refute the legitimacy of the religious fervor that appeared to draw them together and to call it individualist obsession instead.

If the female figures of *Ancient Vision* also appeared to be characterized by individual atomization, it was because they were not truly representative of the harmony of the ancient world. Geffroy suggested that despite Puvis's attempts in *Ancient Vision* to capture the "serenity" of the ancient world, the "burning interior" and "fervent nostalgia" that characterized the figures in *Christian Inspiration* had also infiltrated *Ancient Vision* and had "even obscured the faces of these Greek women, meditating on their interior dream, sad and hallucinatory, like Gothic virgins."[32]

But why had Puvis de Chavannes allowed the ancient harmony that should have permeated the whole of *Ancient Vision* to be tainted with gothic hallucination?

To answer that question, we must add one more piece to the puzzle: Puvis de Chavannes had been born in Lyons. The city of Lyons was famous for its religious painters and infamous for its historical connections to religious mysticism and fervor—connections that Geffroy noted had been sustained even throughout the secularizing reforms of republicanism. The tenacity of this mysticism, said Geffroy, made Lyons an anomaly—a city "where even revolutionaries were mixed up with religiosity." Puvis's Lyons origins, said Geffroy, made him "the man in whom the mysterious and melancholy soul of our race lives."[33] He was thus, the critic argued, instinctively prone to imprint his paintings with mysticism whether he willed it or not.[34] Given the artist's origins, said Geffroy, it was natural for him to paint *Christian Inspiration* with such conviction and to fail in his attempt to picture ancient harmony. By claiming that Puvis had unwittingly imbued his ancient women with gothic mysticism, the socialist critic Geffroy attempted to redirect the viewer not only away from the atomized reverie of the women but also from the religious aspects of the medieval heritage. His ideal remained a vision of willful male solidarity, which was represented, if only distantly and momentarily, in the charging horses.

Christian Inspiration pictured France's origins and the making of art as masculine and fraternal; *Ancient Vision* pictured them as feminine. Yet, even though the paintings were officially commissioned by the republican arts administrations, they undermined republican associations between fraternity and ancient democracy: in *Christian Inspiration*, fraternity was set in a medieval Christian, rather than an ancient, context; and the only image of fraternity and collective will included in *Ancient Vision* was so hazy and distant as to seem inaccessible. The socialist Geffroy and the republican Michel were disturbed by the solicitation of individual desire in *Ancient Vision* and the way the painting asked them to participate in structures of mind widely construed as feminine. *Ancient Vision* instilled a desire for plenitude, and its compositional and narrative ambiguities encouraged pleasurable fantasies. But its subversions of the viewer's mastery always kept the inaccessibility of that plenitude—an inaccessibility that was itself the motor of desire—ever present to the viewer. Even though Michel and Geffroy acknowledged that the power of Puvis's style came from its evocation of sensuality and dream—two aspects of subjectivity associated with the feminine—both of them wanted to link France's origins in ancient democracy to fraternity. The mural encouraged Michel and Geffroy to fantasize a position of plenitude—the position of the charging horses—which existed before modern man was denied access to "noble and voluptuous beauty."

But at the same time, both the subject matter of *Ancient Vision* and the difficulties of Puvis's visual language denied them belief in this fantasy. The plenitude was always just beyond reach. The fantasy was continually disturbed.

Yet what might initially seem to be the failure of *Ancient Vision* was ultimately its greatest strength. Rather than simply offering plenitude, the mural instilled in its viewers the desire to recapture lost plenitude. And it cast that desire at the origins of France. The power of *Ancient Vision*, then, derived not just from what it pictured but also from what it withheld and from the way it made its viewers *feel*. I have been arguing that *Ancient Vision* asked its viewers to participate in creativity. Guyau claimed that the refined aesthetic experience, in which one "desir[es] immeasurably," could amplify desire to the point of disturbance. Looking at the mural through Guyau's lens suggests that the painting did just that in oscillating between pleasure and disturbance, in asking viewers to participate in a pleasurable vision of France and then denying them the possibility of fully mastering their dreams: it mimicked the kind of creativity that Guyau described—creativity rooted in desire and inextricably linked to the body.

This address to emotion and feeling, an address that was embedded in the structure of the painting as much as in its subject matter, was the defining feature of what I have been calling Puvis's modernism. Indeed, it was that conjuring of desire in a dream that made *Ancient Vision* seem particularly modern. "Puvis de Chavannes's painted reveries," said André Michel, "express some of the ways we commonly dream or regret a loss of well-being." It was Puvis's ability to capture the feeling of loss associated with modernity that made him "one of the most truly modern artists of our school of painting," even though he had "never reproduced . . . the formal appearances of contemporary life."[35]

The critical responses to *Ancient Vision*, then, were conditioned by a mixture of aesthetics and politics. Geffroy, whose dream of origins involved a solidarity and oneness with the world that he imagined was characteristic of ancient democracies, thought the kind of retreat into individual fantasy that the individualist-anarchist Octave Mirbeau had celebrated in *Ancient Vision* was far from desirable. Mirbeau, on the other hand, embraced an aesthetic devoted to the cult of the individual. Despite his leftist politics, he was not worried by the atomization that such a retreat into individual fantasy might entail. Instead, he embraced the role of desire and fantasy in Puvis's painting. In addition, he linked them to the sensuous aspects of the work and described sensuousness, fantasy, and dream as the elements that made Puvis's painting modern.

Like Michel, Mirbeau claimed that Puvis's art was much more authentically modern than the modern-life scenes of realist painters. Mirbeau caricatured the tenets of realism, mocking a conception of art in which modernity could be achieved only by copying scenes from modern life. In fact, said Mirbeau, the most modern characteristics of Puvis's art were also those for which realist critics disliked him. The realist critic, said Mirbeau, "reproaches Puvis de Chavannes for *sensing* nature too deeply and expressing it in glorious syntheses. He will not tolerate this procedure of suggestive simplification; nature must not be explained or interpreted; one must copy it without understanding it, just as a typographer composes a text in Chinese or German without knowing how to read it. It is only in this way that one is *modern*."[36]

By making a distinction between "copying" and "reading," Mirbeau implied that Puvis, in his art, not only saw nature but understood it. The particular kind of understanding that Mirbeau attributed to Puvis's work is signaled by the emphasis that he placed on the words *sentir* and *moderne*. *Sentir*, which evokes smells and tastes but also feelings, operates as the hinge in Mirbeau's account, between thought and visceral stimuli, between body and mind. The full meaning of *sentir* becomes clearest when Mirbeau goes on, with a similarly ironic tone, to describe those elements which, according to the optical realist, must not enter into modern art.

In a remarkable passage whose poeticism was meant, I think, to capture some of the feeling that emanated from *Ancient Vision*, Mirbeau catalogued what he believed to be the central elements of Puvis's painting and suggested in a backhanded way that they were, in truth, more modern than anything a realist might produce:

> To be *modern* [says the realist] is obstinately to close one's ears to the music of things, one's nostrils to the scent of things; it is to repress the beatings of one's heart before the evocation of realities condensed in the dreams that rise from the earth and fall from the sky. Everything in this immobilized and mute nature will thus consist only of relations of tone and questions of color value; imagination, enthusiasm, observation, and poetry can never enter here; thought will not have the right to slip for a single instant beneath the deceitful surfaces, to descend into the depths in order to refresh itself, revivify itself, at the very sources of life. There is no need to refute this absurd and barbarous doctrine, because it refutes itself. It makes the painter into a simple machine, a sort of thoughtless and passive tool, and forbids him all the emotion, all the joy, all the painful voluptuousness, of creation [*enfantement*].[37]

Puvis's art is *modern* because it makes the effect of the natural world on the senses—the "music" and "scent" of things—into its material. It is an art shot through with desire that does not repress "the beatings of the heart," an art characterized by "imagination," "enthusiasm," and "poetry," an art in which thought slips through the realm of visual observation into the "very sources of life." In this description, Mirbeau meant to evoke the play of imagination, dream, and fantasy and to link creative thought to emotional response, bodily pleasures, and even sexuality. The process of creation is not transcendent or intellectualized, but emanates from the very body of the artist. Mirbeau's phrase "the painful voluptuousness of creation" emphasizes this link to bodily feeling—particularly because *enfantement* has a double meaning—it is both "childbirth" and "creation." Thus, in Mirbeau's description of Puvis's aesthetic, modern creativity is inextricably linked to the body and, further, to maternal femininity.

If Puvis's paintings are aimed at returning both himself and the viewers to a "lost paradise," perhaps the paradise that Mirbeau longs for is, at the most fundamental level, a form of subjectivity as stability, wholeness, and plenitude. This fantasy is put in play, Mirbeau suggests, by Puvis's murals. Representation, then, becomes the means by which attempts to secure a sense of wholeness, to project images of "soul," take place. What is crucial about *The Sacred Grove* and *Ancient Vision* is that they both instill desire for that wholeness, even hint at what it might feel like, and at the same time make it impossible by constantly making the process of representation go out of control, by constantly undercutting meaning through an unresolvable play between figures. The viewer of Puvis de Chavannes's murals never achieves the plenitude promised by them but is constantly aware of the desire for it. And it is that integration of desire and its visceral effects in the process of viewing that constitutes the modernity of Puvis de Chavannes's painting.

DREAMING THE NATION

In September 1886, *Ancient Vision*, *Christian Inspiration*, and *The Rhône and the Saône* were installed in the main staircase of the Musée des Beaux-Arts in Lyons, completing the decorative scheme that had begun with *The Sacred Grove* (fig. 30). The official interpretation of the cycle can be found in a pamphlet written by the director of the museum, Edouard Aynard, which was sold to museum visitors as a guide. In this text, Aynard was forced to grapple with the contradictions of Puvis's murals as well as with their political implications. These murals were meant to teach visitors to the museum and prepare them for their experiences of the work within. Yet, as we have seen, Puvis's style made them formally elusive and opaque. The murals portrayed two strands of French patrimony, but they also associated the republican virtue of fraternity with Christianity at a moment when the state was battling with both institutional Catholicism and burgeoning neo-Christian movements. In the murals Puvis imagined the origins of French cre-

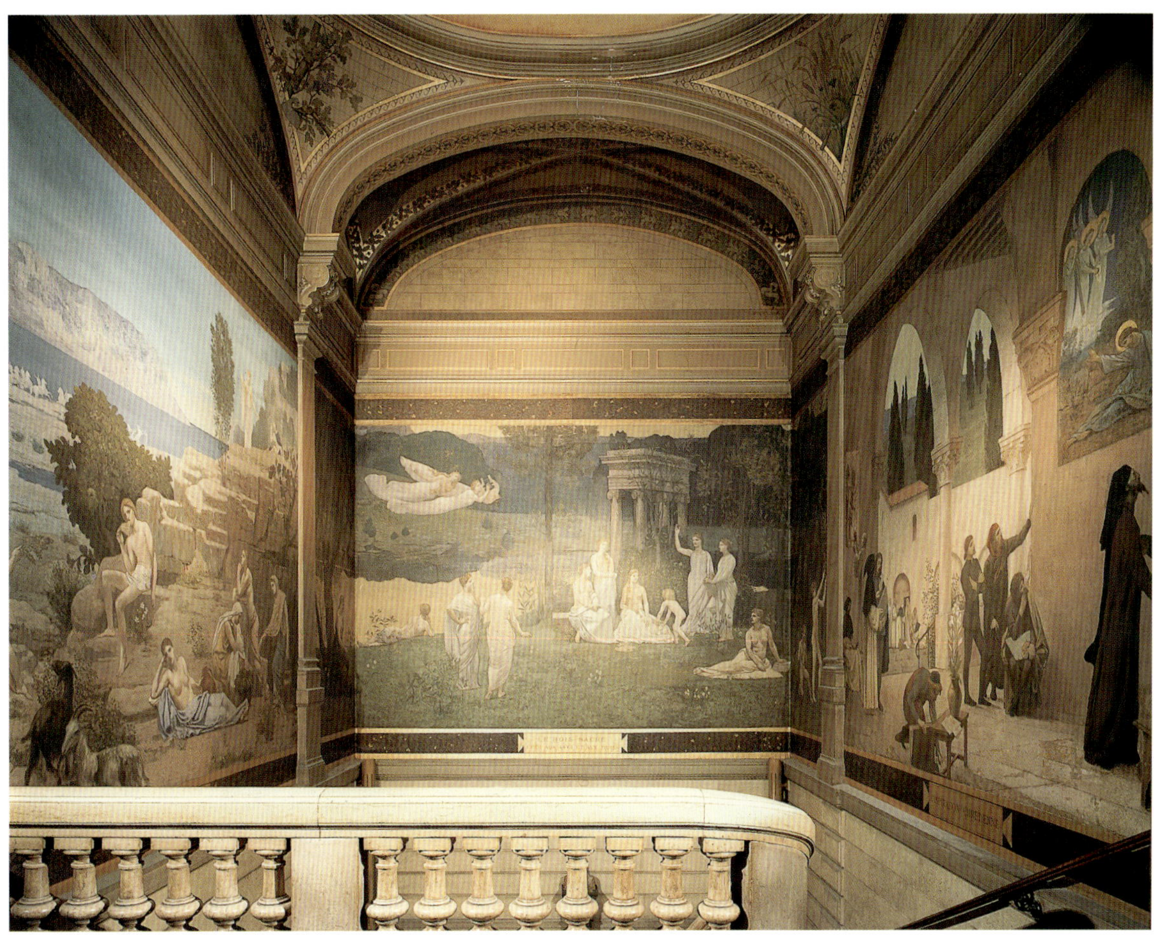

30
Pierre Puvis de Chavannes, decorative cycle in the Musée des Beaux-Arts, Lyons, 1884–86

ativity in the ancient world but associated this aspect of the French sensibility with desire, sensuality, and dream. How would the state interpret work such as this for the populace?

Given the interpretations of the murals, it should strike us as somewhat surprising that the official interpretation emphasized the dreamlike nature of Puvis's style. Regardless of the educational function of the murals, Aynard embraced their indeterminacy. Indeed, he claimed that the paintings themselves were like dreams:

> The caressed eye enjoys resting for an instant in this indeterminacy and, above all, in partaking of the sensation of dream, which is one of the cycle's qualities. These are our sweetest and noblest dreams floating there on the walls, and they attach themselves without appearing to clash. Muses that we have all invoked at least once, sublime antiquity, which sustains our spirit and conserves for us the vestiges of its grandeur, tender Christianity, which saved the world by speaking so softly and quietly to the heart, memories of our country of birth, which remind us of the modern religion of *la patrie*—all of this mingles in a painted synthesis of our spiritual life.[38]

In this poetic and provocative passage, Aynard depends heavily on the language of the unconscious and, most important, references dream and memory. He describes not a picture of a dream but an experience of viewing, which is likened to a pleasurable "caress." Understanding the paintings is less a matter of intellect than of "sensation." However, Aynard suggests, the viewer does not passively take the murals in. Instead, the viewer actively "partakes" of this "sensation of dream"—the viewer dreams along with Puvis, evokes the Muses with him. Aynard's emphasis is not on the subject matter of the murals but on the way they make viewers feel and on the activities of dreaming and remembering that they stimulate. In Aynard's description, as in the Salon reviews, the activity of viewing hinges on sensation, emotion, and fantasy. Never before had critics so forcefully used a vocabulary of dream to describe Puvis's murals. Never in the context of Puvis's public paintings, that is, had the description of the artist's formal means been so directly linked to the unconscious. If the Lyons murals pictured a "synthesis of our spiritual life," they surely offered a conception of the French sensibility that integrated, even capitalized on, desire and fantasy.

Like *Young Girls by the Seashore*, which asked viewers to empathize with the pictured reverie, the Lyons murals gave the sensation of dream. Unlike the easel paintings, the Lyons murals also fulfilled their purpose as public paintings by using that sensation of dream to instill collective devotion to France. By repeating the first-person plural pronoun in the passage—these are "*our* sweetest and noblest dreams," "Muses *we* have *all* invoked," "antiquity, which sustains *our* spirit," "memories of *our* country of birth, which reminds *us* of the modern religion of *la patrie*"—Aynard emphasized that the dreams were not merely about individual pasts, but about collective origins, origins whose memory would strengthen solidarity in the present. Rather than being a hindrance to the public mission of the cycle, the dreamlike indeterminacies were tied to Frenchness, to the "our" of collective identity.

When Aynard referred to "the modern religion of *la patrie*," he invoked a civic morality rooted in ancient republics. This republican sensibility was, Aynard implied, more directly linked to *Ancient Vision* than to *Christian Inspiration*. Aynard abandoned the plural pronouns—"our" and "we"—when he described *Christian Inspiration*: "tender Christianity, which saved the world." The specific and possessive "our" was replaced by a more general description, "the world." That Aynard chose a language less directly tied to collective identity for *Christian Inspiration* had everything to do with the major political battles of the time—battles between the ardent royalist Catholicism that developed toward the end of the century and the democratic secular morality of the republican state. His evocation of *Christian Inspiration* was marked by generality and understatement. This aspect of "spiritual life," said Aynard, speaks "softly" and "quietly." It is more diffuse and generalized, less directly linked to French collective identity.

Still, Aynard claimed that both the Catholic and the republican elements of French identity could appear side by side in the cycle—could "attach themselves without appearing to clash." And here the "indeterminacies" of Puvis's murals work to Aynard's advantage. Precisely because paintings were like dreams, Aynard suggested, they allowed the elements of the French "soul," in conflict in the 1880s, to occupy adjacent walls. Yet something bubbling below the surface of this characterization of the murals needs to be addressed. In saying that the medieval Christian and ancient elements of the French sensibility "float" on the walls "without appearing to clash," Aynard came close to admitting that appearances are deceptive. In one sense, this claim points to a deep desire to end the political divisions of the time or at least to disavow them, to find one place where a vision of France as whole might be experienced, even if only in a "dream."

In addition, Aynard seems to have recognized, along with Fouillée and Guyau, that the unconscious was the means by which art would secure collective identity. Indeed, Aynard did not mean to refer to religious spirituality when he described Puvis's cycle as a synthesis of spiritual life. Instead, he was calling on a vocabulary for collective identity that was part and parcel of republicanism. Perhaps the most famous example of the link between spirituality and collective identity was described by one of Puvis's close friends, Ernest Renan, in his famous "What is a nation?" lecture of 1882.[39] Renan was anything but an apologist for Catholicism.[40] Yet he, too, used a language of soul and spirituality to describe collective identity. "The modern nation," said Renan, "is a historical outcome brought forth by a series of facts converging in the same direction. . . . It is the glory of France to have proclaimed, through the French Revolution, that the nation exists in itself."[41] By this Renan meant that the nation was not (as legitimists would have it) a matter of dynasty set up by divine right. Neither, claimed Renan, was nationhood simply a result of common race, language, or religion. Instead, it came about because of a sense of belonging felt by its citizens and their desire to participate in nationhood. This sense of belonging was not just a result of conscious consent. It went much deeper and was almost impossible to articulate in words. "A nation," said Renan, "is a soul [*âme*], a spiritual principle."[42]

Renan invoked soul and spirit not to point to specifically religious content. On the contrary (and writing slightly before the notion of the unconscious had been adequately formulated), Renan was searching for a vocabulary that would suggest the depth of feeling involved in a sense of national belonging. Indeed, as he attempted to define this principle, he continually returned to a language of desire: "the desire to live together, the will to continue to value the received heritage . . . we have chased from politics metaphysical and theological abstractions. What is left after that? Man is left, his desires, his needs."[43]

Renan was already proposing in the second half of the nineteenth century what has by now become, thanks to Benedict Anderson, a classic formulation of theories of nation:

> The nation . . . is an imagined political community—and imagined as both inherently limited and sovereign. It is *imagined* because the members of even the smallest nation will never know most of their fellow-members, meet them or even hear of them, yet in the minds of each lives the image of their communion. Renan referred to this imagining in his suavely back-handed way when he wrote that "Or l'essence d'une nation est que tous les individus aient beaucoup de choses en commun, et aussi que tous aient oublié bien des choses" [The essence of a nation is that all the individuals have many things in common, and also have forgotten many things].[44]

Like Anderson, I want to highlight this imaginary component of nationness. And I want also to emphasize the awareness of that imaginary component that existed in Puvis's day and was actively cultivated by those with ideological purposes. First and foremost among them was the republican government, which was actively consolidating its hold on notions of Frenchness in the face of rivals on both the Right and the Left.[45]

Renan's words "spirit" and "soul," Anderson's term "imagination"—each of these designates a realm of subjectivity for which no adequate description seemed to exist: the deep sense of belonging, a sense characterized more by emotional affect than by intellectual understanding, that makes collective identity possible. And each points us to processes of mind that are more or less unconscious. Frenchness existed only to the degree to which it commanded belief, and inevitably it did so to varying degrees and with different content in the individuals who made up France. This belief was not just consciously chosen. Rather, it depended on memory and forgetting and on those unconscious processes, those desires and identifications, that were beyond conscious control and that made a sense of belonging seem to inhabit the very depths of subjectivity.[46]

In addition to highlighting the fantasmatic components of national belonging, Anderson makes the powerful claim that nations are distinguished from one another by "the style in which they were imagined."[47] As Anderson implies through his quotation of Renan, France's sense of itself depended on a dialectic of forgetting and remembering. Both Renan and Anderson thus capitalize on fantasy and desire as the impulses that drive the creative process by which the notion of France is constructed. As Renan and Anderson indicate, the two cannot truly be separated. Puvis's painterly mode, like Renan's description of Frenchness, employs a rhetoric of erasure and recapitulation. In Puvis's murals, too, Frenchness and creativity are intertwined.[48]

DREAMING FRENCH CREATIVITY

In the Lyons murals, the patrimony is described as encompassing both antique and medieval, both feminine and masculine, both the individual and the collective, both the grounded and the transcendent. When we look at *Ancient Vision* and *Christian Inspiration* together, it is tempting to go along with Aynard's claim that the two sides of French patrimony appear together without clashing. Puvis, who described the paintings as complementary, seems to have meant to depict Frenchness as wholeness and universality. The responses to his paintings suggest, however, that the story is more complex than that. The disagreements between critics about the murals and the struggles by individual critics to make sense of *Ancient Vision* show that no such consensus existed. The two sides of Frenchness depicted here, the two sides of human subjectivity that are engaged by the paintings, do clash. The critical reception of the murals suggests that in both form and content

Christian Inspiration was at odds with the other paintings in the cycle. Which aspect of art should be taken as dominant in Puvis's oeuvre, which aspect dominated his artistic personality, remained central to critical debates about Puvis as his reputation as a national painter grew.

I have been arguing that precisely because of the way *Ancient Vision* subverted normal expectations and instilled desire, it spoke profoundly to viewers. Puvis's allegiance is perhaps best discerned by looking again at *The Sacred Grove*—the painting that was meant to be a synthesis of *Ancient Vision* and *Christian Inspiration*. Puvis described *The Sacred Grove* as a representation of the well of creativity from which each aspect of the patrimony had sprung. Yet, as we saw in Chapter 2, *The Sacred Grove* was all about an address to the unconscious through the provocation of desire and fantasy. Its mode of address depended on the ambiguity coded into that most material and uncontainable subject, the body. It is tempting, then, to place Puvis more on the side of *Ancient Vision* than on the side of *Christian Inspiration*.

Octave Mirbeau would have agreed with this interpretation of the vision of modern genius proposed in *The Sacred Grove*. And so would Judith Gautier. Slightly more surprising, even Gustave Geffroy, for whom *Ancient Vision* was so powerfully disturbing, would have done the same. Geffroy characterized *The Sacred Grove* as an image of the origins of French civilization. But he was not speaking of historical origins. Instead, he described the subject of *The Sacred Grove* as creativity itself—the force from which all of the products of civilization had sprung.

Geffroy called the original creative endeavor the "legend" and described *The Sacred Grove* as "legendary." His description of the legend suggests that he believed that the legend in general and *The Sacred Grove* in particular were both inextricably tied to the disturbance of desire. Geffroy claimed that the legend, in its attempt to "recount the beginnings of a civilization," described the "gropings of a mind that searches for the meaning of things, the disquiet of man in the face of nature and himself." And such an endeavor is a particular kind of labor that is permeated by desire and located in the body. It is, said Geffroy, "the mysterious phrase, perhaps not even understood by the one who pronounces it, which exits from the mouth like a beast's cry or a bird's song; it is the first attempt at industry, at the work of legislation, of poetry; it is the first trembling step taken in a light that surprises us as the night lifts on unknown soil."[49] If *The Sacred Grove* taught its viewers about Frenchness, this was because it returned them to those origins by making them feel that "disquiet"—the desire that spurs on acts of imagination. The painting was therefore both modern and legendary. The most modern painting, Geffroy suggested, paralleling Guyau's ideas, would return its viewers to the desire at the origin of aesthetic experience—an experience inextricably tied to the body.

Geffroy summed up his interpretation of *The Sacred Grove* in a passage that links the issues of desire, creativity, and Frenchness.[50] Puvis, said Geffroy, had synthesized all the achievements of Western civilization. He was "fashioned by all the men who have preceded him" and had "inherited all their . . . discoveries." Not only had he traced all the achievements of civilization to their primitive origins, but he had taken the best from them and crystallized them into an image of "ideal man." Later in the same passage, Geffroy described *The Sacred Grove* as "the beautiful work that is French in both conception and execution." It was there that the subtext is manifest. France becomes the bearer of the universal memory, the culmination and synthesis of what has come before; Frenchness synthesizes the powers of creativity to be found in all civilizations.

What is most interesting about Geffroy's description is the way that familiar claims about Frenchness, claims that mix chauvinism and universality, are undermined from the start by the very terms on which they are based. Puvis's task is not just to synthesize the achievements of civilization but to return to them the original sense of lack, that sense of desire that drives imagination. When we look at the qualities that Geffroy thought were necessary to realize "the ideal"—qualities peculiar to Puvis's paintings—we see qualities not of clarity and transcendence but of confusion, undecidability, and groundedness. They are the "gropings of a mind that searches for the explanation for things." They are the "disquiet of man before nature and himself." They are "mysterious," "misunderstood." And the artist who can tap into them is not described as positive and intellectual but as "complicated," "skeptical," "changeable and multifarious." Thus, *The Sacred Grove* was for Geffroy both "naive" and "knowing." Puvis takes the knowledge of the centuries—"the harmonies and colors that are the result of centuries of painting" and reinstills in them "the light of disappeared dawns."

Clearly, the understanding of Frenchness that *The Sacred Grove* represents has little to do with any kind of transcendent, unifying thought. The groundedness—in the contradictions of the material past and in the bodily experiences of individual beings—a groundedness that is part and parcel of this ambiguity, is emphasized when Geffroy likens the expression of the primordial by the artist to a beast's cry. In this case "an intellectual labor" involves a breakdown of mind-body divisions. Thought escapes without understanding, through the body. Like the cry of a beast or a bird's song, it is sensed by others, understood instinctively. Comparing it to a cry (of pain) or a song (of joy) also implies its origins in the senses. Geffroy implied that *The Sacred Grove* would teach its viewers more about French patrimony than would the history paintings and religious paintings that surrounded it at the Salon. This is true, I would argue, because rather than picturing that quality of Frenchness, Puvis's paintings make viewers actually experience it. *The Sacred Grove* does not represent Frenchness but demonstrates it in its very structure. Ultimately, Geffroy's description encodes the contradictions involved in attempting to formulate a version of Frenchness that is both materialist and universalistic. We could even say that this passage is symptomatic of the paradoxes involved in such self-definition from the Left. And it is perhaps because his project is somewhat analogous to Puvis's formulation of a materialist high art that Geffroy's writings about the artist seem so poignantly to describe both the seduction and the disturbance of Puvis's work.

In the Lyons murals, Puvis pictures not the patrimony itself but the desire giving rise to creative endeavor. Geffroy was not the first to cast the creative impulse as the French quality par excellence. This was the impetus behind the notion of patrimony. What is particularly revealing about his account, and what is unique to Puvis's paintings at this moment, is that they do not, like an idealized image, stand as testimony to the overcoming of the lack that spurs desire. Rather, the artifacts of Puvis's imagination declare desire to be constitutive of the work of art, of creativity, of subjectivity. In the most powerfully disturbing works in the cycle—*The Sacred Grove* and *Ancient Vision*—viewers are asked to participate in an experience of desire. Faced with undecidable compositions and strange configurations of the body, viewers are put to the task of idealizing and completing the works at hand. The desire spurred by these works is not just an intellectual curiosity but a deep-seated and visceral feeling that demands a response. Individual fantasies are put to the task of (re)creating the patrimony.

4

THE EPISTEMOLOGY OF DREAM

The Sorbonne Mural

When Puvis de Chavannes accepted the commission to paint the mural for the largest and most central lecture hall of the New Sorbonne, he must have known he was entering territory that was both prized and embattled (fig. 31). Picturing knowledge, its achievements, and its possibilities could never be a simple affair. But in France in the 1880s, when the New Sorbonne was built, such an endeavor carried with it particular difficulties. The Sorbonne, which had begun as a theological college under royal sponsorship in 1253, had been under state control since the French Revolution. The new building, part of a controversial plan by the republican state to expand and restructure higher education, became a symbolic site where the conflicts between royalism and republicanism, Catholicism and secularism, were played out.

The mural was to be mounted under the dome that became one of the major landmarks of Paris. If the building gave the republican educational reforms a literal space, Puvis's hemicycle gave it explicit and prominent visual form. The mural would unavoidably meet the eye of anyone and everyone seated in the hall for a lecture, ceremony, or convocation. Critics across the spectrum knew, when they wrote about Puvis's mural, that it was to occupy the symbolic and literal center of the Republic's secularizing reforms. The reception of Puvis's mural for the Sorbonne was therefore, from the outset, caught in a web of violent disagreement about the purpose of education and the origin and content of knowledge. Looking at the reception of the mural provides a window onto these debates, which inevitably brought epistemology together with politics. More than that, because of Puvis's visual style and because of the associations that had already been established in the public mind between Puvis's painterly style, modernism, and the unconscious, the conjunction of issues raised by the Sorbonne mural was even more complex. What, the mural seemed to ask, was the role to be played by the unconscious in knowledge and belief? How were the visual and the bodily implicated in knowledge and belief? And what were the moral and political ramifications of the answers to these questions?

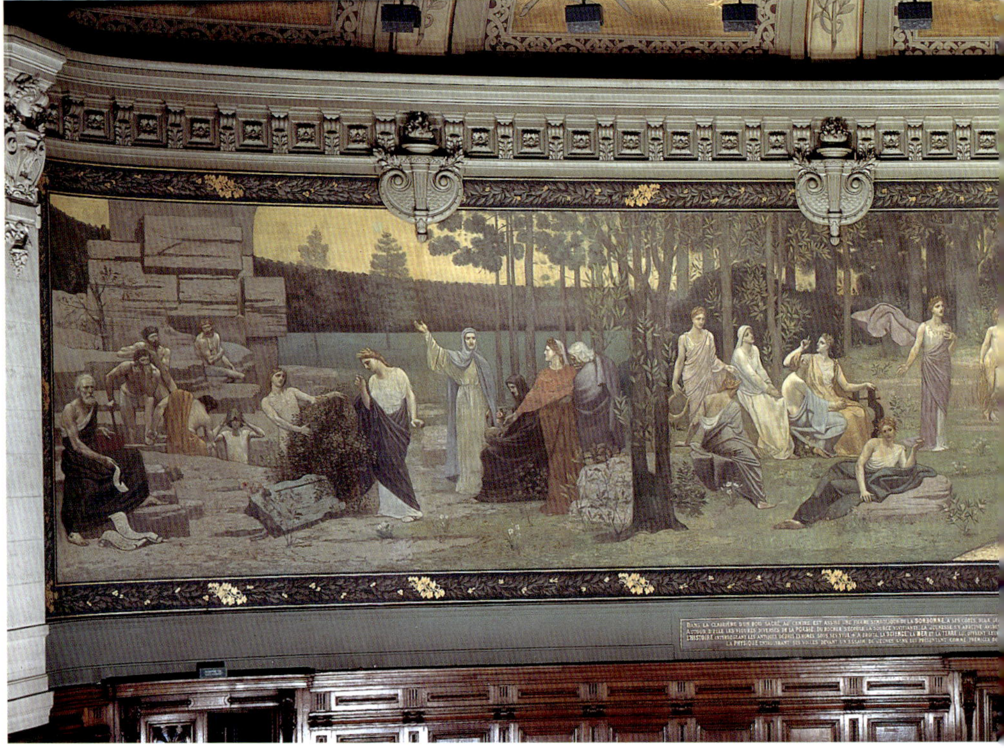

Puvis's Sorbonne mural was commissioned in May of 1886, just after the opening of the Salon in which the second installment of his highly successful Lyons murals *Christian Inspiration* and *Ancient Vision* was exhibited. The commission for those murals had been signed by none other than the government minister Jules Ferry, who had dubbed Puvis de Chavannes "Knight of the Ideal."[1] Although the architect in charge of building the Grand Amphithéâtre chose Puvis to paint its most prominent mural, Ferry may have contributed to that decision.[2] Ferry was most directly responsible for instigating a series of reforms in the 1880s meant to secularize all aspects of the French state. The most important site of this laicizing program was the school system *morale laïque* (civic morality), by which the republican values of liberty, equality, and fraternity would be taught to all.[3] Education became the means of consolidating the bourgeois Republic by replacing Catholic morality with republican virtues, devotion to God with devotion to country. The New Sorbonne was central to this project. It would therefore be fitting for Ferry to have contributed to the choice of Puvis to paint the hemicycle.

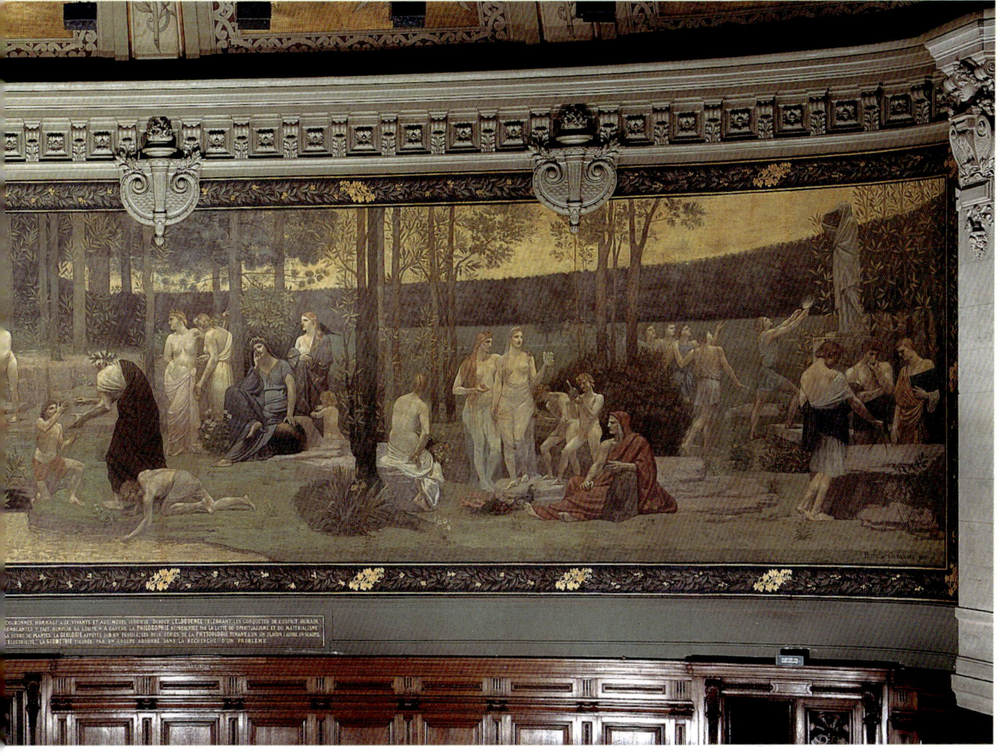

31
Pierre Puvis de Chavannes, *The Sorbonne*, 1889. Oil on canvas affixed to wall, 14 3/4 ft. x 196 3/4 ft. (4.5 x 60 m). Grand Amphithéâtre de la Sorbonne, Paris

A preliminary sketch for the mural that contained all of its basic elements was exhibited at the Salon of 1887. The final version of the mural was unveiled in 1889, when the New Sorbonne was inaugurated. Nowhere was the program of civic morality celebrated with more pomp and ceremony than at the inauguration, which, along with the Universal Exposition that summer, was tied to a celebration of the hundredth anniversary of the French Revolution. The Centenary was a time for taking stock of the legacy of the French Revolution and the principles upon which the Republic had been founded. In the celebrations the state, which had recently survived the turmoil of Boulangism, attempted to consolidate support for republicanism.[4] Inaugurating the New Sorbonne, the state intended not only to provide badly needed educational facilities but to recast the university, which had theological origins, as a secular temple of learning and knowledge. The inauguration was one of the crowning moments of the state's effort to showcase republican achievements for domestic and international audiences. The New Sorbonne would offer the meeting ground for an intellectual community promoting the advancement of all scholarly endeavor, but would focus in particular on the development of science and on positivist approaches to other disciplines. Puvis de Chavannes's mural in the Grand Amphithéâtre was at its center. Here was the place where great minds would gather and share ideas. Here, in the largest and most central hall, intellectual solidarity would be achieved. And all the while, those illustrious citizens and their students would be looking at Puvis de Chavannes's mural as an image of the achievements of and possibilities for the French mind.

THE SORBONNE MURAL

An immense painting, peopled with more than forty figures, the Sorbonne mural was Puvis de Chavannes's most ambitious work yet. He described the setting for the allegory as a "sacred grove." In painting this setting, Puvis returned to and refined many of the aspects of his murals for Lyons. He again used the landscape to envelop the viewer and to structure the visual experience rhythmically. Because of the shape of the room and the size of the mural, the hemicycle literally wraps around the viewer, emitting a golden glow. The landscape is divided horizontally approximately one-third of the way from the top by an intersection of light and dark colors. The large dark area—a thick forest of trees in the distance—prevents a sense of recession. The tops of the trees rise gradually and evenly from center to edge to meet the upper corners of the mural at each side, thus echoing the shape of the room and enhancing the feeling of a landscape enfolding its viewers. Above this relatively undifferentiated band of trees is a golden yellow sky. Between the green foreground and the base of the trees is a monochrome area of blue gray paint. Its function is largely compositional. Along with the trees and sky it reads most emphatically as a band of color, which flattens the composition and emphasizes the shape of the wall behind it.

The most evidence about the reception of the Sorbonne mural can be gleaned from responses to the preliminary sketch exhibited at the Salon of 1887 (figs. 32–34).[5] In the Salon brochure, Puvis offered his viewers a step by step explanation of the central elements of the allegory.[6] An abridged and slightly modified version of this text was inscribed on the wall below the final version of the mural.[7]

The central panel, we are told by Puvis, shows us "l'antique Sorbonne" (fig. 35). Here, set back from the viewer, a robed figure, with covered head, sits stiffly, eyes gazing intently forward, arms crossed. Her rigid and upright posture contrasts markedly with the supple bodies of the ephebes holding laurels at her side. Seated on her block of marble, a block extending out to form the ground that the figures of Poetry inhabit, she seems both to guarantee and to oversee all that unfolds. But what exactly does she represent? Already in the seemingly innocuous description, Puvis has opened up

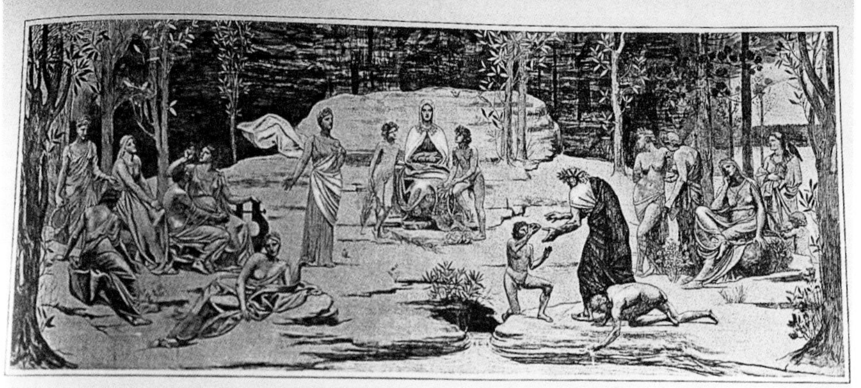

32
Pierre Puvis de Chavannes, cartoon for hemicycle of the Sorbonne, center panel, "La Sorbonne," 1887. Photolithograph. *Figaro-Salon*, May 1887, p. 1

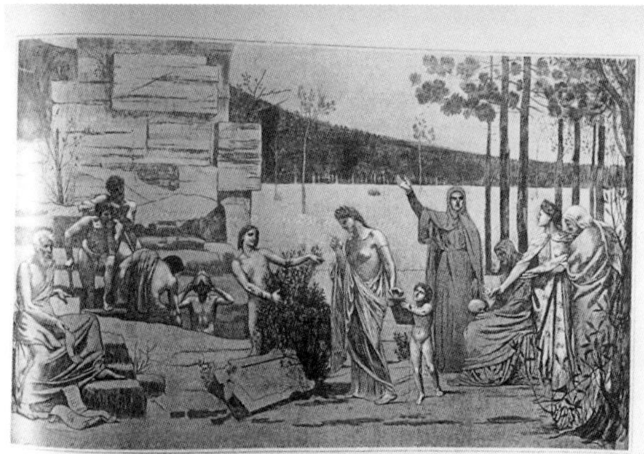

33
Pierre Puvis de Chavannes, cartoon for hemicycle of the Sorbonne, left panel, "La Philosophie et l'Histoire," 1887. Photolithograph. *Figaro-Salon*, May 1887, p. 2

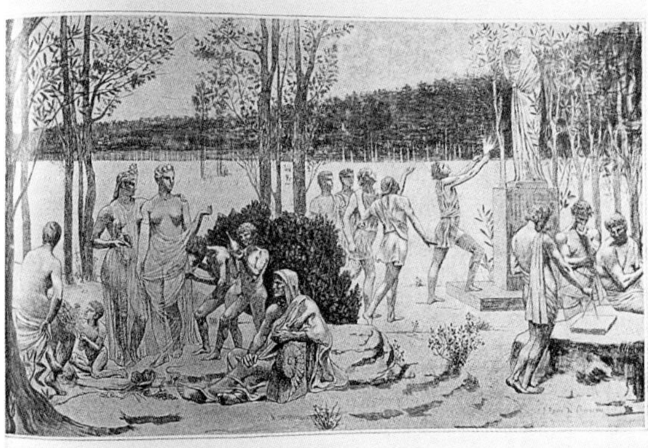

34
Pierre Puvis de Chavannes, cartoon for hemicycle of the Sorbonne, right panel, "La Science," 1887. Photolithograph. *Figaro-Salon*, May 1887, p. 3

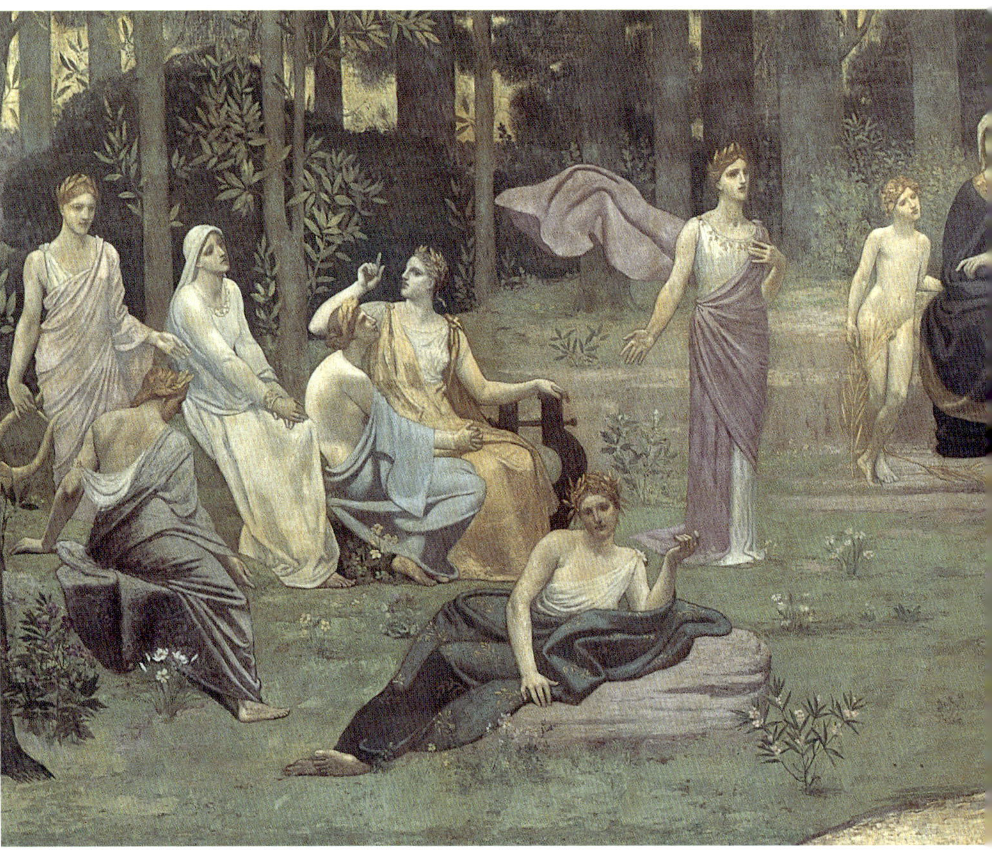

a political can of worms, for what he claims to be showing us is "*l'antique* Sorbonne." The term "antique" is ambiguous. It can refer to the old or classical Sorbonne. Given that Puvis's mural *Ancient Vision*, exhibited only the year before, was widely interpreted as a pastoral landscape of ancient Greece, here "antique" would surely have carried the latter connotation. Regardless of the Sorbonne's historical origins in monarchic medieval Paris, then, Puvis suggested the possibility that its ultimate origin—the origin of true knowledge—was in antiquity, where Christian theology did not yet exist and where government took the form of a republic.[8]

This ambiguity was a point of contention among the critics. Although Gustave Geffroy praised the relative clarity of the allegory, he also noted that "one is forced at first glance to recognize that the medieval Sorbonne is personified in a woman with an archaic physiognomy and posture."[9] The critic for the *Journal des Débats*, Jules Lemaître, on the other hand, described the figure of the Sorbonne as

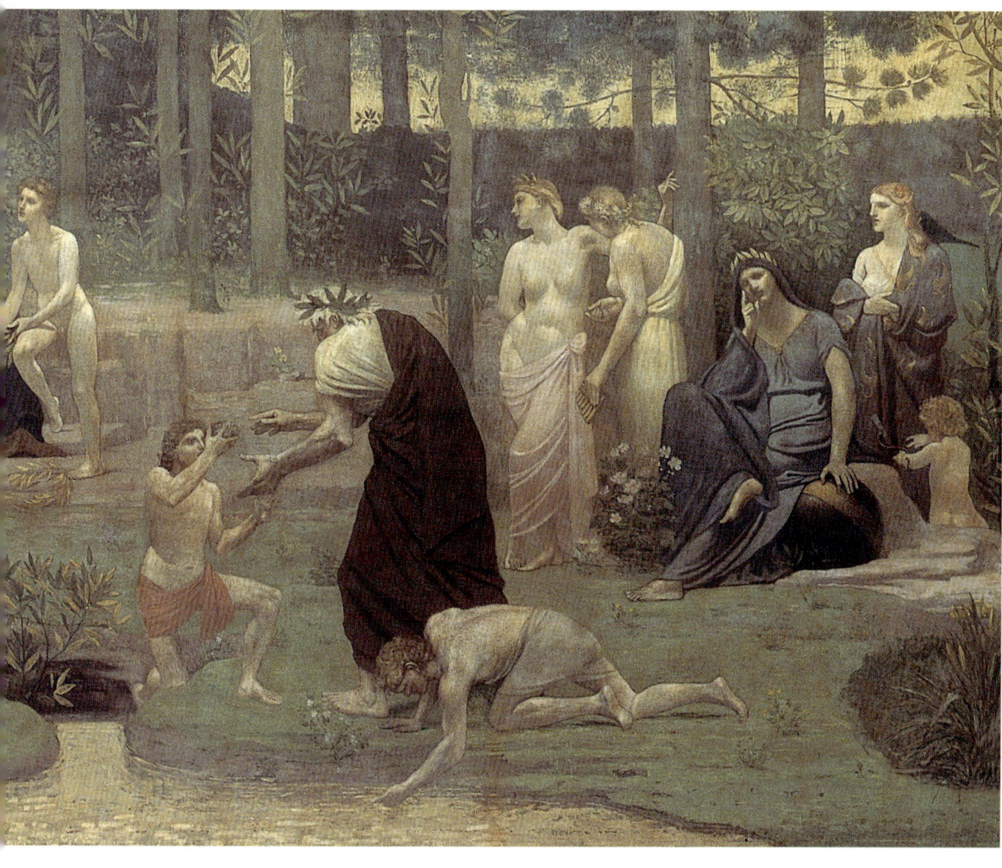

35
Pierre Puvis de Chavannes, *The Sorbonne* (detail of fig. 31; figure of the Sorbonne with Muses of Poetry)

"enclosed in veils, like a great nun or an austere monk." The veils were enough to make Lemaître recall "the religious character" of the Sorbonne's origins. Yet for him this "religious" aspect "symbolize[d] the studious and reclusive life, the solitude in which works of the mind ripen."[10] He thought the robes signified the imaginative withdrawal necessary for a concentrated life of the mind, rather than a sustained religious foundation for the university.

Catholic critics, by contrast, complained that the mural as a whole was nothing but an effort to deny the religious and monarchic origins of the Sorbonne. Here, for example, is Georges-Claudius Lavergne: "This plan of falsifications and subtractions, this impious vandalism . . . tries to pluck our ancient Sorbonne from the royal mantle under which generations of national and foreign masters and students have taken refuge for five successive centuries. . . . One would never have predicted then that in the nineteenth century her palace would be burned and her schools and even her sword would be laicized and . . . that one would go so far as to repudiate her history and throw the diamonds of her crown to the wind."[11] This repudiation of the Sorbonne's history was symbolized by Puvis's stripping it of any overt Catholic or royalist reference. The description of the figure as antique must have raised Lavergne's ire as much as its being pictured with neither crown nor scepter nor cross.

The laicization of the Sorbonne was central to republican rhetoric at the inauguration. M. Fallières, the minister of public education, recounted a history of the university that, like Puvis's mural, left the theological origins of the Sorbonne out of its account. Fallières attributed the decay of the university under the ancien régime to the inability of the monarchy to recognize and reinforce the importance of new scientific and rational principles in higher education. He contrasted this with the educational spirit of the Revolution—a spirit of unified and harmonious intellectual life based in materialism. This, he claimed, was what the New Sorbonne would seek to encourage in the young intellectuals of France.[12] The speech made by M. Gréard, rector of the Sorbonne, emphasized the secular roots of this national esprit. From the moment in the Middle Ages when the nation was founded, until the Revolution, Gréard claimed, the French mind was forced to transform foreign theological and monarchic influences into authentic secular and democratic French thought. The *esprit français* had thus found its free expression only since the Revolution. Even though the nineteenth century was troubled by monarchy and military defeat, the French mind, informed by the secular and positivist principles of 1789, had never before been so intensely and productively active. The consolidation of the French intellectual elite by the rejuvenated Sorbonne would guarantee the final consolidation of the Republic.[13]

The youth of France when properly educated by the state would play a central role in strengthening the Republic. It was therefore fitting for Puvis to include an image of youth in the central panel of his mural. Although the antique Sorbonne occupies the literal center of the canvas, the focus of this section of the mural is unquestionably the group of Youth and Old Age drinking at the spring in the foreground (see fig. 35). The overall composition of the mural suggests that Puvis wished to emphasize these figures. Running down into the space of the viewer, the water offers itself most insistently to the occupants of the Grand Amphithéâtre. Other elements of the composition frame the drinking figures, thus amplifying their importance. The trees that divide this central element from the sides are paralleled by other trees, which recede back and toward the figure of the Sorbonne. The leaves that extend across the top of the central section form a kind of proscenium arch whose theatrical effect is then undercut by the waters flowing past the bottom border. The surrounding figures, too, frame this central group through their gestures and positions. On the left, the reclining figure in the foreground parallels, in the main lines of her body, the angle of the edge of the water. She looks out at the viewer, and her raised left hand points to the action taking place in the center foreground. Further back, in purple and white, a figure of Eloquence extends her arm and continues the framing angle established by the reclining figure. Indeed, virtually all of the figures in this area take on poses that echo one another in such a way as to emphasize the central area of the spring.

Puvis described this section as a "vivifying spring" from which "Youth drink avidly" and "the Aged take new strength." What did it mean to imagine the "life-giving" source—the source of all knowledge and truth—as a spring bubbling up from the ground? What kind of knowledge did Puvis mean to imply flowed from the source? And who had most direct access to the knowledge flowing forth? In both the sketch and the final version two adolescent males ("la Jeunesse") and an old man crowned with laurels ("la Vieillesse") drink from it. One of the youths offers a cup to the old man, who reaches for it eagerly. The gesture of transferring the source of inspiration from young to old is emphasized by the arrangement of their bodies. In the cartoon for the mural, their positions seem to signify an imminent embrace as much as a transfer of the cup (see fig. 32). In the final version, the old man's hands are magnified as if to emphasize his open reaching (see fig. 35). In front of them, the other youth crouches on all fours and leans over the bank, scooping out a handful of water. In the final version, Puvis compares the large empty hand of the old man with the full hand of the crouching figure by aligning their arms along a diagonal. Thus, although the mural suggests an attempt by the young to aid the old by handing off the cup, it is the young—those who have direct contact with the source of inspiration—upon whom the old must rely if they are to continue. This contrast is made even stronger by the inscription below the painting, which was modified for the final version to describe the old man's hand as "trembling."

If the young have greater access to the source of knowledge, they also seem to be more willing to undertake a direct, bodily relation with the waters of the source. The kneeling youth appears almost to climb out of the water in order to hand over the cup, and the crouching figure is shown at the moment when his hand dips into the spring. Several critics commented on their closeness to the earth. In a typical response, Jules Lemaître woefully suggested that "the crouching Genius, who sucks [*hume*] the water from the source displays distressing hindquarters [*étale un arrière-train desolant*]."[14] The term "hindquarters" associates the figure with the animal rather than the human world, and the figure is described as if he has put his mouth to the water like an animal taking drink. Both of these suggest a bodily relation to knowledge and inspiration, which come not from the heights of the heavens but from the earth.

Changes from the cartoon to the final version of the mural reinforce this interpretation. The drapery on the kneeling boy, now painted orange, includes a hanging excess of fabric. Its folds are perpendicular to the ground and echo the line of the youth's lower leg, emphasizing both the force of gravity and his stepping motion. The other young male, the one on all fours, is closer to the spring in the final version than he was in the cartoon. Puvis has emphasized the thrust of the younger figure's arm by making the line of his entire body, from leg to buttocks to spine, lead up to it. Whereas in the sketch the boy's hand hovers slightly above the water, in the final version, the boy's hand is in the water. This makes the contrast between the young boy's access to the water and the old man's desire for it all the more forceful.

The art historical precedents for the figures in this group support the notion that Puvis wanted to represent closeness to nature, for the figures are derived from Poussin's *Landscape with Diogenes* (1648), which depicts the impoverished philosopher who lived in the fourth century B.C. (fig. 36). Poussin shows the moment when Diogenes sees a youth dipping his hand into the water to take a drink and is inspired to throw away his cup, casting off the last of his worldly possessions and thus becoming closer to nature. In Poussin's painting, Diogenes faces the viewer and looks attentively at the youth, thus allowing the viewer to participate in the lesson he has learned. In contrast to Poussin, Puvis represents an older generation that refuses to take its cue from youth. The old man's figure turns away from the viewer, hunched, straining, and empty-handed. Although he is crowned with laurels, suggesting past achievements, he does not set an example for the viewer to follow but remains a relic dependent on the young for his survival.

Taken together, this central image of the spring and Puvis's description of it make an important statement about the sources and proper possessors of knowledge—a statement, moreover, that reinforced the republican program of civic morality. The source of knowledge pictured here is earthbound, found in nature, rather than a transcendent ideal guaranteed by God. Furthermore, the central place given to youth in both the composition and the description resonates with the republican emphasis on the devotion of French youth to the materialist values of the Republic.

This emphasis on the devotion of youth to republican values was central to the rhetoric employed by the republican state when the Sorbonne was inaugurated and the mural unveiled. Gathering together students representative of all the faculties of France in celebration of the Republic, the inauguration ceremony

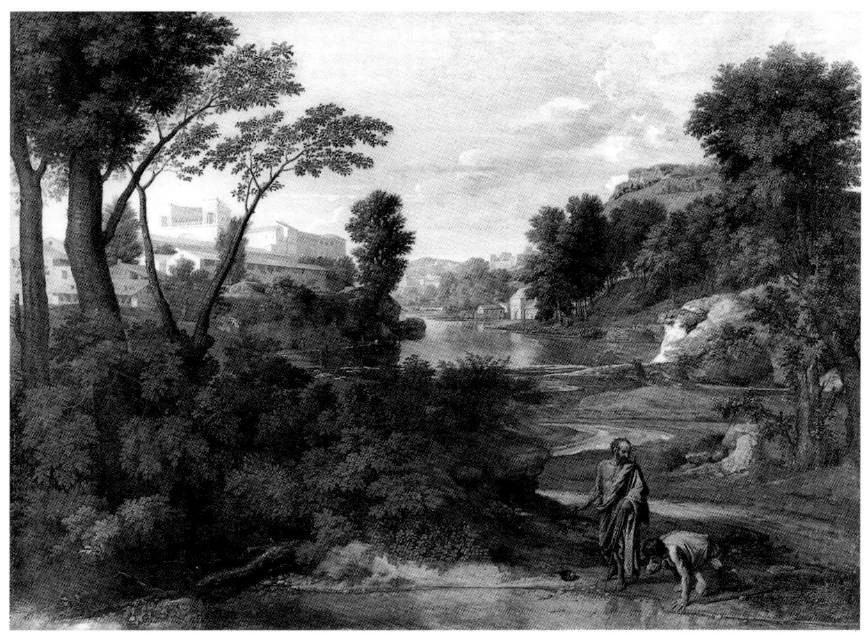

36
Nicolas Poussin, *Landscape with Diogenes*, 1648. Oil on canvas, 63 x 87 in. (160 x 221 cm). Musée du Louvre, Paris

emphasized the "unbreakable attachment" of Youth "to liberty" and the "worship of the principles of 1789."[15] The audience at the inauguration included not only French officials, educators, and students but delegations of students from many different countries, "united in the same sentiment of fraternity, in the same worship of the great principles" of republicanism. Both Fallières and Gréard emphasized the devotion of Youth to these principles, devotion that would guarantee a democratic future for the French state. France was demonstrated to be the wellspring of all intellectual activity. "It was possible to believe," claimed one journalist, "that we were participating for a moment in the celebration not only of our glorious University of France, but in the true University of the Universe."[16] This internationalism ran through many of the commemorations celebrating the Centenary, often with the dual purpose of exalting the superiority of France and demonstrating the solidarity among democratic republics.[17]

It is important to recognize, however, that these speeches were made at a time when French culture was divided over such issues. This was, in fact, the time of a neo-Catholic revival in which many of France's best young minds participated. Led by intellectuals such as Paul Desjardins and Eugène Melchior Vicomte de Vogüé, many of France's most creative youth were turning away from republican values and toward a revamped version of Catholic tradition. Maurice Denis, whose essay "Definition of Neotraditionism" was discussed in Chapter 1, was one example. The republican state's account of the situation of French youth was thus a political move aimed at consolidating its strength and international prestige rather than a description of current trends.[18]

In the Sorbonne mural, Puvis de Chavannes took a stand in the debate. By making the spring into the source of knowledge, Puvis promoted the notion that knowledge was based in the material world of nature, rather than in the spiritual world of transcendent truths. He thus aligned himself with the secularism of the Republic. By using Poussin's *Landscape with Diogenes* as a source for his mural, he set this belief in secular materialism within a tradition of classicism that originated in antiquity (the time pictured in Poussin's landscape) and continued as the central thread of the French tradition (as embodied by Poussin's own classicism). Given the participation of the central group in this rhetoric of aligning knowledge, secularism, and classicism, it is hardly surprising that right-wing critics lambasted it. The neo-Catholic writer Paul Desjardins, for example, criticized the central group as being "without interest" and "empty": It "leaves a gap in the whole."[19] In contrast, republican critics generally had the opposite reaction. For example, Georges Lafenestre found all of Puvis's symbolism ingenious and praised the figures kneeling before the stream.[20]

In the central section, then, we already have the beginnings of a republican epistemology that is reinforced in the rest of the mural. Indeed, the terms of the debate spurred by the central panel are explicitly pictured in the allegory of philosophy. To the left of the Sorbonne figure, beyond a group of Muses representing Poetry, lies the group representing Philosophy (fig. 37). The three female figures allegorize "the battle between spiritualism and naturalism in the face of death," according to the Salon brochure. Meanwhile, an old philosopher dressed in blue passively looks on. Seated at the center of this group, Death, a thin woman cocooned in dark robes, gazes down at a skull on her lap. To her right, Naturalism, a young woman in opulently embroidered red garb, reaches out, holding a flower, an "expression of terrestrial joys and the successive hidebound transformations of matter." From her drapery to the detail of her hair, this figure is drawn with a flowing and sinuous hand. Her beauty is metaphorized in the flower, which is associated, through proximity and gesture, with the skull.

To the left of Death a stoic figure, Idealism, dressed in spare, unembellished clothing, "asserts herself by a gesture of ardent aspiration toward the idea" (Puvis's description again). She is drawn with a correspondingly stiffer and heavier hand. The contrast between the femininity and light beauty of the figure of Naturalism reinforces contemporary associations between visual pleasure, femininity, bodiliness, and materiality, while the image of Idealism suggests the shrouding or renunciation of the flesh in favor of the life of the mind. Here, in strikingly explicit terms, Puvis allegorizes the most central intellectual debate of his time—the debate between materialism and idealism—and points to its ultimate significance as an attempt to attribute meaning to life and to imagine the consequences of death. The blue cape that shrouds the head of Idealism and falls down over her shoulders is similar in tone to the drapery that clothes the old philosopher who looks on. Like the old man at the spring, he turns away from the viewer. A notion of knowledge based on transcendent idealism is thus explicitly associated with the old. Significantly, this shift from the intellectual and transcendent to the bodily and material also involves a shift from the use of predominantly male to predominantly female figures. The architect who commissioned the mural, Henri-Paul Nénot, "had a Raphael-like *School of Athens* in mind."[21] In contrast to Raphael, Puvis depicts the modern debate through female, rather than male, figures. Puvis appears once again to be aligning himself with materialism.

But the situation is not so simple. The figure of Idealism also looks extremely similar to that of the Sorbonne, seated on her block of marble. As in the image of the Sorbonne, no clear stand is taken as to which philosophical attitude is preferable. What remains constant throughout all of these groups, however, is the lack of any explicit reference to Christianity. Still, as with the figure of the Sorbonne, critics debated the degree to which Idealism should be aligned with Christianity. When Puvis's sketch for the mural was exhibited in 1887, the critics could not agree on the meaning of this allegorical group. The critic for *L'Artiste* believed that the figure of Idealism, "with the emaciated head of a saint dying of the desire for Heaven," proffered a religious meaning. The figure, he said, "point[ed] to the sky, toward Christianity." The critic was not sure that a reference to Christianity was Puvis's intention, however. He assumed that Puvis meant to evoke Platonic idealism but had failed. Instead, "whether M. Puvis de Chavannes wanted to or not, this feminine figure . . . emanates a feeling of religiosity, of suffering, and, above all, of renunciation of and disdain for earthly joys quite distant from Platonic thought."[22]

Other critics suggested that the group represented a set of epistemological proposals without a firm conclusion. Said Paul Mantz, critic for the republican paper *Le Temps*, "We see Philosophy teaching less what she knows than what she would like to know, and visibly nourished with hypotheses."[23] Here it is the process of inquiry rather than the source of its resolution that is emphasized. In an article for the conservative *Le Correspondant*, Paul Fresnel lamented what he saw as Puvis's refusal to promote idealism, "to take sides in the battle between spiritualism and materialism." Rather than "tip[ping] the scales to the right side," said Fresnel,

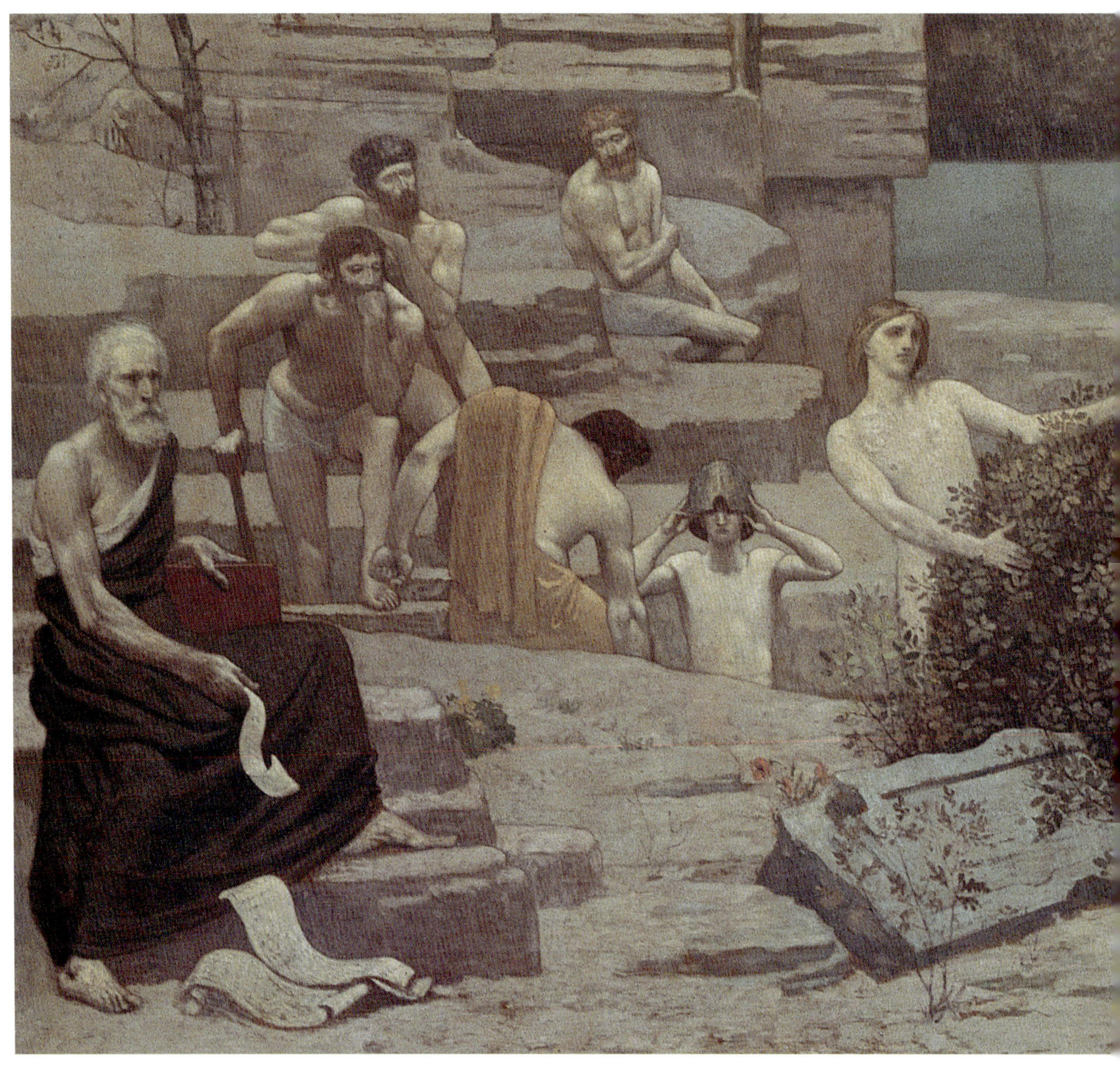

37
Pierre Puvis de Chavannes,
The Sorbonne (detail of fig. 31;
History and Philosophy)

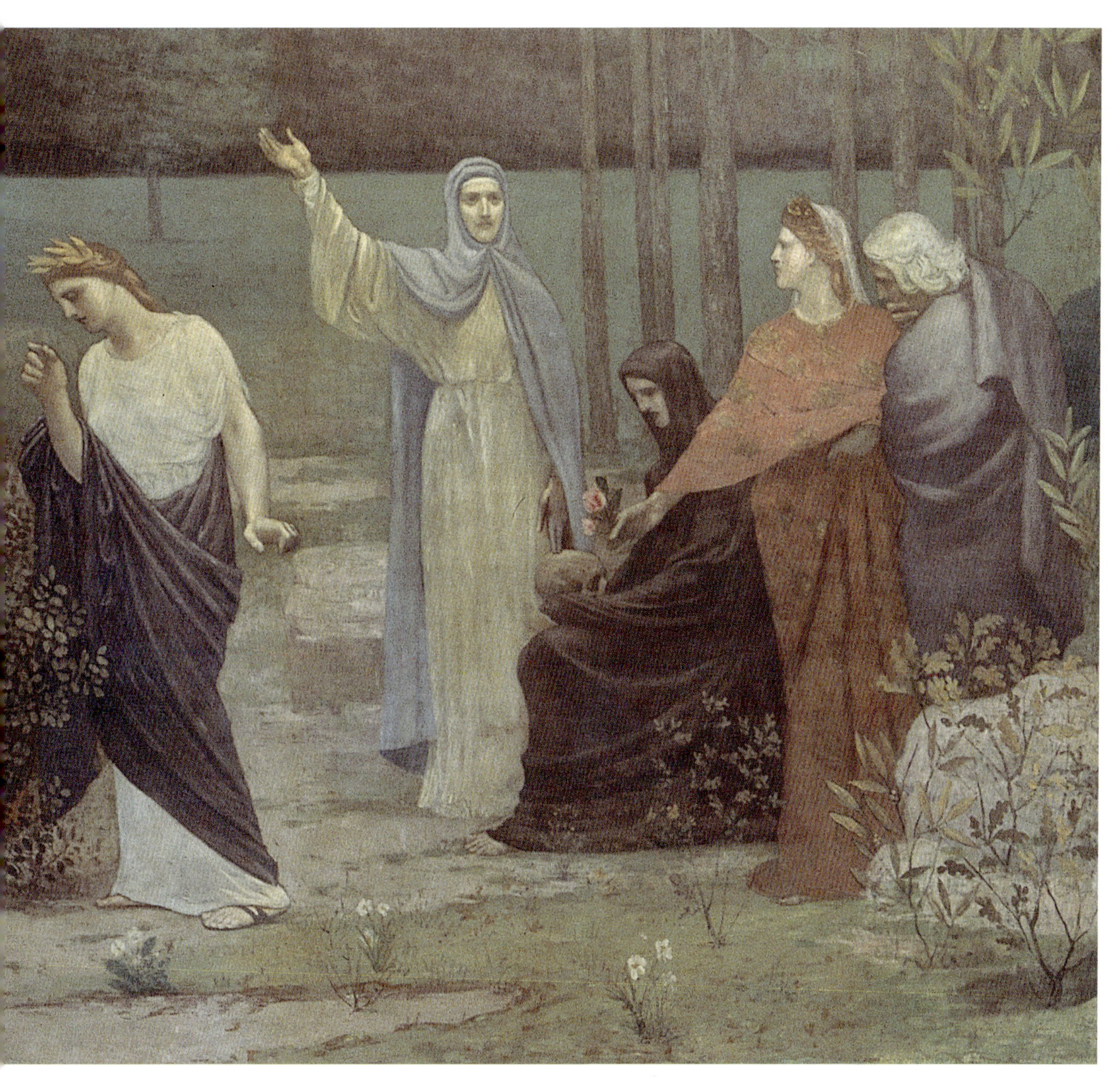

Puvis had remained "in a prudent neutrality, pronouncing himself no more for the ideal than for matter."[24] Not all critics felt that Puvis's refusal to come to a resolution was a problem. Some even celebrated it. The conversation between the three figures was most explicitly imagined by Jules Lemaître: "One says: 'Higher! There is another life; there is a reason for things—I affirm it and I want it.' And the other: 'There is nothing but the eternal enchantment of Matter. None of it makes any sense; but to live and feel is sweet.' And the old woman: 'They are both right, because nothing exists but dream.'"[25] In this striking conversation Materialism is imagined not merely as a scientific reliance on perceptible and quantifiable facts but as an enchantment rooted in feeling and grounded in the actual life of the body. Idealism, on the other hand, seeks a final cause, a "reason for things" beyond the material world. The final sentence, the phrase meant by Lemaître to be the conclusion to be drawn from this passage—"nothing exists but dream"—comes from the old woman, Death. Yet rather than take sides on the issue, her role is to emphasize the desire that drives both philosophical approaches—the dream of ultimately finding a truth of existence. Thus, in Lemaître's description knowledge and its pursuit are most forcefully linked to desire. When the debate between Materialism and Idealism pictured in the Philosophy group is evaluated within the entire framework of the mural, it remains clear that Puvis de Chavannes refused to take the side of transcendent idealism. Instead, he privileged the process of inquiry over the result and imagined that process to be materially based. His failure to offer a clear resolution—a refusal of transcendent truths ultimately guaranteed by God—was what most irked the conservative critics.

The emphasis on materialism was most explicit in the groups that dominate the left and right sides of the mural, the panels devoted to History and Science. At the far left of the mural, we see the Muse of History, whose "interrogation" of the past is represented by several male figures digging up historical evidence from the earth (see fig. 37). One male figure pulls back the branches of a bush, showing the Muse of History a fragment of the past. Several other male figures unearth more treasures. In this panel, Puvis referred to the archaeological method of the Ecole de Chartres, which had replaced the faculty of theology in the New Sorbonne.

The panel devoted to Science occupies the far right of the mural (fig. 38). There are three particularly important themes that run through this section. First, the pursuit of science is a form of materialism. Second, the pursuit of science is a form of devotion. Third, this devotion is communal. Throughout the panel a community of young men demonstrate solidarity as they pursue their scientific goals with fervor. In the center of the panel, four branches of science are allegorized.

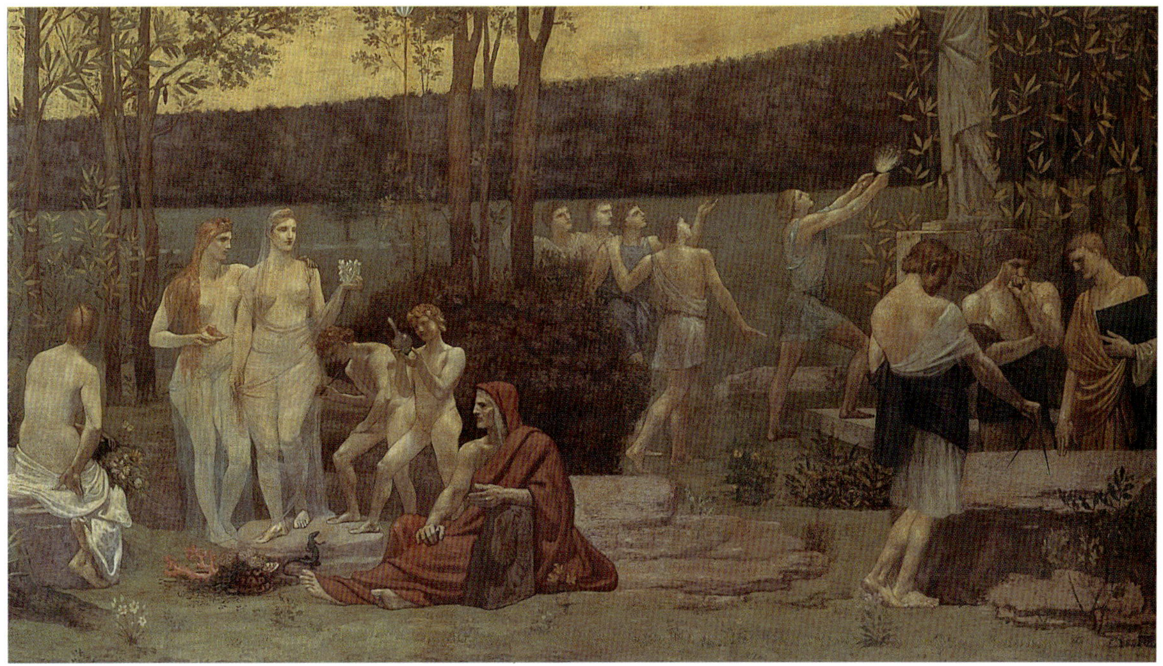

38
Pierre Puvis de Chavannes, *The Sorbonne* (detail of fig. 31; panel on right)

Botany sits nude, her back toward the viewer. Next to her stand two transparently draped Muses. The Sea, positioned in an alluring pose, holds out the mouth of a seashell with one hand, more shells and sea creatures at her feet. Her other arm wraps around the shoulder of Mineralogy. Next to her, two young male figures, one holding a flask, the other a scalpel, investigate unspecified materials. Puvis described them as young men who marvel at Science's riches. Seated squarely in the foreground to our right is the Muse identified by Puvis as Geology. These allegorical figures are paired with young, male figures who scrutinize them, presumably pursuing the scientific knowledge being offered. The theme of solidarity is enforced in the foreground at the far right, where a male figure uses a compass while two others look on with attitudes of concentration. These are Puvis's "three young men, absorbed by study, [who] close the composition."

Devotion to science is most explicitly pictured toward the center of the panel, where, in Puvis's words, "young men . . . , grouped before a statue of Science, pledge a common impulse to devote themselves to her." With a foot on the base of the statue, one of them holds his hands forward, offering or receiving a gift of light. In 1887 one critic identified this as an image of electricity.[26] Louis de Fourcaud criticized Puvis for lifting these figures from his 1882 mural *Ludus pro Patria*

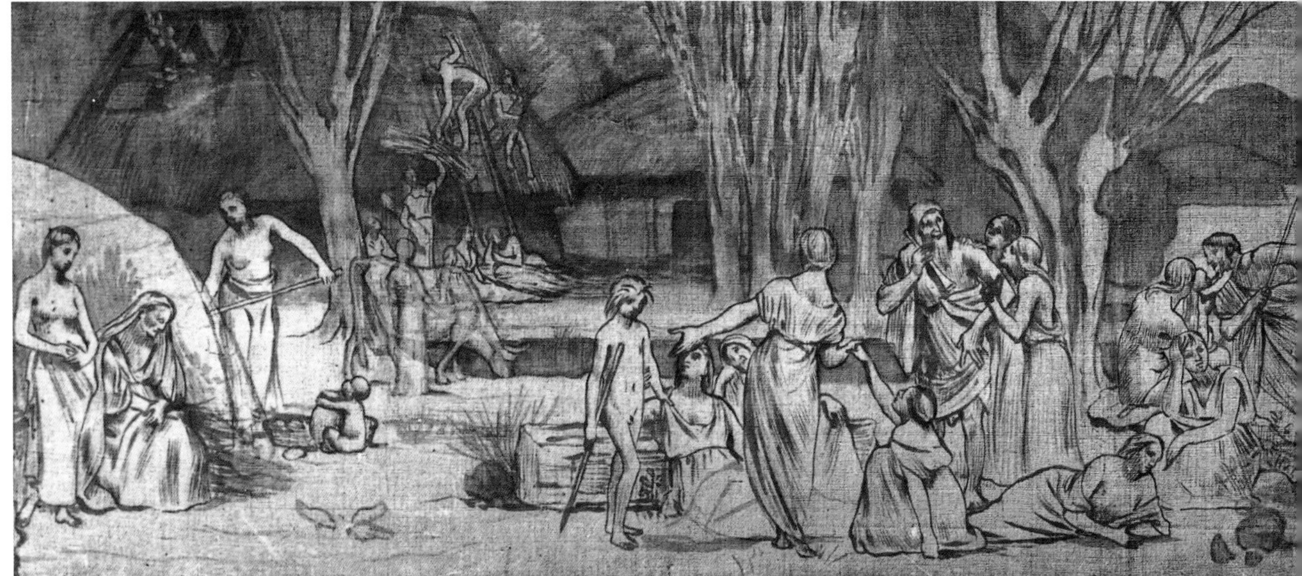

(fig. 39).[27] However, he failed to see what that gesture might have signified: the men devoting themselves to science in the Sorbonne mural are the very figures who had thrown the javelins, practicing "games for the Fatherland," in the other mural. Surely Puvis must have hoped that this reference to scientific activity as another means by which Youth would strengthen and defend the nation would be apparent to viewers familiar with his work. The strengthening of France's scientific community was seen to be an issue of national defense. Many attributed France's defeat in the Franco-Prussian War to inferiority in science.

If we trace the changes that Puvis made from the preliminary cartoon (see fig. 34) to the final version of the mural, we see that most of the changes in the Science panel helped to emphasize the messages of materialism and solidarity. When Puvis set out to make an allegory of positive science, he was faced with an interesting paradox: trying to allegorize scientific endeavors that themselves were based on scrupulous investigation of the material world. He was being asked to allegorize, that is to say, a subject that militated against the very notion of making abstractions. How, then, could the artist retain the allegory while keeping intact the notion of materiality? In this group, Puvis took much the same tack as he had in the panel picturing Philosophy. He implied the material by evoking that which, for the nineteenth century, was the most material of entities—the female body.

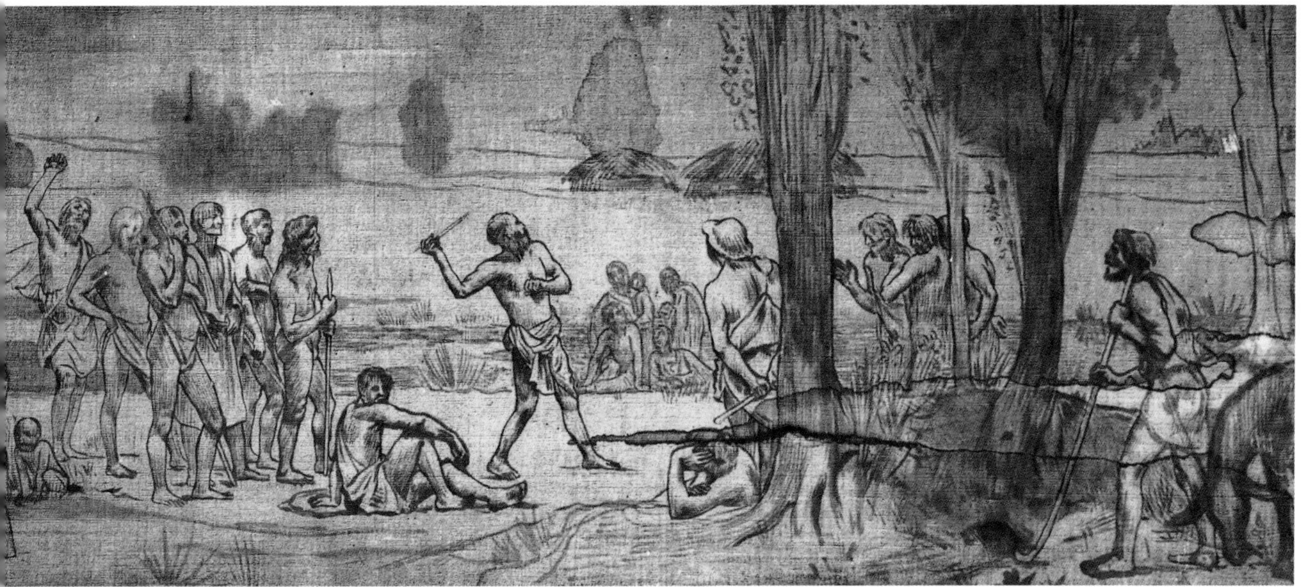

39
Pierre Puvis de Chavannes,
Ludus pro Patria, 1881.
Pencil, red chalk, and oil on canvas,
24 1/2 x 98 3/4 in. (62 x 251 cm). Musée d'Orsay, Paris

To begin with, in the group allegorizing the four types of scientific pursuit, Puvis enhanced the eroticism of the figures (see fig. 38). In the figure of the Sea, for example, the headpiece worn in the cartoon has been made smaller and the hair let down to drape seductively over the front of her shoulder. If her sexual seductiveness is increased, this is also partly through her relationship to Mineralogy, next to her. As in the cartoon, the Sea's arm wraps around this figure and rests on her shoulder. In the cartoon this figure was stonelike and statuesque, but in the final version she has been made supple and given veils and a crystal formation as an attribute. Now the interaction between the two figures has a definite erotic edge. Both figures represent matter—one in flux, the other crystalline. In using a sexualized portrayal of the female body for this purpose Puvis called upon a long established convention of imagining the material world of nature as feminine and the cultural world that shaped and explored it as masculine. Puvis also made changes that evoked materialism by referring to the evanescence of physiological beauty. The figure of Botany, for example, holds a bouquet of flowers in the final version, instead of the branch she held in the cartoon. This suggests a parallel with Materialism in the allegory of Philosophy, who also holds a flower that will, like that figure, grow old, wither, and die.

Not surprisingly, when the cartoon for the mural was exhibited in 1887, antirepublican critics reacted negatively to the patriotic theme. The critic for the royalist *Gazette de France* mocked the panel of Science by alluding to the republican origins of its devotional theme as "something like the 'Marseillaise' of mineralogy." He complained that "nothing in this composition . . . recalls the true story of the Sorbonne."[28] The royalist Catholic critic Georges-Claudius Lavergne was even more explicit in his critique. According to Lavergne, Science had usurped the place of devotional inquiry that should have been taken by Theology.[29] Lavergne engaged in a lengthy diatribe against the "banishment of theology" from the composition. He addressed the three male students absorbed in study. He was speaking, through them, to a generation of young men to be educated by the state. Lavergne chastised the students for not repaying their debt to theology. The Sorbonne, he suggested, was open to Catholicism when it was necessary for its existence but, by banishing theology from its public image, refused to pay its debt.[30]

Lavergne went on to define what he saw to be the true nature of the Sorbonne. In order to try to maintain the appearance of objectivity, Lavergne cited a short history of the institution from a guidebook and emphasized its royal and theological origins. He then gave his own history of the Sorbonne after the Revolution, in which he focused on the persistence of the church's role in education despite state efforts to ban it: "The state was able to enlarge the buildings and augment the physics labs, but neither the royalty of 1830, nor the empire, nor the republic suppressed the teaching of theology."[31] Only Puvis's mural had gone so far as to banish theology completely from the image of the Sorbonne. At the heart of Lavergne's hostility to Puvis's hemicycle was his opposition to republican secularization of education. Puvis's mural—"the allegorical page in which we are shown a laicized Sorbonne"—was part of this process, part of what Lavergne called the "system of falsifications and subtractions [and] impious vandalism that attempts to pluck our ancient Sorbonne from the royal mantel." Lavergne was most critical of Puvis's substitution of Nature for God as the ultimate guarantor of meaning.[32]

When Lavergne attacked the replacement of faith in God with devotion to republican materialism, he focused on the figure of the Sea, the quintessential metaphor for material nature in flux.[33] The young men pursuing science were distracted, said Lavergne, by "the fear that the Sea and the fish will run away and, with them, one of the principal successful elements of the composition."[34] This claim was meant to be a joke. But it was also meant, I think, to suggest that the young men of France feared that they would lose access to the material world—access that they mistakenly believed to be provided by science. For them, as for others who were part of the Catholic revival, a belief in science would eventually be replaced, once again, Lavergne implied, by theology. "You fear above all," said Lavergne, "that Theology, benefiting from the flow of the waves, [will] land with dry feet at the Sorbonne, that she will make an attempt to retake her domain, to reclaim her prerogatives and assert her legitimate and historical right of supremacy. Theology? you respond, what is that?. . . We no longer need theology!"[35]

Lavergne was alluding to the battles over control of education taking place between the state and the Catholic church. But he also had a subtler and more important point to make. By attributing to the students not only the fear of the return of theology but also the fear of the flight of the material world, Lavergne suggested that even those devoted to republican materialism harbored the suspicion that republican values could not provide an adequate form of devotion. The students, said Lavergne, knew the "true motives" for the proscription of theology. Speaking to the three figures who "close the composition," Lavergne continued: "You know all that; but, young rogues, go ahead, close your ears, close your eyes, close whatever pleases you—I will not pose personal questions."[36] Returning the issue to the level of personal belief, Lavergne alluded to the fragility of French youth's faith in republican civic morality by implying that the students knew, deep in their hearts, that science would cease to capture the material world and that religious belief would take hold. In the end, Lavergne read the complete banishment of any reference to theology in the mural as a sign of the Republic's resistance to the Catholic church. The image of the positivist figures having to close their ears and eyes to avoid the "truth" of which he speaks, however, implies that as far as Lavergne was concerned, the process of laicization would never be completed.

A more explicit critique of republican devotion to science was put forth by one of the leaders of the neo-Christian movement, the Vicomte de Vogüé. Vogüé was an aristocrat and a prominent member of the literary Academy.[37] In a series of articles on the Universal Exposition written for the conservative *Revue des Deux Mondes*, Vogüé argued that the state's focus on science would lead the next generation—was already leading them—to reject the principles of 1789 and to yearn for spiritual truths much deeper than the Republic could offer. For him, the prime example of a lack of faith in the Republic was evinced by the very group of people upon whom supporters of the Republic had staked everything: the students of France, represented by those attending the inauguration of the New Sorbonne, who, he claimed, "no longer have faith in the fundamental dogma."[38] Vogüé argued that when positivist principles were brought to bear on the fundamental values of republican doctrine, republican values were shown to be false. The principles of social Darwinism—"determinism, hereditary selection, the right of strength"—refuted the values of "liberty, equality, fraternity" that had been set out in the founding document of republicanism, the Declaration of the Rights of Man. By emphasizing the rational, republicanism would negate itself. Said Vogüé, "Aren't we rather far from the philosophy that inspired the Declaration of Rights? Hasn't this philosophy ended up at a formal negation of its premises? . . . Reason has returned the scalpel against the idol; . . . she has opened the stomach [of the familiar image] and seen that there was nothing inside. . . . Thus was born the crisis of the principles of 1789; they are caught between two fires, between theological protests, which follow them at a distance, and scientific protests, which rise up suddenly in front of them."[39] Even if the celebrations of the Centenary of the Republic at the Universal Exhibition were meant to convince the population that these principles were still the best guarantee of the social order, for Vogüé they represented only the deification of a false idol—an idol he predicted would soon crumble.

Vogüé envisioned a transformation in the social order, a transformation that depended on the very foundation of Gréard's and Fallières's confidence in the future of the Republic—on Youth. Vogüé thus attacked the state on its own terrain, refuting the characterization of the generation to come as devoted to republican principles. Rather than describing 1889 as a consolidation of one hundred years of republican spirit, Vogüé diagnosed "a state of moral perturbation very similar to that of 1789": "Perhaps in one hundred years someone will write that the revolutionary institution was as seriously injured on the day when, for the first time, we taught Darwin's doctrine in France."[40]

The positivist principles of the Republic would, in Vogüé's view, lead inevitably to its downfall. But he worried that when the republican idol had fallen, a moral vacuum would be left. Avoiding this necessitated a rejection of science as the basis of morals: "The metaphysical dream of the past century proposed to men an unrealizable ideal. . . . Physical realism in our century . . . reestablishes summary order, at the price of servitude, fatalism, a return to the life of the animal horde. To avert these results . . . would require that a moral principle, representing the reaction of conscience against the harshness of natural laws, come to soften that which would be intolerable in legislation inspired only by the teachings of physiology. . . . One will search in vain in the world of rational ideas for this principle, which was the only one able to give a solid foundation to the notion of duty: humanity will find it again only in the stronghold where it resides, in religious sentiment."[41] Having taken on the Republic on the terms set out by the state in its celebrations of the Centenary, Vogüé thus argued for the reestablishment of religious faith against the materialism of the Declaration of the Rights of Man. His diagnoses of a religious revival among the young intellectual elite was proven, he said, by the popularity of books like Paul Bourget's *The Disciple*, which questioned the ideals of the scientific approach to life, and paintings like Dagnan-Bouveret's *Bretons at a Pardon* and Millet's *Angelus*.[42]

The paintings were popular, he claimed, not for their representation of rural life but for their religious meanings. These signs that religious faith was a solution for discontent with the Republic reinforced his prediction that a great social change was imminent.

Vogüé proclaimed himself in support of an absolute, rather than a constitutional, monarchy. But he realized that such a drastic change in government would entail civil war. He was forced to acknowledge that "the political faith that remains in our people is at the Republic's disposal; and one can only constitute a people by using the sum of the faith that lives in it."[43] He cited the funeral for Victor Hugo and the inauguration of the Sorbonne as examples of popular feeling for the Republic. In the end, he resigned himself, as had the Albert, fourth duc de Broglie, in *Views of the French Government*, to the Republic as the form of government that, as Broglie put it, "divides the least, and permits the most public spirit to form." Because he saw signs that *l'esprit public* was on his side, he decided to follow Broglie's advice, "only to consider the republican regime as a last resource, as a state of transition."[44] Vogüé felt that the most effective way to work toward the replacement of faith in the principles of 1789 was by holding to and instilling faith in the spiritual values that were, in his account, the true basis of the French soul.

THE MATERIALIZATION OF ALLEGORY

The question of whether theology should have a role in education was linked to more fundamental ontological and epistemological debates. What was the source of knowledge? What means were appropriate to pursue knowledge? As the examples of Lavergne and Vogüé show, the answers to these questions had profound political consequences. For the most part, those who believed that theology ought to be the basis of all knowledge and learning also desired a return to monarchy and the divine right of kings. Clearly, in the mural for the Sorbonne, Puvis was attempting to fulfill the desire of the republican state to put forth a materialist epistemology. And although he largely succeeded, as we have seen, the degree to which the artist himself embraced the kind of crude positivism that was proffered in the speeches inaugurating the Sorbonne remains to be seen.

We will be able to gauge Puvis's attitude to positivism by looking further not only at the subject matter of the mural but also at its allegorical and painterly style. The mural is an allegory, a fact that alone moves us away from the realm of positivism and toward the realm of the ideal. However—and this is the key to understanding the aesthetic significance of Puvis's mural—the allegory is by no means a traditional one. Indeed, counterintuitive though it may sound, Puvis's mural was seen to represent what I shall call a materialist idealism. In it Puvis undertook the task not only of allegorizing the Sorbonne but of bringing the allegory into keeping with republican aims by materializing it. In doing so, Puvis was formulating a modern, forward-looking version of high art. He abandoned the traditional academic paradigm of allegory as transcendence and its associations with the spiritual realm and proposed instead a kind of allegory amenable to the republican state. This, too, was viewed as an attack by Catholic critics for whom allegory itself—as a mode of knowledge and a form of visual representation—had important political and epistemological implications.

Looking further at Lavergne's attack on Puvis's mural makes extremely clear the degree to which aesthetics—and aesthetic idealisms in particular—had become sites of a battle that had political significance. Said Lavergne: "When M. Jules Ferry conferred upon M. Puvis de Chavannes the title *Knight of the ideal*, of what had he wanted to speak? It must have been the *opportunist* ideal. Well! I declare that the opportunist ideal is much too mealy/floury [*enfariné*] for my consumption; I myself remain firmly in favor of the *intransigent* ideal. From which it follows that if I come to touch on decorative painting, on the ideal, on the serenity of M. Puvis de Chavannes, I will raise the opposition of the liberal conservative factions, those more or less united on the Left, and those supporting universal suffrage; it is serious! still, that is what awaits me, I know it, but a person forewarned is equal to four who are ignorant."[45] Lavergne's comment about Puvis de Chavannes was aimed at criticizing admiration for Puvis that came from the political Center and Left—admiration such as we have already seen voiced in response to Puvis's previous works by such critics as Vachon, Lafenestre, and Michel. These critics, we should remember, felt that Puvis's murals might be able to rejuvenate the idealism that had become stale in the hands of academic practitioners. Lavergne named as the republican admirer of Puvis no one less than Jules Ferry, the man who, as minister of education during the early 1880s, had been responsible for the reforms that wrested control of education from the Catholic church and put it in the hands of the state. Such reforms were anathema to this ultramontane Catholic critic.

Lavergne opposed his own *l'idéal intransigeant*—a form of idealism derived from the steadfast traditions of academic high art—to Ferry's *idéal opportuniste*: an ideal at odds with academic tradition and, like Ferry's educational reforms, aligned with the secularizing and materialist impetus of republican philosophy.[46] Lavergne's intransigent ideal is quite similar to the academic notion of art as a transcendent ideal expressed in the writings of Charles Blanc. It imagines a truth guaranteed by God and accessible to the privileged. The last bastions of academic theory were dominated by critics, like Lavergne, who held to a peculiar mixture of neo-Kantian ideas of aesthetic disinterestedness (in which the experience of beauty was divorced completely from physical desire and pleasure) and traditional notions that art should be the servant of morality. As we saw in Chapter 1, both parts of this unstable amalgam depended on the fiction that aesthetic ordering would transform the vulgarities of the physical world into an ideal form with a moral message. The concept of ideal form was thus associated with both spirituality and esprit, with mind as opposed to body. Underlying all of this was a belief in the ability of the mind to transcend the physicality of the body and to keep the fantasmatic elements of bodily pleasures under intellectual control. This paradigm for high art imagined human subjectivity (of healthy French males anyway) as autonomous and unified, as capable of intuiting the ideal via high art through an act of the intellect. By the late nineteenth century, this vision of the relation between subjectivity and representation was sustained by those, like Lavergne, who saw themselves as the upholders of tradition.

As Lavergne defined it, allegory was a visual mode that militated against the display of its own materiality and aimed instead to point to an absolute truth beyond the visual image. Here is Lavergne: "What is understood by this word 'allegory'? *Allegory* (says the dictionary): '*fiction that presents to the mind one object in order to designate another.*' In this case, it is the *other* that is the dominant objective; the allegory must not shift its meaning, it must shed light on it. Why, then, paint a Sorbonne that would be unrecognizable if its name were not inscribed on the painting?"[47] Allegory, for Lavergne, required reading through the represented object (an object represented "to the mind" rather than to the senses) to the "truth" that lay beyond it. It was this truth and not the representation itself that was the dominant objective. If the allegory was to be successful, the material of representation could not get in the way, as it did in Puvis's mural. Lavergne, in his version of allegory, imagined something akin to the transparency of the sign. According to him, the truth pointed to by the allegory should not be transformed in the process of representation, but should only be magnified, made to shine forth more clearly than it did in the material world. This is far from the struggle with representation that we have already seen is a characteristic of Puvis's paintings—far, too, from debates about truth that are alluded to in the Sorbonne mural. Lavergne was putting forth a version of the allegorical mode that was meant to counteract the imaginative reveling in a play of meanings that the materialist opportunist ideal represented, in order "to ruffle . . . the idol of contemporary aesthetics." In place of the republican aesthetic he posed "*the intransigent and militant ideal*," an ideal that was explicitly Catholic and would "encamp in the studio of *Nazareth*, not far from the Tiber, two steps from Calvary."[48]

In contrast to the transcendence of the intransigent ideal, Lavergne described the opportunist ideal as too "enfariné" for his consumption. On one level, the term *enfariné*, which means "floury" but can also mean "mealymouthed" or "smattered" with something, was meant to belittle opportunism as a doctrine without principles. Yet the term also evoked the materiality of substances meant for bodily consumption, in particular the flour (*la farine*) in daily bread. His description of Puvis's painting as enfariné is extremely multivalent. It suggested the materiality of flour, its heaviness when in large quantities, its similarity to the powder of pigment and to the dry look of Puvis's canvases. It also alluded to lightness or insubstantiality, as well as the ability to coat with a thin film, to act as disguise, as in makeup. The metaphor was thus linked to the superficiality commonly attributed to the material world by academic idealists and the metaphorization of this deceptiveness as a feminine quality.[49] In addition, *enfariné* was used to describe mimes and actors who regularly donned white, possibly flour-based, face paint. In this context, the term connoted artifice and a certain cheapness, the shoddiness and unavoidable materialism of the lower reaches of the entertainment business.[50] With the description "enfariné," Lavergne opposed the spirituality of his intransigent ideal to the materiality, even materialism, of republican aesthetics, which he characterized using metaphors for the body's materialism—for a body that consumed in accordance with its basic needs, a body associated with low-brow popular entertainments.

By employing metaphorics of the body, Lavergne made clear that Ferry's version of the ideal—and Puvis's as well—was diametrically opposed to his own. After all, for Lavergne, idealization was meant to lead to transcendence of the mere physicality of the world and point to higher truths. Lavergne seems to have felt that Puvis's aesthetic was doing to high art what Ferry's reforms were doing to French culture: transforming it from a spiritual into a material enterprise. Indeed, the quotation suggests that Puvis's very mode of representation struck Lavergne as the visualization of a challenge to an aesthetic epistemology guaranteed by God. At the heart of the controversy, then, was whether materialism was the appropriate frame for knowledge. It is counterintuitive to imagine Puvis as an advocate of materialism if we imagine the term to connote a crude form of positivism. However, it is less difficult to imagine him as an advocate for the kind of knowledge in which sensation and bodiliness were integral to operations of mind. As we shall see, although Puvis saw his own work as intellectual, he also always stressed its rootedness in sensation and shied away from descriptions of it as transcendent and overly idealizing.

Another critic who espoused a definition of allegory similar to Lavergne's was Saint-Ange. He refused to acknowledge that Puvis's mural for the Sorbonne functioned allegorically at all. Initially, Saint-Ange challenged viewers to find anything other than bodies—"women who are seated, standing, lying down according to their whims, men who think of drinking, men who think of nothing."[51] It was this emphasis on the body as a material entity with physical positions and needs, the critic suggested, that made the mural fail as allegory. It never pointed beyond itself to transcendent truth. Writing in 1887, before the mural had been installed with the explanatory text in the border, Saint-Ange lamented the absence of Puvis's explanatory text from the mural, for it could mitigate the multivalency of the mural. He suggested that Puvis would never want to attach it to the mural anyway, because "it is his least desire to be understood by his contemporaries." Using terms that Brunetière soon used to attack the Symbolists, Saint-Ange said Puvis was obscurantist and his work was hermetic: "He makes a profession of living in his dream and never emerging from it."[52] Saint-Ange had trouble imagining that the Sorbonne mural could say anything definitive without the constraining text. "If you attempt an interpretation," he complained, "I hold in reserve a dozen that will apply with equally as much exactitude to the scene that is figured there."[53] Indeed, behind the deceptive simplicity of Puvis's composition, said Saint-Ange, were so many possible readings that the work could never be understood: "I do not believe painting has ever been destined to make us understand so many things and to contain so many innuendoes. . . . Despite an appearance of simplicity, [Puvis de Chavannes's] art is extremely complicated."[54]

Contrary to Saint-Ange's prediction, in 1889 the final mural was mounted in the New Sorbonne along with an explanatory text on the wall below. We do not know whether the inclusion of this text was Puvis's choice. There is some evidence to suggest that he protested against inscribing it. In a letter written to a friend who was going to see the mural for the first time, Puvis complained about the decoration of the base of his painting, suggesting that both the gold leaf that surrounds it and the text that frames and limits the allegory were put there against his will. The artist gave these words of warning: "I had nothing to do with the ornamentation at the base of my painting. On the contrary. There are, among other very ugly things, two damn books that have no common sense and against which I battled with such an ardor that it finished by burning itself out."[55] If Puvis was referring to the text inscribed on the wall below the mural, this would suggest that he wished to keep alive the indeterminacy for which he was so well known.

Unlike Saint-Ange, the republican critic Jules Lemaître saw the value in Puvis's painterly mode. Although Lemaître believed that when allegory was functioning properly, it would make the viewer think beyond that which it represented, his was not a rigid definition of allegory.[56] He asked of it no universal and transcendent truths. After quoting Puvis's explanation of the central Sorbonne group, Lemaître commented that Puvis's explanation of the allegory would be useful if one wanted to know the significance Puvis attributed to each figure. Knowing this, however, was not really necessary to experience the effect the artist was seeking to convey: "When one does not fully understand, it's not such a bad thing, because one remains free to dream and to interpret the allegory in one's own way!"[57] Lemaître described Puvis's painting as a prime example of an allegory that managed genuinely to stimulate the viewer's imagination. And Puvis's painterly mode, which sensualized and materialized allegory, seems to have been what drew Lemaître to him. "M. Puvis de Chavannes," said Lemaître, "is a great poet, or even better a great magician. . . . There is sorcery in his case, and almost a contradiction between the means he employs and the effects he attains. He is able, with drawing that is often poor and incorrect . . . to give us an impression comparable to that which we receive from the most perfect works of antiquity, for example, the Parthenon frieze; and he manages, with a palette that is more than sober and purely conventional in color, to caress our eyes as deliciously as Rubens or Veronese. He draws superb human figures with the pencil of a child, and he creates enchanted paradises with shadows of colors."[58] This description recalls Puvis's Lyons murals, especially *The Sacred Grove* and *Ancient Vision*. Puvis was like a magician and a sorcerer because his work conjured up an image in the mind of the viewer, hinted at a possible form. Rather than giving the viewer a perfected body or a richly colored landscape, he offered shadows of each, and this stimulated the viewer to dream them in their plenitude. Puvis's shadows of color and awkward drawing encouraged the viewer to resolve the insufficiencies of the picture in fantasy. There was in the end, then, no real contradiction between the "poor drawing" and the impression of perfection given by the murals; and no paradox in Puvis's ability to make "a more than sober palette" produce a color as sensual as one of Rubens's or Veronese's.

Even those critics on the Left who were hostile to allegory altogether found some value in Puvis's work. At this very time, a heated debate was taking place over the appropriateness of allegory in public decoration. The municipal and state arts administrators were arguing over the decorative scheme for the Hôtel de Ville in Paris, which had recently been rebuilt after burning down during the Paris Commune of 1871. Extreme Leftists on the Paris municipal council declared that modern life scenes should cover the walls in lieu of allegory. These suggestions were made in the name of democratization. Allegory was thought to be an elite and outdated mode of communication, inaccessible to the general population. Nevertheless, many critics on the Left found Puvis's particular mode of allegory accessible, even laudable. Félix Fénéon, the modernist critic best known for his support of Neoimpressionism, would have preferred to see modern life scenes by the Impressionists on the walls of the Hôtel de Ville rather than realist painting or allegory. However, he still supported the inclusion of work by Puvis de Chavannes. He proclaimed: "The genius of a master such as Puvis de Chavannes imposes itself completely, even when he treats the most formally allegorical subjects."[59] Fénéon was, of course, less interested in the allegorical message of Puvis's work than he was in its formal impact. When he treated the cartoon for the Sorbonne in 1887, he advised viewers to look past the specific iconographic elements of the allegory, which were so prominent in the cartoon, and imagine the finished work, completed by the colors and textures of paint: "When we forget the childish incoherence of this pictorial symbolism, we find ourselves in front of a serene vision where the groups coordinate themselves in a solemn and magnificent rhythm . . . already those familiar with the work of M. Puvis de Chavannes will be able to have a vague idea of the colors that will flow there and the vague emotional symphony that will fill up this forest boundary and these distant skies."[60] Similarly, writing for the Leftist *Le Radical*, Paul Heusy suggested that it was not the intellectual exercise of deciphering the allegory that was important, but the rhythmic effect of the composition: "If, without searching for the abstract ideas that it symbolizes, one restrains oneself to contemplation, one tastes the particular pleasure given by the beautiful symmetries and rhythms. To the two sides of the Sorbonne, the figures descend in parallel groups, and the parallelism continues to the two opposite extremes of the canvas. Here is great art, with admirable simplicity of means. Once accepted, you enter a serene region."[61] Both Fénéon and Heusy were most interested in the sensual effect that the formal qualities of Puvis's mural would have on the viewer. They focused exclusively on the material effects of the mural. They were articulating, then, a version of what I have been calling modernism. At least in the overtly politicized case of the Sorbonne, the clearest articulations of modernism came from critics on the Left, whereas the most explicit criticisms of Puvis came from the Right.

I am not trying to imply that there is always a one to one correspondence between attitudes toward allegory—or signification generally—and political positions. Still, a few things are clear. First, without exception, critics writing for Catholic and royalist papers espoused a conception of allegory as an image pointing transparently beyond itself to a transcendent truth guaranteed by God. Given the secular message of the mural and Puvis's mode of address, there was never any possibility that it would meet their criteria. Second, many critics and administrators on the radical Left dismissed allegory altogether as an elitist mode yet found

Puvis's allegories to be an exception. Between these two poles are many positions. Clearly, the republican administration wanted the allegory to allude to the association between the university and positivist secularism. But it also wanted to link positivism to high thought, and to do so chose a mode associated with high art. In a sense, then, Puvis's Sorbonne mural was not just about the secularizing reformation of an educational institution but about the secularization of all modes of knowledge—including artistic ones. This is why Puvis's materialization of the allegory—through the play of meanings provoked by his formal means, as well as through the materialist messages the mural was made to portray—must have been so appealing to the state. The primary goal was to offer a secular vision of knowledge, and this necessitated the elaboration of processes of imagination that did not find their ultimate goal or sanction in divine truth.

In addition, the state wanted to retain its claim to sponsor high art while shedding the associations of decadence and conservatism associated with academic allegory. Allegory had been the primary mode of the classical French tradition in high art. In Puvis's era, the degeneration of high art, especially painting, was thought to be epitomized by the conventionalization and limitedness of allegory. As in literature, allegory was rejected by a younger generation of artists for "the Symbol." Puvis held a fascination for Symbolist painters and poets alike. Indeed, many of them referred to his paintings as symbolic. But Puvis himself never did. He was more interested in a rejuvenation of allegory that might offer the possibility of a renewal of the French tradition of high art.

POETRY, FANTASY, AND THE FEMALE BODY

The notion of knowledge based in materiality went against all the presuppositions of right-wing Catholic critics. They were unable to imagine (or unwilling to admit) the possibility of an allegorical mode that communicated through a play of meaning sustained by the materiality of the representation without universalizing or coming to definite conclusions. Yet, I will suggest, it was just this kind of engagement with a play of meaning that Puvis de Chavannes intended to depict. And the privileged representative of this kind of depiction was a group dispersed across the central panel, the group most directly tied to the "life-giving force" of the spring—the source of knowledge—Poetry (see fig. 35). Arranged on either side of the Sorbonne figure, surrounding the central allegory of the spring and separating all of these figures from the allegories of Philosophy and Science, the Muses of Poetry stand on the rocks from which the source of knowledge escapes. What Puvis has designated as "the life-giving source" from which "the Youth drink avidly" and "the Aged take new strength" is most closely linked neither to science nor to philosophy, but to poetry, suggesting that the imaginative processes involved in the poetic are the most powerful forms of intellect. The kind of engagement encouraged by the figures of Poetry differs markedly from the more straightforward symbolism of the other groups we have examined so far. Puvis tells us that the standing figure with flying robes is Eloquence. Aside from that, we are given few clues as to exactly what any of the women are meant to personify. Several of the critics attempted to identify the figures. It is perhaps significant that the only figure they seemed to agree on was the draped Muse at the left with her hands on her knees. She, the critics said, was absorbed in a dream.

I want to suggest that the Sorbonne mural, like many of the works we have looked at so far, solicited a kind of attention from its viewers that was akin to dream. Although dream was personified in the seated figure, an allusion to imaginative fantasy formed the very structure of the Poetry section. Indeed, although the artist was forced to negotiate the iconographic demands of his commissioners in other sections of the mural (for example, the vial of bacterial culture and scalpel were included in the allegory of Science at the request of D. Kaempfen, minister of public instruction), the Muses of Poetry seem to have offered Puvis the opportunity to put forth his own version of mind, one in keeping with earlier works like *The Sacred Grove Dear to the Arts and Muses*.[62] In the Sorbonne mural, as in *The Sacred Grove*, the play of imagination involved in the poetic was symbolized by the entity that was thought in the nineteenth century to be both the most material and the most provocative in a play of fantasy—the female body. In Puvis's mural, the female body is neither idealized nor materialized in any traditional sense, but is seen instead as the place where, for the male viewer at least, the powers of imagination are not only pictured but provoked. This part of the mural, then, involves not a mere personification of the fantasmatic elements of knowledge but also a demonstration of them. The viewer is asked to engage with these bodies not as if they were keys to a transcendent truth but as if they are spurs to imaginative reverie.

As in previous murals, Puvis has juxtaposed female bodies in associative ways. We are asked to compare bodies through echoes of pose and contrasts between naked and clothed. At the center of the group to the left of the figure of the Sorbonne, two seated figures sit in similar positions, arms stretched out before them, one naked, one clothed (see fig. 35). In the Muses of Poetry to the right of the Sorbonne, a similar relationship is established between the two figures farthest to the left of the group, one barely draped and seen from the front, the other with a bared shoulder, seen via a three-quarters view from the back (see fig. 35). Aside from being extremely ambiguous in terms of their allegorical meaning, the Muses have multivalent bodily positions. It is difficult to tell, for example, whether the "dreaming figure" in the group on the left is holding her hands out before her or resting them on her knees. Similarly, the semidraped seated figure (possibly a figure of Melancholy) who echoes her pose might be either holding her hands above her own knees or resting them on the knees of the seated figure with the lyre. These echoes and elusive poses were meant to set the imagination to work. In the dreaming figure and in the echoes of the group as a whole, then, poetry was integrally linked to fantasy.

The figure that most explicitly embodies and demonstrates such reverie is the half-draped Muse to the right of the old man, who, in a sinuous contrapposto leans, with extended arm, on a tree (fig. 40). This was the female figure most praised by the critics in 1887. Her face angles away from the viewer, her eyes in shadow; the serpentine curve of her body stretches and displays the torso to maximum effect. Her drapery falls just below the hip and is given a semitranslucency that allows the viewer to follow her legs underneath it. One leg forms a diagonal which emphasizes the thrust of her hip. The other is lifted, toes pointed delicately on the ground. The expanse of her torso is largely unspecified. Puvis uses shadows to give the slightest indication of the meeting of legs, a fold of belly, the weight of breasts. But nowhere is anything close to detail even tried for. The shifting undecidability of her flesh is made more intense by its sharp contrast with the precision of her drapery. Here is the epitome of Puvis's incompletion, but with the more difficult aspects of bodily distortion drained away. Fantasization of her ideal form is invited, and, in this particular case, the sexual nature of that desire for completion is made explicit by her enticing pose.

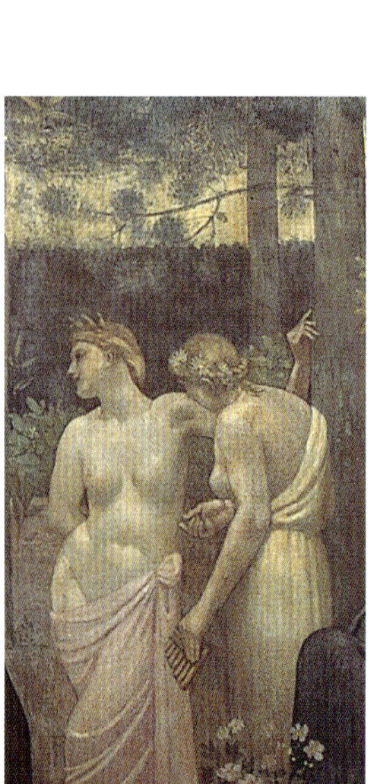

40
Pierre Puvis de Chavannes, *The Sorbonne* (detail of fig. 31; seductive/solid figures of Poetry)

Grouped with this seductive figure is another female figure who embodies a very different kind of strangeness. In this figure, the distortion of the body is all about massiveness and weight. A huge and elongated arm ends in a hand that holds a syrinx. The hand looks so similar to the pipe—so stiff and wooden—that from a distance, the two become one. The massive figure is hugely hunched. Her breast, seen in profile, is given a strange solidity. Virtually everything about her contrasts with the seductive figure. But nowhere is this contrast made more apparent than in the gesture of her other hand. Lined up exactly with the edge of the seductive figure's body, her heavily outlined fingers make a pinching gesture. In this gesture contact between solid body parts with precise boundaries is emphasized. The sense of solid flesh touching flesh is juxtaposed with the seductive figure's body, where flesh seems infinitely transmutable. Thus, Puvis offers us a contrast between two kinds of bodies—the solid and determinate against the vague and undecidable—and these become figures for two modes of representation and two kinds of intellectual engagement with the material world, which, when taken together, create the play of meaning that Puvis so prized.

There is one other place where the contrast between precision and indeterminacy is even more forcefully rendered, and that is in the leaning arm of the seductive figure. Behind the shoulder of the solid figure, the forearm of the seductive figure carries a hand whose individual fingers are clearly and delicately rendered. Yet her forearm does not easily line up with her upper arm. In addition, the hand's flesh is somewhat darker than the rest of her, more beige than pale white. The more one looks at the hand, the more it appears to be a dismembered limb (like the hand in *Young Girls by the Seashore*). This effect is emphasized by the shadow that cuts through the upper portion of her arm just near the shoulder. In addition, her other arm seems to disappear behind her massive hip. Thus, seen from one perspective, she is armless, and importantly so. I am suggesting that the seductive figure could call to mind the Venus de Milo—the work that made explicit better than any other at this moment the drive toward a fantasization of wholeness (fig. 41).

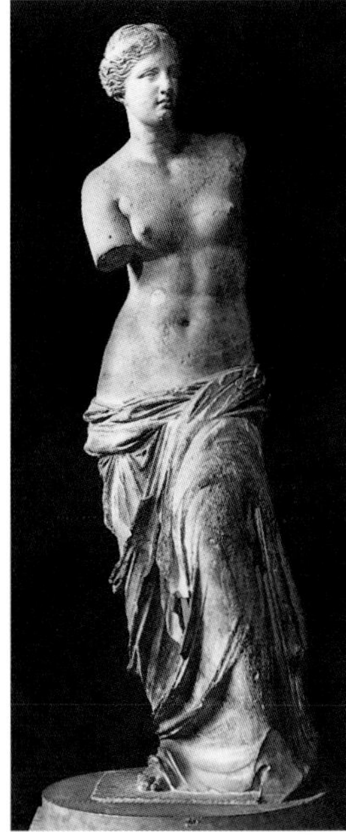

41
Venus de Milo, ca. 100. Marble. Musée du Louvre, Paris

Lest this seem like a forced interpretation, it is worth remembering that when Puvis was painting the Sorbonne mural, another "artist," the scholar M. Ravaisson, was attempting to imagine the Venus de Milo whole again.[63] Ravaisson reconstituted the positions of the Venus de Milo's arms; he gave her gestures significance by making Mars part of the original sculpture. Gustave Geffroy, who had recognized that in *The Sacred Grove* and *Ancient Vision* Puvis's use of indeterminacy and incompletion was a spur to dream, had a predictably hostile reaction to Ravaisson's attempt to fix the meaning of the Venus de Milo. In fact, Geffroy's negative reaction to this project has many connections to his analysis of Puvis's work, providing us with an explicit account of how indeterminacy of visual form was seen to function during this period: "The Venus de Milo must remain and will remain isolated and without arms. . . . Such a Venus is no longer localized within Greek mythology, she escapes her particular role, she demonstrates generalities and symbols to a much higher degree. . . . She has emerged from a virile brain, made fecund by the idea and not the presence, of a woman. . . . Yes, so much the better if the arms are missing. One has a better view of that incomparable torso. One's thought conceives more perfectly the being toward whom all desire tends—the one who remains unmoved and immutable—the one who will never be embraced and will never give herself away—supreme Beauty, eternal attraction of life."[64] Ravaisson's attempt to reconstruct the Venus de Milo was in some ways analogous to the viewer's process of fantasy upon viewing Puvis's strange and distorted figures. The incompletion of the Venus de Milo's body became the motor of Ravaisson's desire and spurred his idealizing fantasies. Ravaisson's project, his attempt to fix once and for all the true form of the sculpture, indicated his wish for the resolution of desire. It is hardly surprising, given the structure of desire, that his attempt to complete the Venus de Milo was unsatisfactory. Geffroy, on the other hand, emphasized the creative potential spurred by indeterminacy. He recognized that the power and fascination of the Venus de Milo derived from the fact that it set desire and fantasy into motion.

Puvis's fragmentation of the female body—in the seductive figure of the Sorbonne mural, as well as in a variety of figures found in earlier work—was meant to emblematize the centrality of desire and fantasy to processes of creativity. We have already seen that the emphasis on sensuality and fantasy—on two aspects of subjectivity aligned with the feminine—was disturbing to traditional critics and exciting to many others, including the anarchist critic Octave Mirbeau and the female critic Judith Gautier. It also needs to be emphasized, however, that the ability to embrace experiences of imagination and fantasy *and* transform them into products of creative endeavor—poems or paintings—was generally conceived as a male prerogative. Indeed, Puvis surely imagined his main audience to be male, because at the time the mural was inaugurated, women were not admitted to the Sorbonne.[65]

In an article on women and modern painting published several years after Puvis painted his mural, Camille Mauclair made the gendered and heterosexual nature of this model clear. Using portraiture as an example, Mauclair contrasted two modes of address, each of which assumed a male viewer. The male portrait, said Mauclair, commands and directs meaning. One does not interpret the masculine image; rather, "one reads it, one verifies it. Its meaning moves from inside to outside, imposes itself on the viewer. The countenance of a man is a definite map." The portrait of a woman, on the other hand, exists only to prompt creative fantasies on the part of its male viewers. It "represents less a being than an accumulation of sensibilities and passions attributed to her by all the admirers of her beauty." Even in a portrait, the subjectivity of the woman depicted is overshadowed by "the shock, the magnificence, of her physical body." Rather than telling us anything about her, it "superimposes there, in the guise of a soul, the reflection of men's desire": "The absolute sensation of feminine beauty given by the painting is precisely that of a harmonious and impersonal organism to which each person's dream easily adds itself."[66]

This openness to a variety of individual fantasy is, Mauclair said, specific to the female portrait. The face (*la face*, a word meaning either "face" or "surface") of a beautiful woman, says Mauclair, "is an unknown country with neither trails nor roads . . . where each explorer traces a route that is immediately effaced after him." Woman is "unknowable," said Mauclair, because, unlike a man, she is "absolutely simple" and "purely physical": "Our soul recognizes there nothing similar to itself and dwells there bewildered and fascinated. The beauty of woman, like all harmony, is perhaps only constituted by its emptiness. It is a space in which we place our dreams."[67] Mauclair's description operates through a set of binary oppositions similar to those invoked by Puvis's paintings—oppositions between masculine and feminine, meaning and ambiguity, mind and matter, directed meaning and undirected dream, substance and void. The constitution of woman as completely Other ("our soul recognizes nothing similar to itself") makes her open to the projection of fantasy. And it is through this projection that male subjectivity is secured. Said Mauclair, "She waits, like a white page, for the sensibility of man to inscribe its dream. She is a permanent spectacle, open to admiration, like a landscape. And what our meditation looks to find there is itself."[68]

Although Mauclair is ostensibly discussing portraiture, the general structure he describes initially seems to extend quite easily to the Venus de Milo as she was described by Geffroy, as well as to Puvis's seductive figure and almost any of the female bodies depicted in Puvis's murals. Bewilderment and fascination, harmony, emptiness, openness to a range of individual fantasy—all of these terms were used to describe Puvis's murals—from *The Sacred Grove* and *Ancient Vision* to the hemicycle for the Sorbonne. And the aim in contemplating these images is also the same. One looks at the image of a woman, said Mauclair, not to learn about her but to find oneself.

As should be clear from the critical reception of the Sorbonne mural, as well as from Brunetière's criticisms of the Symbolists (see Chapter 1), the debate over whether to privilege the productivity of desire (by celebrating a multiplication of meanings) or imagine its resolution (by attempting to fix—if unsuccessfully—a single meaning) took place in a range of contexts. For the most part, it was a debate carried on between men. And the chief medium for this debate, the figure through which it was metaphorized and understood, was the female body. The question of what should be done with the fragmentariness of the Venus de Milo was in some sense (and in a less complicated form) the same question that haunted the debates over Puvis's painting. In both cases, the incompletion of the female body became the material for processes of imagination that were, in the nineteenth century, generally seen to be the purview of the male subject.

It is therefore no accident that Puvis always emblematized incompletion through the female body. Yet there is a very real sense in which Puvis's figures operated quite differently from the way the Venus de Milo did. The difference is epitomized by the contrast between Ravaisson's reconstruction of the Venus de Milo and Puvis's refusal to offer a complete or idealized female form. The critical aspect of Puvis's work was the explicitness of his thematization of incompleteness, the way that ambiguities in the depicted bodies made the viewer aware of fantasmatic processes of compensation. But in Puvis's case—and this sets him apart from his contemporaries—the impossibility of fixing the body was made apparent at the same time that the desire for idealization was instigated. And as viewers were thrown back to their own desires, this sense of incompleteness was shifted from the depicted body to the viewing subject. Puvis's figures could never secure a sense of control over signification because the effect of their incompletion was always so shifting, so dependent on the relations between bodies and between the body and the landscape. Puvis's female bodies were neither the fragmentary Venus without arms nor the academic "whole," although they made reference to both. If we are to see Puvis's seductive figure as another version of the Venus de Milo, we are also forced to see her dismembered arm. Thus she, like most of Puvis's female bodies, speaks of contingency rather than certainty and holds an irresolvable play of meanings in balance.

I mean this description to evoke associations with the contingency of language and knowledge in general—associations that directly contradict the traditional academic notion of allegory as a form of absolute knowledge. I believe that Puvis was asking his viewers to think in these terms. Once we focus on the seductive figure's arm, it leads us back—along the curve of the solid figure's drapery and her own massively distorted arm, then along the pink folds of drapery on the seductive figure's legs—back to the central group of drinking figures. What else, we might ask, could it have meant for Puvis to juxtapose this space of fantasy so closely to the figures below, those figures who are working so hard—so straightforwardly—at the generation of allegorical meaning?

I would suggest that in the Sorbonne mural, poetry is a metaphor for the structures of imagination that form the basis of any pursuit of knowledge. The contingency, ambiguity, and multivalency associated with this part of the cycle were meant to be a counterproposal to those traditional notions of absolute knowledge guaranteed by God. The imaginative processes attributed to poetry were also implied to be central to the pursuit of knowledge undertaken in the rest of the mural. As we continue to look at the figures of Poetry it becomes evident that the echoes so strongly established among them also subtly permeate the rest of the painting. So, for example, in the Philosophy group (see fig. 37) the woman personifying idealism appears to be a standing version of the dreaming figure in the Poetry group, to the left of the Sorbonne (see fig. 35). Similarly, Materialism (the woman holding the flower in the Philosophy group) is repeated in the Muse of Poetry, to the right of the Sorbonne, who stands with the bird on her shoulder. They have similar features, although Materialism's head is covered. And both wear brocaded robes, albeit of different colors. A similar association can be made between the massive figure of the Sea in the panel of Science (see fig. 38) and the heavy Muse who sits on a ball in the group to the right of the Sorbonne. The painting is replete with these kinds of parallels, repetitions, and echoes. Although Puvis's use of echo and association had obvious compositional advantages, it was more than a formal strategy. The artist knew by now, from the responses to his other paintings, that critics considered the combination of indeterminacy and repetition that he employed here as a way to visualize a dream. Indeed, it seems to me that the source of knowledge according to Puvis was neither the "objective" observation of positivism nor the transcendent "truth" of Platonic or neo-Platonic thought, but the play of imagination, dream, and fantasy as they engaged the material world. And he chose the female body as his ultimate symbol for that materiality.

CIVIC MORALITY AND THE USES OF DREAM

A model of the pursuit of knowledge that integrated imagination, dream, and even fantasy was at odds with neither the materialism of the state nor its attempts to promote civic morality. As we saw in our discussion of the Lyons murals, republican theorists such as Guyau and Fouillée had already proposed the integral role played by the unconscious in aesthetic experience and the centrality of aesthetic experience to the promotion of republican solidarity. Furthermore, psychological research on the unconscious was itself a developing branch of science promoted by the state. Research into the unconscious was seen as part of a materialist project aimed at providing a scientific explanation for many phenomena previously described as religious ecstasy or spiritual possession. In addition, some psychologists theorized that techniques for the manipulation of the unconscious mind—especially hypnosis and suggestion—could be used as educational tools.[69] It is therefore not surprising that republican critics explicitly employed theories of the unconscious, dream, and suggestion when they discussed the effect that the Sorbonne mural would have on its viewers.

In an essay for the *Journal des Débats*, the republican André Michel predicted the potential of the Sorbonne mural to promote republican values through its access to the unconscious. First, Michel defined the role of the Sorbonne mural. He emphasized that the mural was situated in a place where "the highest pursuits of the human mind" were debated. The entire architectural and decorative scheme of the building was meant to assure that "even the least prepared listener would be aware of [the high seriousness of the site] from the moment he cross[ed] the threshold." Sitting in the hall, each student took his place alongside the great minds who had founded and perpetuated the traditions of the Sorbonne. They were represented by the statues that decorated the pillars framing the edges of the auditorium. Each of these statues faced the front of the hall, "turned toward the professor." They, along with the students, would "partake of all the lessons." But they were not only facing the professor. They, like the entire audience, were also directed toward Puvis's mural. Better than the individual examples of the Sorbonne's founders, better than any individual professor, Puvis de Chavannes's mural "summariz[ed], condens[ed], and evok[ed] the highest thoughts to which the site [was] consecrated."[70]

This "high thought" had nothing to do with the absolute truths sought by conservative academics. If viewers focused on interpreting the mural as an allegory tied to the written text, Michel suggested, they would fail to open themselves imaginatively to the general atmosphere of the painting—to the feeling given by the rhythms and colors of the landscape and the dreamlike quality of the figures.[71] The power of the mural came from its overall visual form, its "eloquence" from the "very simple lines and very calm and disciplined tonalities that are synthesized and associated in the composed whole." This overall feeling and the imagination it encouraged were the true messages of the mural, not a specific allegorical meaning. Here Michel explicitly took up Guyau's and Fouillée's emphasis on feeling and dream and saw these as the keys to the mural's power. He saw the indeterminacy of the figures to be another key to the relation between the mural and the unconscious. Thus, argued Michel, "the beings of dream evoked by [Puvis de Chavannes], strangers to all particular action, seem as though they are bathed in a psychic atmosphere; but they propose us no enigma; and the very general feelings, the intimate and solemn things they have to tell us, find, without difficulty, the road to our hearts, where they evoke long reveries. A good and superior life animates them without agitating them; their unusual and slow gestures, their pensive attitudes, made beautiful with an indecipherable mixture of familiar grace and epic grandeur, give them the feeling of apparitions found in distant and present visions. They offer us less to understand than to feel, and we have no use for a written commentary."[72] The reverie incited by the mural was its most important effect. For it both encouraged participation in imaginative structures of thought and left viewers receptive to the professor who stood speaking at the podium before the mural.

Michel was predicting, in effect, that the student-viewer would ignore the intellectual message of the allegory and fall into a quasi-hypnotic dream state, which the professor, if his personality was strong enough, would then inhabit. While he gazed on Puvis's mural, Michel said, "a delicious peacefulness, a great serenity descends on me. . . . The professor can mount the pulpit; I am quite prepared to receive all the important thoughts that he will bring me and to take communion with great minds."[73] In this description of the experience of Puvis's mural, Michel replaced the priest at the altar imparting transcendent truths with the professor at the podium offering materials for the imagination. Just as Firmin Javel had in his 1884 response to *The Sacred Grove Dear to the Arts and Muses*, Michel used the language of suggestion—of hypnosis and identification—and drew on current theories of the way suggestion could be used as an educational tool. According to these theories, understanding was gained not merely through an intellectual grasp of concepts but also through an identification with the professor and an absorption of his thought processes, his *haut esprit*, as well as the information conveyed.[74] He thus employed the widespread republican strategy of substituting republican materialism for Catholic idealism. Michel's invocation of the unconscious was a kind of materialism. As we have already seen, the burgeoning field of psychology already was considered very much a scientific endeavor, and it was supported by the state.

But Michel also acknowledged another side of the dream that Puvis's work incited in the viewer. He imagined a situation in which the "professor was only a pedant and a babbler" and did not have the powerful intelligence necessary to infiltrate the student's unconscious. In this case, the student-viewer would ignore him, engaging instead with the figures in the hemicycle: "In the silent interview, the Muses appear, powerful and sweet, above his poor head, at which point I console myself and forget what he is speaking about."[75] Michel described this dialogue as a fantasy instigated by the kinds of distortion and incompletion that so many critics had identified in Puvis's murals. They were the product of "very simple and very simplified means," of a "series of unconscious or premeditated eliminations." They emerged from "tendencies native to his meditative and generalizing mind, by lacks, perhaps, as much as by virtues of his eye and hand."[76] Through this interaction between conscious and unconscious activity, Puvis had "made his visions and daydreams live on the walls of our monuments."[77] Puvis had mounted his dreams on the walls in a public space—a project that might at first seem strange, perhaps even dangerous. According to Michel, however, this act deserved gratitude. If Puvis's mural was, as Michel described it, "an addition to the treasury of French art," then, in a sense Puvis himself embodied the best side of Frenchness. Michel hoped that when viewing the mural the student would thus partake not of his own fantasies but of Puvis's dreams and reveries. He would have access to Puvis's dream via his work and through it would assume—if momentarily—the artist's high moral character.[78] If the lesson offered by the professor was inadequate, Michel suggested, the presence of the mural would fill the potential space of individual fantasy with a dream held in common with others in the room, all of whom would be mesmerized by the mural—a French dream of high thought and intellectual solidarity.

PUVIS DE CHAVANNES AND THE NEO-CHRISTIAN RIGHT

Critics who were both aesthetically and politically conservative, such as Lavergne and Saint-Ange, strongly disagreed with republican critics, such as Michel, about the value of Puvis's Sorbonne mural, but other critics on the Right were more aesthetically open-minded. Even though they were unhappy with the politics of the republican state and strongly skeptical of the state's promotion of materialism, many of them praised Puvis de Chavannes's hemicycle. One critic who wrote about the Sorbonne mural was Paul Desjardins, a writer who in the 1890s became a leading figure of the neo-Christian Right. Desjardins was a participant in a movement that called for the spiritual rejuvenation of France and believed that this necessitated the rejection of republican materialism and the program of civic morality in favor of spiritual faith. Desjardins felt that in general the decorative schemes for the Sorbonne reflected and reinforced the atomization of the public under the republican promotion of individualism. Unlike the works commissioned as decorations for the building, Desjardins claimed that Puvis's hemicycle had "something elysian and depersonalized" about it, which gave it a spiritual quality.[79] Desjardins's assessment of Puvis's mural for the Sorbonne was part of a general trend in which aesthetically adventurous, but politically reactionary, artists and critics attempted to recruit Puvis and his art for their own anti-republican purposes.[80]

In an article written in 1890, the painter Edmond Aman Jean—a student of Puvis de Chavannes and a regular exhibitor at Péladan's Salon de la Rose + Croix—gave one of the first overt neo-Christian interpretations of Puvis's work.[81] Although he could not claim the Sorbonne mural to be representative of the religious mysticism he so prized, his overall project was to characterize Puvis's work as tied to a neo-Christian revival. Aman Jean described Puvis's oeuvre as an ideal that was not progressive and secular but traditional, mystical, Christian. He described the artist as the new savior—a "consoler" who would combat the "official materialism and coarseness of analysis" of the republican state with his "abstract and synthetic art."[82] In fact, according to Aman Jean, it was in Puvis's "Christian" works—in *Prodigal Son* (1879) and the *Beheading of St. John* (1869), both of which were exhibited at the Universal Exhibition in a display of a hundred years of French art—that the artist's intent was best illustrated. (Never mind that when these were originally exhibited, many critics thought that they, like *Poor*

Fisherman, were mocking the whole enterprise of religious painting.) Aman Jean read signs of a religious message even in works that had no explicit Christian references. "Certain faces," he said, had been endowed by Puvis with "the calm and the care of priests of the past." Puvis was one of the only living painters who could evoke the spirituality of landscape—the "serene impression" that exuded from nature: "It is thus that after so many years he has revisited with an intensity so penetrated with truth and mystery the cypresses that dominate the slopes of the Arno, because he has the great gift of memory that the years cannot erase."[83] This last comment, including its reference to the landscape with cypresses in *Christian Inspiration*, was strategically formatted around a reproduction of one of Puvis's drawings for the *Beheading of St. John*. *Christian Inspiration* and the *Beheading of St. John* were thus transformed, in Aman Jean's text, into the products of Puvis's "gift of memory"—into memories of the artist's own origins in France's Christian heritage. By locating Puvis's origins on the banks of the Arno, Aman Jean equated Puvis specifically and French art and Frenchness more generally with a genealogy of Latinity that extended from antiquity to the present.[84] He also emphasized that Puvis's feeling for landscape was a great influence on a whole generation of young painters. Aman Jean claimed that the compelling nature of Puvis's work was evidence of a revival of right-wing mysticism, which we have already seen diagnosed by Vogüé and Desjardins.

This characterization of Puvis de Chavannes's work was surely also aimed at combating the more general claims of republican critics that the artist was a "pagan thinker" in whose work "the poetic sentiment of nature dominates." The critic for *Le National*, Alfred Paulet, said that even Puvis's "Christian" works were "the absolute negation of Christian sentiment."[85] Significantly, although Aman Jean's essay was entitled "Puvis de Chavannes," it included a discussion of the state's use of the Sorbonne to promote secular morality. The essay thus appears to be a response to the overt association of Puvis with republicanism that resulted from the Sorbonne mural. In the face of Puvis's alignment with overt republican rhetoric, neo-Christian admirers of the artist openly proclaimed him to be one of their own. There was more at stake than the aesthetic alignment of Puvis's work with their cause. If Puvis was beginning to be recognized as the national painter who best embodied Frenchness, their annexation of Puvis was also an attempt to define his representation of the nation and its values as coincident with theirs. This was, as we shall see in the next chapter, a trend that would continue as the 1890s wore on.

Aman Jean began by putting forth a definition of the purpose of art that was both antidemocratic and antimaterialist. In the hands of a materialist republican state, said Aman Jean, art has lost its true role and meaning. It had become "analytic." Although this made it "more comprehensible to everyone," it had also lost its defining character: "It is lying to itself and is no longer art. It has followed science instead of preceding it . . . it has forgotten that it lives with eternity and dies from analysis."[86] In his description of the true function of art, Aman Jean both refuted any association of art with positivist observation and alluded to the language of feeling that had already been used to describe Puvis's work. "Although eyes look," said Aman Jean, "it is the heart that sees." Because the French viewing public had "closed its heart" to art, the French tradition of creative endeavor was in peril. Art in its proper role, he claimed, should be the domain of "an elite that translates the feelings of the crowd using means that it [the crowd] does not understand."[87] Not surprisingly, the point of Aman Jean's narrative about the current state of art was to proclaim Puvis master of the elite and to distance his work from the analytic (and democratic) tenets of republicanism. And yet Aman Jean accurately captured something about Puvis's work by contrasting the (often false) sense of possession that comes from analysis with a mode of making and receiving art that kept the truth of the work always just beyond reach—and thus kept desire constantly in play. The problem with Aman Jean's analysis was that he assumed that there was an elite who had access to that truth (even if the truth was hard won).[88]

Aman Jean's neo-Christian agenda was carried through to his analysis of the iconography of the Sorbonne mural. He described the central figure, for example, as "the most serene Sorbonne, having two hands that cross over her arms." His description calls to mind medieval images of saints and royalty at prayer, such as those found in the *Belles Heures* of the Duc du Berry. In addition, Aman Jean transformed the symbolism of the figures drinking at the spring from a celebration of the inspiration of the young to a focus on the influence of the old. "As he raises the cup to his lips," said Aman Jean, "the old man's trembling hands will allow most of the vivifying beverage to escape, and it will fall back into the spring as the symbol of the experience of the old from which the young profit."[89] What many critics had interpreted as the need for elders to accept the inspiration of the young was transformed by Aman Jean into a message of respect for tradition.

Logically enough, Aman Jean predicted that Puvis's mural would distract students from the lectures on secular and materialist subjects that would be given in the Grand Amphithéâtre and provide them instead with a message of spirituality and tradition. Aman Jean, like the republican critic Michel, attributed a great deal of power to Puvis's modernist mode of depiction. He, like Michel, felt that the vision of Puvis's mural could easily overtake the message of the speaker at the podium. He "pit[ied] . . . the person who, standing under the fresco, will address himself to an audience who will forget to listen to him as they look at it." Puvis's hemicycle would make the walls sing, and, Aman Jean predicted, many who had come "to listen to a professor with abstract concepts" would "carry away with them what they had undoubtedly not come to seek and with great surprise [would] feel this unknown peace, which [the professor's] wise words did not give!"[90] The message Aman Jean thought that viewers would take from the mural was diametrically opposed to the one that Michel thought emanated from the mural. What a stroke of luck, Aman Jean must have thought, that the Republic itself was providing an image of tradition that would replace the positivist message being given by the lecturer with a spiritual one. Once again, the republican state was undermining its own secular agenda and helping spiritualism to take hold.

By the 1890s the Christian appropriation of Puvis de Chavannes was so strong that the artist made public statements refuting it. An interview of 1892 published in the radical republican *La Justice* in a series on "the idealist reaction" was the first of many explicit attempts to refute any alignment with a Catholic or neo-Christian agenda.[91] Throughout the interview, Puvis emphasized his interest in nature and the material world. Responding to the interviewer's characterization of "mystical art" as claiming that "the body is nothing, Soul, idea is all," Puvis replied ironically: "No more matter, is that it? No more men, no more women, no more nature! . . . which is to say, no more painting."[92] Here Puvis made it eminently clear that he saw his project as a materialization of the idealizing pretensions that were threatening French painting. When describing his creative process, he emphasized the material aspects of making: "When the idea for a painting torments me too strongly . . . when I have it plastically in my eye . . . I make it." He differentiated his work from artists who started from an "aesthetic formula" by acknowledging that "with me, there is a large part that is unconscious that is very difficult to describe precisely."[93] Over and over, he emphasized the materialism of his practice: "I always apply myself, in materializing my dreams, in giving them a form on the canvas, to do the *possible*, the *probable*, the *reasonable*."[94] Puvis did not want to be aligned with mysticism and idealism.

In an interview with *La Semaine de Paris* published in 1895, Puvis attempted to dissociate his work even further from neo-Christian resonances. The interviewer, Paul Gsell, posed the following question: "Is it with your consent that the Catholics and the neo-Christians align themselves with your work? You know, no doubt, the opinion they have of you: that you are a mystical primitive and believer straying in the nineteenth century." Puvis answered in strongly dismissive terms. His response (as narrated by Gsell) deserves to be quoted at length:

He [Puvis] shrugged his shoulders and brought me in front of the reproduction of the fresco from the Lyons Museum. Around the allegorical figures of the Rhône and the Saône are placed two large scenes: on one side "Christian Inspiration," on the other "Antique Vision": If I had painted only the subject on the left, one could have correctly affirmed that I have been haunted by the Christianity of the Middle Ages, but look, this pagan landscape, which manifests so clearly the joy of life on earth—doesn't it make a sufficient counterpoint to the panel for which it is the pendant? Now, if one really wishes to take the trouble to look at my "Christian Inspiration," does one find there the glorification of ecstasy and mortifications? Not at all. Here is what I have done: a religious painter, a sort of Fra Angelico, is in the process of finishing a decorative mural. Far from being swallowed by the infinite, he seems taken with a fever to work, he has the appearance of wanting to throw himself into his work in order to put on the final touches: all his being is in movement. Behind him, as the evening approaches, another religious man begins to light the lamps; and then two young men arrive, two young artists who lean on the wall in order to take a lesson from the master by watching him work. I would certainly like to know if there is anything in all this other than a testimony in honor of earthly activity. These men think of God, but, above all, they live, and they work with their hands, they enjoy exercising their physical and moral force: that is my own philosophy and not the overly contemplative spirit of the Middle Ages.[95]

In this passage, Puvis gave a secularizing and materializing interpretation of painting, even when it was carried out by monks. Even the Christian side of the patrimony, he implied, should be seen in materialist terms. For Puvis, the painting that was most often mobilized as proof of his alignment with the neo-Christians—*Christian Inspiration*—was properly about the material processes of making art and about "terrestrial activity." This emphasis on the material is even more clearly invoked in his other work—above all, *Ancient Vision*. The bodies in *Ancient Vision* were precursors to the figures of Poetry in the Sorbonne mural; and it was in the group of Poetry that Puvis's own conception of knowledge was most strongly articulated.[96]

5

IMAGINING THE MOTHERLAND

Modernism and Fantasy in the Hôtel de Ville

Listen well: The City Hall! This is not a banal corner of wall in an official building, not any old place where nobody ever goes that must be covered with colored subjects. This is everyone's home, the summary of Paris, an architectural assembly of staircases and rooms that the population moves through, a book open to all whose pages must tell of yesterday and today, the history of the beings and things of our time and the times that preceded us.

GUSTAVE GEFFROY ON THE HÔTEL DE VILLE IN PARIS

Puvis de Chavannes's *Summer* (1891) and *Winter* (1892) are not typical allegories of the seasons (figs. 42, 43). Given their author and the political circumstances of their making, they could never have been just that. These murals were part of a decorative scheme for the Hôtel de Ville in Paris, to which the artist contributed several works.[1] The Hôtel de Ville was burned during the Paris Commune in 1871, in the aftermath of the Franco-Prussian War, at the very moment when the Third Republic itself was established. In the 1880s it was reconstructed by republican administrations wishing to promote the success of the republican state and to wipe away the memory of the German occupation of Paris and the violence of the Communard experiment. Conservative opponents of the Republic pointed to the Commune as an example of the dangers of revolutionary politics whose origins lay in 1789. For republicans, on the other hand, the Commune was, by the end of the century, generally regarded as an aberration in the history of democratic politics.[2] The resurrection of the Hôtel de Ville gave the state an opportunity to temper the events that reminded the nation of division and trauma. The opportunist Republic rebuilt the Hôtel de Ville in the image of its predecessor, only on a grander scale. The new building represented continuity with a past in which the Franco-Prussian War and the Paris Commune had been edited out, along with prospects for a future of France no longer marked by those traumas. Integral to this reconstruction was a decorative campaign in which Puvis and many other artists participated.[3]

The Hôtel de Ville epitomized the style of national imagining defined by Renan, in which imagining and forgetting go hand in hand. Puvis was by now

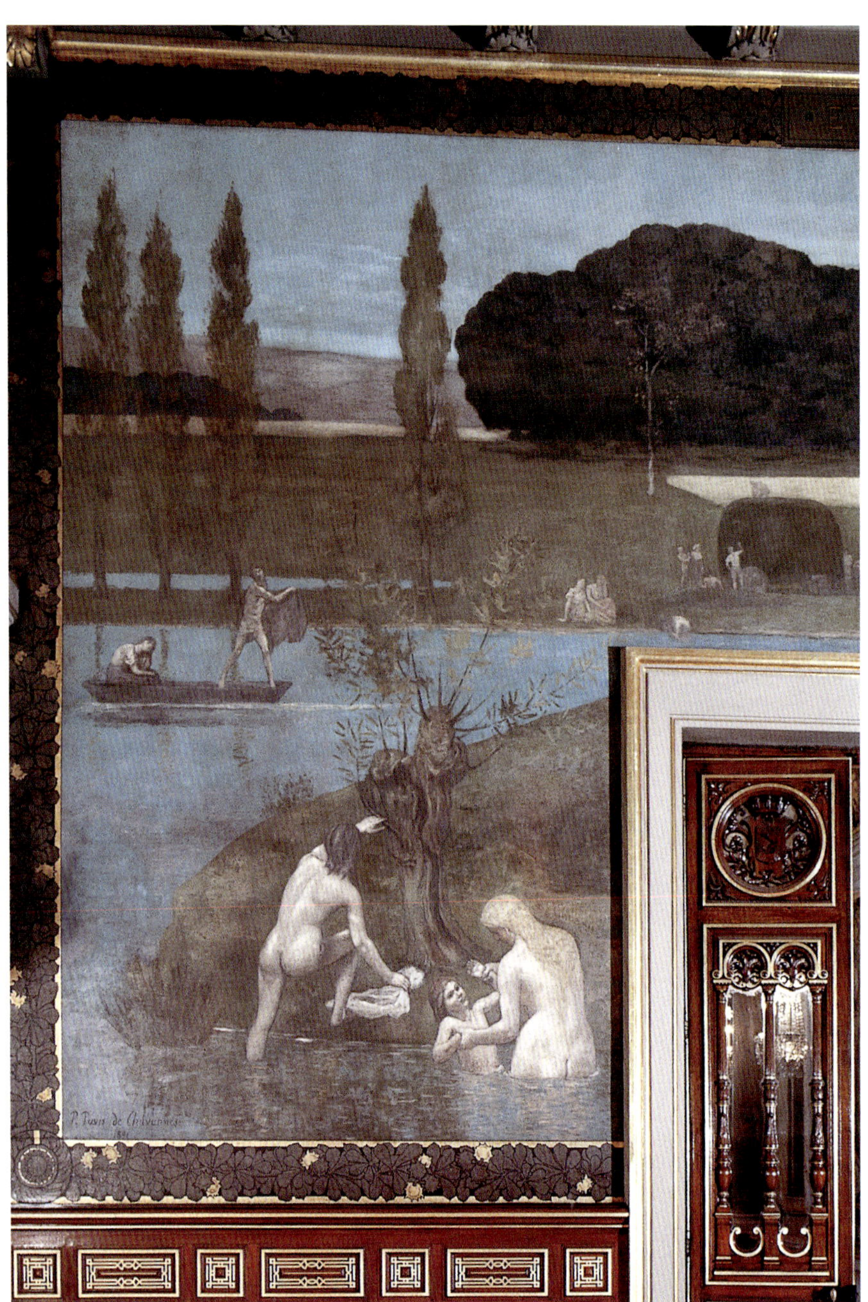

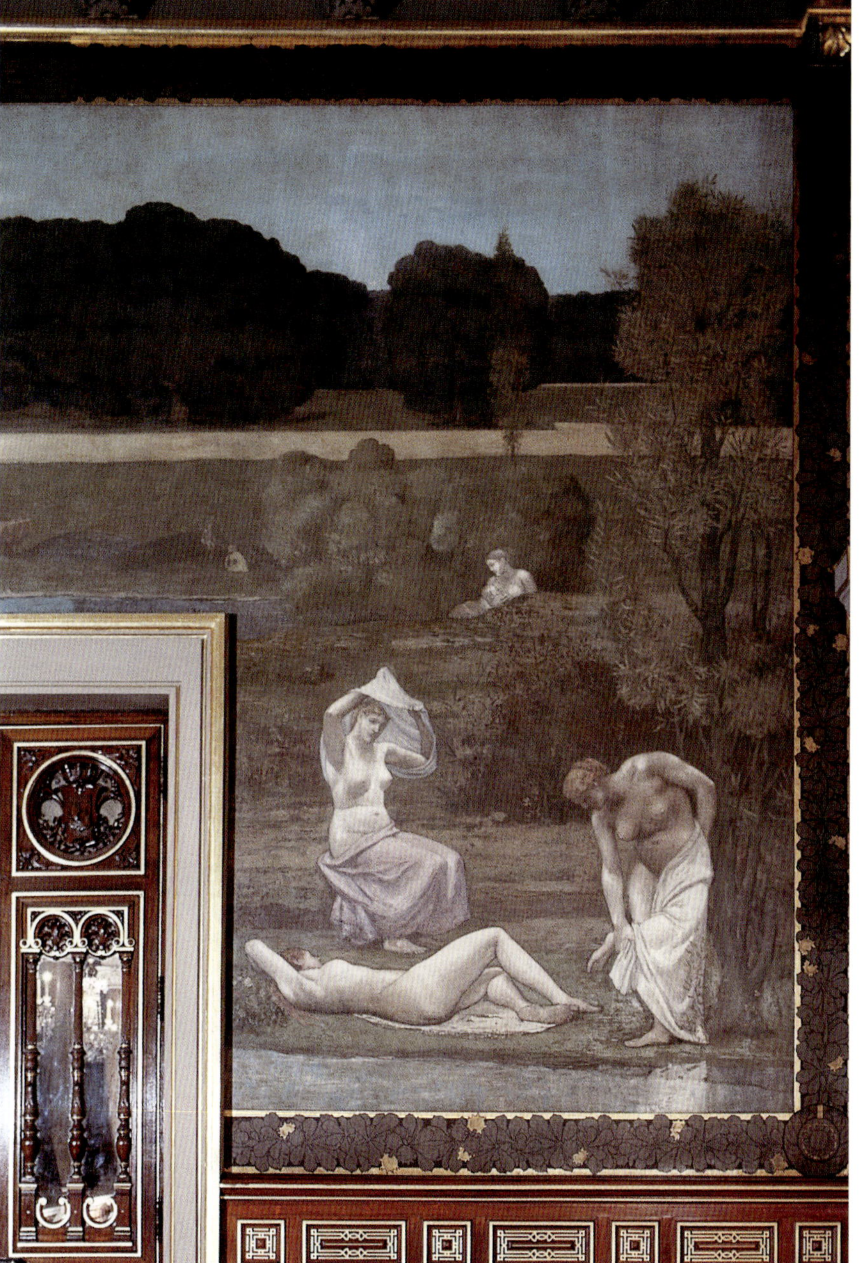

42
Pierre Puvis de Chavannes, *Summer*, 1891. Oil on canvas affixed to wall, 19 1/3 x 29 3/4 ft. (5.9 x 9.1 m). Hôtel de Ville, Paris

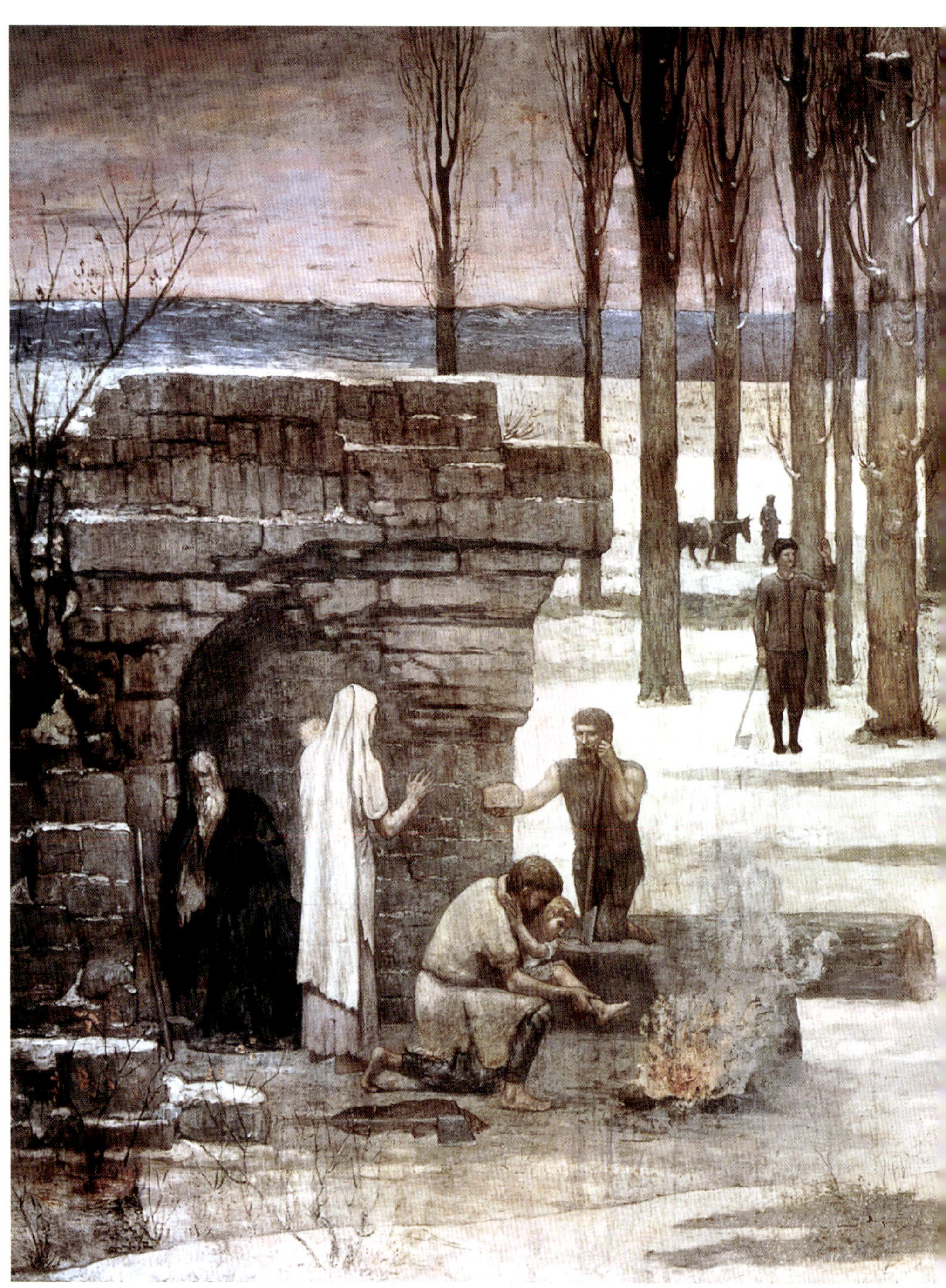

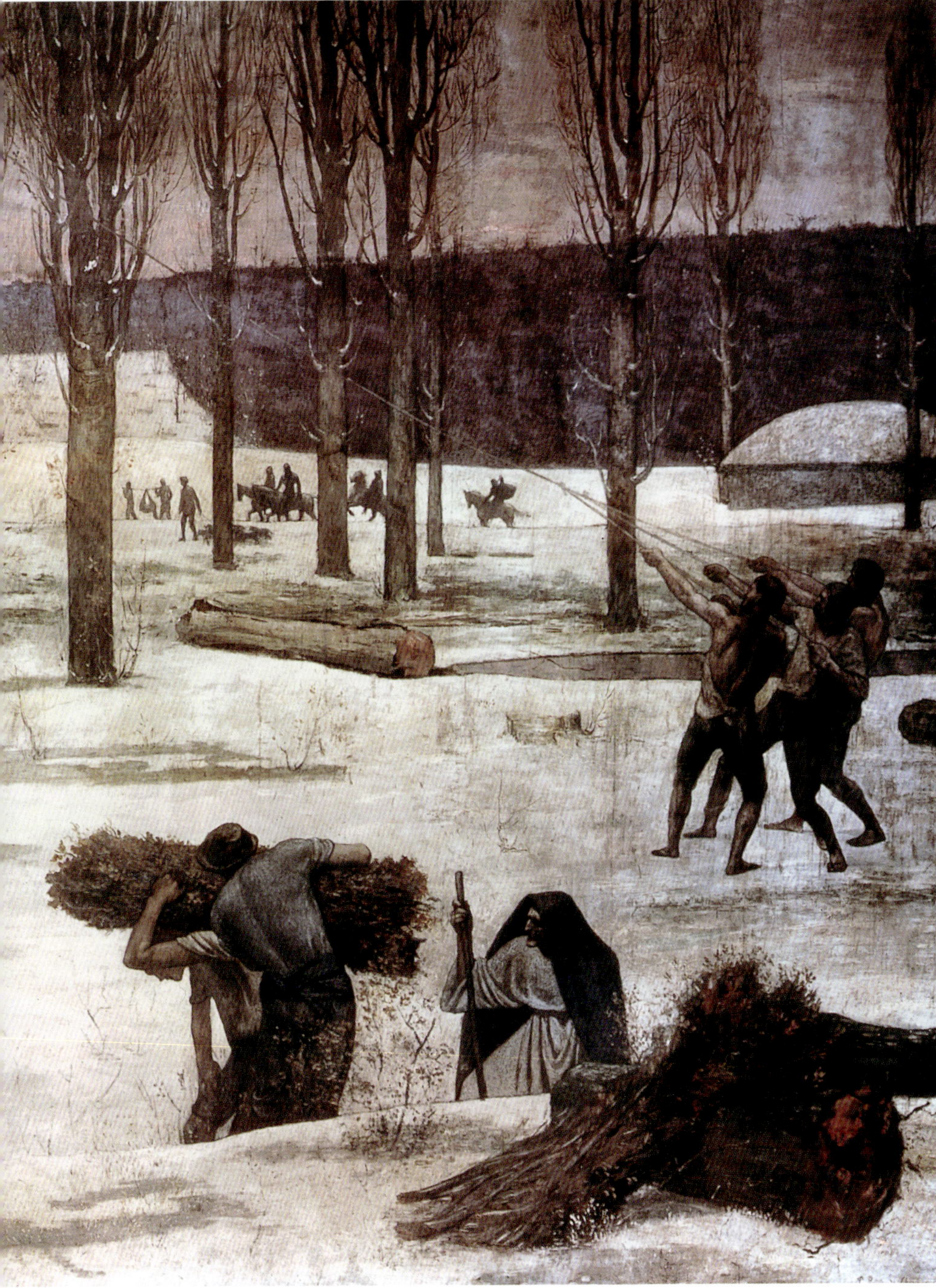

43
Pierre Puvis de Chavannes, *Winter*, 1892. Oil on canvas affixed to wall, 19 1/3 x 29 3/4 ft. (5.9 x 9.1 m). Hôtel de Ville, Paris

famous for the patriotic images of Paris he had painted during the war and the time of the Commune. He was ardently anti-German and anti-Communard.[4] The commission for a new Hôtel de Ville surely held a special significance for him. And it did for the state as well. The decoration was the visual seal over the wounds to the collective body of France, a site for imagining France while forgetting that the Commune and the Franco-Prussian War had ever taken place.

In addition, the building was a monument to national unity. Despite the cultural distance between Paris and the rest of France, it was meant to be not just the place where Parisians could gain access to their municipal government but also a *maison commune* in which the entire population could take part in Frenchness. The reconstruction of the Hôtel de Ville was thus a tool in the implementation of an ideology of civic participation promoted by the Republic. Puvis was given the commission for the Salon du Zodiaque on January 29, 1889. The choice of Puvis as the decorator of one of two entrance halls for the new building was adopted without dispute by the commission. No subject matter appears to have been stipulated, but Puvis surely knew about the architect Théodore Ballu's 1884 proposal that the room be decorated with allegories of the four seasons, and seems to have chosen to follow his wishes. There is evidence, however, that some members of the commissioning body would have liked Puvis to do otherwise.[5] The body was made up of a combination of state-appointed arts administrators and municipal councillors. The Paris Municipal Council was far more radical than the central government, and the debate was charged with disagreements between Left and Center about the kind of subject matter and painterly mode that would be most appropriate.[6] As Edouard Vaillant, a socialist member of the municipal council who participated in the debate, put it: "We do not want . . . [the walls] to be covered with allegories, which is to say, with subjects that no longer correspond to the current idea of art."[7] This attitude, which was expressed in 1886, shows how politicized the issue of allegory already was and resonates with the critical conflicts over allegory that arose when Puvis exhibited his cartoon for the Sorbonne mural. After much debate, new recommendations were issued, but the commissioners never rejected outright the allegorical program proposed by Ballu. Instead, they added the stipulation that "subjects connected to the history of Paris, the enfranchisement of the communes, the life of Etienne Marcel, and the great events of the Revolution will be imposed on all vertical surfaces presenting a sufficient expanse."[8]

In 1889 the state tried unsuccessfully to commission Puvis de Chavannes to paint a mural apotheosizing the French Revolution. It seems quite likely that this mural was destined for the Hôtel de Ville.[9] Puvis's response to this request suggests the attitude he took toward the allegories of Summer and Winter that he had already agreed to paint for the building: "To others the glory of singing this colossal mystification! . . . If Michelet were still living, we would favorably replace the cold, deceitful, and pretentious account by several of this master's paragraphs, which would redress things and return them to their point of departure—and form a sort of moral catechism purified of all historical lies in which the *duties* of men would have as much place as their *rights*."[10]

If we take seriously Puvis's comment that "the *duties* of men would have as much place as their *rights*," we can see these murals as representing Puvis's rather anti-didactic picturing of the way France ought to be. In *Summer*, Puvis instilled in his viewers his hopes for France if the best circumstances prevailed, leaving room for the play of individual fantasy. In *Winter* he pictured the way the community ought to behave in times of hardship. The dichotomy set up in *Summer* and *Winter* in the Hôtel de Ville echoes the division between plenitude and asceticism that we saw in the Lyons murals. If the Lyons murals were implicitly about the definition of the French soul, this theme is on the surface here. What Puvis offered in his murals for the Hôtel de Ville instead of the opportunity to worship the saints and martyrs of the Revolution was his own version of a secular moral catechism: he pictured and idealized the structures of sociality in times of bounty and hardship. But the anti-didacticism of *Summer* and *Winter* left the social and political meanings of the national ideal an open question—a question that haunted the interpretation of these paintings for years to come.

SUMMER'S EMBRACE

The decorative scheme for the Hôtel de Ville included works by many different artists. When the building was inaugurated, critics complained that it was too eclectic and pandered too much to the tastes of the market.[11] It looked more like an exhibition of works for private consumption than a program meant to educate the public. But even the harshest critics thought Puvis's murals provided something quite different from what was offered by most of the works on display. In fact, his contributions were virtually the only paintings unanimously found to be worthy of praise—none more so than *Summer*, the mural destined to decorate the space around the doorway of the Salon du Zodiaque, a reception room leading to the southern entrance halls. Puvis completed an oil sketch that closely resembles the mural in both color and composition in 1891 (fig. 44). The final version of the mural was first exhibited at the Salon de la Société Nationale des Beaux-Arts in 1891 and then again at the Durand-Ruel galleries later that year before being installed in its place at the Hôtel de Ville.[12] Its pendant, *Winter*, was installed on the opposite wall the following year.

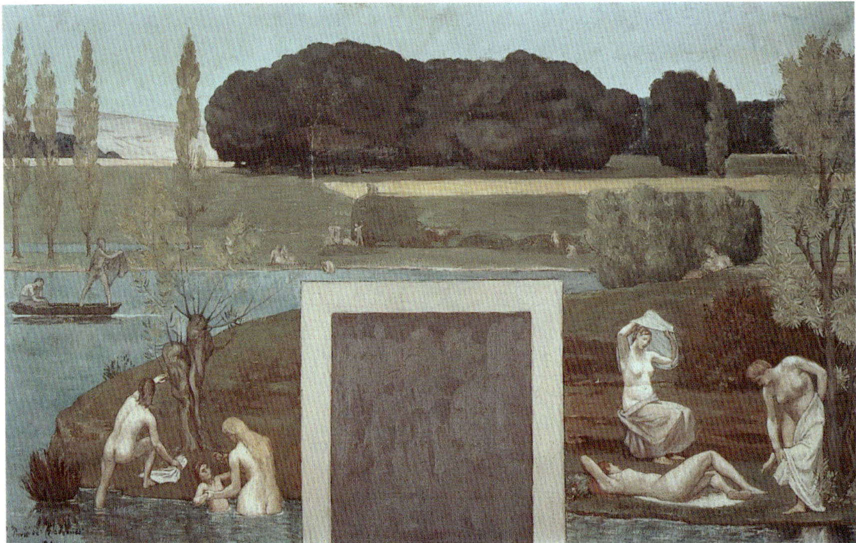

44
Pierre Puvis de Chavannes, *Summer*, 1891. Preliminary sketch for mural in the Salon du Zodiaque, Hôtel de Ville, Paris. Oil on canvas, 213 3/4 x 340 1/2 in. (543 x 865 cm). Musée du Pétit Palais, Paris

From the very outset, critics responded to the formal qualities of *Summer*. In it Puvis embedded local distortions and disjunctions into an overarching rhythmic and coloristic design. This rhythmic interaction of color—which is as direct and sensual as Puvis ever gets—is surely meant to captivate the viewer. And the critics in 1891 *were* captivated. One, the republican administrator and champion of the decorative arts Louis de Fourcaud, explicitly linked the appeal of *Summer* to the simplified formal means that were powerfully visible even from afar: "The more distantly one perceives it," he suggested, "the more it attracts and enchants, if only by its masses and its radiant harmony." He saw the landscape as a series of alternating bands of color: "very blue sky; distant violet coasts; a zone of tender green cut by a band of golden wheat; . . . a blue river that cuts across the landscape in a soft curve; some thin trees bordering the shore whose tops rise vaporously toward the azure; finally, personages enveloped in the whole form an integral part of this dreamed reality."[13] This description is particularly interesting for the way the rhetorics of distance and desire intermix. The seductiveness of the painting is attributed to the play of light that results from the alternating masses of blue, violet, green, and gold, stitched together by the curve of the river and the vertical tree trunks. The figures are the last to pull the critic in. From a distance, anyway, it is not the bodies but the sensual effect of color and the bold abstract pattern that attract and enchant. This emphasis on large areas of color and abstract patterning is an important element of Puvis's modernism—it is surely one of the things that made him so important for painters like Matisse and Picasso. What needs to be emphasized in this context, however, is that the pleasurable sensuality of the patterning had meaning. It lent the painting a dreamlike atmosphere. And nowhere was a dream of national unity more desperately needed than in the new Hôtel de Ville—a building meant to be a monument to national healing in the aftermath of war and at a time when political and social divisions in France were polarized.

The dreamlike nature of the composition can also be attributed to certain strange disjunctions. A sense of the flatness of the surface—established by the decorative color patterning—alternates with a sense of recession, which is achieved through the diminishing size of the figures. Rather than presenting us with a seamless gradation into space, Puvis provides us with three distinct planes. The first is peopled by large figures, on either side of the doorway, who seem to have little narrative purpose. The second, at the vertical center of the canvas, is occupied in the wings by smaller figures—a fisherman in a boat on the left and a nursing mother on the right. Finally, just above the fisherman on the far banks of the river, is the third, with smaller and less clearly articulated figures who reap the harvest of the fields or lounge on the riverbank. The painting seems to shift perspectival registers as the viewer's eye moves from foreground, to middle ground, to background. In both the preliminary sketch and the final mural, the background scene is clearer than the foreground scene from a narrative point of view. We can identify the activities of fishing and reaping. But in each painting Puvis exaggerates the rules of perspective to make the figures in the background much smaller and less accessible than they need logically to be. Indeed, in the final mural, the middle ground has been made slightly larger and more legible, with emphasis on the mother nursing her child, and the background figures have been slightly diminished. In each case we almost have the sense that the action in the background is part of a different perspectival world than the foreground is, both because of the disjunction in size and because of the difference in narrative strategy in the two registers. Puvis had employed this compositional strategy a few years earlier in *Ancient Vision*, where tiny white horses inhabit a background that seems impossibly distant from the foreground figures. He used it again in *Winter* the next year, placing tiny horses and riders at the hunt in the background. In the final version of *Summer*, there is even more discrepancy than in the sketch between the harvesters of the hay who occupy this impossible distance and the figures who lounge inexplicably in the foreground.

Many of those who responded to the painting commented on the contrast between background and foreground. This underlines the importance of the compositional device that Puvis employed here. The painting hinges on the disjunction between a background that is so small and so roughly painted that it verges on the illegible—seems always just out of reach—even though it is comprehensible from a narrative point of view, and a foreground that is impressively present, yet also disturbing. This contrast between the inaccessible and the disturbingly present was also considered to be part of the painting's language of dream.

An additional way in which *Summer* draws viewers in—into a dream—is by the arrangement of the figures. They are not arranged hierarchically or logically; instead, they are dispersed in a circle that both echoes the movement of the river around the central grassy area and surrounds the gap formed by the doorway. The viewers are thus made physically to traverse the center of the picture, to be encircled by these figures as they cross from room to room.

Fourcaud's reaction to the mural provides some clues to the processes of identification and desire that were thought to be evoked by the painting. His description of the figures is particularly striking: "Enveloped in the whole," they "form an integral part of this dreamed reality." We should remember that Fourcaud used this sentence to sum up his analysis of the alternating bands of color. Indeed, Fourcaud had just been describing his own feelings of envelopment by the color and design of the composition—recounting, that is, how he was "attract[ed] and enchant[ed]" by its masses of color and "radiant harmony." Fourcaud's rhetoric thus involves a telling slippage between what the composition does to the figures on display and what it does to Fourcaud himself, as a viewer. Who, after all, is dreaming the reality of the painting? Fourcaud the viewer or the figures that occupy the space of the mural? Standing in front of the mural, Fourcaud, like the figures, has the experience of being enveloped in the landscape.

This shift in Fourcaud's rhetoric between his experience of the painting and his description of the bodies on display becomes even more interesting when we look closely at the figures themselves. If Fourcaud (and other viewers) somehow "dreamed" *Summer*, the dream is dependent on both the pleasures of the painting and its disjunctions. The critical responses to the painting make clear that those disjunctions hinge on the experience of viewing Puvis's strange configuration of the body. In *Summer*, incomplete or inexplicable bodies are set into what had seemed from a distance to be a pleasing composition aimed at delighting, rather than disturbing, its viewers. The painting taken as a whole appears harmonious because of its decorative patterning, it is less so when the viewer focuses on individual figures.

The foreground of the mural wraps around the frame of the door. Each side is dominated by nude or semidraped figures. Their large size encourages careful examination of their bodies. When we undertake such an examination, the figures become increasingly strange, even unintelligible. To begin with, it seems as though their bodies have been brought in line with the overall design of the landscape, even at the risk of distortion. In the group to the left of the doorway, the side of the woman's body is stretched to an uncomfortable rigidity as it is made to parallel the vertical of the door frame (see fig. 42). The figure who emerges from the water is perhaps even more difficult to read. Because it is seen from behind, we have no clear signs of gender. The general body type seems to hover between male and female. It is neither strongly muscular nor excessively curvaceous. The hair does not give much more information, because it is neither short nor long. There was no critical consensus as to the sex of this figure, in fact. Several critics found it to be masculine—the husband and father to the bathing mother and child.[14] Others saw it as not only feminine but one of the most seductive of all the female figures.[15] Thus, where the foreground initially seems to promise a simple narrative of bathing by showing a family group, this figure raises uncertainties about gender that destabilize the meaning of the scene. As in *Ancient Vision*, Puvis did not, in *Summer*, fulfill expectations of legible narrative and correct anatomy. Instead, the painting set parameters for reading by hinting at narrative content, then raised questions rather than providing a story. The narrative was left open to individual interpretation.

The figures to the right side of the doorway push this refusal of narrative closure to an even greater extreme (fig. 45). Indeed, the three women seem to have no narrative purpose whatsoever. These figures are even more impressively massive than those on the left. Situated at eye level, they have enough sheer size to command attention. We could argue that the women are drying themselves after a bath, but their gestures seem too bizarre and belabored for that explanation to carry much weight. If their gestures serve no logical purpose, neither do their positions suggest conventional allegorical meanings. The figures hold no allegorical attributes with which a viewer might be familiar. Instead, they evince various stages of undress and a variety of bodily positions. A nude figure reclines on the bank, the line of her back echoing the edge of the shore. To her right, another female figure stands half draped, precariously clutching her left foot, with her right arm in a strange and inexplicable self-reflexive pose. Yet another woman is seated and holds drapery above her head.

All three figures, with their classical drapery and bather's poses, invoke a tradition of depicting the female body that aims at idealization. Yet none of them provide the sense that the body has been mastered by the artist and presented in an idealized form to the viewer. Especially in these three figures, Puvis is aiming to make the body as evocative as is possible within the parameters of public painting. Each of the three bodies is deliberately painted to look indeterminate and strange. For example, instead of providing us with the body as a harmonious whole, the reclining woman threatens to decompose into ungainly parts (see fig. 45). Her arm looks cut off at the elbow, and her head looks almost detached. It is difficult to decide exactly where her lower legs sit in relation to her huge hips and torso. Puvis outlines her body starkly, but this line distorts rather than idealizes her form, emphasizing even more the disjunctiveness of the body. Within the boundaries of this outline the artist uses modeling, light, and shadow in ways that work against their conventional functions. The upper half of her body is characterized by a confusing play of light and shadow: The side of her shoulder could as easily be her armpit. It is difficult to determine the position of her breast in relation to her head. The more we look, the more the side of her body becomes a shadowy field stretched and magnified in size to emphasize its blankness and indeterminacy.

Similar difficulties arise with the other two figures. In the seated figure shadows obscure the relation between arms and torso, between head and neck. In the standing figure at the far right, the arms and feet seem to stretch and fall away as they are aligned with her massive body. They are elongated to the point of distortion. Similarly, the modeling of the chest, shoulders, and head does less to define her body than to obscure it. The breasts look almost detached. The head is very oddly connected to the shoulders. Lest one think that these distortions are

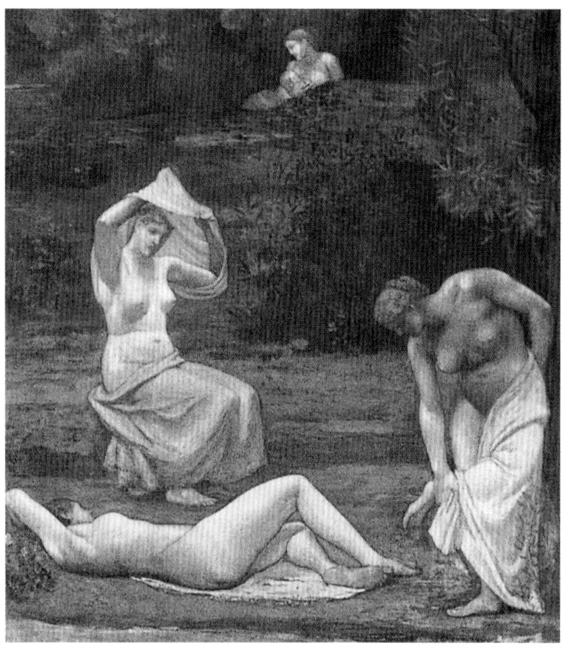

45
Pierre Puvis de Chavannes, *Summer* (detail of fig. 42; right foreground)

accidents of bad draftsmanship, it is worth noting that the distortions were arrived at in the sketch for the mural and carried into the final version without correction. Indeed, Puvis employs the same strategy of using drawing and modeling to evocatively distort his figures in order to encourage the viewer's own desire for idealization, as we have seen in previous examples.

All three figures in this group are positioned in a rhythmic interaction with one another and with the landscape. This whole section of the mural is composed of a series of bodily echoes that send the eye from figure to figure and encourage viewers to make comparisons between them. The gesture of the seated figure, arms over head, echoes that of the reclining figure. The lower half of the seated figure's right leg is aligned with the thigh of the reclining figure. The lower half of the seated figure's left leg parallels the standing figure's down-stretched arm. The standing figure's limbs are arranged in a series of verticals and angles that echo the edge of the canvas, the frame of the door, and the angled limbs of the other two women. This repetition and variation of generalized body types—naked and half draped, hair held up and hair let down, standing and sitting and reclining—seems to be more about portraying the body as a site for imaginative theme and variation than about employing it as a vehicle for narrative or allegorical knowledge. The purpose of these figures seems to be to evoke bodiliness without ever specifying it too concretely—a bodiliness that is instinctive, in which some deep-seated and innate principle rather than knowledge and convention governs the interactions between figures and landscape.

The more we look at these figures, the more we want to look. The more we look, the more disturbing they become. The more we look, the more we feel a desire to compensate, in the mind's eye, for these indeterminacies—to find some way of imagining these bodies whole again. This was not the first time that Puvis had treated the body in such a manner. This strange undecidability of the body permeates his work. And critics had already established a mode of reading Puvis's figures that took into account their evocative nature, even made it central. In 1884, in response to Puvis's murals for the Museum of Fine Arts, Lyons, the critic Henri Fouquier had done just that when he stated: "Instead of searching for an ideal the artist contents himself with evoking the notion in our minds. He leaves us, in sum, to make three quarters of the painting."[16] Gustave Geffroy had put the matter even more clearly: "Puvis de Chavannes's willed abbreviations are not drawing errors, but voluntary and necessary sacrifices. Nothing has been precisely indicated in the bodies and clothing of these noble young women who only live in our imagination."[17]

When *Summer* was exhibited at the Salon, the critics who complained about the three women used terms that indicate the problematic nature of Puvis's configuration of the body. One critic described the women as "too athletic in their richness."[18] Another thought they were "constructed . . . with a vigor that sometimes seems to have gone too far."[19] These critics were seemingly overwhelmed by the abundance of distorted and undifferentiated matter-cum-flesh. Not surprisingly, conservative academic critics were the most hostile both to Puvis's painting and to the general republican message of the Hôtel de Ville as maison commune. They were thus also most likely to give detailed descriptions of the ways the composition was incoherent. The royalist critic Georges-Claudius Lavergne predictably denigrated Puvis's "trees and bathers," which, he said, were "only decorative if we agree to observe them from a distance."[20] He mocked the praise showered on the artist by republican critics.

Alphonse de Calonne, who wrote for another royalist newspaper, *Le Soleil*, was also hostile to the mural. He described *Summer* as a dream and contrasted its dreamlike composition with the clear intellectual communication of ideas that he expected from decorative allegory. Calonne's vituperative rhetoric was not just a defense of worn-out formulas for academic composition. In the most extreme invective Calonne spoke eloquently of the anxiety induced by the painting's evocation of fantasy. The figures in *Summer*, he said, did not "lift themselves from the background." They were "feeble and limp." "They pass as if in a dream, without vigor or movement." Distinctions between things were becoming blurred, he suggested, just as they are in a dream. Even worse, the overall composition did not display the orderly and unified thought expected of high art. Rather than making a clear and hierarchical composition, Puvis dispersed his figures across the canvas: "He doesn't compose," said Calonne. "He scatters the figures. Never a mass, never a group, nothing but isolated personages."

The problem was not just Puvis's disregard for academic convention. Calonne was also worried about the effect these figures might have on their viewers. Puvis's figures did not use conventional gestures to transmit legible ideas. Describing the artist's refusal to direct meaning using conventional strategies, Calonne said: "He places them on the canvas *for the viewer*, not for the action, not to create a subject to be interpreted, not to bring an idea to light. Everything is nebulous in thought and execution. In addition, his paintings are enigmatic and empty. If he uses allegories, which is the defining character of his compositions, he imagines them to be obscure, hidden, even shadowy."[21] Colonne contrasts the legibility and clarity that the critic expects from high art with the indeterminacy he feels Puvis's painting actually delivers. The point of the painting, Calonne suggested, is not to portray an action with a moral message or to "bring an idea to light" that might edify the viewer. Rather than being placed to secure a definite meaning, the figures are depicted "for the viewer."

Responsibility for the meaning of the work is transferred, the critic implied, from artist to audience. That is, it is the viewer, rather than the artist, who ultimately supplies meanings for the allegorical body. What Puvis gives instead of the usual fare is a combination of indeterminacy and sensuality that encourages a far greater range of individual response than this critic thought was wise.

The lack of differentiation between figure and ground, the shadowiness, even "emptiness" of the canvas—these are descriptions of Puvis's tendency toward abstraction. Clearly, this pictorial mode threatened to provoke the viewer's own imaginative processes rather than tell the viewer what to think. And the processes set in motion, I would argue, had less to do with intellect as Calonne conceived it than with sensation, memory, and desire. To admit this play of fantasy as a legitimate effect of high art would have been to acknowledge that intellect and desire were intertwined. Thus Calonne, who proffered the aesthetic views of a royalist paper invested in upholding the academic tenets of aesthetic disinterestedness, could not fully admit the power of Puvis's mural. To do so would have lent legitimacy to materialist aesthetics and to all that they implied about human subjectivity.

Yet even this conservative critic, who inveighed against the compositional incoherencies of *Summer,* had to grant that the painting afforded pleasures. These he attributed to the very qualities he had been denouncing. Suddenly, in the midst of his complaints, the disgruntled critic waxed poetic and pointed metaphorically to the absences he had complained about. "It seems," he said, that one has exited "from an infernal music, and enter[ed] into an imaginary country where even the birds themselves refuse to sing."[22] Despite his academic biases, Calonne recognized that the rhythmic sensual structuring in the painting transported him into an "imaginary country"—a world of the imagination. Like so many other critics, he was seduced by the dreamlike structure of *Summer.* Yet he was also uncomfortable with its effects on him—with the way it asked him to fill in the imaginary spaces, which he poetically described as an emptiness left by silent birds. Summarizing the painting, Calonne declared: "It is a lot, but it is not enough." He was not sympathetic to the evocativeness of *Summer.* Indeed, he was worried that Puvis had opened up a space meant to encourage the imagination of individual viewers.

Although he wanted to dismiss Puvis's painting for political reasons, Calonne identified and described Puvis's mode of address rather accurately. Not only was he able to link Puvis's compositional and painterly strategies to the seduction of the viewer, but he also made clear, through the conflicted nature of his own rhetoric, the movement in Puvis's work between pleasure and disturbance. The very tone of the criticism admits the sensual pleasure provided by *Summer* and suggests a longing that, I would argue, is provoked by the way the figures themselves undermine that initial pleasure, providing in its place a sense of disturbance and a desire to regain the sensual plenitude that the painting at first (and from a distance) proffers. This double address to the viewer—this embedding of distorted and evocative bodies into an overall decorative patterning—is one of the key aspects of Puvis's painterly mode. It both defines his modernism and provides power to the work's address to the imagination. Any painting, especially any painting of the body, will address the unconscious desires of its viewers. However, Puvis's painting wears its fantasy on its sleeve, so to speak. It does not even attempt to maintain the fiction that viewing should lead to knowledge and edification. Instead, as the critical responses to it make clear, it aims straight for the fantasmatic elements of imaginative processes. And this, it was recognized even in Puvis's own day, was the very property that made Puvis de Chavannes such a powerful public painter.

The majority of critics viewed the qualities that were the source of Calonne's dissatisfaction with Puvis's mural as positive. The often overdetermined critical rhetoric used to describe the mural demonstrates how badly the critics wanted to see in *Summer* a vision of France as a plentiful land without dissonance of any kind. Many thought the bodies of the three female figures epitomized the general theme of the painting. One critic, for example, said that *Summer* was a scene of both painterly and material plenitude—replete with "infinite depth, all exuberant with vigor," with "warm light," "harvesters who load wheat on an overflowing cart," and "fishermen tending their nets."[23] He described the massiveness of the female bodies as a metaphor for the fertility and plenitude of the landscape. In particular, the "supremely beautiful" standing woman who has an "abundant torso" becomes an emblem of "summer itself, in all its majesty." In a striking choice of vocabulary, this critic characterized the woman's torso as "plantureux" (abundant, fertile, rich)—a word that could equally apply to the landscape and which is commonly used to describe a meal (as in the phrase "un repas plantureux").[24]

Such descriptions of the fertility and bounty of *Summer* are commonly matched by attributions of sensual plenitude to its form. We have already seen an instance of this in Fourcaud's account of the enchanting and radiant harmonies. Fourcaud provides just one example of an extremely common response that emphasizes the feeling of the viewer as he or she stands before *Summer*. Another critic commented that the mural "would not suffice to convince our minds if our eyes did not also get their due, thanks to an incomparable sense of harmony and a voluptuous concordance of tones."[25] This passage underlines the extent to which the power of Puvis's paintings was attributed to those aspects of his painterly mode that should be aligned with modernism—the large expanses of color and decorative patterning. It also makes clear that Guyau's and Fouillée's theorizations of the importance of feeling as a component of aesthetic address was already integral to art criticism. Like Fouillée, the critic Alfred Ernst, who was writing for the republican paper *Le Siècle*, described the requirement that a painting make its viewers *feel* in the same way before it could be convincing. It was only through an emphasis on the sensual aspects of light and paint (on the "voluptuous concordance of tones") that the sense of design was achieved.

Such comments indicate that Puvis's critics imagined color to offer the most direct address to feeling. For us, what is important is that all of the critics who commented on color associated it with fantasies of an enveloping caress—"so sweet," said one writer, "and yet so powerful!"[26] The same critic who remarked on the standing woman's "torse plantureux" attributed particular meanings to the feeling of sensual plenitude that the painting provided: "It is experienced like a caress. . . . Once more it is this same enveloping poetry of the master that we find again and that cradles us [*que nous retrouvons et qui nous berce*]."[27] In language that has striking parallels to his description of *Ancient Vision* in Chapter 3, this critic described the painting as a place where something akin to an enveloping and cradling maternal body might be reexperienced. Indeed, both the form and subject matter of Puvis's *Summer* led critics explicitly to link the landscape pictured in *Summer*, the landscape of France, to a fantasy of the maternal body: rediscovered, voluptuous, abundant, enveloping, nourishing, cradling. It is fitting that critics who wanted to promote the unifying message of Puvis's painting called on such maternal rhetoric, for in using it they were evoking a fantasy of origins that cut across political affinity, race, class, and gender: everyone who exists has been born to a woman.[28]

The analogy between *Summer* and the maternal body was also encouraged by another element of the painting. Directly behind the standing figure, reclining at the far edge of the near bank, a woman nurses an infant. Through this figure the abundance of the French landscape is linked with the productivity of the female body in no uncertain terms. A formal echo is established between the heaped haycart in the background and the nursing woman before the bush in the middle ground, making plain the comparison between the productivity of the earth and the fruitfulness of the female body (see figs. 42, 45). Though relatively small, the nursing mother, like the harvesting figures, was often remarked on by the critics. One wrote explicitly: "There is a young woman who nurses her child; in addition, the harvesters reap the hay; and a sense of the calm nature extends throughout this pleasant countryside."[29] The sequence of the description, from the suckling infant to the gathering of hay, makes the final phrase seem like a summary of the first two. *Summer* thus provoked in critics a vision of the French landscape as a nourishing, maternal power.

What needs to be emphasized, however, is the overdetermined nature of all the rhetoric of the maternal that we have seen so far. Indeed, *Summer* was particularly convincing as an image of nation because it combined gaps, distortions, and absences within an overall pleasurable design. The painting set up expectations of pleasure and abundance and mimicked the maternal embrace in its sensual address. It reinforced those associations through its subject matter. But it also withdrew that comfort in its deployment of figures, which disturbed conventional viewing patterns. It asked its viewers to react to both the pleasures and the disturbances on the level of feeling. It demanded that its viewers submit to the sensual pleasures of the design, that they identify with the stretches and pulls of the bodies on display, and that they compensate for the bodily distortion of Puvis's figures through their own imagination. The disturbing qualities of the painting played dialectically off of its pleasurable aspects to set up a desire for a plenitude that could never quite be achieved. That plenitude was literalized by Puvis in the middle ground and in the distant landscape and through these elements was implied to be a property of France itself. And it was this France that viewers were encouraged to desire. If Calonne and others made clear the extent to which the insufficiencies of the painting called for imaginative compensation on the part of its viewers, in describing the painting they also gave examples of such compensation. The descriptions are of the painting as a dream—as Fourcaud put it, a "dreamed reality"—a "reality" dreamed by the critics themselves. But they did not dream it without the guidance of Puvis, who set the parameters of their dreams through a careful choice of subject matter.

The depth and poignancy of the response to *Summer* could never have been evoked if this subject matter had been more overt—if, for example, we had been given one big nursing mother on a pedestal formed by a haycart in the foreground. Such explicitness would have turned the experience of *Summer* into the kind of intellectual decoding game that viewers expected from decorative painting cycles, with their allegories and narratives. Instead, the disjunctions, the gaps in meaning, induced the flights of imagination that gave the painting its power, that prompted in its viewers a desire to be cradled by Mother France. Puvis did not tell his viewers, "You belong to France." He inspired in them a feeling of desire for Mother France. Describing his style, Alphonse Germain, the critic who was convinced that the artist's "thusness" would be responsible for making French art "national again," chose the term "the indecipherable" (*l'indéchiffrable*) to describe Puvis's style: "He enigmatizes so perfectly . . . that no one performing pictorial exegesis would know how to fathom it."[30] Puvis's painterly style was itself representative of France's style of national imagining, an imagination dependent on forgetting and guided by the desire to recapture what had been lost.

THE POLITICS OF PLENITUDE

I have been arguing that *Summer* evoked—in both its form and its subject matter—the desire for pleasures and comforts retrospectively fantasized as having existed in infancy. And because *Summer* was universally assumed to be an image of France, the painting aligned the maternal with the national. It is worth noting that Puvis painted a reduced version of *Summer* meant for private sale and consumption. In this market-oriented canvas, Puvis eliminated the cutout door and, more significantly, left out the elements that made the analogy between nation and mother most explicit—the harvesters and the mother suckling her child (fig. 46). The reduced version centered on the three female figures, and because it no longer aimed to promote national solidarity, its fantasmatic power was limited to inducing individual fantasies of femininity.[31] The contrast between the two versions of *Summer* suggests that Puvis was well aware of the links to be made between maternal imagery and national sentiment. During the period when the mural was painted and exhibited, France was at the height of a nationalist, pro-natalist campaign meant to address fears about France's falling population.[32] Maternity and national sentiment were being linked across the cultural sphere.

The background of the mural, with its inclusion of a nursing mother and rich fields, is explicitly figured as a site where France placidly renders up its bounty to its human population, both the fruits of the breast and the fruits of the earth. But

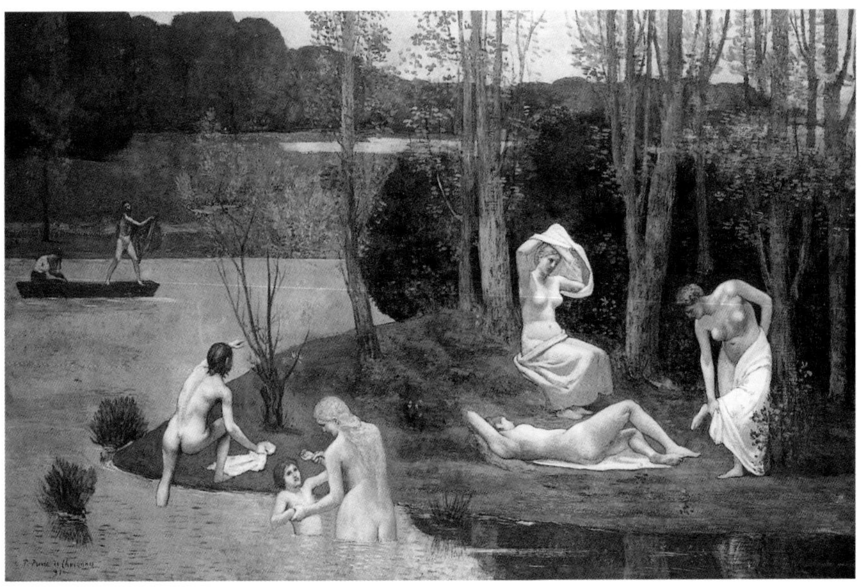

46
Pierre Puvis de Chavannes, *Summer*, 1891. Oil on canvas, 59 x 91½ in. (149.8 x 232.5 cm). Cleveland Museum of Art, Gift of Mr. and Mrs. J. H. Wade

here its explicitness ends. Rather than representing an immediately available bounty, it seems to represent a past that might be regained or a future that might be attained. Puvis, I am arguing, had found a way not to picture plenitude but to hint at it just enough to provoke the viewer's desire for it.[33] In *Summer*, a feeling of what plenitude might be like is provided by the pleasurable form of the picture. This feeling was meant, in Guyau's phrase, to "unite [viewers] in the same pleasure." But, as we have seen, the painting offered a feeling of pleasure through its decorative harmony only to disturb it with inexplicable bodies and unclear meanings. These disturbances set up a desire for the pleasures initially promised. Pleasure and desire were intermixed. Ultimately, the painting provoked a common desire for plenitude: a desire for the mother was recast as a desire for the motherland.

Although virtually all the critics who wrote about *Summer* thought that the painting pictured an ideal France, the consensus ended there. In the charged political situation of the 1890s, no one could agree on an ideal of France. Puvis's mural allowed for great variation in images of both mother and nation—the images in the painting were open to a wide range of maternal and national fantasies. The evocativeness and inexplicitness of the painting were therefore the key to its power.

Given that *Summer* was a republican commission, it is hardly surprising that responses to the painting from republican critics disavowed its compositional disjunctions. Often the vision of plenitude on offer in *Summer* was linked to the classical origins of France. The degree and kind of classical heritage pictured in *Summer* became one issue around which debates over the ideal nature of France crystallized. In the 1890s classicism came to signify much more than a painterly or literary style. It became a politically embattled category, appropriated (like nationalism) by a variety of groups on the Right even while republicans tried to reclaim it and transmute its meanings back to their own purposes.[34] In the minds of most French citizens, especially educated males, there was no contradiction in evoking both Virgil and Poussin as part of the French tradition. Particularly for those on the Right, defining a classical lineage for the French race was both a defense of tradition and part of an exclusionary strategy with both racialist and specifically anti-Semitic aims. Writing for *Gil Blas*, the critic René Maizeroy described *Summer* as a dream of antiquity, a "calm landscape from the eclogues" peopled with "young, white, blond women."[35] Maizeroy's description of a *race blonde* smacks of the kind of rhetoric that became prevalent on the Right a few years later, especially as the Dreyfus Affair polarized the population around issues of the "French race."

As classicism began to be claimed by the Right in the 1890s, it became even more important for the Republic to stake its claim to define this aspect of the

French heritage. As the numerous examples of classical subject matter in the Hôtel de Ville make clear, the state still wanted to promote its possession of the classical legacy. Thus several critics writing for solidly republican journals promoted the ancient roots of French civilization. In *Le Rappel*, Charles Frémine was explicit about this transposition of the classical pastoral to the French countryside. Frémine described Puvis's painting as an evocation of all of the classical heritage at once. It transported viewers "into the Serena temples that Lucrèce spoke of." It was a "Virgilian dream" that reminded viewers of the places where archaeological traces of France's classical heritage remained, in Lyons, on the banks of the Saône. This area of France was conflated with the banks of the Seine in Paris, and the poplar trees scattered around France were "poplars from Italy." The women pictured by Puvis were likened to the sculptures of Phidias. The landscape of *Summer* was a timeless one in which all the classical aspects of France were integrated. For Frémine this timelessness was allegorized by the chariot–hay cart, which was "both ancient and modern and which traverse[d] the ages while conserving its simple rustic structure."[36] Clearly, for Frémine, the idealized French landscape par excellence was the French landscape reduced to its classical essence. The essential France was rural and classical.

André Michel's account of Puvis's painting was perhaps the most explicit example of the need for republicans to negotiate the difficulties posed by classicism in the 1890s. In his article for the *Journal des Débats*, he had two related goals. First, he wanted to dissociate Puvis from Symbolist painters, whom he thought were too elitist with their dabblings in obscurantism and mysticism. Although Puvis was born near Lyons, his family had its roots elsewhere. Puvis's painterly mode derived more from his Burgundian rationality than from Lyonnais mysticism. "Beneath the Lyonnais dreamer," there was "a healthy and eloquent Frenchman who followed in the tradition of Buffon, Edgard Quinet, and Lamartine," all of them members of a republican pantheon of great minds.[37] Second, Michel wanted to align Puvis with a particularly French tradition of painting. He traced a lineage from Poussin through Corot and Millet to Puvis. Michel offered a definition of French classicism derived from Poussin's letters. Michel cited passages in which Poussin described the rationality and measuredness, the moderation and determined order, of his practice.[38] Michel linked this to Poussin's strategy for provoking feelings in his viewers tied to those represented by the bodies of his figures. Thus, claimed Michel, taking a line of argument that (somewhat ironically) had parallels to Brunetière's criticism of Symbolist poetry, what the Symbolists conceived in obscure terms and they thought they had invented was really what the classicists had been doing all along: "If Symbolism is, in effect, only a renewed form of a very old desire to note or arouse a mysterious correspondence between certain states of mind or imagination and the inert matter of our works, between our thought and our dreams and inanimate nature . . . couldn't one say that the classical landscape, as it was understood by Poussin in his admirable bacchanals, is the symbolic work par excellence, and if we look a little closer, isn't there continuity between Poussin and Puvis de Chavannes?"[39]

By making this claim, Michel was trying to rescue Puvis from associations with Symbolist mysticism and align him with the rationalism of a classical tradition in tune with republican positivism. The classical tradition was rational, he implied by using the bacchanals as his example, even when picturing or analyzing the passions. Puvis did address the passions, but he was not a Symbolist painter. He was, rather, a classicist in the tradition of Poussin. Michel (and Brunetière, for that matter) had a point in making their critiques of Symbolist claims to a completely innovative project. Yet Poussin's description of his own classicism has a tone of extreme confidence that the passions he pictured in his figures would be directly passed on to the viewer. Poussin's was a description of the academic paradigm, where the narrative order of the composition and the gestures and expressions of the figures were meant to be legible and to direct the viewer's experience of the painting straightforwardly. This was not the way Puvis's paintings operated.

Michel wanted to apply Poussin's rational mode to Puvis's painting. Thus, when he tried to cast *Summer* as an example of the classical French landscape, his description seemed inadequate to the painting. *Summer* was, he said, a "classical landscape, which is to say, true to the tendency toward plastic synthesis and studying in all things their most general expression and most comprehensive signs." Puvis's aim was to use form and color "to sum up . . . the essential character of the hot season."[40] In this description, Michel left out the disjunctive and dreamlike aspects of Puvis's painting and emphasized "plastic synthesis" beyond all accuracy. He disavowed the ambiguities of the painting, describing it instead as "concerted." What he failed to understand was that the power of *Summer* came from the feeling of overall harmony combined with the experience of dissonance.

Michel, like Frémine, made Puvis's landscape into a vision that was ideal, timeless, and essential. It was not representative of summer in any particular site, but of "summer in itself, absolute and eternal."[41] Despite Michel's refusal to link the landscape to a particular locale within France, he clearly saw it as representing an ideal of France. Both the subject matter and the structure of the painting were, for Michel, quintessentially and classically French: "Because of the rhythm and the eloquent and simple ordering of lines, the powerful and gentle resonances of broadly juxtaposed tonality, this is an admirable piece of natural architecture, and at the same time, it is the most intense expression and plastic exaltation of the ardors, fecundities, and splendors of Messidor."[42] Messidor is the summer month of the republican calendar.

In this passage Michel marked out a particular definition of French classicism, one that was first and foremost a republican one. We are not given just any summer, but a bounteous republican summer. Even this fecundity had a rational order, a "rhythm," and a "natural architecture." Michel thus described Puvis's image of France as the direct result of the republican values of reason, liberty, equality, and fraternity—the values that the republicans claimed had been initiated in the French Revolution and now sustained the Republic. Ironically, despite Michel's best efforts to emphasize the classicism of *Summer*, the sense of fraternity in this ideal republic was to be achieved through the seduction of dream: viewers would be enticed into an experience that conjured modes of subjectivity more commonly associated with the "feminine."

The socialist critic Gustave Geffroy described the painting in terms that even more explicitly evoked the themes of dream, plenitude, desire, and the maternal body. But these added up to something quite different from Michel's republican vision. Geffroy began with a description of the three female figures in the foreground and emphasized the way their bodily positions were meant to harmonize with the design of the landscape: "These are large and strong creatures, quickly indicated and summarily modeled, conceived, above all, with sights set on achieving harmony between the positions of figures, their fleshtones, and the landscape that unfolds behind them and on celebrating summer by showing the wholesome joy of their damp bodies and their calm countenances."[43] The sense of bodily well-being that Geffroy attributed to these figures, a sense with which he believed the viewer would empathize, was, he thought, encoded into the picture by the overall compositional harmony among bodies and between the bodies and nature. This harmony resulted from Puvis's summary mode of depiction. Even more than the female figures, the landscape, with its gently curved blue river and encompassing bands of green and gold intersected by vertical gray poplars, enticed the viewer to participate in the pleasures of summer. Geffroy, like Fourcaud, described the painting as a series of interlocking color planes over which the eye, like the pictured river, could wander at ease.

At the center of this pleasurable space Geffroy identified an unexpected element of darkness and shadow, whose meaning was inaccessible to the viewer: "And look, at the height of this beautiful cultivated slope, in the midst of these fields, beyond the light bushes, under the profound and luminous sky, which is penetrated by the sun's ardor, here is an impenetrable clump of a hundred trees, dark, hoary, opaque, standing at the center of this lightness and fluidity of air. All the shadows of the valley are gathered there, in the interstices of the leaves, which are like the clefts and crevices in the rocks at ground level, surrounding enormous stocky trunks full of low branches."[44] It was as if Puvis had separated out all the threatening aspects of nature and relegated them to the mass of trees.[45] The beneficent space thereby created in the rest of the painting allowed for nothing other than a sense of well-being. This orchestration of pleasure around the central block of trees constituted, for Geffroy, the main activity of the painting. Nature, rather than humanity, became the protagonist of this drama because, aside from the constant reminder of the unknown and of mortality that loomed in the trees, there was no distinction to be made between people and other living beings: "Here and there, human activity is visible. On the water, a boat passes, a woman seated in the front, a man standing behind her throwing a net. A woman takes shelter with a child in the shadow of the willows. Workers come and go around a cart of grasses. All of this is scattered, lost in the landscape; people meld halfway with things, living beings are tinted with the pink and green reflections of the light and soil. It is the life of one day that flutters and unfolds around this formidable mass of trees, so ancient in appearance, so fierce, so overwhelming, so constant, that one could believe them without end, immutable and eternal."[46] The painting, Geffroy suggested, spoke of a dream of unity between human being and nature, of a disintegration of boundaries between subject and object. Puvis's figures blend into the rest of the landscape "tinted with the pink and green reflections of light and soil." Geffroy read this disintegration of boundaries as a metaphor for complete harmony. Such a melding of one being with another is, of course, one aspect of a fantasy of the maternal—of the moment before distinctions between self and world have been firmly established. But in Geffroy's description people meld only "halfway" with things. Rather than fantasizing a return to complete coalescence with Mother Nature, Geffroy imagines a space where human subjectivity can remain separate but harmonious.

Geffroy recognized that this image of utopian unity with all beings and things was only a beautiful dream. But the melancholy poeticism of his rhetoric makes clear how powerfully *Summer* asked him to imagine such a dream as the possible future of France: "It is beautiful to fix thus the surroundings in which we live, the surroundings in which we manifest our vain desire for happiness, the mysterious dream of our destiny, which has no possible explanation. Things are expressive and speak to us. We know what bonds unite us to everything that surrounds us . . . and our spiritual fellow-feeling and our joy and our melancholy all gravitate toward those aspects of matter that existed before us, that will exist after us. This is the highest purpose of . . . the poetry of *Summer* by Puvis de Chavannes. The artist knows how to make the clouds, the waters, the fields, the trees, speak to us—all this unconscious nature in which we take refuge as we would with an accomplice or a friend."[47]

This passage is characterized by longing. It describes the French landscape as a vehicle for social unity and a spiritual bond among the French. But it also admits that the place where "we know what bonds unite us to everything that surrounds us" is only a product of Puvis's production of an imaginary site. In *Summer*, an evocative vision of nature acts as the catalyst for fantasies of unity and wholeness, of a space beyond time and division. In Puvis's painting, nature takes on characteristics of maternal fantasy—it becomes a preexisting and all-powerful form of materiality that provides a sheltering and beneficent home. The French landscape is described as both a physical and emotional refuge, and the collective fantasy of it as the means by which a socialist ideal will be achieved.

The political implications of Geffroy's account of *Summer* were made even clearer in an essay published in 1892, when the mural was inaugurated as part of the decorative scheme of the Hôtel de Ville. The painting represented, Geffroy suggested, not an idealized memory of France but a contemporary vision of a future ideal. *Summer* encouraged its viewers to imagine a vision of "the future of today's man." It pictured the goal toward which past struggles had tended in a building that was a site of those struggles: "here, in the heart of Paris, in this Hôtel de Ville reconstructed on ruins, after so much fire and so much blood, in the full and visible social evolution of today." Puvis, he suggested, had been able to "translate our upheavals into images of restless beauty" and to represent "the desire for justice that one senses trembling in the new masses, the philosophical equity of the enlightened," through an image of "the unconsciousness of nature, eternal scenery of all our sentiments and passions."[48] *Summer* was, for Geffroy, both a spur to envision and a utopian vision of France that partook of socialist values.

The Vicomte de Vogüé provided a very different interpretation of the kind of landscape pictured in *Summer*. Unlike the royalist Calonne, a narrow-minded and predictable academic critic, Vogüé was one of those paradoxical figures of the 1890s (like Germain and Denis) who wed modernist aesthetics to neo-Christian conservatism.[49] Of all the critical voices who addressed *Summer*, the Vicomte de Vogüé offered the most poignant and imaginative account of the painting. His essay "Before Summer" ("Devant l'Eté") became a touchstone for discussions of Puvis's work in the 1890s because it encapsulated and gave power to the whole cluster of issues that surrounded Puvis's oeuvre. According to Vogüé, *Summer* offered an image of neither the republicanism of the day nor a socialist utopia. *Summer* was not, as Geffroy had implied, the picture of the outskirts of Paris. Instead, said Vogüé, "it is far from Paris . . . the true countryside where we grew up when one lived as one should live"—the countryside bound up with Vogüé's childhood memories.[50] The painting, he thought, would evoke in its viewers a memory of the "true" nature of France, characterized by the social hierarchy of a pre-Revolutionary feudal order. And this memory would contrast sharply with the conditions of modernity. Vogüé was one of the many figures on the Right who rejected the French Revolution and the secular values derived from the Declaration of the Rights of Man that went with it. As we saw in the previous chapter, he, like many on the Right, thought France should return to pre-Revolutionary values and morality. *Summer*, he thought, had the power to facilitate such a political transformation.

Vogüé's account of *Summer* is particularly interesting for our purposes because it makes so explicit the way the painting elicited individual and national fantasies of origins that overlapped with a more general symbolism of France as mother: "Of this maternal land men are born: ancient and simple creatures who have elevated the life of these waters, these fields and these woods to the human level without perverting it. They work, but their work evokes the idea of neither loss nor profit; it is a rite, a communion with the Mother."[51] In this passage, Vogüé imagines Puvis to have painted a landscape in which nature and mother are synonymous and man's ritual cultivation of nature is both a transformation and elevation of her and a form of communion. Rural labor is pictured not as work but as an innate and inevitable activity. *Summer* thus elicited from Vogüé a fantasy of the "true" nature of France rooted in his own aristocratic past. His characterization of rural labor as a natural activity was surely meant as a critique of the development of a modern industrial economy. By suggesting that the landscape showed a return to origins, he imagined *Summer* to evoke a nostalgic "memory" of a social order that had disappeared—the feudal hierarchy of which he, as an aristocrat, was a remnant.[52]

At the outset Vogüé valued the mural as an escape from the turmoil of modernity—an escape that worked on the level of feeling. This escape, Vogüé implied, depended on Puvis's use of a modernist formal mode. He pointed to the inappropriateness of both Calonne's criticisms of Puvis's incorrect drawing and Michel's rational, analytic approach to the mural. Instead, he argued, one must allow oneself to be taken in by the depiction of a dream: "They say that there are drawing faults, flaccidity, and indecision in the contours. That is quite possible; I know nothing of it, not having approached the issue myself. Do they need to draw so near to the painting, with their magnifying glass, their compass, their bag of critical instruments, in order to tear open the dream?"[53] Vogüé assumed from the start that this painting was addressed to the unconscious mind, not the the rational mind, which meant that it required a qualitatively different kind of critical attention. He encouraged a mode of viewing that would allow the painting to evoke desire: "One must regard M. Puvis de Chavannes's promised land from a distance; it is necessary to stop thirty steps away, even better, forty, to forget the world around you, which has the crazy pretension of being the real world, and to let the indescribable serenity that permeates the painting penetrate your eyes, descend into your soul, and insinuate itself throughout your whole being."[54] In this passage, Vogüé describes a slow insinuation of desire as the viewer is teased with "la terre promise"—a land promised but not given. From the beginning, then, Vogüé assumed a relationship between viewer and mural that was intuitive rather than rational. In his essay the viewer is first imagined as a passive recipient of a sensation that penetrates and insinuates itself.

Although Vogüé described the sensation proffered by *Summer* as serenity, his language hinges on a metaphor of desire. For example, he recounted the relationship between the viewer and the three female figures in the right foreground thus: "We love them, these anonymous daughters of the Earth, because they are complacent and available forms through which each of us gives body to the ideas, the feelings, the memories, that people these fields for us. They are our lost and our dead, those who rise from the lands we have traveled, reminding us of the parts of life that are already lost to us. Because each of us is left piecemeal in many tombs, there will be very little left to put in the one that carries our name, the one we think will enclose us whole."[55] The "anonymous" bodies of the three female figures in the foreground do not direct the viewer to particular meanings. Instead, their very lack of definition both evokes desire and makes them "complacent"—"available" to individual fantasies. They become spaces where "the ideas, the feelings, the memories" of viewers can be "given body," where the "lost" and the "dead" are conjured, made once again to "people th[e] fields" of the memory and fantasy that structure subjectivity. They become, that is to say, screens for the projection of individual fantasies of plenitude. Yet the "reality" that must be covered over by such fantasies, the reality that the indeterminacy of the women's bodies (and the mural as a whole) represents, Vogüé suggested, is that subjectivity itself is "piecemeal," shot through with desire, division, and loss.

As the passage continues, Vogüé imagines himself standing before *Summer* and, in the space of a dream, trying to fulfill the desire for plenitude provoked by the painting: "We must stay here tonight . . . just as *Summer* must be beautiful when the moon rises from behind the forest. And the moon will surely come. . . . By its light, these women will appear harmonious. Perhaps, during the time when the night liberates these immobile forms, the nebulous site will become a remembered site, the anonymous images will become those we have summoned. Why must it end so soon?"[56] This account of the experience of standing before *Summer* alludes, I think, to the shadowy and distorted forms of the women's bodies and to the way bodily disjunctions provoke in viewers a desire for harmony. Vogüé gives an account of his own attempts to compensate in his imagination for the indistinct, distorted, and ungainly aspects of the women. Furthermore, he suggests that the processes of imagination provoked by the bodies call on his own memories of harmony, memories that are nonetheless inaccessible and difficult to conjure. This fantasy of harmony, it is implied, calls on primordial memories of the female body and is thus related to Vogüé's description of the painting as a return to origins. In the dreams spurred by *Summer*, suggests Vogüé, each viewer will summon particular memories from the nebulous and anonymous images, will attempt momentarily to regain all that is lost: an impossible task. And Vogüé's language, with its constant repetition of what "must be," turns to a desperate pleading. His fantasy of plenitude is shattered by his final question: "Why must it end so soon?"

Vogüé elaborated on the kind of viewing Puvis's modernist formal mode required through a parable in which he allegorized the relationships of viewers to the fantasies of plenitude provoked by *Summer*. He imagined a deluded king seeking to allay the disjunction between the contemporary world and the landscape offered by the painting:

> If I were king of Bavaria, I would have the useless frames that distract attention removed. . . . If I were king of Bavaria, I would have poetry harmonious with the work of the painter engraved on the panel surrounding *Summer*; the verse of Homer in beautiful purple Greek letters; . . . in letters of azure, the verse of Virgil; in letters of gold, the great, calm verse of Leconte de Lisle. . . . If I were king of Bavaria, I would place an invisible orchestra, which would play the *Symphonie Pastorale*, in the neighboring room; and every day, after council, I would come here to forget the foolishness my ministers had recounted to me, I would come here to forget all that a king must suffer when he thinks of the evil his subjects do.—If I were queen of Bavaria, I would pierce this canvas in order to see the horizons that it predicts by way of those it shows; I would shatter the illusion and I would find the wall, the wall that one always finds, the wall that is behind everything.[57]

Three times Vogüé's musings begin with the line "If I were king of Bavaria," and the repeated "if" both emphasizes the impossibility of his wishes and sets up an expectation of repetition. Thus when, in the fourth proposal, Vogüé shifts to "If I were queen of Bavaria," the change shatters the illusion through which the reader had followed Vogüé, just as the queen's tearing of the canvas has shattered the king's fantasy. The king's embellishment of the mural allegorizes the viewer's own relation to the mural, suggesting that the possibilities of plenitude offered by *Summer* depend on the viewer's imaginative compensation. And when the queen shatters the king's fantasy, the parable reminds us of the desire for plenitude that emerges for viewers of *Summer* as the disturbing qualities of the female bodies in the right foreground become more and more evident. It reminds us, that is, of the experience that provoked Vogüé's question: "Why must it end so soon?"

The meanings suggested by the parable are multiple, and they point us to some of the deepest implications of *Summer* and of Puvis's painterly mode in general. Only a king, with the ability to embellish a situation according to his whims, could fail to be aware of the contrast between the images offered by the mural and the contemporary political situation. Only a mad king blinded by his own compensatory fantasies could fail to be disturbed by the disjunctions between elements in the mural. If *Summer* is, for the king, a complete escape from contemporary events, it is only at the price of his own madness. The "truth" about the painting, from Vogüé's point of view, lies in the way it both offers and denies images of plenitude: through the distant vision of France's idealized past and then in the distorted images of the female body. Taken together, these add up to a desire for a return to origins in which individual and national fantasy occur simultaneously. The mural provoked these fantasies, Vogüé suggests, in order to instill a desire for a particular vision of the future of France—for a vision of France as a land of plenitude characterized by feudal hierarchy and an agrarian economy. If this image of France was to be effective, the viewers would have to experience the plenitude depicted as already lost—lost, but perhaps attainable once again.

As we have seen, the sense of plenitude that the painting offered was also withdrawn in several ways: by the disjunctive composition, by the disturbing female bodies, and by the relegation of the nursing mother and reapers to the middle ground and background. The key to the power of the painting came, Vogüé suggested, from the ways it asked its viewer to compensate in fantasy for those lacks. *Summer* did not incite a superficial desire for a feudal past merely by picturing it. Rather, the painting instilled that desire at the deepest levels of subjectivity by making viewers actively participate in their own fantasies of plenitude. Thus, if *Summer* could, as Vogüé stated, actually "predict [horizons] by way of those it shows," it did this by channeling primary and individual fantasies of plenitude toward particular political ends, by aligning those fantasies of the maternal with fantasies of France as a feudal hierarchy.

The desire instilled by the painting, Vogüé implied, would lead to social action, for, even as *Summer* instilled a sense of loss, it offered a particular vision—of rural, pastoral, feudal France as the site of plenitude—that would be an antidote to that loss. Vogüé spoke directly of the power of the painting to use this fantasy to interpellate different kinds of individuals. The king of Bavaria's fantasy was male and aristocratic. So was Vogüé's. And *Summer* offered the aristocrat an image of "the work the richest in memories of childhood joys"—it offered, that is to say, a detached and mythologized vision of the harvesters in the fields whom Vogüé had watched from a distance as a child on a country estate. However, Vogüé believed that the mural would address urban workers just as readily as aristocratic lords. Urban workers, whom Vogüé called "children of the field, suffocated by Parisian factories," would also long for their origins as they stood before *Summer*. "I truly believe," said the critic, "that they will stop before *Summer* as they stop to hear a country song; their lungs will breathe in a gust of native air; they will find what they seek each Sunday at the gates of the city, a little communication with the earth from which they were torn. For them, too, there is peace and recollection in this evocation of origins." This ability to stir a desire for common origins in individuals of different classes and from different regions was, said Vogüé, what made *Summer* the best, perhaps the only, example of "democratic painting."[58]

If *Summer* evoked a common desire for the "true" France, it was able to do so by mining fantasies of the maternal that were common to all, but with infinite variations. Thus, Vogüé described the painting itself as a mother and the experience of viewing it as a moment of desire that taught a moral lesson about the present: "Eternal and indifferent, she [*Summer*] will see the passing, like the harvested hay, of her daily masters; she will suckle them all with the same indulgence, because they are all her children. . . . She will teach them, in addition, truth and piety; she will tell them always that there must be a God to create a beauty such as herself. . . . A station before *Summer* in the morning, that is the best cordial for recharging one's life with obedience."[59]

Summer taught its moral lesson, Vogüé implied, not by presenting legible allegories of universal values (the old academic paradigm) but by making its audience feel a common desire for maternal plenitude and by connecting that feeling to the feudal hierarchy, which he believed was pictured. Ironically, then, this neo-Christian conservative proposed the same means of ideological manipulation though art that the republican theorists Fouillée and Guyau had imagined. *Summer* was, Vogüé said, "like a landscape of last judgment" on the political and social situation of modern France—on the stark divisions between Right and Left that characterized the 1880s and 1890s and on the instability of a political situation recently threatened by Boulanger's near toppling of the government—a landscape that would make its viewers long for the stability of the past. The experience of the painting would be not only a political but a moral balm.

We might ask, however, whether there were limits to the viewing public whom Vogüé imagined to be addressed by the painting. If the efficacy of the painting was determined by an overlap between memories of the maternal and memories of France's past, what place did Vogüé think it could offer to citizens whom he did not consider authentically French—to Jews, to recent immigrants, to colonial subjects? Could the fantasy of the maternal on which the painting hinged operate in the same manner for women as it did for men? Another way to pose this question would be to examine the role of the queen in Vogüé's parable. It is, after all, the queen who shatters the king's illusion. Unlike the king, she does not participate in the fabrication of the fantasy. Yet the reasons for this are left ambiguous. On one reading, we might imagine that the queen pierces through the illusion of *Summer* not because she believes it to be an illusion but because she is so duped by it. We would then imagine the queen looking at the mural as she would look at a window onto an enchanted world, accidentally tearing the mural as she tried to enter that world. In this case, the queen would neither understand nor participate in the processes of signification that the king, even in his madness, can attempt to control. On this reading, only the king has mastery of the production of fantasy, whereas the queen is simply in the fantasy.

We could also interpret Vogüé to imply that the "horizon" suggested by the painting is, because of its decorative flatness, the wall. On this reading, the king would seem to be not the controller of representation but the slave to his own fantasy and to his belief in representation without lack. Here the king would occupy the position of a human subject fooled into believing in his own autonomy and in the complete transparency of language and representation. Now the queen would appear as a bearer of truth who shatters the king's illusion by showing him what is behind the painting. And if the queen represents someone who understands the truth about the illusion, if she knows what is behind the fantasy, perhaps that is because she understands the gendered codings of subjectivity in French culture. Perhaps she understands that the place assigned to femininity is, in the model of representation that Vogüé outlines, the place of absence, the place of the "anonymous daughters of the Earth," the loss of the "tomb," the blankness of the wall—an absence, a blankness, that allows for the productivity of the "womb." On such a reading, "the wall that is behind everything" is envisioned as the emptiness that underwrites the subjectivity of both men and women and that is masked by male fantasy through the creative activity of the unconscious. Again, the shift to the shattered illusion suggests the explicit coding of the fantasy as a male prerogative, the incessant warding off of an acknowledgment that human subjectivity is divided by representation and temporality: that it is a "reality" of which the queen is already well aware. But where does this leave the queen?—either so fully within the illusion that she cannot manipulate it or so fully aware of what it is masking that the creative process becomes untenable. The queen remains stuck in an impossible double bind.[60]

Unlike his more conservative literary peers, who held on to a notion of representation as transparent and universal, Vogüé gave positive weight to the individual and fantasmatic aspects of representation. In his parable of the king he imagined not two forms of subjectivity (the king and the queen) but three. Remember that his narrative began with the refrain "If I were king of Bavaria." Clearly, Vogüé saw his own subjectivity as distinct from that of both the mad king and the queen. He represented a position in between theirs—the position of the enlightened subject, the male subject who was aware on some level of the piecemeal nature of his subjectivity, of his own efforts to people the fields of memory and fantasy through a projective enterprise that took Puvis's female figures as its starting point. Unlike the king, whose unselfconscious embellishment of fantasy through representation was a sign of his madness, Vogüé imagined himself to be at least partially in control of this process. What he offered was a model of creative subjectivity that embraced the unconscious, memory, and desire and channeled them to creative ends.

The model of creativity that Vogüé described in his response to *Summer* would apply equally well to the poetry of Mallarmé, with its emphasis on the sensual characteristics of words and its cultivation of the void. This should come as no surprise. This model of creativity was part of the wider cultural matrix known as Symbolism. Puvis's *Summer* was, Vogüé claimed, not only the result of such a creative process but a work that would encourage that process in other creative subjects. Thus, the concluding line of the essay earnestly commands: "Symbolists, my friends, hail your master."[61] Vogüé imagined a model of creativity that was quintessentially modern. It depended on a modernist formal mode, and it capitalized on the discovery of the unconscious. In addition, he suggested that the kinds of fantasy enabled by this modernist model of creativity could be harnessed for ideological manipulation.

The critics who responded to Puvis's *Summer* held widely divergent political views. What they all shared, however, was an appreciation for the aspects of Puvis's aesthetics that made him an important early participant in modernism: decorative patterning of color, the refusal of traditional composition, narrative, and allegory, and strange and evocative portrayals of the body. As we have seen, Vogüé, a neo-Christian, took the wide appeal of *Summer* as evidence that feudal hierarchy was the natural and appropriate structure for France. He hoped the fantasies of an ideal past that *Summer* provoked would incite a desire for a return to the feudal order, or at least a new piety in a country dominated by secular republicanism. For Gustave Geffroy, a socialist, *Summer* represented not the feudalism of the past but the socialism of the future. Its popularity was evidence of "the desire for justice that one senses trembling in the new masses."[62] In the extremely polarized political climate of the 1890s, Vogüé and Geffroy could agree on only one thing: the importance and poignancy of *Summer*. Each critic tried to make his own political use of Puvis's modernist formal mode and of *Summer's* invocation of the maternal, and each thought that he had mastered the rhetoric of the painting. Yet the language employed by these critics suggests that *Summer* was working on them, too. That it generated such sustained and passionate longings for the motherhood of France in critics with such opposing views is a testament to the power of its invocation of fantasy.

WINTER'S DUTY

If *Summer* represented an ideal to be worked toward, *Winter* described the community relations that were required when that ideal was far from present (see fig. 43). In *Winter*, much more than in *Summer*, Puvis seems to be inciting the viewer to think about duty. Like *Christian Inspiration*, it offered a vision of duty and asceticism. And it placed that image in a medieval context. In the right corner, a ruin suggests the postclassical era. The costume, too, makes reference to the Middle Ages, particularly in the tunic of the crouching man near the arch and the long headdress of the woman behind him. But other signals, particularly the garb worn by the workmen, make a vague reference to more modern times. This is neither a history painting nor a scene from modern life. The elliptical placing of the scene in time suggests a condensation of moments, which encouraged Puvis's contemporaries to make connections between the moment they inhabited and their heritage. By pairing *Summer* and *Winter*, Puvis was, in a sense, reenvisioning *Ancient Vision* and *Christian Inspiration* for a more politically charged context. If ever Puvis's painting was meant to give a moral message, it was here. André Michel described the painting as having been determined by "moral" as well as "plastic exigencies."[63] Another critic, Léon Roger-Milès, saw the painting as testimony to the moral goodness of human beings. For him, it represented "the serenity of life and the resigned happiness of humanity before the mournful but beneficent spectacle of nature." This particular view of humanity was, he said, quintessentially French. Thus, this painting proved Puvis to be "not just one of the masters of our French school but the master before whom we bow down with respect."[64]

In *Winter* the laborers that were pictured in the distance in *Summer* have migrated to the forests for winter work. The figures depicted in *Winter*—that same "proletariat of the woods" that Millet had pictured at the very moment of their disappearance—no longer carried the specific political implications they had at mid-century.[65] But the association of these figures with a migratory working class was certainly still part of their resonance in the 1890s. If *Winter* represented workers, it was so that they could be made to stand for the necessity of community solidarity in times of hardship.

The ruin frames several figures whose roles most blatantly emblematize community solidarity. Under a stone arch huddles an old man, whom critics often referred to as a "beggar"; he is presumably taking shelter from the cold. To his right a woman holding a child faces a man who holds out a loaf of bread. Most critics described the man as a woodcutter taking a moment from his labors to provide sustenance for those less fortunate than he. One critic described the woman as refusing his charity.[66] Sometimes critics imagined the woman to have begged the bread for the old, crouching man. Others, however, thought the woodcutter was himself a beggar who was being given charity by the female figure.[67] Although there was no consensus on the detail of the narrative, the basic message of the interaction between the two—the distribution of charity in times of want—was clear to all. Slightly closer to the foreground and framed by the figures exchanging bread rests a man on bended knee, warming the feet of a child before a fire. Here we are given another image of the community taking care of its own.

The message of communal responsibility is reinforced by the composition of the picture. In the middle ground a group of three woodcutters pull in unison on a rope that will bring down a tree. Next to that tree another man directs their work. The tree that the workers pull down serves as the compositional pivot of the painting. It is situated at the point where two diagonals intersect: the first runs from the lower left corner through the exchange of bread to the tree; the second moves from the right foreground through the wood gatherers in the right foreground to the tree. Finally, the tree is linked to the three woodcutters both by their concentration upon it and by the line of the rope, which runs up to the top center of the composition and back down through the trunk. The workers' transformation of the tree leads to another series of exchanges around which the community is based. Nature is transformed into fuel and into wages that will buy bread. And these wages are shared by the community of workers. Each of the transactions is performed by men. The only women pictured act as onlookers (the old woman watching the wood carriers) and go-betweens (the woman transferring the bread).

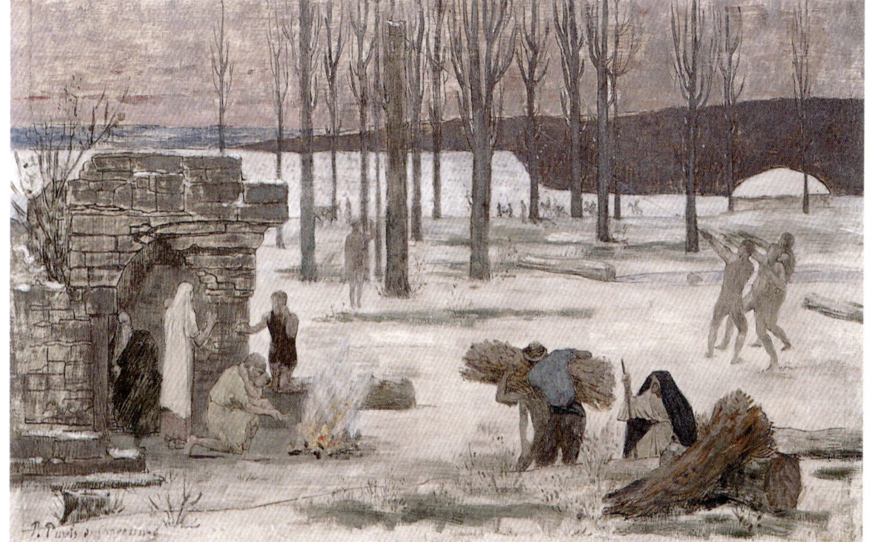

47
Pierre Puvis de Chavannes, *Winter*, 1891–92. Preliminary sketch for mural in the Salon du Zodiaque, Hôtel de Ville, Paris. Oil on canvas, 21 x 33 3/4 in. (53.5 x 85.6 cm). Musée du Pétit Palais, Paris

Critics commonly commented on the desolate atmosphere of *Winter*. The landscape and the trees were barren, they said. The atmosphere was somber and gray. Its color scheme is far more muted than *Summer*'s. Roger Marx described the painting as having "the feeling of cold and sadness everywhere."[68] As in *Poor Fisherman*, nature is pictured as unproductive and dormant, sometimes even hostile. Marcel Fouquier described the plane of canvas that stretched out before him as barren. The sea pictured in the distance in the upper right of the mural was "savage" and "never slept": it was a place where "barques no longer go."[69] With this phrase, the critic referred to the fisherman's barque in *Summer* and suggested not only the possible danger of the sea but the impossibility of harvesting its fish.

In sharp contrast to *Summer*, everything available for warmth or nourishment in *Winter* was provided not by nature, but by human beings' transformation of nature against all odds. Men, in this painting, take the initiative, and transform the harsh environment into a livable social space through integrated, communal work. Here was an image of fraternity analogous to the scene in *Christian Inspiration*, but this time the explicitly religious content was excluded. The man warming the child's feet fits the theme. Roger-Milès described the "crouching father who tenderly warms the feet of his little one."[70] When the "maternal" force of nature has retreated, fathering becomes a necessity. But *Winter* does not appear to be a call to fathers to take over maternal duties, especially when seen in conjunction with *Summer*.[71] Most nineteenth-century men could not have imagined nurturing as a desirable occupation. (Roger Marx thought that the figure warming the child's feet was a woman.) Rather, as in Puvis's *Poor Fisherman*, the message seems to be about the heroism of those fathers who make do when women have forsaken maternal duties—when nature offers not an embracing cradle but a cold wasteland.

When seen together, the heroicization of "maternal" productivity in *Summer* and the lamentation of its lack in *Winter* can be seen to feed into contemporary pro-natalist fervor. Such meanings were particularly appropriate for the Hôtel de Ville—especially when we remember that the resurrection of the building was meant to suture the wounds inflicted by the Franco-Prussian War. After all, the French defeat had for two decades been partially attributed to the decline in the number of French citizens and had provoked a rampant fear of depopulation.[72]

Because Puvis thematized deprivation in *Winter*, the critics could acknowledge Puvis's elliptical composition. Many found that the compositional structure left them unsatisfied and linked this to the theme of the painting. For example, Paul Bluysen praised both the family group on the left and the worker group on the right but complained about "a sort of 'hole'" at the center of the mural "that [was] not filled by the thin silhouettes of denuded trees" or the "minuscule carpenter" who directs the woodcutters. Something was "missing" at the center, and as a result, "the panel becomes hollow and escapes us." He felt that the contrast between *Winter* and *Summer* made clear that *Winter* needed "the frame of serene nature in harmony with the comfort" given by Puvis to his figures.[73] In describing the "gap," he equated the deficiencies in composition, color, and bodily comportment to the general feeling of deprivation that the painting instilled, and contrasted this to the theme of plenitude in *Summer*.

The opposition between *Winter* and *Summer* was more than thematic. It permeated Puvis's compositional choices. In *Summer*, workers were depicted sketchily in the background and thus positioned at a distance from the implied viewer. The viewer was closest to the space of the female figures in the foreground—figures who, if they could be said to belong to a social class, might have belonged to a leisured one. In contrast, all of the foreground figures in *Winter* are manifestly workers. In fact, the class structure of *Summer* has been reversed. Workers dominate the foreground, and hunting aristocrats occupy the distant place that the harvesters took in the first picture (see fig. 42). The moral message of *Winter* was thus conveyed through the noble workers' mutual aid and sacrifice. The community that feeds and supports the poor is a community of workers who also have to combat the perils of hostile nature.

Not surprisingly, for many republican and left critics the main point of *Winter* was the picturing of work. According to René Doumic, critic for *Le Moniteur Universel*, the foreground showed "winter work," with the left side illustrating "the work of indoor life" and the figures on the right displaying "work outdoors."[74] Similarly, Bluysen, writing for *La République Française*, described the foreground scenes as picturing "workers devoting themselves to winter occupations."[75] The critic for the radical republican *La Lanterne* mentioned "men occupied with diverse tasks." He explicitly acknowledged that *Winter*, like *Summer*, pictured the nation, but he also implicitly criticized the idealization of hardship: "Some fell trees, and for this work, despite the snow that covers the earth, they have nude torsos. It is true that this has to do with our ancestors, and that, as everyone knows, they were much stronger than we."[76] He was making a point about the inappropriateness of the male nude in this image. In doing so he also pointed to the danger of classicizing depictions of misery. In addition, his comments exemplify the assumption that *Winter*, like *Summer*, represented a memory of France.

The socialist critic Gustave Geffroy also suggested that the painting might allow its viewers to become complaisant about the misery of their *confrères* in times of hardship. For him, Puvis's mural made winter too innocuous. Geffroy criticized Puvis for failing adequately to depict the harshness of winter: "What we do not see here is a sum of reality that corresponds to this fierce theme of winter that was taken as the subject. The sadness of the harsh season is absent, and also its cold and sparkling sumptuousness. This snow is gray, without contact with the pure light of December frosts—these people and classic groups . . . especially the half-nude men who fell a tree, do not make one think of the rigor of the weather, of the hostile atmosphere, of the brief light of day."[77] Part of the failure came from Puvis's classicizing depiction of the body. He smoothed over the effects of winter's harshness, Geffroy implied, citing the woodcutters, whose exposed bodies were not afflicted by cold.

In addition, Geffroy suggested that the landscape was too beautiful. The experience of pleasure that the viewer would gain from looking at *Winter* would undercut the moral message that Geffroy had hoped the painting would carry. The distant woods and slope extending to the horizon, said Geffroy, "cause the eyes to travel over the expanse that is customary in the works of Puvis de Chavannes. And it is, without a doubt, the depth of beauty in the landscape that makes the principal action in the foreground insufficiently wintry."[78] Geffroy also complained that despite the measured spacing of the figures, there were too many of them in the foreground. Yet this complaint, in the end, had less to do with the compositional structure of the painting than with its ideological effect. Having so many figures grouped together gave the impression of "a happy encampment, of an inalterable security, rather than imposing the poetry of a terrible winter."[79] It was as if, for the socialist Geffroy, the only image of hardship that could have been convincing would have been an image of individual hardship. Perhaps he could not conceive of a cooperative community that involved suffering.

It was not just the figures in the foreground that suggested insufficient hardship. The impression was reinforced by the "heroic line of hunters that appear beyond the large trees, who stand outlined in the procession of a bas-relief. . . . The Greek rhythm found here has the result of rendering this winter fleeting."[80] The "Greek rhythm" of the hunters beyond the trees suggested the fleetingness of the cold because it reminded him of another painting by Puvis. Comparing the hunters to a bas-relief, Geffroy associated them with the figures from the Parthenon—the charging horses in the background of *Ancient Vision* (see figs. 22, 29).

In addition to conjuring up visions of a warmer land, the hunters were rendered so conventionally that they would detract from the viewer's ability to imagine the real effects that cold and deprivation might have had on the pictured bodies. Geffroy called instead for "a vision more bitter with solitude and silence, with a frozen sky and desolate earth—a more absolute winter—with figures less statuesque, better melded with this nature they so narrowly dismiss." His desire for such a landscape came, said Geffroy, despite his "tested admiration" for the "harmoniously pictorial and intellectual work of this great artist, or rather because of this same admiration, which allows for neither partial satisfactions nor reticences."[81] The classicizing aspects of Puvis's depiction of the body and the rhythmic structuring of the landscape meant that rather than speaking of the deprivation of the poor and inspiring the viewer to try to transform the conditions that led to it, the painting mollified the situation of the workers and eternalized it. Geffroy expressed a profound disappointment in the resulting failure of the picture to be morally didactic.

His reaction indicates that at least some critics may have seen *Winter* as a call for social appeasement and the de-radicalization of the working class at the very moment when the Left was gaining strength. In this image, the worker became representative not only of social solidarity and the community but also of resignation and serenity. The worker himself envisioned the imminent dawning of *Summer* represented by the powerful figures in the background. In fact, the background was widely read as an image of the aristocracy at the hunt. Conservative critics remarked on this. Louis de Meurville, writing for the royalist *Gazette de France*, gave the background figures an explicit class interpretation and located the painting in a particular moment: "It is the hunt of the Middle Ages."[82] Just as Michel and Geffroy had done with the charging cavaliers in the background of *Ancient Vision*, René Maizeroy paid more extensive attention to the men at the hunt than their tiny size seemed to merit. He described them as the most important elements of the composition and evoked the figures in the foreground almost as an afterthought.[83]

The republican critic and arts administrator Marius Vachon, on the other hand, understood Puvis's compositional strategy. He thought Puvis had deliberately juxtaposed the workers and the aristocracy to enhance his moral message: "If winter is cruel to those who work outside, to those who have neither bread nor hearth, it has its pleasures for the rich. In the background, at the border of the wood, we see some riders who return from the hunt, pairs of dogs, and the hunters carrying a felled deer on a branch."[84] Viewed from this perspective, the hunters in the background were part of the moralizing quality of the painting. However, there is also a sense in which Vachon's interpretation seems unjustified by the painting itself. The lack of clear narrative and the confusion about the relationships between figures prevented the mural from being overly pedantic. Not for a moment did it offer the moralizing didacticism of some contemporary realist genre scenes. That Vachon tried to give it the kind of overtly didactic reading that Geffroy was unable to justify suggests how much was at stake for Vachon in attributing a moral to *Winter*.

Vachon's secular moral was probably meant to combat the overtly Christian interpretations that many critics gave to the mural. Although the painting included no specific references to Christianity, the vision of deprivation, the generalized placement of the scene in the Middle Ages, and the vision of plenitude in its pendant were enough to align it with *Christian Inspiration* (see fig. 23) in the minds of many critics. Alfred Paulet was one who compared *Winter* to the Lyons painting. He lamented Puvis's failure to paint "beautiful, very well modeled, very graceful, very Greek bodies." Instead, he had depicted bodies that were "shriveled, rather similar to the scanty monks that he showed us in his *Christian Vision*."[85]

Although Paulet, who wrote for a republican paper, was unhappy that Puvis's mural for the Hôtel de Ville reminded him of the Lyons mural, others were delighted. The religious references in some of the responses were intended to recruit Puvis as a promoter of a Christian, rather than a secular, morality—much the way Aman Jean's interpretation of the Sorbonne mural was meant to. Gustave Goetschy compared the method of inspiring piety in its viewers in *Winter* to the effect of organ music in a church service.

> This painting emanates such majesty, such nobility, that it is impossible to stop dreaming of it after one has seen it. These large trees that rise straight and parallel, like the pipes of a calm, deliciously restful organ, sing sweetly in your head, evoking the dreams of a pious and consoling primitive art. . . . Have you noticed, when snow has just fallen, the impressive silence that immediately imposes itself? It comes from a very great, almost religious song . . . nature seems to raise its sheets over its shoulders and slumber while praying. . . . France can be proud of such an artist in a period where everything seems to fall into the most degrading materiality; we must go to him to ennoble ourselves; we must go to him because he elevates our hearts, and in lieu of other things, this is already a great consolation.[86]

Although the critic never overtly compared *Winter* to *Christian Inspiration*, it is clear that he had the parallel in mind. His interpretation of *Winter* seems almost predetermined by that painting. His claims that the painting provoked "dreams of a pious and consoling primitive art" bring to mind descriptions of the Lyons picture. Even though there was no overt religious imagery in the painting, Goetschy made the landscape itself into a protagonist who prayed. He thus described Puvis as source of a spiritual inspiration in a time of materialism and decadence.[87]

In contrast to Goetschy and other conservative critics, republican critics emphasized the success of *Winter* as an image of civic, rather than religious, duty. Writing for the left republican paper *Le Voltaire*, the critic and inspector of fine arts Roger Marx emphasized the appropriateness of the subject matter and style for a site such as the Hôtel de Ville. "No motif could be more accessible" than Winter, "killer of poor people." And "none could be better suited to a *maison commune*." *Winter*, the critic implied, was appropriate to the maison commune both because its subject was an aspect of common experience and because the vision it presented paralleled the function of the building itself. Both painting and building provided a common space for all citizens. Both were meant to facilitate community action. Furthermore, Marx imagined that the rhythms of the landscape and the attenuation of color would "make the viewer's soul serene" and "open it to meditation and dream." Thus, it helped to enhance the "severe architecture of monuments elevated to exalt civic and social duty."[88] Marx's account was a far cry from the conservative description of *Winter* as inspiring Christian piety.

The lengthiest and most elaborate republican response to *Winter* came from André Michel. In his discussion of it, he took much the same route as he had the previous year when treating of *Summer*. Again he used the opportunity to trace a lineage of French classicism from Poussin through Corot and Millet to Puvis. And again he attempted to dissociate Puvis from contemporary academicism, conservatism, and neomysticism. This time, however, he was much more explicit about the enemies he was fighting against.

Michel dissociated Puvis from academicism by proposing that his work was a rejuvenation of the French tradition of classicism. Puvis's painting was "at once very classical and completely outside the banal formulas taught in schools."[89] He believed Puvis was renewing the true French tradition of painting by reinstilling it with "our instinct for clarity and good sense":[90] "The art of Puvis de Chavannes is French art without any foreign impurities, and it is classic art in the best sense of the word.—All the qualities of composition, eloquence . . . and thoughtfulness dear to our genius are found here with this taste for grandeur in which we have always delighted. . . . Over the heads of the Italianizers and the ultramontanes, it gives a helping hand, along with the old masters who founded the French tradition—French and not Latin or Roman—to those who will invent the *opus francigenum*."[91] When discussing *Summer*, Michel was trying to reclaim classicism for the republican cause. In his review of *Winter*, he was even more overt in his attempt to disentangle classicism from associations with the Right—as the final sentence of this passage makes clear. Puvis, he claimed, was bypassing the elitist associations of classicism. His version of classicism was not royalist, not ultramontane. Nor did it have anything to do with those right-wing rhetorics that distinguished between Semitic Frenchmen and those of the "race latine."[92]

Michel also took pains to dissociate Puvis from contemporary neomysticism. This time, he explicitly named Sâr Joséphin Péladan as the leader of the group of neomystics who had recently tried to claim Puvis for their cause.[93] These painters also worshipped the Italian primitives and saw medieval art as a model for their own work. Michel argued that Puvis's quintessentially French classicism was compatible with the state's promotion of the gothic heritage. Both were representative of republican values and the clarity of the French sensibility. "Of all the errors implanted in us since the Renaissance," said Michel, "the most distressing has been to believe . . . that the art of the Middle Ages was nothing but confusion, mystery, and alchemy. . . . M. Joséphin Péladan . . . continues to propagate the idea that all of this old world . . . was a compound of sorcerers, somnambulists, and hallucinating mystics." On the contrary, said Michel, the image makers of the thirteenth century had "clear minds," and their "charming idealism came without the least esotericism." In fact, they mixed with their large figures "many little genre paintings in which one recognizes a populist verve, a familiar bonhomie."[94] In this passage, Michel aligned France's medieval heritage with a classic sensibility and dissociated both medieval painting and Puvis's art from claims of mysticism.

Like Roger Marx, Michel described *Winter* as a painting for the people—a work comprehensible to all: "A plastic work will not be able to touch us by the subtlety of its symbols, by the rarity of its attributes, or by the ingeniousness of its literary allusions. It need be neither a vague abstraction, nor a rebus, nor an enigma, and even less a comedic scene. It must unite the principal characters of the cold season in the simplest action and the most balanced decorative unity. A child would be able to give the scenario: in winter, one is cold; it snows; one cuts wood; one hunts. Let's not look any further than this."[95] This quality of directness and simplicity was, for Michel, characteristic of French classicism. Given Michel's description of Puvis's classicism as a democratic mode of painting, it might at first seem surprising that Michel himself identified a "willed character of indeterminacy" in *Winter*. But for Michel, this quality was to be linked not to esotericism but to a synthesis that was both thematic and formal and that required the details of costume to be held back so that in the painting "we are outside time." More important, said Michel, was that "all the lines, all the forms, the attenuated concert of all the color notes, resolve themselves in a total harmony and a general rhythm that leaves neither the eye nor the mind with any indecision and that penetrates us at the same time as the beauty and the majesty of eternal nature and the sentiments of melancholy and pity invade our hearts in the harsh weather of winter."[96]

According to Michel, then, the message of the painting was put forth not through the details of the figures but through the feeling instilled in the viewer by the formal arrangements of lines and colors. In *Winter*, as in *Summer*, the sensual effect of the painting imparted the meaning of the painting directly to the viewer. To understand it required no special knowledge—perhaps only a French sensibility.

CONCLUSION The Banquet for Puvis de Chavannes	**The idea came from the Right, the Left, the Center, from the Institute, the Napolitain, from the Café de Versailles, frequented by painters who colonized Montparnasse and Plaisance, from the important papers and the small journals, for a banquet for Puvis de Chavannes.** **GUSTAVE KAHN**

In 1895 a banquet was held to honor Puvis de Chavannes on his seventieth birthday. A retrospective exhibition of his work at the Durand-Ruel galleries accompanied the celebration.[1] More than five hundred came to the banquet, filling two rooms at the Hotel Continental. Government officials, artists, and critics gave speeches. The avant-garde journal *La Plume* consecrated a special issue to Puvis, and the Symbolist writers associated with the journal offered Puvis a book of poetry composed for the occasion (fig. 48).[2] The banquet was an occasion to demonstrate approbation for Puvis's oeuvre and to canonize him as France's most important painter. It would not be an exaggeration to claim that by the mid-1880s Puvis de Chavannes seemed to show the best way forward for painting in France.

The Symbolist writer and critic Gustave Kahn described the inception of the banquet in his reminiscences. The event and the discourse generated around it illustrate the widespread appeal that Puvis de Chavannes held for the people of late nineteenth-century France; around him converged, as Kahn's account makes clear, a group of admirers from a broad range of political, ideological, and artistic camps.[3] Describing how much Puvis was admired by the Impressionists, the Neoimpressionists, and "other groups as well," Kahn put the matter plainly: "Puvis was the great painter who divided us the least."[4] But this merging of competing interests inevitably produced tension. If, at the beginning of Kahn's essay describing the banquet, Puvis was a site of convergence, by the end he was a site of contention. A battle arose between supporters of traditional classicism and advocates of modernism, a battle replete with shouting, heckling, and jeers. In the speeches given at the banquet each faction attempted to define Puvis's art on their own terms.

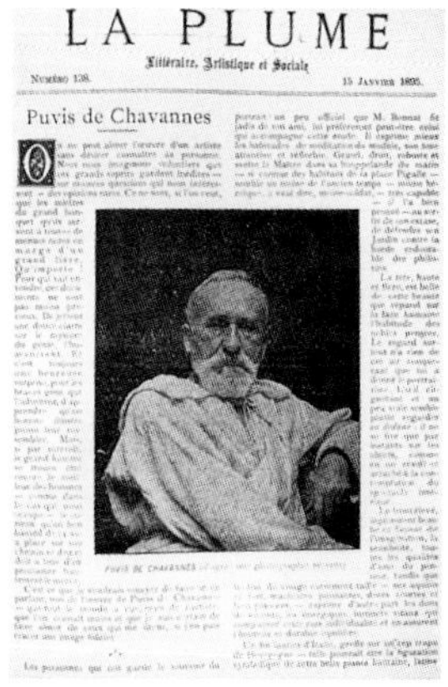
LA PLUME

Littéraire, Artistique et Sociale

Numéro 138. 15 Janvier 1895.

Puvis de Chavannes

48

La Plume, no. 138, January 15, 1895

If the banquet meant to honor Puvis eventually turned into a battle to define his art, this was because Puvis de Chavannes was important to so many different people for so many different reasons. By the 1890s, Puvis did not just offer a future for French national art. He also seemed to show the way forward for young artists trying to imagine where painting might go after Impressionism. As we saw in Chapter 1, Puvis's art offered the possibility of seeing painting as "a flat surface covered in colors arranged in a certain order." His murals and easel paintings focused attention on the sensations caused by the arrangement of lines and colors. Already in the 1880s young artists were captivated by the link that Puvis's paintings proposed between arrangements of line, color, and form and the feelings that those arrangements evoked in viewers, as well as by the links proposed between these feelings and dreams.

A caricature of *The Sacred Grove* (see fig. 11) from the mid-1880s suggests that the attention to feeling in Puvis's painting was in some ways analogous to the Impressionist interest in perception (fig. 49). The title, "La Grenouillère des Muses," connects *The Sacred Grove* to Impressionist renderings of leisure spots.

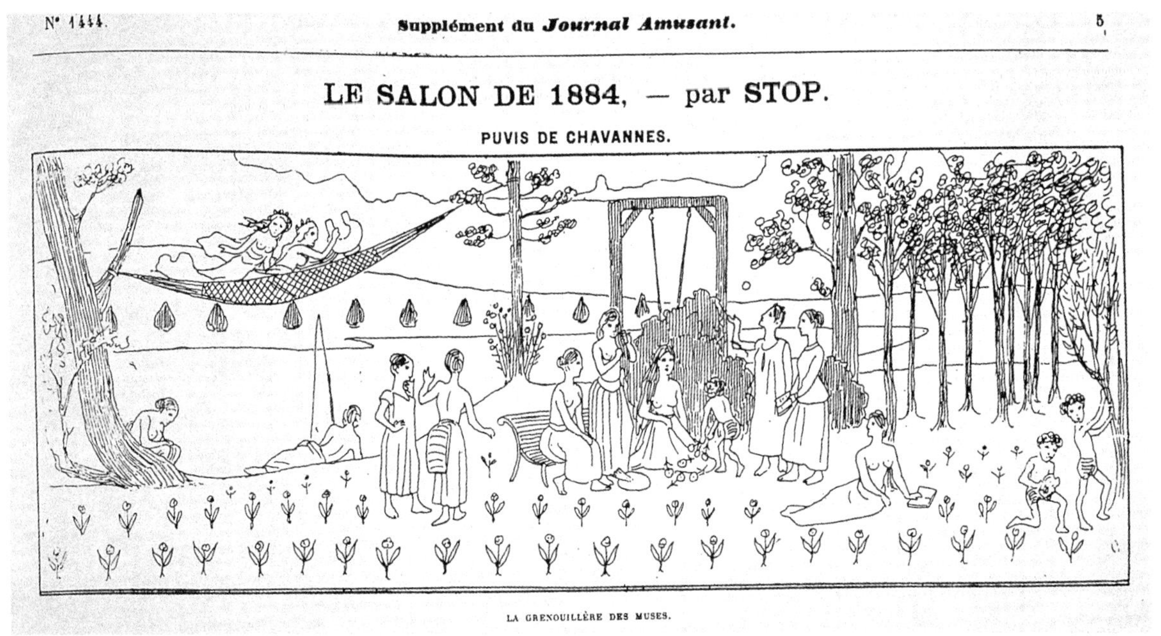

49
Stop, caricature of *The Sacred Grove*, "La Grenouillère des Muses." *Journal Amusant*, May 3, 1884, p. 5

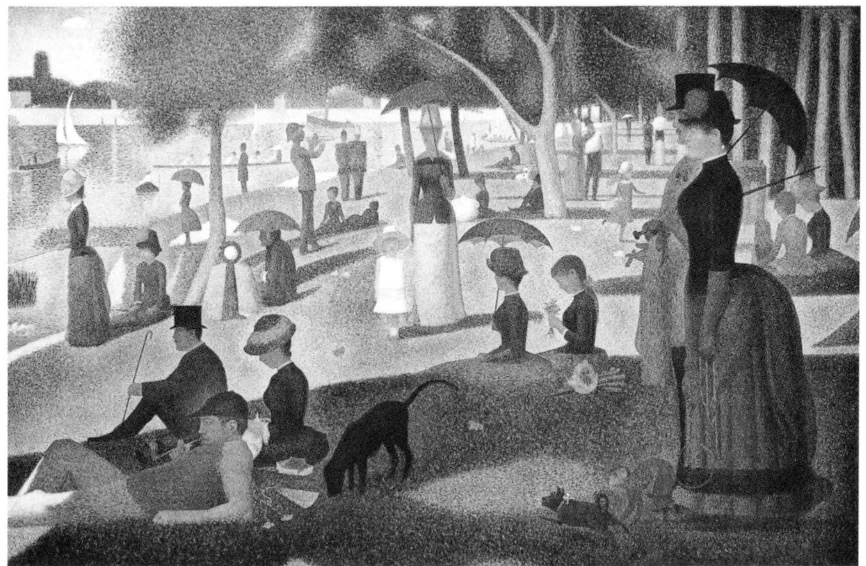

50
Georges Seurat, *Sunday Afternoon on the Island of the Grand Jatte*, 1884–86. Oil on canvas, 81 3/4 x 121 1/3 in. (207.6 x 308 cm). Helen Birch Bartlett Memorial Collection, Art Institute of Chicago

Like Toulouse-Lautrec's parody of the mural, the caricature depends on the differences between Puvis's work and Impressionist painting for its humor (see fig. 15). How silly it would be, the caricature suggests, to imagine that Puvis's painting might be tied to specific places or moments. The caricaturist recognized that Impressionism focused on attempts to capture fleeting and momentary sensory effects on canvas, whereas Puvis de Chavannes's work divorced sensation from its subject matter and from the immediacy of time. Puvis's paintings emphasized the way decorative rhythms of paint might cause sensations in viewers' minds and provoke their imaginations. This shift from the momentary and fleeting to the timeless and perhaps even shareable was one of the things that drew artists attempting to update Impressionism to Puvis's art.

Such certainly seems to have been the case for Georges Seurat, whose *Sunday Afternoon on the Island of the Grand Jatte* (1884–86) bears a striking resemblance not only to Puvis's *Sacred Grove* but to the caricature of it (fig. 50). By regularizing his brushstroke, standardizing color juxtapositions, and simplifying his composition, Seurat attempted to make a painting in which sensation would be shareable. In *Grand Jatte*, he drew directly on Puvis's decorative arrangement of the landscape. He also made use of Puvis's drawing style, as well of his placement of bodies in a rhythm echoing the landscape. The critic Félix Fénéon recognized this

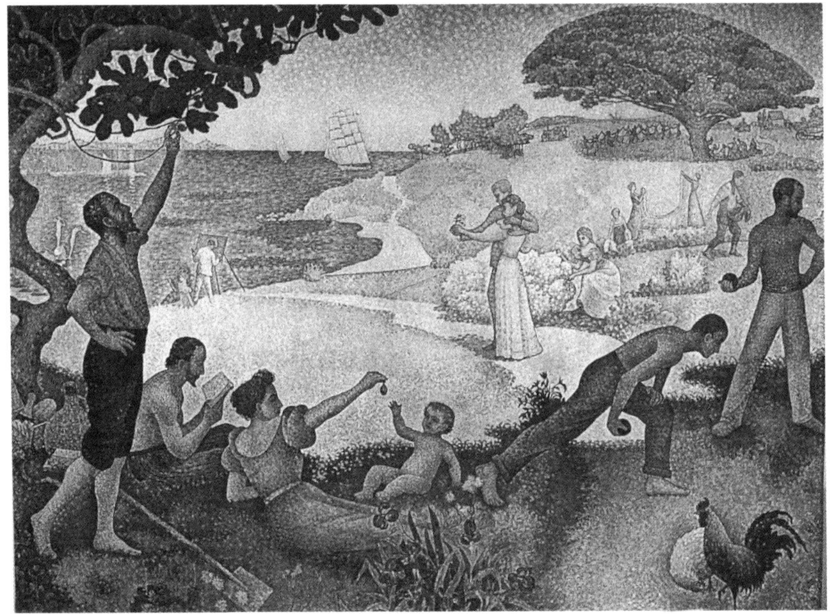

51
Paul Signac,
The Time of Harmony, 1894–95.
Oil on canvas, 9 3/4 x 13 ft.
(3 x 4 m). Mairie du Montreuil

52
Henri Matisse, *Luxe,
Calme et Volupté*, 1904–5.
Oil on canvas,
34 x 45 3/4 in. (86 x 116 cm).
Musée d'Orsay, Paris

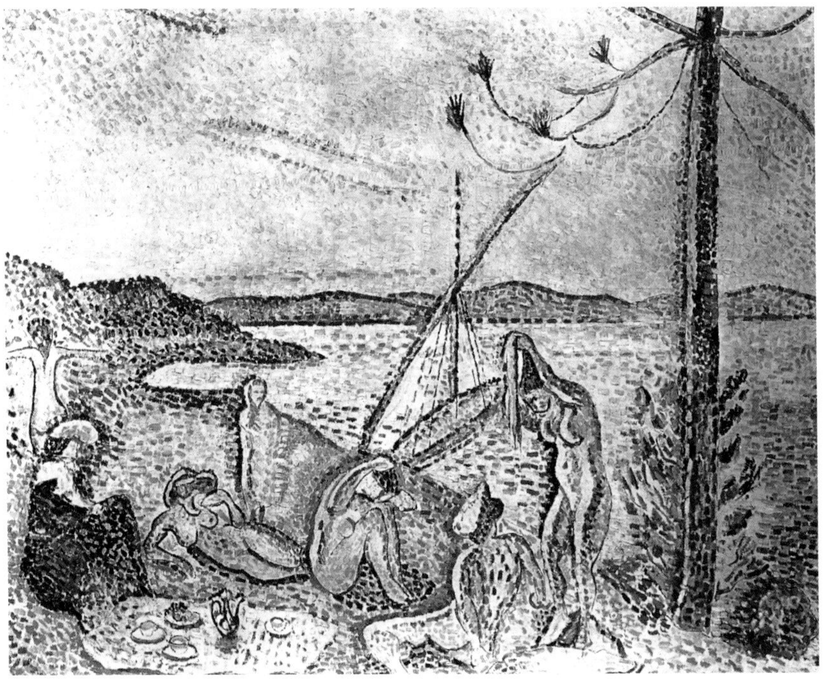

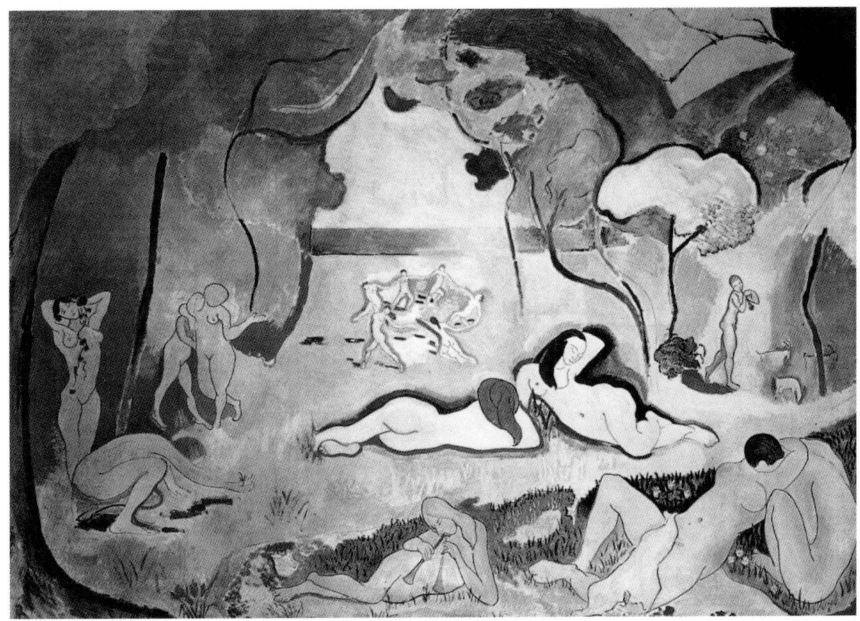

53
Henri Matisse, *Bonheur de Vivre*, 1905. Oil on canvas, 69 x 95 in. (175 x 241 cm). The Barnes Foundation, Merion, Pennsylvania

and called Seurat's *Grand Jatte* a "modernizing Puvis."[5] In the 1890s, Seurat's fellow Neoimpressionists Paul Signac and Henri Edmond Cross took the desire to standardize the sensations produced by works of art even further. They painted idyllic landscapes meant to embody a harmony in tune with their anarchist politics (fig. 51). They so wished that the sensations their work produced would educate viewers about the harmonies of anarchism that they even imagined hanging their paintings in workers' halls.[6]

Others who were informed by Puvis's work took a less systematic approach to feeling. Van Gogh and Gauguin each drew from Puvis's art in their own ways.[7] As we saw in Chapter 1, Picasso took up the emphasis on feeling in such blue-period works as *Poor People on the Seashore* (1903). And Matisse was influenced by Puvis's style. In paintings like *Luxe, Calme et Volupté* (1904–5), he followed the Neoimpressionists in their use of decorative line and lozenges of color, as well as their idyllic subject matter; both technique and subject matter were at least partly drawn from Puvis's work (fig. 52). Puvis's painting style hovers in the background of Matisse's masterpiece *Bonheur de Vivre*, with its large flat areas of color and its overall use of decorative line (fig. 53).[8] Beyond the particular borrowings of any of these painters, however, was the more general conception of painting that Puvis de Chavannes offered to so many of the early twentieth-century avant-garde artists: Puvis de Chavannes had opened up the possibility of imagining paintings as dreams.

The association between Puvis de Chavannes's work and dream was already well established by the mid-1880s. This vocabulary for his painting began to emerge in the reception of his murals for the Museum of Fine Arts, Lyons. It was reinforced in 1887, when a retrospective of his work was held at the Durand-Ruel galleries. This exhibition, which included the cartoon for the Sorbonne mural, Puvis's copies of his murals in reduced size, many important easel paintings, and photographs of the murals in situ, elicited responses from critics whose rhetoric relied heavily on the notion of dream. Writing for *L'Artiste*, for example, Léonce Bénédite described Puvis's paintings as evocations of dream and memory. They embodied, he said, a "profound spirit of divination that plunges us into dream."[9] Others described the exhibition as an escape from the everyday world to a place where "a peaceful and beneficent feeling envelop[ed]" them.[10] One even advised "nervous, tired" readers to go to the Durand-Ruel galleries to "rest": "There is an oasis where you can dream for a few minutes"[11]—a description that may remind us of Marcellin Desboutin's portrait of Puvis de Chavannes (see fig. 20). Taken together, these associations of Puvis's work with an idyllic dream suggest how much this model of painting influenced the approach of Henri Matisse: "What I dream of," wrote Matisse in "Notes of a Painter" (1908), "is an art of balance, of purity, of serenity . . . an art which could be for every mental worker . . . a soothing, calming influence on the mind, something like a good armchair which provides relaxation from physical fatigue."[12]

The relation between representation, sensation, and dream was at the heart of late nineteenth-century conceptions of modernism, and Puvis de Chavannes's work was instrumental in proposing that relation. Not everyone agreed that Puvis's art was modern, however. Some, like the conservative academician and editor of *Revue des Deux Mondes*, Ferdinand Brunetière, put Puvis's work in the lineage of traditional classicism, a placement that had nothing to do with sensation or dream. As it turned out, Brunetière gave the keynote address at Puvis de Chavannes's birthday banquet. Looking at the controversy this caused will underline the terms on which modernism was understood by the 1890s. It will also make clear that Puvis de Chavannes was central to the very definition of modernism.

BRUNETIÈRE VERSUS THE SYMBOLISTS

At the banquet celebrating Puvis de Chavannes's birthday, a battle erupted between the young Symbolist-affiliated poets represented by Catulle Mendès and an old conservative literary guard represented by Ferdinand Brunetière. As we saw in Chapter 1, prior to the banquet Brunetière had launched a moral campaign against Symbolism and condemned the Symbolists' hero Baudelaire as—in Gustave Kahn's words—a "bad poet" and an "obscene maniac." Ironically, Brunetière was given an opportunity by the banquet organizers to speak about Puvis on behalf of the French literary community. According to Kahn, the younger poets' objections to this were so strong that they considered boycotting the banquet. Finally, it was decided that Catulle Mendès would read a poem to Puvis on behalf of the literary avant-garde after Brunetière's speech, and the boycott was called off.[13]

Why, we might ask, was each side so passionately committed to defining Puvis's art in its own terms? Puvis's status as a national painter was surely part of the reason. But we still might wonder why literary enemies would battle over a painter. The answer, I believe, is this: The debates about modernist art and modernist literature in the 1880s and 1890s were never merely about writing and painting. At their heart lay an issue that was far more fundamental and profound—the relation between modernism and human subjectivity. The modernist model of creativity and aesthetic reception called into question the opposition between mind and body that had dominated French academic theory for more than a century. Modernism proposed a model of mind that operated through, was grounded in, indeed, was part and parcel of, a bodily engagement with the sensuousness and materiality of a work. For conservatives who wanted to believe in an educated male subject who was both rational and autonomous, the collapse of the mind-body distinction posed the threatening possibility that if acts of mind could not be bracketed off from the body and desire, subjectivity itself might be determined by those uncontrollable forces.

The Symbolists were attracted to Puvis because his project seemed in many ways to be a model for theirs. Like him, they were formulating alternatives to academic traditionalism—questioning the claims to mastery that were characteristic of academic practice in both painting and literature. The banquet itself was organized, by and large, by the young literati and was a way for them to align themselves with Puvis de Chavannes and to define his art as modernist. Brunetière seems to have realized this. When Rodin wrote to him to request his presence at the banquet, Brunetière replied by asking for the privilege of giving a speech on behalf of France's poets. Brunetière was a major literary figure occupying a powerful position. Circumstances made it impossible for Rodin to refuse his request, even though Rodin knew that many would be angered by Brunetière's participation—many who believed that Brunetière's recent attack on Symbolism employed terms that might just as easily have been applied to Puvis de Chavannes's painting.

Brunetière had criticized modern poetry for its "empty forms" and "hollow rattling words." He feared that the Symbolist poem would have two dire consequences. First, it would threaten to unravel the subjectivity of its viewers. Rather than serving as a focus for the crystallization of the reasoning mind, the sensuous address of the poem would encourage that mind to wander. It would, he said, "dissolve the unity of the self in a diversity of successive states . . . give it over to the wandering voluptuousness of dream."[14] And this enticement of writers and readers into their own associational landscapes would have profound social consequences—would lead to "the glorification of egoism" and the "negation of solidarity." Brunetière wanted so badly to prove that Puvis de Chavannes's work had nothing to do with Symbolist poetry because of what it would mean about French culture if the public murals of France's most important national painter—works meant to edify and socialize their audiences—functioned more like Symbolist poetry than like Brunetière's classical prose, if they replaced "order," "purity," "tradition," "idealization," and "expression" with individual dreams. The controversy at the banquet was about Puvis de Chavannes, but it also was about modernism, about subjectivity, about French culture.

Rodin's solution to Brunetière's request was to find another participant who could counter Brunetière's presence. He approached Octave Mirbeau and asked him to speak at the banquet. For reasons that remain unclear, Mirbeau declined to give a speech, although he did attend the banquet. To Rodin he wrote: "In the end I did not accept the invitation to speak at the banquet for Chavannes for many reasons. . . . It would be good, nevertheless, for a voice to reclaim Puvis de Chavannes from the Institute, of which, by unfortunate bad luck, this banquet has become a celebration! How ironic!"[15] Clearly, when Rodin invited Mirbeau to speak, he was trying to prevent Puvis de Chavannes's work from being aligned with the traditionalism of the Academy. He had evidence from Mirbeau's many essays about Puvis de Chavannes's murals of the kind of speech that Mirbeau might have given. Of all the critics that we have reviewed so far, Mirbeau is the one who most forcefully used the vocabulary of sensation, feeling, and fantasy to characterize Puvis's work as modern. In 1891 he had written an article on Claude Monet in which he compared Monet to Puvis and then to the Symbolist poet Mallarmé, implying that Puvis's art too might be analogous to Mallarmé's poetry. The crux of Mirbeau's linkage between Puvis, Monet, and Mallarmé was the assumption that desire and fantasy were constitutive of subjectivity and that representation was the hinge of that relationship. By inviting Mirbeau to speak about Puvis de Chavannes, Rodin seems to have been hoping to link Puvis's work to modernism, sensation, and fantasy. He seems to have predicted that Brunetière would propose exactly the opposite.

In his speech at the banquet Brunetière did attempt to dissociate Puvis de Chavannes's work from modernism—and especially from Symbolism. Brunetière claimed that unlike the Symbolists, Puvis never tried to make his paintings allusive. Nor did he revel in the possibilities for ambiguity offered by the material qualities of color. Said Brunetière to Puvis, "You have seen absolutely no enigma in blue, nor have you sought mystery in red."[16] Brunetière had earlier defined Symbolist indeterminacy thus: "The Symbolists believe that the vague and the imprecise, the floating and the fugitive, the celestial and the imponderable, are a part of poetry."[17] According to him, instead of using the materiality of painting to address the senses in a way that might spark fantasy, Puvis had always spiritualized what was often too material about the means of painting. In his speech he said to Puvis: "If, because of the powers of seduction they exercise on our senses, color and form sometimes have something too material about them, you have spiritualized them. By subordinating the signification of form to the exigencies of thought, you have simplified [painting]."[18]

This claim stands in direct opposition to any link between Puvis de Chavannes's art and a modernist emphasis on form, feeling, and fantasy. According to Brunetière, in Puvis's work the unruly qualities of color and form were sublimated by thought. And he offered this process as a model not only for Puvis's painterly practice but also for the practice of all true poetry. "By renewing and spiritualizing painting," said Brunetière, Puvis had made painting itself poetic. The artist, Brunetière continued, had shown himself to be "master" of the elements of nature that were "sometimes so coarse" and had taken the role of "interpreting the ideal" that he found in himself.[19] Brunetière claimed that in Puvis's work, the sensual qualities of the material world were bypassed in order to avoid any relationship between representation and sensation that might lead to desire. What separated Puvis's painterly practice from the "Baudelairean" mode employed by Symbolist writers, Brunetière implied, was the degree to which desire and fantasy were operative in each. In Puvis's painting the material world of nature, with its seductive and sensuous elements, was brought under control and reduced to a sign for the ideal. Brunetière left out of his account any acknowledgment of the effects of materiality, sensuousness, or physicality on the desiring body; he had denigrated these qualities in his campaign against Symbolism.

Not only did Brunetière assert that Puvis's paintings were resistant to individual fantasy; he also attributed to them the ability to prevent such fantasy. After invoking four of Puvis's public murals, Brunetière claimed that Puvis's art had "the power to evoke visions that . . . purify the eyes of men."[20] Puvis's public paintings were given an educational role. By purifying the eyes of men, Brunetière implied, they prevented their viewers from entering the space of individual fantasy encouraged by the Symbolist mode. Thus, Brunetière ended his speech by proclaiming the most important effect of Puvis's painting: "You have returned art to the dignity . . . of her social mission."[21] A mural by Puvis placed in the public realm would, according to Brunetière, oppose that atomization of the public that he imagined Symbolism and other forms of modernism as promoting. When he gave his speech at the banquet, Brunetière knew that he would be followed by Catulle Mendès. He thus aimed at invalidating in advance any description of Puvis's painting that might carry a modernist or Symbolist edge.

Brunetière characterized Puvis's work as exemplary of the order and unity of traditional French classicism. Puvis's project demonstrated, Brunetière claimed, the continuing viability of traditional modes, which had been "noisily buried in order to give the illusion of their death." Puvis's painting did not, he said, have anything to do with those styles associated with modernity—Impressionism, Naturalism, Symbolism, and so forth. These Brunetière opposed to the true purpose of the painter: "The painter, like the poet, truly has charge of souls."[22] In Brunetière's speech, then, Puvis was upheld as sustaining a traditional form of classical idealism. Brunetière was, in the end, part of a minority of critics—all of them conservative—who took such a position.

The Symbolists met Brunetière's speech with jeers. They saw Brunetière's characterization of Puvis as an attack on their understanding of Puvis's art and, further, on their own poetry and on modern attitudes toward representation in general. In an account of the banquet written in 1925, the Symbolist writer and critic Gustave Kahn described Brunetière's characterization of Puvis's work as an attack on modernism. Brunetière had "refined his discourse (order, purity, majesty) and chiseled marks against the Impressionists. Respect for art, . . . Classical beauty . . . unity . . . [were his watchwords.] He said his piece on modernism."[23]

After Brunetière's attempt to define Puvis de Chavannes's work as classicism, it was the literary avant-garde's turn to speak about Puvis's work. Catulle Mendès read an ode that began with this stanza:

Master! we celebrate your glory and ours.
Because, fervent poets who celebrate you here,
We have, this day our victory also;
The triumph of God honors the apostle,
And all come, with palms in hand,
Those from the past, those from today, those from tomorrow,
Hugo, Gautier, from their apotheoses on high,

And dear Baudelaire with his great sorrowful heart,
And De Lisle and Banville, shining from happy skies,
And we whose brows are overburdened with sullen years,
Rise still to love or pray,
And Youth mixes its rosy laurels with this ancient tribute.[24]

This invocation of Baudelaire in the face of Brunetière represented a triumph for the young literati who viewed the author of *Les Fleurs du Mal* as their most important predecessor. Indeed, after the line mentioning Baudelaire, many of the young poets hooted and cheered. Clearly, the issue here was not just the status of Baudelaire. Rather, Mendès's evocation of Baudelaire and his progeny was a vindication of authority of this literary circle to speak for the merits and meanings of Puvis's work and stood as a correction to Brunetière's punctilious classicism.

The editors of the Symbolist journal *La Plume* also wanted to make sure that Puvis would be associated most strongly with the avant-garde. The cover photo for the special issue of the Symbolist journal *La Plume* published to coincide with the banquet pictured Puvis in his robe—a sort of monk's habit—thus likening the artist to the monk-artists in his mural *Christian Inspiration* (see fig. 48). In the accompanying article, Puvis is described as spending the whole day in his studio painting, with nothing but bread and water to keep him going. Here was a man uninterested in indulging the pleasures of the senses!

This myth of Puvis's asceticism was meant to counterbalance some of the worries about his art and the desires that propelled it. But it also contributed to those worries. Puvis's withdrawal into dream could also be aligned with the "egoism" disdained by Brunetière and "mysticism" that cultural critics like Max Nordau saw as symptoms of "degeneration." For Nordau, any kind of modernism was the product of a degenerate sensibility and any formal experimentation the result of the "visual derangements" that Charcot had identified "in degeneration and hysteria."[25] Whereas Nordau believed that the vogue for Puvis's work was a symptom of mass hereditary degeneracy rather than its cause, other critics feared that paintings like Puvis's might be promoting the dissolution of subjectivity rather than encouraging aesthetic activity, which focused the reasoning mind. Brunetière's speech was meant to counteract such claims.

In *La Plume*, Brunetière's speech was prefaced by a description of the academician as a "bitter enemy" of the young literati: there was "not a new idea, not a noble thought, that has found favor with the pawn who directs the *Revue des Deux Mondes*."[26] Similarly, in a retrospective account of the event, one of the organizers of the banquet, the poet Mathias Morhardt, discredited Brunetière's characterization of Puvis: "One may say that there was not a word of this speech that the great teaching of Puvis de Chavannes did not protest against with all its energy."[27]

Two years after the banquet, Octave Mirbeau wrote an article that also seems to have been a belated response to Brunetière's characterization of Puvis. Mirbeau began by criticizing those for whom a celebration of sensuality in high art was anathema: "I know few men as resistant to the sensual pleasure of art as men of letters. One counts those who are capable of attesting to it [sensual pleasure in art], and the count is quickly made. . . . Not only do they not understand it, but they go to the extreme of negating its intellectual character and its educational power. Most of them consider it to be a perversion of intelligence and consequently a social danger. For them, this is only one of the forms—and not the least odious—of degraded sensuality, of vice, and of crime." Mirbeau's reference to the "educational power" of the pleasures provided by art is reminiscent of Guyau's and Fouillée's formulations of art's socializing potential. According to Mirbeau, Puvis de Chavannes was the only artist who, "as if by a miracle, has escaped this law of proscription."[28] Mirbeau's essay helps us to see, once again, the degree to which modernism, sensation, and fantasy were linked in the discourse of the late nineteenth century. And it makes clear that no one was more central to that connection than Pierre Puvis de Chavannes.

FROM AESTHETICS TO POLITICS

The debate between Brunetière and the Symbolists was never merely aesthetic in nature. More and more, as the 1890s drew on, aesthetic positions came to imply political ones. Puvis's work provided the terrain for many different kinds of battles, and they crystallized in the proceedings of the banquet and in the texts that surrounded it. As Mathias Morhardt put it in a retrospective account of the banquet: "Once again art and politics confronted one another. But above all, the antagonism that divided the admirers of Puvis de Chavannes into two completely hostile enemy camps dominated, with all its violence, the unanimity of the homage that we gave to the illustrious master."[29]

The banquet was given political resonance by contemporary events, some of them engineered by Brunetière himself and others that were coincidental. Only a few months before the celebration, Brunetière had caused a controversy when, after returning from a visit to the Vatican, where he had been received by the pope, he declared that science was bankrupt. Brunetière's famous essay, "Bankruptcy of Science," received wide coverage in the press and was generally seen as an attack on the republican state. In it he implied that the positivism underpinning the republican civic morality was also morally bankrupt.[30] When Brunetière emphasized the spiritual and idealizing aims of Puvis de Chavannes's work, he was attempting not only to counter Symbolist attempts to define Puvis but to dissociate Puvis from republican materialism.

Yet, as we have seen, republicans believed that Puvis de Chavannes had saved the grand tradition of high art by rejuvenating idealism and reclaiming it from the academicians (like Brunetière), in whose hands it had become so unconvincing. As the republican critic André Michel put it in an article about the banquet that appeared in *Journal des Débats*: "We simply wanted to try, in the context of this celebration, to indicate why we owe him every token of our gratitude for having brought to French art, at a critical hour in its history, the eloquence for which it had the greatest need, for having saved idealism, which had fallen into disrepute, less as a result of attacks from its enemies than by the unintelligent and sterile formalism of its followers and official representatives or defenders."[31] Republican critics like Michel saw Puvis's practice as a modernization and materialization of the means of painting that would allow for a newly rejuvenated French high art.

Marius Vachon's characterization of Puvis represents even more clearly the kind of republican rhetoric that Brunetière wanted to counteract. In an article published to coincide with the banquet, Vachon described the unanimous celebration of Puvis as a sign that "the current generation, despite all the accusations lodged against it, knows how to understand social virtues and admire them."[32] This we should recognize as the same kind of rhetoric employed by representatives of the state at the Universal Exposition in order to claim the adherence of French youth to republican values.

Puvis's painting was, Vachon explained, aimed at celebrating the French worker and consolidating a harmonious insertion of every citizen into the social structure of the Republic. According to Vachon, rather than offering a dreamlike escape from fin de siècle pessimism, Puvis represented socially responsible optimism.[33] Vachon described Puvis's compositional choices as analogues to his moral message. Through his compositional form, Puvis had "made the individual enter into the group and the group into the collectivity."[34] Although Vachon, like Brunetière, insisted that Puvis's art communicated a moral message, he was diametrically opposed to Brunetière in his emphasis on the formal qualities of Puvis's work. He claimed that rather than sublimating and transcending the material qualities of painting, Puvis used those qualities to communicate to the viewer. Just as the hypothetical milieu that Puvis provided for his figures influenced the formation of their characters, his arrangements of color provided a milieu for the viewer of his murals.[35] Vachon explained that "we have observed scientifically that red produces an intense vibration of heat in the brain," but Puvis preferred to use "tender, light, and luminous colors . . . [including] violet, which, in the opinion of the wise, currently represents the highest level of development of the visual sense."[36] This interest in the sensual effects of color was closely aligned with the kind of modernism that Brunetière abhorred.

The political meanings of the aesthetic positions taken by Brunetière and his enemies were amplified by Brunetière's recent antimaterialist stand. Yet, even if the celebration of Puvis had not followed so closely upon the heels of Brunetière's critique of republican materialism, the banquet would have been a political battlefield, for Puvis held a special place in the hearts of the intelligentsia. He was France's national painter.

PUVIS DE CHAVANNES—NATIONAL PAINTER

> All the art critics have been unanimous, once more, in exalting the genius of he whom they call "the most magnificent artist of our time." . . . It has seemed to me that our worship of the art of M. de Chavannes has been a wholly abnormal psychological phenomenon without any correspondence to our admiration for this or that other painter. . . . We are taken by a thirst for dream, emotion, and poetry. Saturated in a light that is too vibrant and too crude, we have breathed in the fog. And this is why we are so passionately attached to the poetic and foggy art of M. de Chavannes. We have loved it for its worst faults, for its drawing errors and lack of color. . . . The art of M. de Chavannes has thus been for us a cure; we have become attached to it like the sick to a new treatment. But we must beware that the treatment does not, in its turn, become a malady.
>
> —*Téodor de Wyzewa*

> Puvis became incontestable, national. There were no more monuments but for him.
>
> —*Gustave Kahn*

> [In the work of Puvis de Chavannes] I can only sense with a sensual pleasure that I cannot describe, a feeling, a taste, an understanding of art that gives me the very idea of perfection, of a fraternal perfection in which I recognize the image . . . of the men of our blood.
>
> —*Charles Maurras*

> If there is one word that, today, seems to express a noble and pure idea, it is the word *patrie*; governments know how to manipulate this word with singular cleverness, and men who sincerely detest tyrannies nevertheless allow themselves to be tyrannized without protest in the name of *la patrie*. Who would dare confess themselves unpatriotic?
>
> —*A.-Ferdinand Herold*

The voices I invoke here—Téodor de Wyzewa, Gustave Kahn, Charles Maurras, and A.-Ferdinand Herold (with the exception of the last)—were speaking of Puvis de Chavannes at the time of the banquet.[37] I juxtapose them to make explicit a claim that has been lurking in this book in various forms. Puvis's paintings held a particular power for his contemporaries, a power that made such critics as Wyzewa uncomfortable. For Wyzewa, the paintings seemed to signal a collective desire for a vision of "the real" that obscured, rather than exposed, its details. For him, the reaction to Puvis's work was proof of the demise of aesthetic realism. Yet, I would claim, the desire for "poetic and foggy art" identified by Wyzewa had a much wider significance. This was implied in Wyzewa's characterization of Puvis's painting as a "treatment" that itself threatened to become a "malady"—something akin to a collective addiction to a drug with narcotic effects.

Puvis's art answered a need (which became stronger as the century drew to a close) for a convincing, cohesive, public representation of France. This need is perhaps most strongly signaled to us by the deeply felt and overdetermined responses given to his works. The quotations also signal an awareness of that need. The lines from Kahn, for example, come from his essay celebrating the banquet as a triumph of the modernist literati over the forces of the Academy and the Institute. Puvis was an honorary member of the younger generation of France, Kahn claimed. And if so, he implied, then the nation was best represented by the voices of modernism. In his description of the painter, Kahn equated "incontestable" with "national." In this single celebratory sentence, he pointed to an aspect of Puvis's importance in the 1890s that I only alluded to earlier: Puvis de Chavannes's status as a national painter.

Kahn's equation signals the depth of the need for a national idiom—a need that Puvis de Chavannes seemed to fill. But it also suggests that it was only through a disavowal of the conflicted and fragile nature of the nation that national identity could begin to be secured. (Remember Renan's statement: "The essence of a nation is that all its individual members have many things in common, and also that they have forgotten many things.") Puvis's paintings, with their address to fantasy, encouraged the mechanisms of disavowal. The range of interpretations of his work we have already seen are evidence of this. Puvis was national, we might say, *because* he was incontestable. Kahn implied that to question the adequacy of his painting to represent France might have also been to undermine one of the last viable public sites of a vision of France that inspired belief. If the rhetoric critics used to describe Puvis's painting seems often to have been overdetermined, this was perhaps because the critics themselves wanted so badly to believe that Puvis met this impossible need for a convincing image of France.

It is therefore fitting that the banquet celebrating Puvis's life and work took place on January 5, 1895, the very day when the fragile political leadership of France was again shifting as President Jean Casimir Périer resigned to be replaced by M. Félix Faure. Mathias Morhardt described the initial worry that the government's homage to Puvis might be left out of the banquet owing to the political crisis. In the end, however, according to Morhardt, the fall of the government did not ruin the celebration. Two ministers, Georges Leygues and Raymond Poincaré, attended, and Leygues "spoke in the name of the government, despite the fact that it no longer existed."[38] What a perfect parallel to the critical responses to Puvis's painting this makes: the minister of a nonexistent government speaking to the painter whose work was made to represent a vision of the collective unity of France when the work itself, in many ways, undermined that very possibility and when the vision it was meant to represent had never, in truth, existed.

The words I quote from Charles Maurras exemplify, in the most extreme form, the part that Puvis's painting was often made to play in the consolidation of nationalist fervor. Maurras began his career in the literary avant-garde but soon became the spokesman for the extreme monarchist Right. He proposed that true Frenchness belonged to an elite intelligentsia.[39] The powers of thought of the intelligentsia were described as the product of a particular lineage linked to classical Greece and Rome, which would properly flourish only under a royal regime. In Maurras's gloss on Puvis's painting we can already see a conservative nationalism that would become more virulently anti-Semitic as the century drew to a close. In his essay, published in the royalist *Gazette de France*, Maurras turned the very interest in sensual pleasure (*volupté*), which had fascinated Symbolist poets, into a sign of innate French taste (*un goût*). "Le goût de Puvis de Chavannes"—the taste for "fraternal perfection in which I recognize the image of the men of our blood"—stood as proof, for Maurras, that "our blood" was passed down (among French brothers) from generation to generation. This racist view, which was at this moment the domain of the extreme Right, permeated the national consciousness all too soon.

The example of Maurras makes clear that if changes in political and aesthetic positions were taking place in the middle of the 1890s, they tended to amplify extreme positions. In December 22, 1894, days before the banquet, Dreyfus was sentenced to deportation. On the very day of the banquet, Dreyfus was publicly degraded in the courtyard of the Ecole Militaire. These events were the prelude to the full flowering of an affair that polarized an entire nation. By the time of Zola's "J'accuse," personal political identity revolved largely around being a Dreyfusard or an anti-Dreyfusard. When the banquet took place, such polarizations were already forming; right-wing nationalism, with its racist and anti-Semitic contingents, was already on the rise. The discourse through which this type of nationalist rhetoric was framed had its origins in the aesthetic discourse of classicism. The terms through which it developed were already well inscribed in the language used to define and describe both literature and painting. Not only Maurras but Brunetière and Vogüé eventually played active roles in the organization representing this most extreme form of exclusionary nationalism, Action Française.[40]

Along with my examples of critical glosses on Puvis's oeuvre, I have quoted from Herold's article on la patrie that appeared in *Entretiens Politiques et Littéraires* a few years before the banquet. This excerpt gives a sense of the climate of the time and the way it forced individuals to proclaim their attachment to the collectivity. The pressures were so strong that they provoked Herold to ask, in a tone both cynical and a bit worried: "Who would dare to confess themselves unpatriotic?" The question was a rhetorical one, and it had its roots in a moment when intellectuals were being politicized and when questioning la patrie could be a rather risky business.

In the 1890s there was a revolt against the increasingly repressive policies of the state with regard to literary production and a collective mobilization of writers in protest against censorship. Initially the petitions against censorship were signed by writers and artists from across the political and generational spectrum, but when the government imposed a law against the "promotion" of anarchism by intellectuals, the literary avant-garde began to take political sides. In July 1893, *L'Ermitage* published "An Artistic and Social Referendum," a poll of intellectuals, offering them "the choice between liberty and discipline." When publication of the second edition of Jean Grave's *La Societé Mourante et l'Anarchie* coincided with the anarchist attacks of Henry and Vaillant, Grave was arrested for his "incitement" of anarchist violence. This led to a protest by writers in support of Grave, which cemented a relationship between intellectuals and politics. (Significantly, Zola refused to sign the petition, because Grave's book was an explicit political tract, not a censored work of fiction; signing it, Zola claimed, would suggest a sympathy with Grave's politics that he did not have.)[41]

In August, during the anti-anarchist Trial of the Thirty, the state rounded up and attempted to prosecute those suspected of anarchist sympathies, not just political agitators. The Neoimpressionist painter Maximilien Luce was arrested as part of this anarchist "conspiracy" but was released after a petition was circulated that bore the signatures of respected national artists. First on the list was the name Pierre Puvis de Chavannes.[42] These and other events suggest that by the time of the Dreyfus Affair in 1894, a new conception of the political role of the intellectual was in place, and along with it new conceptions of the means for expressing political views—including the petition and the questionnaire. The highly publicized banquet for Puvis was, I would argue, another such means. Nor would more have been at stake at any event than at a banquet for the artist who seemed to offer the only viable image of the collective identity of France—Puvis de Chavannes.

NOTES

INTRODUCTION

Epigraph: Alphonse Germain, "Puvis de Chavannes et Son Esthétique," *L'Ermitage* 2, no. 1 (1891): 140–44.

1 The Third Republic began its life in the early 1870s in the aftermath of the Franco-Prussian War and the Paris Commune. By 1885 the Republicans had lost their majority in parliament and had to govern by coalition. Ministries seemed to change from month to month and were beset by numerous scandals (the most important being the Wilson Affair in 1887 and the Panama Scandal in 1892). Despite these political divisions, the period was characterized by a common desire finally to recover from the humiliating defeat of the Franco-Prussian War. The fear that waning birth rates left France still vulnerable to German competition in both the industrial and the military realms was another common denominator among political opponents. Out of this fear emerged nationalist sentiments that often had racist, anti-Semitic components. The desire for the reform of a government viewed as corrupt led, in 1888, to a crisis in which the government was nearly overthrown by General Boulanger, a former cabinet minister and prominent military figure with a strong nationalist agenda, whose support paradoxically came from radicals on the Left and conservatives with Catholic and royalist leanings. The political extremism of the period is perhaps manifested most clearly in the rise of anarchism in the 1890s and the attendant bombings and stabbings carried out in its name. In 1892–94, thirteen anarchist attacks were carried out on institutions of authority, most of them with dynamite. The most famous incidents were the bombing of the Chamber of Deputies on December 9, 1893, and the stabbing of President Sadi Carnot in Lyons on June 24, 1894. See Jean Marie Mayeur and Madeleine Rebérioux, *The Third Republic from Its Origins to the Great War, 1871–1914*, trans. J. R. Foster (Cambridge, England, 1987); Theodore Zeldin, *France 1848–1945: Politics and Anger* (Oxford, 1979); Richard David Sonn, *Anarchism and Cultural Politics in Fin-de-Siècle France* (Lincoln, Nebr., 1989).

2 The artist's hemicycle for the Grand Amphithéâtre of the New Sorbonne inaugurated as part of the centennial festivities was arguably the most important work commissioned to coincide with the event. For a discussion of this mural and the inaugural festivities in 1789 see Chapter 4.

3 My sense of the polarization of the aesthetic milieu comes in part from reading large amounts of criticism firsthand. There are many excellent art historical accounts of this period. See, for example, Carol Armstrong, *Odd Man Out: Readings of the Work and Reputation of Edgar Degas* (Chicago, 1991); T. J. Clark, *The Painting of Modern Life* (Princeton, N.J., 1984); Clark, *Farewell to an Idea: Episodes from a History of Modernism* (New Haven, 1999), chaps. 2 and 8; Jonathan Crary, *Suspensions of Perception: Attention, Spectacle and Modern Culture* (Cambridge, Mass., 1999); Tamar Garb, *Sisters of the Brush: Women's Artistic Culture in Late Nineteenth-Century Paris* (New Haven, 1994); Garb, *Bodies of Modernity: Figure and Flesh in Fin-de-Siècle France* (New York, 1998); Marie-Claude Genet-Delacroix, *Art et Etat sous la IIIème République: Le Système des Beaux-Arts, 1870–1940* (Paris, 1992); Nicholas Green, "'All the Flowers of the Field': The State, Liberalism, and Art Under the Early Third Republic," *Oxford Art Journal* 10, no. 1 (1987): 71–78; Steven Z. Levine, *Monet, Narcissus and Self-Reflection: The Modernist Myth of the Self* (Chicago, 1994); Michael Marlais, *Conservative Echoes in Fin-de-Siècle Parisian Art Criticism* (University Park, Pa., 1992); Patricia Mathews, *Passionate Discontent: Creativity, Gender and French Symbolist Art* (Chicago, 1999); Richard Shiff, *Cézanne and the End of Impressionism* (Chicago, 1984); Debora Leah Silverman, *Art Nouveau in Fin-de-Siècle France: Politics, Psychology, and Style* (Berkeley, 1989); Martha Ward, *Pissarro, Neo-Impressionism and the Spaces of the Avant-Garde* (Chicago, 1996); Margaret Werth, "'Le Bonheur de Vivre': The Idyllic Image in French Art, 1891–1906" (Ph.D. diss., Harvard University, 1994).

4 For example, Alphonse Germain (who, in the epigraph,

praises Puvis for his thusness) was a young, aesthetically advanced critic traveling in circles associated with literary Symbolism and Neoimpressionism; but he was also ardently Catholic and linked his support of modernist aesthetics to an extreme form of neo-Christian idealism. Here is a passage from Germain's 1893 treatise "Pour le Beau": "Supprimer la beauté plastique! c'est-à-dire prostituer la forme par laquelle le divin Révélateur incarna l'invisible substance du Père!" *Essais d'Art Libre*, February–March 1893, p. 48. Germain combined this Catholic stance with right-wing politics and an anti-Semitic emphasis on authentic Frenchness that was influenced by Charles Maurras, the founder of Action Française. On Alphonse Germain's criticism see Marlais, *Conservative Echoes*, 171–83. In the 1880s, Germain wrote for socialist papers, but by the early 1890s his politics had shifted to the right. See Ward, *Pissarro*, 204–10. The Nabi painter Maurice Denis was certainly at the forefront of modernist practice and criticism in the 1890s. However, Denis was also extremely conservative politically and was in fact part of the neo-Christian revival that affected many Symbolist circles. Marlais, 185–219. On the other hand, Octave Mirbeau, the critic instrumental in formulating a Symbolist interpretation of Monet's series paintings and a champion of Puvis, had anarchist leanings.

5 August Strindberg, "Letter to Paul Gauguin," in *Vente de Tableaux et Dessins par Paul Gauguin, Artiste Peintre, Hôtel des Ventes, Salle 7, le Lundi 18 Février 1895*, 3–5, cited in *Impressionism and Post-Impressionism 1874–1904*, ed. Linda Nochlin (Englewood Cliffs, N.J., 1966), 171.

6 André Michel, "Puvis de Chavannes," *Journal des Débats*, January 14, 1895, p. 1.

7 Ibid.

8 Some explicit borrowings by members of the avant-garde include Gauguin's *Young Boys Wrestling* (1888), which reworks figures from the background of Puvis's *Sweet Land* (1882), and Picasso's *Poor People on the Seashore* (1903), which refers both to *Young Girls by the Seashore* (1879) and *Poor Fisherman* (1881). Seurat's *La Grand Jatte* (1884–86) was described by Félix Fénéon as a "modernizing Puvis." See Richard J. Wattenmaker, *Puvis de Chavannes and the Modern Tradition* (Toronto, 1975; rev. ed. 1976); Robert L. Herbert, "Seurat and Puvis de Chavannes," *Yale University Art Gallery Bulletin* 25 (1959): 23. Art historians have long been puzzled by Puvis's wide appeal. Until recently he was dismissed as a watered-down Symbolist or an academic hack (even though he had almost no academic training at all). He was seen as an artist who pleased everyone by inoffensive compromise and whose wide appeal in his own day derived not from aesthetic innovations but from aesthetic conservatism—from what Robert Goldwater described fifty years ago as "the neutral character of [Puvis's] style." Robert Goldwater, "Puvis de Chavannes: Some Reasons for a Reputation," *Art Bulletin* 38, March 1946, p. 33. Most art historians who have endeavored to write extensively about his work have not fully elaborated the intersections between aesthetics and politics that define it. (Two notable exceptions are Claudine Mitchell and Margaret Werth.) The catalogue of the Puvis de Chavannes exhibition held in Amsterdam in 1994 alludes to some of the issues that are central to Puvis's oeuvre, classicism, nationalism, and modernism, without discussing them in detail. See Aimée Brown Price, *Pierre Puvis de Chavannes* (Amsterdam: Van Gogh Museum, 1994); and my review of that catalogue in *Art Bulletin*, December 1995, pp. 688–89. See also Price, "Puvis de Chavannes: A Study of the Easel Paintings and a Catalogue of the Painted Works" (Ph.D. diss., Yale University, 1972); Price, "L'Allégorie Réelle Chez Pierre Puvis de Chavannes," *Gazette des Beaux-Arts*, January 1977, pp. 27–40; Price, "Puvis de Chavannes's Caricatures: Manifestos, Commentary, Expressions," *Art Bulletin*, March 1991, pp. 119–40. For a recent monograph see Brian Petrie, *Puvis de Chavannes*, ed. Simon Lee (Brookfield, Vt., 1997).

For a discussion of the ideological underpinnings of *Ludus pro Patria* (1882; Musée de Picardie, Amiens), see Claudine Mitchell, "Time and the Idea of Patriarchy in the Pastorals of Puvis de Chavannes," *Art History* 10, no. 2 (1987): 188–202. Margaret Werth offers an analysis of the critical discourse on Puvis in the context of idyllic, pastoral, and utopian imagery and its role in French cultural politics, as well as formal analyses of many of Puvis's paintings of the 1880s and 1890s. See Werth, "'Le Bonheur de Vivre,'" 1994. Other considerations of Puvis's work in the context of pastoral landscape include Taube G. Greenspan, "'Les Nostalgiques' Re-Examined: The Idyllic Landscape in France, 1890–1905" (Ph.D. diss., City University New York, 1981); and Joyce Henri Robinson, "A 'Nouvelle Arcadie': Puvis de Chavannes and the Decorative Landscape in Fin-de-Siècle France" (Ph.D. diss., University of Virginia, 1993).

9 Maurice Denis, "Définition du Néotraditionnisme," in *Théories, 1890–1910: Du Symbolisme et de Gauguin vers un Nouvel Ordre Classique* (Paris, 1920), 1.

10 See Herbert, "Seurat and Puvis de Chavannes"; Wattenmaker, *Puvis de Chavannes and the Modern Tradition*.

11 Greenberg's theorizations of modernist formalism and self-reflexivity are extremely complex. I do not wish here to simplify Greenberg's writings, only to signal the way certain

aspects of them have been taken up as tenets of formalism or even prescriptions for writing about art. For a classic debate about modernism between Clement Greenberg and T. J. Clark see *Pollock and After*, ed. Francis Fascina (New York, 1985). Greenberg's writings have recently been collected in *Clement Greenberg: The Collected Essays and Criticism*, 4 vols., ed. John O'Brian (Chicago, 1986–93).

12 In the past few decades, art historians have critiqued modernist formalism. Some have looked anew at subject matter that had been ignored in the name of form. Others have examined the political implications and social meanings of an "art for art's sake" stance. Still others have been interested in the social and political meanings of painterly experimentation. (Ironically, Clement Greenberg's early writings provide some of the best examples of this last approach.) My understanding of nineteenth-century French modernism has been formed in dialogue with the work of many scholars whose work addresses one or more of the concerns described above. They include, among others: Kathy Adler, Carol M. Armstrong, Norma Broude, T. J. Clark, Thomas Crow, Michael Fried, Tamar Garb, Nicholas Green, John House, Linda Nochlin, Fred Orton, Griselda Pollock, Abigail Solomon-Godeau, and Anne M. Wagner. T. J. Clark's recent work on modernism has provided the most provocative and fertile site for intellectual engagement. See in particular his *Farewell to an Idea*, in which he elaborates through a variety of trenchant case studies the proposal that "Modernism and materialism go together." P. 139.

13 For a discussion of the intersections between debates about Puvis's work and debates about Symbolist poetry in the 1890s see Jennifer L. Shaw, "The Wandering Gaze: Modernism, Subjectivity and the Art of Pierre Puvis de Chavannes," in *Moving Forward, Holding Fast: The Dynamics of Nineteenth-Century French Culture*, ed. Mary Donaldson-Evans and Barbara Cooper (Amsterdam, 1997).

14 I am not questioning the value of this kind of art historical revisionism, only proposing another means by which we might reject an empty modernist formalism in favor of a concrete account of what form itself meant in the particular instances in which it was employed. T. J. Clark gives a series of brilliant accounts of modernist form in *Farewell to an Idea*. See in particular pp. 127–34 for a discussion that masterfully captures the complexities of the relation between modernism, Symbolism, and decoration.

15 For a general account of the "discovery of the unconscious" see Henri F. Ellenberger, *The Discovery of the Unconscious* (New York, 1970). Gustave Le Bon and Gabrielle Tarde developed theories of group psychology to which an unconscious component was integral. The psychological research of Bernheim's school of Nancy posited the influence of unconscious processes in the everyday lives of normal human subjects. Bernheim's primary rival was Jean Martin Charcot, whose school of Salpetrière conducted experiments on hysteria in which the visual image played a large part. The French state actively fostered this kind of psychological research. The philosophical theory of Schopenhauer, which was centered on the relation between desire and representation, enjoyed a vogue in France at the end of the century, and there was a similar fascination with the philosophy of Henri Bergson, which focused attention on the issue of memory and posited an analogy between art and hypnosis. This was also the moment when advertising in France began to be explicitly theorized using Bergson's philosophy. For an excellent account of the relation between Freudian theories of the unconscious and the work of his French precursors see Mikkel Borch-Jacobsen, *The Freudian Subject* (Stanford, 1988). On Le Bon see Susanna Barrows, *Distorting Mirrors: Visions of the Crowd in Late Nineteenth-Century France* (New Haven, 1981). On the role of the visual image in hysteria see Georges Didi-Huberman, *Invention de l'Hystérie: Charcot et l'Iconographie Photographique de la Salpetrière* (Paris, 1982); Janet Beizer, *Ventriloquized Bodies: Narratives of Hysteria in Nineteenth-Century France* (Ithaca, N.Y., 1993); Sander L. Gilman, "The Image of the Hysteric," in *Hysteria Beyond Freud*, ed. Gilman (Berkeley, 1993), 345–452. See also Henri Bergson, *Essai sur les Données Immédiates de la Conscience* (Paris, 1991); and Marjorie Anne Beale, "Advertising and the Politics of Public Persuasion in France, 1900–1939" (Ph.D. diss., University of California, Berkeley, 1991).

16 For an excellent account of the relation between the new psychology and the visual arts see Silverman, *Art Nouveau*, chap. 5. See also Clark, *Farewell to an Idea*, chap. 3, for a discussion of the relation between Cézanne's bather images and contemporary psychology.

17 This was the crux of the debate between the Salpetrière and Nancy schools of psychology. See Silverman, *Art Nouveau*.

18 Quoted in Silverman, *Art Nouveau*, 75.

19 "La psychologie contemporaine nous enlève donc l'illusion d'un moi fermé, impénétrable et absolument autonome." Alfred Fouillée, "Les Grandes Conclusions de la Psychologie Contemporaine: La Conscience et Ses Transformations," *Revue des Deux Mondes* 107 (1891): 811.

20 "Il n'est pas d'émotion esthétique qui n'éveille en nous une multitude de désirs et de besoins plus ou moins inconscients." Jean-Marie Guyau, *Les Problèmes de l'Esthétique Contempo-*

raine (Paris, 1884), 27–28. Several chapters from this book were published in 1881–1883 in *Revue des Deux Mondes*, including a version of the chapter from which this argument is drawn, "Principe de l'Art et de la Poésie," *Revue des Deux Mondes* 46 (1882): 750–78. For a philosophical discussion of Guyau's aesthetics see J. W. Harding, *Jean-Marie Guyau (1854–1888), Aesthetician and Sociologist* (Geneva, 1973).

21 For a discussion of the tradition of allegory in French public art see Antoine de Baecque, "The Allegorical Image of France, 1750–1800: A Political Crisis of Representation," *Representations* 47 (Summer 1994): 111–43.

22 No strict distinctions were made in the 1880s and 1890s between public art and painting for the private market. As Nicholas Green has shown, the Third Republic's ideology of civic participation infiltrated its sponsorship of the arts in general. Its goal was to promote an ideology of individualism appropriate to the development of a capitalist marketplace while also encouraging individuals to feel that they collectively participated in the betterment of France. Green has shown that one of its strategies was to cultivate a wide variety of artistic practices through state purchases. Green, "'All the Flowers.'" In addition to this cult of the individual artist, the Third Republic sponsored a range of research and activities meant to explore and take advantage of the individual subjectivities of its citizens. These include the sponsorship of psychological research, the reform of education, an emphasis in the education of males on the cult of the *moi*, and the promotion of decorative art that mimicked the range of individual styles sponsored by state purchases. Marie Jeannine Aquilino has argued that during this period there was "a shift from mural painting as public edification to decorative painting as a new and intimate mode of public art" that emphasized "individual subjectivity and feeling, personal fantasy and taste, and the pure aesthetic of the marketplace." Aquilino convincingly links this shift to the more general transformations of the public sphere theorized by Jürgen Habermas. For an excellent discussion of the way this was manifested in the overall decorative scheme for the Paris city hall see Marie Jeannine Aquilino, "Painted Promises: The Politics of Public Art in Late Nineteenth-Century France," *Art Bulletin* 75, no. 4 (1993): 706–8.

23 The scope of this shift and its implications for our understanding of French nationalism are important areas of study that remain beyond the realm of this book. There are many excellent accounts of the association of Frenchness and fraternity by historians and art historians. Some important historical accounts include Madelyn Gutwirth, *The Twilight of the Goddesses: Women and Representation in the French Revolutionary Era* (New Brunswick, N.J., 1992); Lynn Hunt, *The Family Romance of the French Revolution* (Berkeley, 1992); Joan B. Landes, *Women and the Public Sphere in the Age of the French Revolution* (Ithaca, N.Y., 1988); Dorinda Outram, *The Body and the French Revolution: Sex, Class and Political Culture* (New Haven, 1989). Accounts by art historians include Thomas Crow, *Emulation: Making Artists for Revolutionary France* (New Haven, 1995); Alex Potts, *Flesh and the Ideal: Winckelmann and the Origins of Art History* (New Haven, 1994); Abigail Solomon-Godeau, *Male Trouble: A Crisis in Representation* (New York, 1997). I thank Melissa Hyde for pointing me to valuable references on this topic. I thank Amy Lyford for helping me to think in wider terms about issues of gender and Frenchness.

CHAPTER 1. HIGH ART'S OTHER BODY

1 "Elle a comme toujours, le privilège de ne point vous laisser indifférent; elle a un côté énigmatique qui échappe à la masse, quelque chose d'étrange qui surprend. . . . Tout ce que je sais, c'est qu'elle est empreinte d'une poésie irrésistible, poignante, qu'on subit, et qui échappe à toute analyse et à tout raisonnement. Explique qui voudra la sensation qu'elle procure, j'y renonce pour ma part et je me borne à constater l'impression ressentie. Pour moi c'est tout un poème." Emile Cardon. "Le Salon de 1881, IV: La Peinture," *Le Soleil*, May 10, 1881, p. 3 (also published in "Le Salon de 1881: I," *Le Correspondant*, May 10, 1881, pp. 553–63).

2 Another critic, Charles Flor, had a similar response to *Poor Fisherman*, saying, "This canvas offers something remarkable that is impossible to define; it defies all critical analysis [Cette toile offre quelque chose impressionnant, qui est indéfinissable; elle défie toute critique]." Flor, like Cardon, found something in *Poor Fisherman* that escaped the bounds of intellectual decipherment. Charles Flor, "Le Salon de 1881," *Le National*, May 4, 1881, p. 2.

3 "Une mélodie vague, intraduisible, qui pénètre l'âme, échappe à l'analyse brutale." Emile Cardon, "Salon de 1879, IX: La Peinture," *Le Soleil*, June 1, 1879, p. 3.

4 For discussions of the relation between Impressionism, sensation, and modernism see Clark, *Painting of Modern Life*; Shiff, *Cézanne and the End of Impressionism*.

5 T. J. Clark offers a poignant description of the relations between knowledge, representation, and the body in the work of Paul Cézanne: "Our representation of bodies—our own and other people's—just is some such process of interchange and duplication, of unstoppable weird empathy, of our somehow putting an internal sense of what being in the body feels like into our picture of how another body looks." *Farewell to an Idea*, 157.

6 Georges Lafenestre, "L'Art au Salon de 1879," *Le Correspondant*, June 15, 1879, p. 678–79. Georges Lafenestre was a member of the Conseil Supérieur des Beaux-Arts. From 1875 to 1880 he served as head of the Bureau des Travaux d'Art and from 1880 to 1887 as commissioner general of expositions.

7 For previous discussions of the "crisis of the nude" see Clark, *Painting of Modern Life*, 79–146; Beatrice Farwell, *Manet and the Nude: A Study of Iconography in the Second Empire* (New York, 1981); Lynda Nead, *The Female Nude: Art, Obscenity, and Sexuality* (London, 1992); Jennifer L. Shaw, "The Figure of Venus: Rhetoric of the Ideal and the Salon of 1863," *Art History* 14, no. 4 (1991): 540–70.

8 On academic training see Albert Boime, *The Academy and French Painting in the Nineteenth Century* (New Haven, 1986). It is worth noting that Puvis did not attend the Ecole des Beaux-Arts. He gave an account of his education and training in an interview with *Le Temps* in 1895, which can be summarized as follows: Puvis attended the prestigious Lycée Henry IV in Paris and was encouraged to be an engineer, but decided instead (after a trip to Italy) to study painting. He trained in the studio of the portraitist Henry Scheffer for about a year, then went on a second trip to Italy with an artist friend. Upon his return he entered the studios of Eugène Delacroix, for two weeks, and Thomas Couture, for three months, but claimed not to have learned much from either of them. Thiébault-Sisson, "Puvis de Chavannes Raconte par Lui-Même," *Le Temps*, January 16, 1895, p. 2.

9 On the eclipse of the male by the female nude see Solomon-Godeau, *Male Trouble*.

10 Charles Blanc, *Grammaire des Arts du Dessin* (Paris, 1867), 6–23. Blanc's book reflected and transformed academic theories of art, conceptions of its purpose, and rules for its execution. It became one of the most important sources of artistic theory for years to come. Blanc's theory was based in large part on Victor Cousin's neo-Kantian aesthetics of "the true, the beautiful, and the good." See Victor Cousin, *Du Vrai, du Beau et du Bien* (Paris, 1853). For a more complete discussion of Blanc, Cousin, and the idealizing impulse in nineteenth-century painting see Shaw, "Figure of Venus."

11 Blanc, *Grammaire*, 23.

12 "Nous l'avons dit bien souvent et l'on ne saurait trop le répéter: le nu est la seule base solide du grand art, et l'étude approfondie de la forme humaine est le point de départ nécessaire de toute éducation artistique sérieuse." Charles Clément, "Exposition de 1879," *Journal des Débats*, May 18, 1879, pp. 1–2.

13 "Les nus sont en général très faibles, et plusieurs d'entre eux ne sont que des nudités." Ibid.

14 "Un style à lui dans la langue spéciale qui parle, laquelle est la langue universelle du beau, des formes et des figures, inspirées, inventées pour l'éducation, l'édification esthétique." J. Buisson, "Le Salon de 1881," *Gazette des Beaux-Arts*, June 1881, p. 474.

15 Ibid.

16 Tamar Garb analyzes the way this discourse played itself out with respect to female Impressionists, in "Berthe Morisot and the Feminizing of Impressionism," in *Perspectives on Morisot*, ed. T. J. Edelstein (New York, 1990).

17 Lafenestre, "L'Art au Salon de 1879," 679.

18 Louis de Fourcaud, "Le Salon du Gaulois," *Le Gaulois*, May 16, 1879, p. 2.

19 "Dessin d'une correction infinie; merveille de composition; suavité perpétuelle; modelé ravissant; morbidesse incorrigible. . . . Quant à la pâte, n'en cherchez nulle part." Messire-Jean, "Le Salon IX," *Le Soir*, June 7, 1879, p. 1.

20 P. de Charray, "Le Salon de 1879," *Le Pays*, May 13, 1879, p. 3.

21 Messire-Jean, "Le Salon IX," 1879, p. 1.

22 Ibid.

23 "M. Puvis de Chavannes, afin d'être bien entendu, comme tous les réformateurs, a pu quelquefois insister, plus que de raison, sur ses principes. Il a pu exagérer la simplicité de ses compositions; peut-être a-t-il commis cette faute dans . . . ses *Jeunes Filles au Bord de la Mer*. . . . Mais, ces exagérations mêmes sont de celles qui mènent aux comparaisons utiles. La vue de ces fragments, doux aux regards, où l'harmonie tranquille des colorations laisse si simplement se développer les contours expressifs des figures, a donné à plus d'un l'horreur de tous ces tripotages étranges, d'une cuisine compliquée et généralement sombre, qui nous sont présentés comme des prodiges de peinture." Lafenestre, "L'Art au Salon de 1879," pp. 678–79.

24 Ernest Chesneau, "Le Salon de 1879," *Moniteur Universel*, June 6, 1879, p. 3.

25 "On n'y remarque plus que ses défauts, et ses défauts poussés à l'extrême. Ses figures ne sont plus que des larves sans forme et sans couleur, des ombres sèches et dégingandées. Je ne veux pas entrer dans le détail des incorrections, qui se volent de reste, signaler une jambe qui manque ou un sein placé en trop. C'est le système qui est mauvais, le point de vue qui est faux, la route qu'il faut arpenter en sens inverse." [Edmond] About, "Le Salon—III," *Dix-Neuvième Siècle*, May 17, 1879, p. 1.

26 "Le tableau, tel qu'on l'entend aujourd'hui, le tableau agréable qu'on embordure dans l'or et qu'on suspend dans son salon au milieu des colifichets mondains." Paul Mantz, "Chronique" *Le Temps*, May 25, 1879, n.p.

27 Puvis's distorting mode is amplified when it is translated

from mural painting, which covers large areas and is meant to be taken in from a distance, to easel painting, with its more intimate form of address. However, the distinctions between the two were not so hard and fast. For one thing, decorative paintings were usually shown in the Salon before being mounted at their sites, and it was here that judgment was passed upon them. And there were many academic painters who, when given official decorative commissions, did little to change their style and composition to make them more suitable for the large expanse of a wall.

28 "M. Puvis de Chavannes reste très indifférent aux détails de la forme embellie. Lorsque, au jour suprême, on dressera le catalogue de ses qualités et de ses faites, on verra qu'il a dessiné bien des pieds barbares, bien des mains aventureuses. Dans les *Jeunes Filles au Bord de la Mer*, . . . le dédain pour la beauté ne se dissimule pas. L'une des femmes a les plus pauvres épaules du monde. Ce qu'il y a de surprenant, c'est qu'après avoir constaté les inélégances de l'auteur, on les oublie. La parfaite harmonie de l'ensemble, la justesse de l'impression, la sobriété des couleurs qui parlent si bas qu'elles semble vouloir se taire, et surtout une certaine étrangeté dans l'accent suprême le détail incomplet ou mal venu. Telle est du moins notre impression actuelle. Elle ne s'est pas formulée en un jour. Avec M. Puvis de Chavannes, nous avions commencé par la résistance et il nous fallu quelque temps pour goûter son charme un peu maladif." Mantz, "Chronique."

29 Fourcaud, "Le Salon du Gaulois" (1879), p. 2. Cardon also pointed to this: "M. Puvis de Chavannes's facture is often incomplete." Cardon, "Salon de 1879, IX–La Peinture," 3.

30 "Je ne décrirai point . . . ses *Jeunes Filles au Bord de la Mer*. Inutile d'expliquer le chinois à qui ne veut pas l'apprendre. D'ailleurs, c'est très long à traduire; et je n'ai ni le courage de faire le pédant ni l'envie d'être ennuyeux." Messire-Jean, "Le Salon IX" (1879).

31 "C'est un poète qui sent profondément et qui sait exprimer son sentiment profond." Ibid.

32 "On commence par en être troublé; on finit par en subir le charme." Fourcaud, "Le Salon du Gaulois" (1879), p. 2.

33 "Proteste qui voudra contre le charme pénétrante de sa manière! Moi, je l'aveu que je le subis de la façon la plus absolue et ne tenterai pas d'y échapper." Armand Silvestre, "Le Monde des Arts: Dieux et Déesses au Salon de 1879," *Moniteur des Arts*, 1879, pp. 100–101.

34 "Les . . . tableaux de M. Puvis de Chavannes répondent à un besoin, à un sentiment très actuel et très moderne. Il y a des moments où, las des allées et venues inutiles des bavardages, des énormes bruits affolés, des théories du pittoresque et de l'importance usurpée brutalement par le tohu-bohu des circonstances turbulentes, on voudrait se réfugier dans quelque chose de nu, d'infini, dans un rien de tout qui du moins fût calme et silencieux. Telles ces *Jeunes Filles au Bord de la Mer* qui, réduites à leur expression la plus abstraite, dénouent leur cheveux et songent, nues devant un flot immobile, que rien ne remuera jamais, sous un ciel immuable, dans une atmosphère exempte de mouvement et de vie. Cependant, quoique pures comme l'onde azurée, au moins j'aime à le croire, elles semble désespérées comme les Femmes Damnées de Baudelaire; Elles voudraient aller encore plus loin, près d'une mer encore plus tranquille, et que n'aurait effleurée ni le vol des blancs oiseaux, ni le regard des yeux humains. Ah! je les comprends!" Théodore Banville, "Salon de 1879—IV," *Le National de* 1869, May 21, 1879, p. 1.

35 This is, need it be said, a male fantasy that was widespread in the painting and literature of the nineteenth century and that most often had both misogynistic and homophobic resonances.

36 Charles Baudelaire, *Les Fleurs du Mal*, trans. Richard Howard (London, 1987), 129–30.

Comme un bétail pensif sur le sable couchées,
Elles tournent leurs yeux vers l'horizon des mers,
Et leurs pieds se cherchant et leurs mains rapprochées
Ont de douces langueurs et des frissons amers. (Charles Baudelaire, *Oeuvres Complètes* [Paris, 1990], 84)

37 Baudelaire, *Les Fleurs du Mal*, 130.

Vous que dans votre enfer mon âme a poursuivies,
Pauvre soeurs, je vous aime autant que je vous plains
Pour vos mornes douleurs, vos soifs inassouvies,
Et les urnes d'amour dont vos grands coeurs sont pleins! (Baudelaire, *Oeuvres Complètes*, 85)

38 Baudelaire, *Les Fleurs du Mal*, 127.

39 Ibid., 129.

Descendez, descendez, lamentables victimes,

. . .

Ombres folles, cours au but de vos désirs;
Jamais vous ne pourrez assouvir votre rage,
Et votre châtiment naîtra de vos plaisirs

. . .

Loin des peuples vivants, errantes, condamnées,
A travers les déserts courez comme les loups;
Faites votre destin, âmes désordonnées,
Et fuyez l'infini que vous portez en vous! (Baudelaire, *Oeuvres Complètes*, 86)

40 For a discussion of the intersections between debates about Puvis's work and debates about Symbolist poetry in the 1890s see Shaw, "Wandering Gaze."

41 "Elle est l'art de sentir à l'occasion de l'objet, et comme de s'abandonner aux suggestions qu'il provoque, jusqu'à ce qu'ayant pris elles-mêmes quelque chose de l'inconsistance du rêve, elles se traduisent à leur tour par des sensations qui en imitent le caractère flottant, irréel et bizarre." Ferdinand Brunetière, "La Statue de Baudelaire," *Revue des Deux Mondes*, September 1, 1892, p. 216.

42 Ferdinand Brunetière, "Le Symbolisme Contemporain," *Revue des Deux Mondes*, April 1, 1891, pp. 685–86.

43 "L'art, en général, peut corriger, rectifier, modifier, continuer, prolonger même ce qu'il imite." Ibid., pp. 683–84.

44 "Nous voulons déchirer le voile; et nous voulons atteindre enfin l'essence dont les manifestations se jouent à la surface des choses. . . . Les symbolistes estiment que le vague et l'imprécis, que le flottant et le fugitif, que l'aérien et l'impondérable sont une partie de la poésie." Ibid., 684–85.

45 "Le moins 'spirituel' de tous, l'odorat est le sens dont les impressions s'échangent le plus aisément avec celles des autres." Brunetière, "La Statue," 214. What Brunetière calls *baudelairisme* is an engagement with the reader's most debased sensual faculties—a cultivation of them, we might even say. He describes Emile Zola, Joris Karl Huysmans, and Paul Verlaine as writers whose work falls under the category of *baudelairisme* because they all represent a debased materialism and a lack of focus on moral messages. For a conservative like Brunetière, both the Symbolists and Zola stood for a kind of materialism that was quintessentially modern—materialism that should be contrasted with the morality and idealism of traditional culture. Significantly, these three writers are usually seen to be in opposing camps—Zola as a naturalist novelist and Huysmans and Verlaine more closely aligned as Decadent and Symbolist. This points to the problem of defining Symbolism as a reaction to realism when addressing the literature and art of this period. See Christophe Charle, *La Naissance des "Intellectuels," 1880–1900* (Paris, 1990).

46 "Tandis que les couleurs ou les formes limitent, pour ainsi parler, la liberté du rêve, en dessinant les contours avec quelque précision, les odeurs au contraire l'émancipent, la favorisent, et l'exaltent," Brunetière, "Le Statue," 215.

47 Ibid.

48 Brunetière's characterization of Baudelaire becomes even closer to Banville's description of Puvis when he analyzes particular poems—for example, his assessment of Baudelaire's poem "Rêve Parisien." The narrator of the daydream refers to himself as a "peintre fier de mon génie" and the stanzas of the poem that Brunetière quotes recount a fantasy landscape similar to those painted by Puvis, replete with classical colonnades and self-reflective naiads. Brunetière is particularly worried about the combination of such subject matter with the emphasis on the sensual aspects of words. The repeated sounds and rhythms of the poem are so incantatory, suggests Brunetière, that Baudelaire's poem is ultimately "nothing but empty forms; and the only impression one keeps of it is of hollow rattling of words." Brunetière, "La Statue," 220–21.

49 "Au lieu donc de tyranniser la liberté de l'imagination et du rêve, ils demandent que la poésie les rende à leur essor." Brunetière, "Le Symbolisme," 685.

50 "L'unité du moi dans une diversité d'états d'âme successifs . . . de le rendre à la volupté vagabonde du rêve." Ibid.

51 "L'une des pires conséquences qu'elles puissent entraîner, c'est en isolant l'art, d'isoler aussi l'artiste, d'en faire pour lui-même une idole, et comme de l'enfermer dans le sanctuaire de son *moi*. . . . il n'y a plus rien qu'il respecte ou qu'il épargne, . . . la vraie définition de l'immoralité. . . . c'est la glorification de l'égoïsme, et par suite la négation même de la solidarité." Brunetière, "La Statue," 221.

52 Brunetière, "Le Symbolisme," 691.

53 Henry Havard, "Le Salon de 1881," *Le Siècle*, May 14, 1881, p. 1.

54 Edmond Villetard, "Le Salon de 1881," *Le Français*, May 25, 1881, p. 1.

55 "Le Salon de 1881," *La Patrie*, May 27, 1881, p. 3. Charles Flor even suggested that by exhibiting *Poor Fisherman* at the Salon, Puvis was thumbing his nose at the Academy. Flor, "Le Salon de 1881," p. 2. Even though the government had ceded control of the Salon jury to the artists, the Salon jury remained in the hands of the Academy because the artist members of the Société des Beaux-Arts had voted them onto the jury of their own accord. They had voted Puvis on, too, but he refused to serve.

56 "A force de vouloir transfigurer son *Pauvre Pêcheur*, l'artiste l'a bien moins divinisé qu'il n'en a fait un triste personnage." Edouard Thierry, "Salon de 1881," *Moniteur Universel*, May 17, 1881, p. 1.

57 "Qu'est-ce que ce lamentable Ecce Homo, ce faux Christ demi-nu les mains jointes devant lui, un vieux linge autour de la tête en guise de couronne d'épines, en contemplation douloureuse devant son mât comme devant l'instrument de sa passion?" Ibid.

58 Edmond About, "Salon de 1881," *Le Dix-Neuvième Siècle*, May 12, 1881, p. 1.

59 Ibid.

60 Fourcaud, "Salon du Gaulois," *Le Gaulois*, May 2, 1881, p. 1.

61 "Jamais ils ne se jugeront assez pénétrants, assez avancés dans l'intimité des êtres, assez maîtres de leurs conceptions. Leur art est véritablement, suivant un mot célèbre, le culte extérieur qu'ils rendent à leurs idées. S'ils dominent le métier, ils méprisent tout artifice; en tout cas, ils arrivent à des concentrations si grandes, à de si puissantes synthèses, qu'on les tient au-dessus du métier et que tout leur est permis." Ibid.

62 Ibid.

63 "Je comprends qu'on s'irrite contre une pareille oeuvre; ce qui est certain, c'est qu'elle finit par émouvoir. Elle s'est échappée du profond d'un rêve humain; elle est d'une humanité profonde." Ibid.

64 This notion of the exteriorization of the idea would become one of the theoretical bases of Symbolism. See, for example, Jean Moréas, "Un Manifeste Littéraire: Le Symbolisme," *Le Figaro, Supplément Littéraire*, September 18, 1886, p. 150. Many of the early attempts to define Symbolism were reprinted in *Les Premières Armes du Symbolisme* (Paris, 1889). For a recent account of literary Symbolism see Richard Candida Smith, *Mallarmé's Children: Symbolism and the Renewal of Experience* (Berkeley, 1999).

65 "Ceux qu'étreint et qu'éperonne le tourment de la nouveauté produisent . . . des oeuvres inégales et parfois incorrectes, mais profondes, synthétiques, et qui valent des symboles." Fourcaud, "Salon du Gaulois" (1881), p. 1.

66 "Engage-toi dans ton propre chemin disent les deux autres; sonde la vie, sonde l'âme qui est la tienne, livre-toi à tes propres sensations, seconde tes propres désirs, soulage tes obsessions propres, va droit à l'avenir et ne tourne jamais la tête." Ibid.

67 Arthur Schopenhauer, quoted in Albert Hofstadter, *Philosophies of Art and Beauty* (New York, 1964), 449.

68 Philippe Burty, "Salon de 1881," *La République Française*, May 2, 1881, pp. 1–2. Burty attributed this problem not to Puvis's modernity but to his "mysticism," a quality often associated with the region of France surrounding Lyons, the area where Puvis was born. Puvis's natural tendency toward "mysticism," said Burty, led him to "shun everything that might materialize his intention." Another critic parodied Puvis's use of allusion in similar terms, saying that the artist had taken it upon himself to "inaugurate in France painting by signs." He felt that *Poor Fisherman* was a manifesto—"a veritable declaration of principles," and the general principle was a refusal to use the means of painting to fully indicate any part of the material world: "This fisher, who is neither flesh nor fish, occupies the center of a simulacrum of a painting, in an insinuation of a raft, which goes to the mouth of an absent river. To call things by their names, this canvas is only the stenographic summary of a sketch." A. Baluffe, "Le Salon de 1881," *L'Artiste*, June 1, 1881, p. 830.

69 Dieu de Dieu! . . . Juste ciel!. . . .
Son Pauvre pêcheur, grisaille enluminée par plaques,
est un défi au sens commun.
De l'Epinal chlorotique.
Pas de couleur sur la toile. Pas de chair sur les os. Pas
de créature dans les vêtements. Pas de. . .
Total: zéro. ("Chronique Parisienne: Le Salon de 1881, *Journal Amusant*, May 7, 1881, p. 2)

70 In a similar, though more serious, vein, the critic for the Catholic paper *L'Univers* commented that "M. Puvis de Chavannes has exhibited a Poor Fisherman. Very poor fishermen, in fact: by virtue of being simplified, M. Chavannes's figures become 'phantoms without bones.'" "Salon de 1881." *L'Univers*, May 11, 1881, p. 2. Here, as in *Young Girls by the Seashore* (whose figures, we should remember, were described by About as "larvae without form or color"), the body is said to be dematerialized by Puvis's technique, but in such a way that lack of structure leads to distortion and the evocation of death. And as we saw in the previous critic's response, death can easily suggest the body in its most material but least sensuous state. There are many other examples of this invocation of the dead or decaying body. Edmond About referred to the "poor fisherman, his poor wife, and his poor dropsical child." About, "Salon de 1881," p. 1. Messire-Jean moved even more explicitly from the spiritual to the bodily in his description of the painting. And his account included not only death but sexuality. This critic, among others, punned upon the word "fisher" (*pêcheur*)—or "sinner" (*pécheur*)—and linked the joke to sexuality. The deformed figure of the child is referred to as a "fetus," presumably dead, which is the offspring of the sinner/fisherman. Messire-Jean, "Le Salon—V," *Le Soir*, May 26, 1881, p. 2. Similarly, Edmond Villetard complained that the fisherman was "badly drawn," that the child was "swollen, sleeping or dead," that the figure on the bank was a "poor fisherwoman or poor sinner-woman who, I believe, cuts flowers so as not to tear out her hair." Distortions of drawing transmute into attributions of illness, madness, and death. Villetard ended with confusion: "What does all this mean? Infantile composition, drawing that would make an Impressionist recoil." Edmond Villetard, "Le Salon de 1881," *Le Français*, May 25, 1881, p. 1. Similarly, Burty described the woman as having "gestures of a lunatic" and the child as "abandoned like a cadaver." Burty, "Salon de 1881," p. 1.

71 "Le pêcheur est veuf; il emmène ses enfants avec lui ne sachant où les laisser. Il est anéanti dans sa solitude. Il est écrasé dans la grandeur de la nature. L'eau s'étend, morne et solennelle jusqu'à l'infini." Fourcaud, "Salon du Gaulois" (1881), p. 1. That Fourcaud's fantasy should take such a form is hardly surprising given the general malaise about the fecundity of women, which had been increasing since the Franco-Prussian War. It plays upon depopulation fears that had been sparked by the war, fears that were focused on a campaign to keep women securely within the maternal role. In this particular case, the fantasy spun out of Puvis's painting is anything but threatening to the social order. See Karen Offen, "Depopulation, Nationalism and Feminism in Fin-de-Siècle France," *American Historical Review* 89 (1984): 648–76.

72 "Un pays extraordinaire, étrange, surprenant, déconcertant, mais sublime et d'une magie si spéciale qu'on s'oublie à méditer ce poème et qu'on ne songe pas à regarder comment il est exécuté. M. Puvis de Chavannes nous fait entrer dans son tableau dans sa vision." Fourcaud, "Salon du Gaulois" (1881), p. 1.

CHAPTER 2. DREAM'S BODY

1 "Les Arts et les Muses, en effet, symbolisent et enfantent toutes les créations que comporte un monument consacré à l'art." The artist went on to elaborate: "Au centre du tableau, au pied d'un double portique ionien qui les relie, apparaissent les trois Arts plastiques: l'Architecture assise sur un fragment de colonne, la Sculpture debout à ses côtés, et la Peinture accueillant l'hommage d'un enfant qui répand des fleurs sur sa robe blanche (allusion à l'art particulier où se sont illustrés les artistes lyonnais); près d'elles sont éparses les Muses inspiratrices: Polymnie, un bras levé, les charme et les exalte par son éloquence; Clio, tenant ses tablettes, s'apprête à écrire l'impartiale Histoire; Calliope, assise, déroulant la page épique sur laquelle on lit: Arma virumque can, va chanter la gloire des héros, pendant que deux génies cueillent des branches de laurier et tressent des couronnes. Sur la gauche, Thalie, la Muse de la Comédie, s'arrête attentive, et d'Euterpe, les deux arts de la Poésie et de la Musique, qui traversent mystérieusement l'espace dans leurs longues robes flottantes. Au second plan, Uranie, étendue sur le bord d'un lac, contemple les constellations que se reflète dans les eaux éclairées par l'or du couchant.—A l'écart, sous un saule, Melpomène médite les scènes de la Tragédie. Le paysage, baigné par la silencieuse lumière du soir, est limité par des hautes montagnes qui ferment l'accès de ce lieu de prédilection, et ne laissent voir qu'une étroite bande de ciel.—Sur le sol, semé d'arbustes et de fleurs, se dressent des arbres des altitudes épiques, le laurier, le pin, le chêne." Henri Lechat, "Puvis de Chavannes au Musée de Lyon: La Décoration de l'Escalier Neuf du Palais des Arts," *Gazette des Beaux-Arts*, October 1920, p. 236. Lechat notes that the explanatory pamphlet was printed in Paris and suggests that Puvis probably provided the description.

2 In paintings like *Charles Martel Saving Christianity by His Victory over the Saracens near Poitiers* (1874), for example, Puvis showed both the triumphant and the vanquished on the eve of the Battle of Poitiers. Other murals offered more generalized depictions of the places where they were situated, often with historical reference points. In the pair of murals for Marseilles, *Marseilles, Greek Colony* and *Marseilles, Gateway to the Orient*, the characteristic landscape of the port is pictured at two defining moments in its history.

3 Antoine de Baecque, "The Allegorical Image of France, 1750–1800: A Political Crisis of Representation," *Representations* 47 (Summer 1994): 111.

4 Ibid., 116.

5 See L.-F. Alfred Maury, *Le Sommeil et les Rêves*, 4th ed. (Paris, 1878); Edmond Colsenet, *La Vie Inconsciente de l'Esprit* (Paris, 1880). For historical accounts of the dream in the nineteenth century see Yannick Ripa, *Histoire du Rêve* (Paris, 1988); Henri F. Ellenberger, *The Discovery of the Unconscious* (New York, 1970).

6 "Borné par de hauts rochers noirs, qui ferment l'horizon, le bois se développe dans le calme profond des solitudes sereines." Edmond Jacques, "Le Salon 1884," *L'Intransigeant*, May 1, 1884, p. 2.

7 "Le Salon de 1884," *Le Français*, May 6, 1884, p. 3.

8 Gustave Geffroy, "Salon de 1884," *La Justice*, May 7, 1884, p. 2.

9 "L'emploi presque exclusif des verticales et des horizontales, le choix d'une tonalité grise et éteinte." "Le Salon de 1884," *Moniteur des Arts*, May 6, 1884, p. 1.

10 One exception was Joséphin Péladan. When he reviewed the Salon exhibition in 1884, he probably had access to special information about the painting provided by Puvis or someone close to him. Péladan's identification of the figures corresponds exactly with the description provided to viewers at the Museum of Fine Arts in Lyons when the painting was installed in 1886. Nevertheless, even with this information, Péladan did not think the painting signified in the conventional fashion. He marveled at Puvis's ability to "disengage himself from the entire history of art and treat this subject as if he were its inventor." Péladan praised the composition and the grouping of figures, but he was most interested in "the character of each figure taken in isolation." Puvis, he suggested, was able to make each individual figure signify without the use of conventional allegorical attributes. The Muses were specified, said Péladan, not by the attributes they carried but through the disposition of their bodies. He identified the reclining figure who contemplates the reflection of the moon in the water as Urania, the astronomer. He marveled at the "stylish modernity" of Thalia, the actress—a quality he attributed to the distribution (*le piètement*) of her limbs: "a hand on hip and her chin in hand." Using a vocabulary associated with furniture building (*le piètement* refers to the legs and crosspieces in furniture), Péladan emphasized the objecthood of her body and the way that its horizontals and verticals echoed the general design of the canvas. Rather than reading past the bodies to an allegorical meaning fixed by the attributes, Péladan suggested that viewers would find meaning in the bodies themselves: "When one dreams that these twelve allegories are recognizable without *the least* attribute, when one compares this *Sacred Grove* to all the other exhibition entries . . . one is definitely forced to proclaim, and without any reticence, that Puvis de Chavannes is the greatest master of the time." Joséphin Péladan, "Salon de 1884—II. La Peinture Lyrique M. Pierre Puvis de Chavannes," *L'Artiste* (June 1884): 424–52. Péladan's analysis points out the demands these bodies made on contemporary viewers and the way they claimed priority as a site of meaning without an appeal to conventionalized poses, gestures, or attributes. However, Péladan implied that the body itself would successfully replace the allegorical attribute as the key to meaning, whereas I would suggest that the bodies in *The Sacred Grove* never offered the kind of stable meaning that Péladan attributed to them. Most responses to the painting when it was displayed at the Salon failed to give specific readings of the figures, although most who wrote described them as generally powerful and captivating.

11 "On peut se promener à l'aise dans ces grandes toiles; on vole à droite, à gauche, sans risquer de se cogner. A peine rencontre-t-on de loin en loin quelque figure pensive et solitaire, contre laquelle on pourrait même se heurter sans grand danger, tant elle est diaphane. On dirait d'ailleurs que c'est pour nous, peuple des oiseaux, que peint M. de Chavannes: Il place toujours la scène de ses compositions dans des lieux ravissants et mystérieux où ces lourdauds d'humains n'ont jamais pénétré." "Le Salon de 1884," *Le Français*, May 6, 1884, p. 3.

12 "Nulle action précise, nulle occupation définie. Ces figures dont le geste et la marche sont une cadence, dont la physionomie dit le repos que rien ne peut troubler, apparaissent dans ce bois silencieux, comme des visions de rêve." Geffroy, "Le Salon de 1884," p. 3.

13 Geffroy was not the only critic to react this way. An anonymous critic for *Le Gaulois* thought that Puvis's painterly means had "a particular magic" that was derived from this combination of indeterminacy and sensual pleasure. Although the figures had a certain familiarity—"the Arts and Muses are known to me," said the critic—they also left him dissatisfied. "I have the need to rebel," he complained, "to demand more innocent figures, more human action, a more precise set of facts." Like a memory, the figures were too hazy and imprecise to be satisfying. Despite his dissatisfaction, he went on to describe how, as he gazed at *The Sacred Grove*, his faculties of critical judgment gave way to the enjoyment of the sensual pleasures offered by the work: "This general harmony where the blue dominates with the yellow is delicious; . . . I have before me a tapestry; it is impossible for me to take it as a work of truth, but my eye submits to ravishment. M. Puvis de Chavannes has never been further from the real, but his poetic fantasy imposes itself on me despite myself." "Le Gaulois Salon," *Le Gaulois*, 1884, supplement, p. 2. The original French reads: "M. de Chavannes a atteint son but par des procédés d'une magie particulière. Les figures des Arts et des Muses, . . . me sont des figures connues . . . j'ai envie de m'insurger, de réclamer des figures plus neuves, une action plus humaine, un ensemble de faits plus précis; mais le charme opère et je me prends à admirer tout net. Cette harmonie générale où le bleu domine avec le jaune, est délicieuse. . . . J'ai devant moi une tapisserie, il m'est impossible de la tenir pour une oeuvre de vérité mais mon oeil subit le ravissement. M. Puvis de Chavannes n'a peut-être jamais été si loin du réel, mais sa fantaisie de poète s'impose à moi, malgré moi-même."

14 "Les abréviations voulues par M. Puvis de Chavannes ne sont pas des erreurs de dessinateur, mais des sacrifices volontaires et nécessaires. Il n'y avait rien à préciser des corps et des vêtements de ces nobles filles qui ne vivent que dans nos imaginations." Geffroy, "Le Salon de 1884," 2.

15 "M. Puvis de Chavannes, au lieu de chercher à formuler un idéal impossible à atteindre se contente d'en éveiller la notion dans les esprits. Il nous laisse, en somme, faire les tableaux pour les trois quarts." Henri Fouquier, "Le Salon," *Gil Blas*, May 1, 1884, p. 2.

16 "Il ne fait pas jour là-dedans et il n'y fait pas même nuit, quoiqu'une lune absente au ciel reflète son croissant dans quelque chose de jaune qui cependant n'est pas de l'eau. Quelques arbres chétifs et mal venus qui voudraient bien être des chênes, des saules, des pins et des lauriers, mais qui s'en tiennent à l'intention, s'élèvent." [Edmond] About, "Salon de 1884," *Le Dix-Neuvième Siècle*, May 8, 1884, p. 1.

17 "Mannequins informes, de larves pâles, molles et disloquées qui ne rappellent la figure humaine que de bien loin. . . . Un enfant qui a les bras sensiblement plus longs que les jambes contemple avec étonnement la main énorme de sa mère et lui demande avec naïveté si son mal ne serait pas l'éléphantiasis." Ibid. The language he chooses is reminiscent of his descriptions of Puvis's work beginning with the exhibition of the *Young Girls by the Seashore* and becomes a kind of formula for About when talking about Puvis's work, which he modifies to accommodate particular pictures.

18 Hayward Gallery, *Toulouse-Lautrec* (London, 1992), 122–25; quotation on p. 124.

19 "M. de Chavannes a atteint son but par des procédés d'une magie particulière. Les figures des Arts et des Muses . . . me sont des figurés connues . . . j'ai envie de m'insurger, de réclamer des figures plus neuves, une action plus humaine, un ensemble de faits plus précis; mais le charme opère et je me prends à admirer tout net. Cette harmonie générale où le bleu domine avec le jaune, est délicieuse. . . . J'ai devant moi une tapisserie, il m'est impossible de la tenir pour une oeuvre de vérité mais mon oeil subit le ravissement. M. Puvis de Chavannes n'a peut-être jamais été si loin du réel, mais sa fantaisie de poète s'impose à moi, malgré moi-même." "Le Gaulois Salon" (1884), p. 2.

20 "Il faut prendre son parti de voir ce qu'il y met et ne pas s'obstiner à y chercher ce qui ne s'y trouve pas. Ce qui s'y trouve, c'est le rêve incomplètement formulé d'un artiste très sincère, à l'esprit élevé, distingué, poétique qui ne sait donner une expression précise et, au point de vue technique, parfaitement satisfaisante à sa pensée, mais qui dit assez pourtant pour se faire comprendre et pour entraîner le spectateur après lui dans les plus hautes régions de l'art." Charles Clément, "Exposition Annuelle de 1884," *Journal des Débats*, April 30, 1884, p. 2.

21 "Les figures sont trop égrenées, trop dispersées, et que l'ensemble manque à un trop haut degré de concentration et de cohésion." Ibid., 1.

22 "Maître dangereux, il est un artiste admirable. Mais il ne peut plaire à tous et j'ajouterai qu'il serait déplorable qu'il fait trop goûter de tout le monde. Il doit rester dans notre école à l'état d'exception singulière et charmante." Fouquier, "Le Salon" (1884), p. 2.

23 Clément, "Exposition Annuelle de 1884," 1.

24 "Naturalisme . . . chez qui la notion . . . de transformation esthétique en un mot, n'existe que peu ou point, qui mettent au premier rang les qualités d'exécution matérielle et ces idées de *vie*, de *vérité atmosphérique*, de *trompe l'oeil*." Ibid.

25 See Marie-Claude Genet-Delacroix, *L'Art et l'Etat sous la IIIème République: Le Système des Beaux-Arts, 1870–1940*, vol. 31, *Histoire de la France aux XIXe et XXe siècles*, ed. Université de Paris I (Paris, 1992), 129 n. 53.

26 "En dépit des railleries truculentes qu'on lui adresse si fréquemment sur son idéalisme éthéré, sur son ascétisme esthétique, M. Puvis de Chavannes est un vrai *naturaliste*, qui sait, il est vrai, allier l'ampleur du style, l'originalité de l'imagination, à un sentiment profond du réalisme." Marius Vachon, "Le Salon II: M. Puvis de Chavannes," *La France*, May 13, 1884, pp. 2–3. This was a strategy typical of republican and Left-leaning critics, including Geffroy and Mirbeau, who, if they even used the notion of idealism to describe Puvis, attempted to redefine it as something that was not transcendent and universal but immanent in humanity.

27 Mirbeau was also a well-known novelist and member of the literati who would eventually associate with the Left, even flirting with anarchism. In 1884, however, he was still writing for conservative newspapers, such as *Le Gaulois*. According to Reg Carr, his "conversion" to anarchism did not begin until 1885. His aesthetic opinions, however, seem to have been ahead of his political ones. On Mirbeau's anarchism see Reg Carr, *Anarchism in France: The Case of Octave Mirbeau* (Manchester, England, 1977).

28 "Comme si le Beau s'apprenait ainsi que la grammaire, et comme s'il existait un Beau plus Beau, un Beau vrai, un Beau unique; comme si le Beau n'était pas la faculté toute personnelle." "Il ne nous est pas permis de casser ces formes et de plier ces lignes sous la pression d'une idée personnelle ou d'une vision particulière." Octave Mirbeau, "Notes sur l'Art: Puvis de Chavannes," *La France*, November 8, 1884, reprinted in *Combats Esthétiques*, vol. 1 (Paris, 1993), 72.

29 "Le rêve abstrait et charmant où l'humanité se décolore et se volatilise." Ibid.

30 "Ce qui m'émeut profondément dans Puvis de Chavannes, c'est que ce grand artiste, qui est aussi un grand poète, n'est d'aucun temps, d'aucune école, d'aucune coterie et d'aucune routine. Il me fait l'effet d'un attardé en cette époque de civilisation à la vapeur et de préjugés persistants: attardé ou réminiscent, je ne sais au juste; attardé aux poésies latentes et non révélées, ou réminiscent des paradis perdus?" Ibid., 73.

31 "Il ne le voit, de la vie, il s'est renfermé, en quelque sorte abstrait, en un rêve magnifique que comme une grande et lente palpitation d'ailes dans l'azur. Il voit en dedans." Ibid.

32 A. Robida, "Le Salon Comique: Modernisme, Antiquisme," *La Caricature*, May 17, 1884, p. 161

33 See, for example, Richer's "Tableau Synoptique de la 'Grande Attaque Hystérique Complète et Régulière' avec Positions Typique et 'Variantes.'" *Etudes Cliniques*, 1881, reproduced in Georges Didi-Huberman, *Invention de l'Hystèrie: Charcot et l'Iconographie Photographique de la Salpetrière* (Paris, 1982).

34 Janet Beizer, *Ventriloquized Bodies: Narratives of Hysteria in Nineteenth-Century France* (Ithaca, N.Y., 1993). This very process of inscription, this transformation of the female body into a hysterical body to be diagnosed and categorized by science, becomes, Beizer suggests, a method of control. Carol Armstrong relates the "reflexive physicality" and "disordered bodily vocabulary" of Degas's nudes to representations of the dysfunctional body in psychological discourses such as Charcot's and Richer's in which "bodily disorder and asymmetry were seen as signs of deviant social and psychological states." Armstrong notes that "their accounts . . . seem to be based on the assumption that *any* form of corporeal expressiveness denoted deviance and excess" and that "the equation between expression and the dysfunctional was most often located in the female body." Carol Armstrong, *Odd Man Out: Readings of the Work and Reputation of Edgar Degas* (Chicago, 1991), 186. I have learned much from Armstrong's work on Degas's treatment of the nude.

35 "Un respect involontaire vous saisit, un charme inexpliqué vous cloue sur plan." Firmin Javel, "Le Salon," *L'Evénement*, May 4, 1884, p. 2.

36 "Dans la contemplation du beau, dans l'effet que peut produire sur nous une oeuvre d'art, il y a quelque chose d'étrange, et que l'on n'a pas encore bien expliqué. Il est tout naturel que nous regardions les belles choses avec plaisir. Mais ne nous arrive-t-il pas, après les avoir contemplées quelques temps, de tomber dans une sorte d'extase qui se prolongerait indéfiniment si quelque accident extérieur ne nous rappelait pas à nous-mêmes? Dans les illusions que produit la peinture n'y a-t-il pas de l'hallucination? . . . En réfléchissant à ces faits, on ne pourra manquer de constater l'analogie qu'ils présentent avec certains phénomènes troublants, déconcertants, qui depuis quelques années surexcitent vraiment la curiosité publique: je veux parler de l'hypnotisme. . . . Entre cet état d'hypnose et l'extase du beau, entre ces effets de la suggestion et ceux de l'art, il y a une ressemblance singulière, qui donne à penser. Bien qu'ils diffèrent évidemment par le degré, ne seraient-ils pas au fond de même nature?" Paul Souriau, *La Suggestion dans l'Art* (Paris, 1893), 1–2. Werth discusses this text in "'Le Bonheur de Vivre.'" Souriau was more than familiar with Puvis's painting. Indeed, he used Puvis as one of his main examples when formulating a general theory of creativity. See Paul Souriau, *L'Imagination de l'Artiste* (Paris, 1901).

37 The dangers of hypnotism and whether it could be used to incite people to crime was a subject of much popular debate. Demonstrations of hypnotism and somnambulism were common; hypnotists and their subjects were the main characters of novels and the subjects of journalism. The city of Marseilles even went to the extreme of banning shows put on by "saltimbanques en hypnotisme." There was extensive coverage in the Parisian press of a conference on hypnotism in Paris in 1889. See "L'Hypnotisme à Paris," *Le Siècle*, August 9, 1889, p. 3; "L'Actualité, Mesmer Vengé," *L'Eclair*, August 10, 1889, p. 1.

38 "L'objet de l'art est d'endormir les puissances actives ou plutôt résistantes de notre personnalité, et de nous amener ainsi à un état de docilité parfaite où nous réalisons l'idée qu'on nous suggère, où nous sympathisons avec le sentiment exprimé. Dans les procédés de l'art on retrouvera sous une forme atténuée, raffinés et en quelque sorte spiritualisés, les procédés par lesquels on obtient ordinairement l'état d'hypnose." Henri Bergson, *Essai sur les Données Immédiates de la Conscience* (Paris, 1991), 11.

39 Toward the end of the century, theories of suggestion were explicitly integrated into theories of education. Educational treatises often suggested the ways the teacher could, by the very strength of his personality, positively influence his students on an unconscious level. See, for example, Thomas, *La Suggestion, son Rôle dans l'Education* (Paris, 1898).

40 Margaret Werth analyzes the relationship of this discourse of healthy Frenchness and nationalism with Puvis de Chavannes, in "'Le Bonheur de Vivre.'"

41 Guyau hailed from a solidly republican background. In 1877 his mother wrote *Le Tour de France par Deux Enfants* under the pseudonym G. Bruno. This educational tract, aimed at teaching republican values to schoolchildren, helped to mold generations of French children into good French citizens. See Mayeur and Rebérioux, *Third Republic*, 87.

42 "Le besoin et le désir, c'est-à-dire l'agréable . . . voilà le critérium primitif et grossier de l'esthétique." J.-M. Guyau, *Les Problèmes de l'Esthétique Contemporaine* (Paris, 1884), 24–25.

43 See, for example, Cousin, *Du Vrai*; and Blanc, *Grammaire*. These texts are discussed in Chapter 1.

44 "En somme, rien de plus inexact que cette entière opposition . . . entre le sentiment du beau et le désir: ce qui est beau est désirable *sous le même rapport*. . . . Il n'est pas d'émotion esthétique qui n'éveille en nous une multitude de désirs et de besoins plus ou moins inconscients. . . . Il y a du plaisir dans le désir même et la période de désir nous reste souvent dans l'esprit comme plus délicieuse que la jouissance." Guyau, *Problèmes*, 27–28.

45 "Le désespoir de l'artiste et ce qui l'entraîne facilement au pessimisme, c'est de désirer ainsi démesurément et de ne pouvoir que dans une faible mesure satisfaire ses désirs." Ibid., 27–28.

46 Ibid., 23.

47 Ibid., 25.

48 Guyau died at a young age, and his theories were taken up and expanded by Alfred Fouillée, who had close ties to the state arts administrations. Fouillée was the second husband of Guyau's mother and thus technically Guyau's stepfather. He was also Guyau's student.

49 "Du fond incohérent et discordant des sensations et sentiments individuels, l'art dégage un ensemble de sensations et de sentiments qui peuvent retentir chez tous à la fois . . . qui peuvent ainsi donner lieu à une *association* de jouissances. Et le caractère de ces jouissances, c'est qu'elles ne s'excluent plus l'une l'autre, à la façon des plaisirs égoïstes, mais sont au contraire en essentielle 'solidarité'." Alfred Fouillée, "Introduction," in J.-M. Guyau, *L'Art au Point de Vue Sociologique* (Paris, 1889), ix.

50 "Tout art est-il un moyen de concorde sociale, et plus profond peut-être encore que les autres; car *penser* de la même manière, c'est beaucoup sans doute, mais ce n'est pas encore assez pour nous faire *vouloir* de la même manière: le grand secret, c'est de nous faire *sentir* tous de la même manière, et voilà le prodige que l'art accompli." Ibid., x.

51 Alfred Fouillée, "Les Grandes Conclusions de la Psychologie Contemporaine: La Conscience et Ses Transformations," *Revue des Deux Mondes* 107 (1891): 811.

CHAPTER 3. DREAMING THE FRENCH PATRIMONY

Epigraph: André Michel, "Salon de 1886," *Journal des Débats*, May 6, 1886.

1 This order would be reversed when the paintings were mounted in Lyons in September 1886. Walking up the museum stairs toward *The Rhône and the Saône*, viewers have *Christian Inspiration* on their left and *Ancient Vision* on their right. Someone standing at the top of the landing and facing *The Sacred Grove* has *Ancient Vision* on the left and *Christian Inspiration* on the right. *The Rhône and the Saône* is on the south wall at the top of the stairs, opposite *The Sacred Grove* and at the viewer's back. Thus, the alignment, within the triptych, between masculine and feminine that helped to structure the understanding of the paintings at the Salon no longer holds upon seeing the murals in the museum. All of the criticism I discuss in this chapter is taken from Salon reviews. Furthermore, I believe that the strong thematization of gender in the compositions themselves is enough to sustain the arguments I make in this chapter.

2 "La composition primordiale et génératrice autour de laquelle se grouperont des sujets complémentaires. Les Arts et les Muses, en effet, symbolisent et enfantent toutes les créations que comporte un monument consacré à l'art." Quoted in Henri Lechat, "Puvis de Chavannes au Musée de Lyon: La Décoration de l'Escalier Neuf du Palais des Arts," *Gazette des Beaux-Arts* (1920): 236.

3 The commission for the cycle was formalized in 1883. In the contract designating the program for the cycle, Puvis was explicit about his desire to provide paintings that were both appropriate to an art museum and "characteristic of Lyons and the region." *Puvis de Chavannes, 1824–1898* (Grand Palais, Paris, 1977), 194.

4 See André Chastel, "La Notion du Patrimoine," in *Les Lieux de Mémoire*, ed. Pierre Nora (Paris, 1984), 405–50.

5 The qualities that should be associated with each aspect of the heritage, as well as the relative weight that each moment should be given, were subjects of a dispute that had political implications. There was a strong republican tradition of associating the gothic heritage with individual creativity. In addition, republicans emphasized the democratic nature of the classical past, whereas the Right appropriated France's ancient heritage in the 1890s as the guarantor of racial purity. For a discussion of this phenomenon in the early twentieth century see Kenneth E. Silver, *Esprit de Corps: The Art of the Parisian Avant-Garde and the First World War, 1914–1925* (Princeton, N.J., 1989).

6 Daniel J. Sherman, *Worthy Monuments: Art Museums and the Politics of Culture in Nineteenth-Century France* (Cambridge, Mass., 1989).

7 Louis de Meurville, "Le Salon," *La Gazette de France*, May 7, 1886, p. 2.

8 "En bas les femmes rêvent, se reposent, ou travaillent. L'une souffle dans ses pipeaux; l'autre lève des yeux calme sur la beauté du site." Edmond Jacques, "Le Salon," *L'Intransigeant*, May 1, 1886, p. 2.

9 "Quelle absence de modelé, quelle négligence du détail, quel mépris de la forme et de la couleur dans cette Vision antique!" Meurville, "Le Salon" (1886), p. 2.

10 Saint-Ange, "Le Salon de 1886," *Le Français*, May 7, 1886, p. 3. Firmin Javel saw the two simply as lovers. Firmin Javel, "Le Salon," *L'Evénement*, May 3, 1886, p. 2.

11 Alfred Gassier, "Salon de 1886," *Le National de 1869*, May 2, 1886, pp. 1–2.

12 "D'un geste noble, inspiré, qui embrasse le paysage de terre, de mer et de ciel, elle semble dire à l'homme éveillé: 'Regarde, remplis tes yeux de cette vision, et travaille à nous faire des dieux!'. . . . L'artiste toujours contemple le spectacle qui se déroule devant lui." Octave Mirbeau, "Le Salon," *La France*, May 9, 1886, pp. 1–2 (reprinted in *Combats Esthétiques*, vol. 1, pp. 257–58). In André Michel's account the female figure on the cliffs was a muse handing a golden mallet to a sculptor. André Michel, "Salon de 1886," *Journal* *des Débats*, May 6, 1886, p. 3. Judith Gautier described the two as lovers and then suggested that they might be poet and muse, marking the intersection between physical love and creativity. Judith Gautier, "Le Salon," *Le Rappel*, May 1, 1886, pp. 1–2.

13 "Disséminées plutôt que disposées. . . . Nous nous sentons dépaysés. Et cela suffit pour que nous nous prêtions à la fantaisie de l'évocation." Saint-Ange, "Le Salon de 1886," *Le Français*, May 7, 1886, p. 3. The choice of vocabulary is interesting here. "Dépaysés" evokes associations with *unheimlich*, Freud's word for the "uncanny."

14 "Le regard circule librement, va, vient, s'arrête et se perd." Gustave Geffroy, "Salon de 1886," *La Justice*, May 9, 1886, p. 1.

15 "Il se dégage de ce paysage éthéré, élyséen, une solennité, si troublante, si empoignante, que l'émotion, cette qualité suprême de l'artiste, gagne le spectateur et le fait penser, songer, rêver malgré lui." Alexandre Georget, "Le Salon de 1886," *L'Echo de Paris*, May 1, 1886, pp. 1–3.

16 "Du ciel immense, profond, fluide et doux, tombe une paix magnifique, une paix fait de paresses et de voluptés." Mirbeau, "Le Salon" (1886; reprinted in *Combats Esthétiques*, vol. 1, p. 258).

17 "La rêverie peut s'égarer à l'infini." Ibid., 259.

18 Judith Gautier was the daughter of Théophile Gautier, who before his death had been a longtime friend of Puvis's. She was an extraordinarily well educated woman (she knew several languages, including Chinese) and one of the few women art critics to write under her own name instead of a male pseudonym. See Joanna Richardson, *Judith Gautier* (London, 1986).

19 "Tout dans cette toile respire le bonheur et la paix de l'âme bercée dans la beauté des choses." Gautier, "Le Salon" (1886).

20 For an excellent discussion of the aesthetic, political, and psychological ramifications of fantasies of origins in Puvis de Chavannes's and Matisse's work see Werth, "'Le Bonheur de Vivre'"; and Werth, "Engendering Imaginary Modernism," *Genders* 9 (1990): 49–74. Theorists of psychoanalysis in the twentieth century have described the fantasy of the maternal body as a site of pre-Oedipal fullness—of a time before the infiltration of language, culture, and the father's law. The problem posed to male critics by the desire to recapture the maternal is that it is a desire to return to a pre-subjective state associated with femininity. See Luce Irigaray, "Any Theory of the 'Subject' Has Always Been Appropriated by the 'Masculine,'" in *Speculum of the Other Woman*, trans. Gillian C. Gill (Ithaca, N.Y., 1985). For discussions of the pre-Oedipal maternal in relation to representation see Julia Kristeva, *Desire in Language: A Semiotic Approach to Literature and Art*, trans. Thomas Gora, Alice Jardine, and Leon S. Roudiez (New York, 1980). For discussions of Kristeva's writings about the maternal see Jacqueline Rose, *Sexuality in the Field of Vision* (London, 1976); Kaja Silverman, *The Acoustic Mirror: The Female Voice in Psychoanalysis and Cinema* (Bloomington, Ind., 1988). Richard Candida Smith discusses Kristeva's analysis of Symbolist poetry in the introduction to *Mallarmé's Children*.

21 "S'élèvent du regard à la contemplation et de la contemplation à l'extase." "Le Salon," *Le Radical*, May 4, 1886, p. 2.

22 Albert Wolff, "Le Salon," *Figaro-Salon*, May 17, 1886, pp. 3–4.

23 "Une idée de calme, de la paix sereine, du silence, du charme de mystère et de recueillement," "impavidité égoïste des coeurs païens," "se tournent vers un idéal de fraternité," Mirbeau, "Le Salon" (1886; reprinted in *Combats Esthétiques*, 260).

24 On homosociality in David's studio see Crow, *Emulation*. On the Primitifs see George Levitine, *The Dawn of Bohemianism: The Barbu Rebellion and Primitivism in Neoclassical France* (University Park, Pa., 1978). For an excellent case study of friendship between artists in the early nineteenth century see Stacy Garfinkel, "Painting and the Language of the Private in Early Nineteenth-Century France" (Ph.D. diss., University of California, Berkeley, 1998), 1–56. Some scholars have suggested that the heads of the artists are modeled on nineteenth-century Lyons painters and that the scene is meant to represent modern artists admiring the work of the Renaissance. See Anne Condon Peterson, "A Vision of Antiquity: A Re-Evaluation of Puvis de Chavannes" (M.A. thesis, University of Pittsburgh, 1961). Aimée Brown Price concurs with this suggestion. See Price, *Puvis de Chavannes*, 191.

25 "La mort attristant la vie, le tourment de coeur émaciant la chair, le mépris des joies présentes pour l'espoir et la terreur d'une existence future." "Les cagoules jouant le suaire" "le miracle et l'extase remplaçant dans l'esprit de l'homme les merveilles de la nature et les ivresses des sens." "Cette retraite d'où la femme est exclue et l'amour banni." Gautier, "Le Salon" (1886).

26 "Un moine, sorte de Fra Angelico, est occupé à peindre; Il est tout entier isolé dans son oeuvre, artiste d'un art immatériel, pieux ouvrier pour qui peindre, c'est prier." Saint-Ange, "Le Salon de 1886," 3.

27 "Des trois panneaux, voilà de beaucoup le meilleur. L'atmosphère est profonde, le calme et le recueillement dominent toute la scène; c'est la paix du Seigneur régnant sur le monde de la pensée." Meurville, "Le Salon" (1886), p. 2.

28 "Créatures de rêve dont les fronts bas paraissent habilités de pensées sereines et sérieuses et dont les gestes lents sont comme enveloppées de douceur." Michel, "Le Salon de 1886," 3.

29 "Dans le déroulement paisible des lignes synthétisées et un peu raides, dans les notes rabattues des bleus, des havanes, des roses, des verts argentés ou bleussans, des jaunes pâles au-dessus desquels vibre le bleu intense de la mer, on a la sensation de la fuite de ce rêve antique, inaccessibles désormais." Ibid.

30 "Un galop qui obéit une cadence"; "volonté agissante." "Les femmes du premier plan ne présentent pas des preuves aussi évidentes de la compréhension de l'antiquité, elles ont de la Grèce les attitudes et les gestes figés de statues, mais elles semblent mener sur cette terre joyeuse des existences isolées et inquiètes. Elles s'accoudent, elles se couchent sur le sol; une lassitude les envahit; leurs tristes regards errent dans le songe." Geffroy, "Salon de 1886," 1.

31 For a discussion of hysteria in men see Mark S. Micale, "Hysteria Male/Hysteria Female: Reflections on Comparative Gender Construction in Nineteenth-Century France and Britain," in *Science and Sensibility: Gender and Scientific Enquiry*, 1780–1945, ed. Marina Benjamin (Oxford, 1991), 200–239. I thank Amy Lyford for pointing me to this reference, as well as for helpful discussions of this topic.

32 "Qui obscurcissent même la sérénité des visages de ces femmes de la Grèce, recueillie en leur rêve intérieur, tristes et hallucinées comme des vierges gothiques." Geffroy, "Salon de 1886,"1.

33 "Où même le révolutionnaire se complique d'un religiosâtre"; "l'homme en lequel vit l'âme mystérieuse et mélancolique d'une race." Ibid.

34 Geffroy made this claim even though Puvis de Chavannes came from an old Bordelais family that had only recently moved to Lyons. Whether the artist was truly Bordelais or Lyonnais was a point of debate that had political implications. The artist himself always emphasized his lineage in Bordeaux, and so would his republican supporters who wished to distance the artist from Lyons, with its associations with religiosity and mysticism. See, for example, Vachon, *Puvis de Chavannes* (Paris, 1895), 3.

35 "Les rêveries peintes d'un Puvis de Chavannes expriment . . . quelques-unes de nos manières habituelles de rêver ou de regretter le bonheur, et c'est pourquoi [ce] maîtr[e], qui n'[a] jamais reproduit les côtés extérieurs et les apparences formelles de la vie contemporaine [est] cependant [l'un des artistes] les plus vraiment modernes de notre école." Michel, "Le Salon de 1886," 3. Michel also described Delacroix, Moreau, and Cazin as painters capable of evoking such dreams.

36 "Reproche à Puvis de Chavannes de *sentir* trop profondément la nature et de l'exprimer en de glorieuses synthèses. Ce procédé de simplification suggestive, il ne l'admet point. Suivant lui, la nature ne s'explique pas, ne s'interprète pas; on doit la copier sans y rien comprendre, de même qu'un ouvrier typographe compose, sans savoir le lire, du chinois ou de l'allemand. C'est ainsi seulement qu'on est un *moderne*." Mirbeau, "Le Salon" (1886; reprinted in *Combats Esthétiques*, vol. 1, pp. 257–58).

37 "Etre *moderne*, c'est fermer obstinément ses oreilles aux musiques, ses narines aux parfums des choses; c'est comprimer les battements de son coeur devant l'évocation des réalités, condensées en rêves, qui montent de la terre et tombent du ciel. Tout, dans cette nature immobilisée et muette, ne serait donc que rapports de ton et question de valeurs; une imagination, un enthousiasme, une observation, une poésie n'y pourraient jamais pénétrer; la pensée n'aurait pas le droit de glisser, un seul instant, sous les trompeuses surfaces, de descendre dans les profondeurs, pour aller se rafraîchir, se vivifier aux sources mêmes de la vie.

"Il n'est pas besoin de réfuter cette doctrine absurde et barbare, car elle se réfute d'elle-même. Elle fait du peintre une simple machine, une sorte d'outil inconscient et passif, elle lui interdit toutes les émotions, toutes les joies, toutes les voluptés douloureuses de l'enfantement." Ibid.

38 "L'oeil caressé aime à se reposer un instant dans ce vague et à goûter tout d'abord la sensation de rêve, qui est une de celles que l'oeuvre apporte. Ce sont nos songes les plus doux et les plus nobles, qui sont là flottants sur l'édifice, et qui s'y fixe sans avoir l'air de le heurter. Muses que nous avons invoquées au moins une fois, antiquité sublime qui soutient notre esprit et lui conserve les vestiges de sa grandeur, christianisme tendre qui a sauvé le monde en parlant si doucement et si tristement au coeur, souvenirs du pays natal qui nous rappellent la religion moderne de la patrie, tout se confond dans une synthèse peinte de la vie spirituelle." Edouard Aynard, *Les Peintures Décoratives de Puvis de Chavannes au Palais des Arts* (Lyons, 1884), 6–7.

39 "Qu'est-ce qu'une nation?" was delivered as a lecture at the Sorbonne on March 11, 1882, and subsequently published in a volume of collected essays, *Discours et Conférences* (Paris, 1887). See Ernest Renan, *Qu'est-ce Qu'une Nation? et Autres Essais Politiques*, ed. Joâl Roman (Paris, 1992).

40 Renan began a seminary education in 1838 and intended to pursue an ecclesiastical career. But in 1845 he abandoned both his faith and his pursuit of the priesthood for a life of letters that included translating the Old Testament (Book of Job, 1858; Song of Songs, 1860) and histories and interpretations of religion (*Histoire Générale des Langues Sémitiques*, 1855; *Etudes d'Histoire Religieuse*, 1857; *Vie de Jésus*, 1863; *Les Apôtres*, 1866; *L'Antéchrist*, 1873; *Les Evangiles*, 1877;

L'Eglise Chrétienne, 1879; *Histoire du Peuple d'Israâl*, 1887–91). Renan was named professor at the Collège de France in 1862 but was suspended four days after his first class owing to a "Catholic plot." He did not recover his chair until 1870. In *Vie de Jésus*, Renan controversially described Jesus less as a god than as a man. Renan attempted to enhance the moral message of his account by making the reader identify with Jesus' feelings to such a degree that *Vie de Jésus* has been compared to romantic novels. See Ernest Renan, *Vie de Jésus*, ed. Jean Gaulmier (Paris, 1974). In the words of Jean Gaulmier, Renan "a démoli la lettre de la religion et rendu le divin sensible à la conscience." P. 26.

41 Renan, "Qu'est-ce Qu'une Nation?" 42–43.

42 Ibid., 54.

43 Ibid., 54–55.

44 Benedict Anderson, *Imagined Communities* (London, 1983), 15. The translation of the quotation from Renan is mine.

45 Anderson describes the proliferation of printed material as contributing to the imagining of community in the modern era. Reading the newspaper is, he says, an "extraordinary mass ceremony: the almost precisely simultaneous consumption ('imagining') of the newspaper-as-fiction. We know that particular morning and evening editions will overwhelmingly be consumed between this hour and that, only on this day, not that. . . . The significance of this mass ceremony—Hegel observed that newspapers serve modern man as a substitute for morning prayers—is paradoxical. It is performed in silent privacy, in the lair of the skull. Yet each communicant is well aware that the ceremony he performs is being replicated simultaneously by thousands (or millions) of others of whose existence he is confident, yet of whose identity he has not the slightest notion. . . . At the same time the newspaper reader, observing exact replicas of his own paper being consumed by his subway, barbershop, or residential neighbors, is continually reassured that the imagined world is visibly rooted in everyday life. . . . Fiction seeps quietly and continuously into reality, creating that remarkable confidence of community in anonymity which is the hallmark of modern nations." Ibid., 39–40. The periodic press proliferated in France in the second half of the century. I would suggest that the widespread campaign to decorate public buildings from post offices to town halls that took place in France in the 1880s and 1890s was meant to have an effect similar to the one that Anderson describes.

46 For an excellent discussion of the fantasmatic elements of nation formation see Stathis Gourgouris, "Notes on the Nation's Dreamwork," *Qui Parle* 7 (1993): 91–101. A classic formulation of the relation between ideology and individual subjectivity comes from Louis Althusser, "Ideology and Ideological State Apparatuses," *Lenin and Philosophy* (London, 1971).

47 Anderson, *Imagined Communities*, 15.

48 I want to make it clear that what I am calling a style of national imagining should be understood as historically contingent. The kind of imagining I elaborate is not just a product of Puvis's painterly style. It is also dependent on wider cultural phenomena—a deep desire for national unity in a time of instability and division, the lingering need to come to terms with the humiliations of 1870–71, and the sense, which infiltrated virtually all realms of culture at this moment, that human subjectivity itself was far from autonomous, that human subjects were moved by things to which they had no conscious access, and that many of these things were found in the realms of representation and the arts. Without this conjunction of circumstances Puvis's painting could never have meant as much as it did.

49 "Raconte les débuts d'une civilisation, les tâtonnements de l'esprit qui cherche l'explication des choses, l'inquiétude de l'homme en face de la nature et de lui-même; c'est la phrase mystérieuse, incomprise peut-être de ceux qui la prononçaient, et sortie de leur bouche comme un cri de fauve ou comme un chant d'oiseau; c'est le premier essai d'industrie, de travail, de législation, de poésie; c'est le premier pas fait en tremblant, au sortir de la nuit, dans la lumière qui surprend, sur le sol inconnu." Geffroy, "Le Salon de 1884," 1.

50 "Quel est l'artiste d'aujourd'hui, l'artiste qui a derrière lui cinq mille années de littérature et d'art, l'artiste qui a contemplé tous les ciels et coudoyé toutes les races, l'artiste façonné par tous les hommes qui l'ont précédé, qui a hérité de tous leurs efforts, de toutes leurs découvertes, quel est cet artiste compliqué, sceptique, ondoyant et divers qui va s'abstraire de son temps, remonter les âges, et entreprendre cette tâche effrayante de nous raconter, non pas même l'homme primitif, qui a laissé des traces de son passage, mais l'homme qui n'a jamais existé, l'homme créé par le cerveau de l'homme, l'homme idéal, né de la pensé, et vivant comme elle. C'est là un labeur intellectuel plus que pictural, pour lequel il faudra un pinceau à la fois savant et naïf, sachant mêler les harmonies de couleurs qui sont le résultat de siècles de peinture, à la lumière des aubes disparues.

"Beaucoup s'essayent à cet art qui demande un dégagement presque absolu des formules apprises et des habilités de métier: peu réussissent. . . . Une oeuvre exposée au Salon au milieu des peintures de religion et d'histoire, nous le dirons avec une autorité et une clarté saisissante. . . . C'est la toile de M. Puvis de Chavannes . . . qui nous apparaît ainsi, démonstrative et suggestive." Ibid.

CHAPTER 4. THE EPISTEMOLOGY OF DREAM

1 Arrêté, July 21, 1883, Archives Nationales, F21/2106.

2 Puvis de Chavannes was selected to decorate the Grand Amphithéâtre by the architect Henri-Paul Nénot, and this choice clearly met with the approval of the republican administration. The mural was commissioned on May 17, 1886, for thirty-five thousand francs, with an additional one thousand francs later offered for the state's right to photograph and reproduce the cartoon. The sum was paid in installments of twelve thousand francs. The artist painted the final version of the Sorbonne mural in 1888 and 1889. By mid-August 1888, Roger-Ballu, having visited Puvis's studio in Neuilly, reported that "the most important panel is entirely painted. The second is at least one-quarter painted." Puvis was later informed that the mural must be finished by July 1, 1889, in time for it to be mounted on the wall of the Grand Amphithéâtre for the inauguration ceremony on August 5, 1889.Archives Nationales, Paris, F21/2106. Aimée Brown Price gives a short account of the Sorbonne mural in Price, *Pierre Puvis de Chavannes*, 200–209. See also Dominique de Fournoux, "Puvis de Chavannes et le Grand Amphithéâtre," in *La Sorbonne et sa Reconstruction* (Lyons, 1987), 175–76.

3 These secularizing reforms included, for example, in 1880, the annulment of the law of 1814 forbidding work on Sunday; in 1881, the abolition of the denominational nature of cemeteries; in 1884, the legalization of divorce; and in 1887, a law on funerals that favored civic funerals and the laicization of hospitals. See Mayeur and Rebérioux, *Third Republic*. The most important reform was the establishment of compulsory, free, secular, primary education, which (in theory at least) included a course in civic morality. The historian Pascal Ory has described the new Sorbonne as the edifice that most explicitly promoted the government program of morale laïque. Pascal Ory, "Centenaire de la Révolution: La Preuve par 89," in *Les Lieux de Mémoire*, ed. Pierre Nora (Paris, 1984), 523–60. The New Sorbonne represented "the exaltation of a new sacred history, completely aiming toward social betterment and the progress of the mind by means of secular, free, obligatory school." In February 1880 clergy were excluded from the Conseil Supérieur de l'Instruction Publique; also in 1880 university exams were required to be held before state boards, and only state institutions were allowed to take the name "university," which meant the exclusion of Catholic schools of higher learning from this category. See Phyllis Stock-Morton, *Moral Education for a Secular Society* (Albany, N.Y., 1988).

4 In the months preceding the inauguration, the republican government was nearly toppled by popular support for the minister of war, General Boulanger. For a discussion of these events and their causes see Mayeur and Rebérioux, *Third Republic*, 127–37.

5 The large, three-paneled cartoon for the Sorbonne mural was exhibited in 1887 in the vestibule of the painting section. It is best known to us today through photolithographic reproductions that appeared in the *Figaro-Salon*, May 1887, p. 1. Critics referred to it as both an "esquisse au fusain" and a "toile grise." This suggests that it was probably a work on canvas as yet uncolored. See Meurville, "Le Salon," *Gazette de France*, May 1, 1887, p. 3; and Emile Hervet, "Le Salon," *Le Pays*, May 2, 1887, p. 2. Because Puvis's preliminary sketch was a large monochromatic drawing, the critical response to it focused on its iconography rather than on the decorative layout and color, which had taken up so much commentary on other works exhibited at the Salon in previous years. Although Puvis's final version of the mural was usually mentioned in accounts of the inauguration, there were few extended visual analyses of it in 1889. Many simply quoted the text that Puvis had inserted in the Salon brochure in 1887.

6 "Au centre, sur un bloc de marbre, est assise l'antique Sorbonne ayant à ses côtés deux génies avec des couronnes et des palmes, hommage aux vivants et aux morts glorieux. Debout, l'Eloquence célèbre les luttes et les conquêtes de l'esprit humain. A droite et à gauche sont groupées des figures attentives, symbolisant les diverses poésies. Du rocher qui les porte s'échappe la source vivifiante; la Jeunesse y boit avidement, la Vieillesse y puise une nouvelle force.

"Le compartiment de gauche est réservé à la Philosophie et à l'Histoire, symbolisées, la première par un groupe de figures représentant la lutte du spiritualisme et du naturalisme en face de la mort: l'un s'affirme par un geste d'ardente aspiration vers l'idéal, tandis que l'autre montre une fleur, expression de joies terrestres et de transformations successives limitées à la matière.—Le second groupe montre l'Histoire interrogeant le passée, figuré par d'antiques débris que l'on vient d'exhumer.

"Le compartiment de droite est consacré à la Science. Le premier groupe faisant suite aux Muses, se compose de quatre figures: la Botanique, la Mer, la Minéralogie et la Géologie. Des jeunes gens s'émerveillent de ces richesses, tandis que d'autres, groupés devant une statue de la Science, jurent dans un commun élan de se vouer à elle. Trois jeunes hommes, absorbés par l'étude, ferment la composition."

This text was cited in many Salon reviews, including M. de Théminus, "Salon de 1887," *La Patrie* (1887), p. 2.; Henri Havard, "Le Salon de 1887: Les Commandes Officielles," *Le*

Siècle, May 7, 1887, p. 1; Auguste Dalligny, "Le Salon de 1887," *Journal des Arts*, May 10, 1887, p. 1.

7 The text inscribed below the mural reads thus: "Dans la clairière d'un bois sacré est assise une figure symbolique de la Sorbonne: à ses côtés, deux génies porteurs de palmes et de couronnes, hommage aux vivants et aux morts glorieux. Debout, *l'Eloquence* célébrant les conquêtes de l'esprit humain. Autour d'elle, les figures diverses de *la Poésie*. Du rocher s'écoule la source vivifiante. La jeunesse s'y abreuve avidement. La vieillesse aux mains tremblantes y fait remplir sa coupe.

"A gauche, *la Philosophie* représentée par la lutte du spiritualisme et du matérialisme, *l'Histoire* interrogeant les antiques débris exhumés sous ces yeux. A droite, *la Science*: la mer et la terre lui offrent leurs richesses. *La Botanique* avec sa gerbe de plantes, *la Géologie* appuyée sur un fossile; les deux génies de *la Physiologie* tenant l'un un flacon, l'autre un scalpel. *La Physique* entrouvrant ses voiles devant un essaim de jeunes gens lui présentant comme prémices de leurs travaux la flamme de *l'Electricité, la Géométrie* figurée par un groupe absorbé dans la recherche d'un problème."

8 Robert de Sorbon founded the Sorbonne in 1253 as a theological college under royal sponsorship. It was rebuilt in 1629 under the direction of Cardinal Richelieu. The state had controlled it since the 1789 Revolution. See Rivé, *La Sorbonne*.

9 Gustave Geffroy, "Salon de 1887," *La Justice*, June 22, 1887, p. 1. The sense that the description of the figure as "antique" may have been problematic is amplified when we look at the differences between the initial Salon catalogue entry and the inscription on the final mural—a modified version of the explanatory text that Puvis provided in 1887. The text begins much the way the previous version did, although the qualifier for the Sorbonne figure ("antique") has been left out.

10 Jules Lemaître, "Le Salon (premier article): Réflexions Préliminaires—M. Puvis de Chavannes," *Journal des Débats*, May 7, 1887, p. 2.

11 Georges-Claudius Lavergne, "Le Salon de 1887," *L'Univers*, June 3, 1887, p. 2: "le système de falsifications et de soustractions, ce vandalisme impie . . . tend à dépouiller notre antique Sorbonne du royal manteau sous lequel s'abritèrent, cinq siècles durant, les générations successives des maîtres et des écoliers nationaux et étrangers . . . l'on ne prévoyait pas alors qu'au dix-neuvième siècle ses palais seraient incendiés, que ses écoles et même son épée seraient laïcisées et galvanisées, et qu'on en viendrait jusqu'à répudier son histoire et à jeter au vent les diamants de sa couronne."

12 Fallières, "Discourse Pronounced at the Inauguration of the New Sorbonne," Paris, August 5, 1889. There were many accounts of the ceremony in the press. See, for example, "La Nouvelle Sorbonne," *La République Française*, August 6, 1889, p. 2; G.D., "La Nouvelle Sorbonne," *Journal des Débats*, August 4, 1889, pp. 2–3; "Inauguration de la Nouvelle Sorbonne," *Le Monde*, August 7, 1889, p. 1; "Inauguration de la Nouvelle Sorbonne," *Moniteur Universel*, August 7, 1889, p. 854.

13 Gréard, "Discourse Pronounced at the Inauguration of the New Sorbonne," August 5, 1889.

14 Lemaître, "Le Salon . . . M. Puvis de Chavannes," 2.

15 "Son attachement inviolable à la liberté, son culte pour les principes de 1789." Hector Depasse, "La Nouvelle Sorbonne," *La République Française*, August 6, 1889, p. 1.

16 "Qu'on assistait pour un moment à la fête non pas seulement de notre glorieuse Université de France, mais de la véritable Université de l'univers." Ibid.

17 See Ory, "Centenaire de la Révolution," 548. The critic for the more conservative *Journal des Débats*, despite being impatient with much of the recent Republican flourish, described the purpose that the New Sorbonne would serve. It would "donne une solide unité et une âme collective." G.D., "La Nouvelle Sorbonne," 2.

18 For an excellent account of the relationship between critics like Vogüé and Desjardins to Puvis's imagery see Werth, "'Le Bonheur de Vivre.'"

19 Paul Desjardins, "Salon de 1887, II: Peinture Décorative," *La République Française*, May 8, 1887, p. 1. In general, Desjardins was sympathetic to Puvis's work and even commissioned the design for a poster from him in the mid-1890s. Werth discusses this in "'Le Bonheur de Vivre.'"

20 Georges Lafenestre, "Le Salon de 1887," *Revue des Deux Mondes*, June 1, 1887, p. 608.

21 See Price, *Puvis de Chavannes*, 199–206. Other figures that are clearly reminiscent of the *School of Athens* include the old academician in the group of History and the three men representing Geometry in the panel of Science.

22 Charles Ponsonailhe, "Le Salon," *L'Artiste* (1887), pp. 423–24.

23 "On voit la Philosophie enseignant, moins ce qu'elle sait que ce qu'elle voudrait savoir, et visiblement nourrie d'hypothèses." Mantz, "Le Salon," *Le Temps*, May 15, 1887, p. 1.

24 "De faire pencher la balance du bon côté, au lieu de rester, comme il l'a jugé à propos, dans une prudente neutralité en ne se prononçant pas plus pour l'idéal que pour la matière." Paul Fresnel, "Salon de 1887," *Le Correspondant*, May 10, 1887, p. 567.

25 "L'une dit: 'Plus haut! Il y a une autre vie; il y a une raison d'être des choses, je l'affirme, je le veux'. Et l'autre: 'Il n'y a rien que l'éternelle féerie de la Matière. Tout cela n'a aucun sens; mais vivre et sentir est doux'. Et la vieille femme: 'Elles ont raison toutes deux, puisque rien n'existe que le rêve'." Lamaître, "Le Salon . . . M. Puvis de Chavannes," 2.

26 Saint-Ange, "Salon de 1887," *Le Français*, May 3, 1887, p. 3.

27 Louis de Fourcaud, "Le Salon," *Le Gaulois*, April 30, 1887, p. 4.

28 Meurville, "Le Salon" (1887), p. 1.

29 Lavergne, "Le Salon de 1887," p. 1. In fact, the Ecole de Chartres, which took an archaeological approach to history, replaced the theological faculty. See Price, *Puvis de Chavannes*, 199; and Rivé, *La Sorbonne*.

30 "Le coffre-fort d'Arpagon était toujours ouvert les jours de recettes, toujours fermé les jours d'échéances. C'est le fait de votre opération. Je vous prends la main dans le sac." Lavergne, "Le Salon de 1887," p. 1.

31 Ibid.

32 Ibid. Other critics called upon this theme in their reviews of the cartoon, though few with as much hostility as Lavergne. Writing for the republican paper *Le Soir*, the critic Paul Lafage played on the replacement of religious faith by devotion to science by parodying the "Lord's Prayer" and replacing all the references to God with references to Nature and Science. See Paul Lafage, "Le Salon," *Le Soir*, April 30, 1887, p. 1.

33 The sea was the metaphor that brought together the materiality of nature with the notion that woman was subject to her own uncontrollable physicality. In the mid-nineteenth century Jules Michelet compared woman to the sea and gave this comparison a physiological basis in the female menstrual cycle. Lavergne thus invoked not only a fear of Nature but also a fear of femininity in this passage. See Jules Michelet, *La Mer* (Paris, 1861); Michelet, *L'Amour* (Paris, 1859); and Michelet, *La Femme* (Paris, 1858). Thérèse Moreau discusses these texts in her excellent book *Le Sang de l'Histoire: Michelet l'Histoire et l'Idée de la Femme au Dix-Neuvième Siècle* (Paris, 1982). For a discussion of these texts in relation to academic idealism see Shaw, "Figure of Venus."

34 Lavergne, "Le Salon de 1887," p. 1.

35 "Vous redoutez surtout que la *Théologie*, profitant de l'écoulement des eaux, n'aborde à pied sec la Sorbonne, qu'elle fasse une tentative pour reprendre son domaine, pour revendiquer ses prérogatives, pour faire valoir son droit légitime et historique de suprématie.

"La théologie? Répondez-vous; qu'est que c'est qu'ça? . . . Il ne faut plus de théologie!" Ibid.

36 Ibid.

37 In an article for *La Justice*, Geffroy described Vogüé as "le chef franco-russe de cette école de littérature neo-chrétienne." Vogüé is often characterized as a Christian socialist, but I think we should follow Geffroy in being skeptical both of such a characterization of him and of the possibilities for the existence of real socialism with a Christian agenda in France at this moment. Geffroy noted that the new generation that Vogüé predicted will take up a Christian socialist mantel was characterized by Vogüé himself as (1) uninterested in politics but disturbed about social problems; (2) skeptical of traditional forms of spiritualism; and (3) possessing "une âme collective et fraternelle" and "rebelle à la domination romaine." Geffroy's ironic tone in his description of Vogüé's writings implies that he did not see these characteristics as necessarily leading to socialism—Christian or otherwise (he implied in fact that the two are incompatible). See Geffroy, "Le Mouvement Neo-Chrétien," *La Justice*, March 30, 1892, pp. 1–2. Although Vogüé proclaimed himself to be promoting a form of social solidarity, it is clear from many of his writings that he would have preferred a pre-Revolutionary form of solidarity but acknowledged the impossibility of this. Furthermore, he was certainly not interested in international socialism but in promoting "la sève gauloise." This stance led him to become a participant in the nationalist racism of Action Française.

38 Eugène-Melchior de Vogüé, "A Travers l'Exposition, IX: Dernières Remarques," *Revue des Deux Mondes* 96 (1889): 177–78.

39 "Il serait superflu d'insister sur les conséquences sociales de ces doctrines; elles pivotent autour de trois points fondamentaux, le déterminisme, la sélection par l'hérédité, le droit de la force.—Liberté, égalité, fraternité. Sommes-nous assez loin de la philosophie qui inspira la Déclaration des droits? Comment cette philosophie a-t-elle abouti à une négation formelle de ses prémisses? Par une marche très logique sous les contradictions apparentes. . . . La raison a retourné son scalpel contre l'idole; qu'on me passe l'image familière, elle lui a ouvert le ventre, et elle a vu qu'il n'y avait rien dedans. . . . Ainsi est née la crise des principes de 1789; ils sont pris entre deux feux, entre la protestation théologique, qui les suivait de loin, et la protestation scientifique, qui s'est dressée subitement en face d'eux." Ibid., 175–76.

40 Ibid., 179.

41 "Le rêve métaphysique du siècle passé proposait aux hommes un idéal irréalisable; il leur a procuré quelque allègement, au prix de l'anarchie, de l'instabilité, d'un excès d'individualisme incompatible avec la garantie sociale et la grandeur nationale. Le réalisme physique de notre siècle ramène les hommes à la stricte imitation de la nature; il rétablirait un ordre sommaire, au prix de servitude, du fatalisme, d'un retour à la vie animale du troupeau. Pour conjurer ces conséquences, il faudrait que la nouvelle théorie des rapports humains fût complétée par le correctif qui a manqué à l'ancienne; il faudrait qu'un principe moral, représentant la réaction de la conscience contre la dureté des lois naturelles, vint adoucir ce qu'il y aurait intolérable dans une législation inspirée par les seuls enseignemens [sic] de la physiologie. . . . Ce principe qui peut seul donner un fondement solide à la notion du devoir, on le chercherait en vain dans tout le monde des idées rationnelles: l'humanité ne l'a jamais ressaisi que dans le fort où il réside, dans le sentiment religieux." Ibid., 180. In 1895 Ferdinand Brunetière would cause a stir by making a similar remark about the "bankruptcy of science" after visiting the Vatican and having an audience with the Pope. See "Le Banqueroute," *Le Figaro*, January 3, 1895, p. 1; "Le Banqueroute de la Science," *Dix-Neuvième Siècle*, January 15, 1895, p. 1.

42 The news right about then that Millet's *Angelus* was to be sold to a buyer outside France caused an uproar that was reported in many newspapers. The painting was bought back by the state the following year.

43 "Ce qui reste de foi politique dans notre peuple est au service de la république; et l'on ne peut constituer un peuple qu'en utilisant la somme de la foi qui vit en lui." Vogüé, "A Travers l'Exposition, IX," p. 188.

44 "Divise le moins, et qui permet le mieux à l'esprit public de se former." "De ne considérer le régime républicain que comme un pis-aller, comme un état de transition." Broglie, quoted in ibid.

45 "Et lorsque M. Jules Ferry a décerné à M. Puvis de Chavannes le titre de: *paladin de l'idéal*, duquel a-t-il voulu parler? Ce doit être de l'idéal *opportuniste*. Eh bien! Je déclare que l'idéal opportuniste est beaucoup trop enfariné pour ma consommation; je tiens plutôt et même je tiens ferme pour l'idéal *intransigeant*.

"D'où il suit que si je viens à toucher à la peinture décorative, à l'idéal, à la sérénité de M. Puvis de Chavannes, je vais soulever contre moi l'opposition du parti libéral conservateur, celle des gauches plus ou moins réunies, celle du suffrage universel; c'est grave! Et pourtant c'est là ce qui m'attend, je le sais, mais un homme prévenu en vaut quatre." Lavergne, "Le Salon de 1887," p. 1.

46 "Opportunism" is a term that defines the strategies of the republican state between approximately 1870 and 1890 to secularize and democratize the Republic. For a discussion of opportunism in connection with the ministers most closely associated with it—Thiers, Ferry, and Gambetta—see Theodore Zeldin, *France, 1848–1945: Politics and Anger* (Oxford, 1979), 241–75. Zeldin points out the contradictions in this kind of centralized, top-down approach to republicanism, which, on the one hand, "saw the republic as a defense of the individual against the state, as a means of social ascension, and as an instrument for the emancipation of local communities from traditional tyrannies" and, on the other hand, stressed "not the defense of the individual but the creation of order, unity, glory, all of which required sacrifice from individuals for the attainment of higher principles." P. 241.

47 "Deuxième question: Qu'entend-on par ce mot: allégorie?

"*Allégorie* (répond le dictionnaire), '*fiction qui présente à l'esprit un objet pour désigner un autre*.' Dans ce cas, c'est *l'autre* qui est l'objectif dominant; l'allégorie ne doit pas le métamorphoser, elle doit le faire resplendir. Pourquoi donc peindre une Sorbonne qui serait méconnaissable si son nom n'était pas inscrit sur le tableau." Lavergne, "Le Salon de 1887," p. 1.

48 "Ira camper dans l'atelier de *Nazareth*, non loin du Thabor, à deux pas du Calvaire." Ibid.

49 A more explicit vocabulary of *maquillage* was available at the time, and many critics used it to describe avant-garde painting by Manet, Degas, and other Impressionists. For a discussion of this see Jean Clay, "Ointments, Makeup, Pollen," *October* 27 (Winter 1983): 3–44; and Carol Armstrong, *Odd Man Out*, 61, 80, 166–67. For a fascinating discussion of overlaps between discourses of painting and makeup in the eighteenth century see Melissa Hyde, "The 'Makeup' of the Marquise: Boucher's *Portrait of Pompadour at Her Toilette*," *Art Bulletin* 12, no. 3 (September 2000): 453–75.

50 I wish to thank Marcus Verhagen for drawing my attention to this point. For a further discussion of the intersections between painting and popular entertainment in the late nineteenth century see his "Re-figurations of Carnival: The Comic Performer in Fin-de-Siècle Parisian Art" (Ph.D. diss., University of California, Berkeley, 1994).

51 "Je vous défie de trouver là autre chose que des femmes qui se sont assises, levées, couchées suivant la fantaisie qui leur en a pris, des gens qui pensent à boire et des gens qui ne pensent à rien." Saint-Ange, "Salon de 1887," p. 3.

52 "C'est son moindre désir d'être compris de ses contemporains. Il fait profession de vivre dans son rêve et de n'en pas sortir." Ibid.

53 "Si vous tentez une interprétation, j'en tiens en réserve une dizaine qui s'appliqueront avec tout autant d'exactitude à la scène qui est ici figurée." Ibid. A. D. de la Rue also refused to see the painting as allegory: "cela ressemble, en somme, à toutes les autres compositions de M. Puvis de Chavannes et pourrait s'intituler comme elles toutes: *Nymphes dans les*

Bois." A. D. de la Rue, "La Peinture au Salon," *Observateur Français*, May 9, 1887, p. 3.

54 "Or je ne crois pas que la peinture soit destinée à nous faire entendre tant de choses et à contenir tant de sous-etendus. . . . Avec une apparence de simplicité, son art est d'une extrême complication." Saint-Ange, "Salon de 1887," p. 3.

55 "Il y a là, entre les autres choses bien laides, deux coquins de livres qui n'ont pas le sens commun, et contre lesquels j'ai lutté de toute une ardeur qui a fini par s'éteindre." L. Wehrlé, "Lettres de Puvis de Chavannes, 1888–1898," *La Revue de Paris* 11 (1911): 456. There is no indication in any reproductions of the Grand Amphithéâtre of sculpted ornamentation to which Puvis could be referring. I have compared the mural in its current state with images of the inauguration, which indicate that the wall below the mural remains in its original state. I understand the phrase "coquins de livres" as being a way of personifying, in dismissive terms, the text.

56 Lemaître, "Le Salon," 2.

57 "Quand on ne comprend pas bien, ce n'est pas un grand malheur, puisqu'on reste libre de rêver et d'interpréter l'allégorie à sa façon!" Ibid.

58 "M. Puvis de Chavannes est un grand poète, ou pour mieux dire un grand magicien. Peut-être aimerait-il mieux qu'on dit de lui tout simplement qu'il est un grand peintre. Il l'est, si vous voulez, mais de si singulière façon! Il y a du sortilège dans son cas, et presque une contradiction entre les moyens dont il dispose et les effets auxquels il atteint. Il arrive, avec un dessin souvent pauvre et incorrect . . . à nous donner une impression comparable à celle que nous recevons des oeuvres les plus parfaites de l'antiquité, et, par exemple, des frises du Parthénon; et il parvient avec une palette plus que sobre et une couleur de pure convention, à caresser nos yeux aussi délicieusement que Rubens ou Véronèse. Il dessine des figures superbes et plus qu'humaines avec un crayon d'enfant, et il crée des paradis enchantés avec des ombres de couleurs." Ibid.

59 "Le génie d'un maître tel que Puvis de Chavannes s'impose souverainement, même quand il lui plaît de traiter les sujets les plus formellement allégorique." Félix Fénéon, "Au Salon de 1887," in *Oeuvres Plus que Complètes*, ed. Joan U. Halperin (Geneva, 1970), 78–79.

60 "Que l'on oublie la puérile incohérence de ce symbolisme pictural, et l'on est en face d'une sereine vision dont les groupes se coordonnent sur un rythme grave et magnifient . . . déjà les familiers de l'oeuvre de M. de Chavannes peuvent avoir l'obscure conscience des colorations qui vont y fluer, et de l'émotionnelle symphonie voilée qui emplira cette forêt limitante et ces lointains du ciel." Ibid.

61 "Si, sans chercher les idées abstraites qu'elle symbolise, on se borne à la contempler, on goûte le plaisir particulier que donnent les belles symétries et les belles ordonnances. Des deux côtés de la Sorbonne, les figures descendent en groupes parallèles, et le parallélisme se poursuit jusqu'aux deux extrémités opposées de la toile. Il y a là un grand art, avec une admirable simplicité de moyens. L'allégorie une fois acceptée, vous pénétrez dans une région sereine." Paul Heusy, "Le Salon," *Le Radical*, May 2, 1887, p. 1.

62 For accounts of the roles played by particular administrators who influenced the commission see Price, *Puvis de Chavannes*, 199–201; and Rivé, *La Nouvelle Sorbonne*.

63 Gustave Geffroy, "Les Bras de la Vénus de Milo," in *La Vie Artistique*, vol. 1 (Paris, 1892), 10–14; originally published June 28, 1890. By June of 1890, the result of Ravaisson's reconstruction of the Venus de Milo was on view in the vestibule of the institute. A summary of the most important attempts to imagine the original form of the statue was published in the *Gazette des Beaux-Arts* that year, complete with illustrations. See Salomon Reinach, "La Vénus de Milo," *Gazette des Beaux-Arts*, May 1, 1890, pp. 376–94.

64 "S'il s'agit de donner au chef d'oeuvre sa forme définitive, c'est peine perdue. La Vénus de Milo doit rester et restera isolée et sans bras. . . . Vénus, ainsi, n'est plus localisée dans la mythologie grecque, elle échappe à son rôle spécial, elle monte au plus haut degré des généralisations et des symboles. Saint-Victor, dans son idéalisme mal compris . . . s'applaudit de ce qu'il n'y ait pas un atome de chair dans ce marbre auguste: 'Ces traits grandioses, dit-il, ne reflètent aucune ressemblance, ce corps . . . accuse la généralisation de l'esprit. Il est sorti d'un cerveau viril, fécondé par l'idée et non par la présence d'une femme.' . . . Oui, tant mieux si les bras sont absents. On voit mieux l'incomparable torse. La pensée conçoit plus parfaitement celle vers laquelle vont tous les désirs—qui reste impassible et immuable—qui n'étreint pas et ne se donne pas—la souveraine Beauté, éternel appât de la vie." Geffroy, "Le Bras de la Vénus de Milo," 11–14.

65 The first women were admitted to the Sorbonne in 1893 in the face of much protest.

66 "Le portrait de femme crée une émotion exactement contraire à celle du portrait d'homme. On n'interprète une effigie masculine: on la lit, on la constate. Son expression va du dedans au dehors, s'impose au spectateur. La face d'un homme est une carte définie. . . .

"Il représente moins un être que l'accumulation de sensibilités et de passions réunies sur lui par tous les admirateurs de sa beauté. . . . Il exprime les traits, l'éclat de la figure physique—et il y superpose en guise d'âme, le reflet du désir des hommes. La sensation absolue de beauté féminine, donnée par la peinture, est précisément celle d'un organisme harmonieux et impersonnel où s'ajoute commodément le rêve de chacun." Camille Mauclair, "La Femme devant les peintres modernes," *La Nouvelle Revue* (1899), pp. 190–91. I thank Charlotte Eyerman for pointing me to this reference.

67 "La face d'une femme belle est une contrée inconnue où il n'y a ni traces ni routes où les mouvements secrets ne doivent rien déranger, où chaque explorateur trace son chemin aussitôt effacé derrière lui; elle est inconnaissable précisément parce qu'elle est absolument simple, purement physique, et que notre âme n'y reconnaît rien de semblable à elle-même, et en demeure éperdue et fascinée. La beauté de la femme, comme toute harmonie, ne se constitue peut-être que de son vide. C'est un cadre ou nous plaçons nos rêves." Ibid.

68 "Elle attend, comme une page blanche, que la sensibilité de l'homme y inscrive son rêve. Elle est un spectacle permanent, ouvert, comme un paysage, à l'admiration. Et ce que notre contemplation cherche à y découvrir, c'est soi-même." Ibid.

69 See, for example, Thomas, *La Suggestion, Son Rôle dans l'Education.*

70 André Michel, "Le Grand Amphithéâtre de la Nouvelle Sorbonne," *Journal des Débats*, August 6, 1889, p. 2.

71 Ibid. Michel complained about the presence of the text at the base of the mural, and his complaints suggest the way he believed the painting should function for the viewer. For one thing, said Michel, those standing back far enough to see the mural in its entirety found the text impossible to read.

72 "Tout son éloquence est dans la vertu des lignes très simples et de tonalités très calmes, disciplinées, synthétisées et associées dans des ensembles composés. Les êtres de rêves évoqués par lui, étrangers à toute action particulière, sont comme baignés dans une atmosphère psychique; mais ils ne nous proposent aucune énigme; et les sentiments très généraux, les choses intimes et solennelles qu'ils ont à nous dire trouvent sans peine le chemin de nos coeurs, où ils éveillent de longues rêveries. Une vie propre et supérieure les anime sans les agiter; leurs gestes rares et lents, leurs attitudes pensives, belles d'un indicible mélange de grâce familière et de grandeur épique, leur donnent l'air d'apparitions amies de visions lointaines et présentes. Elles nous offrent moins à comprendre qu'à sentir et nous n'avons que faire d'un commentaire écrit." Ibid.

73 "Un apaisement délicieux, une grande sérénité descendent en moi. . . . Le professeur peut monter en chaire; je suis bien préparé à recevoir toutes les grandes pensées qu'il m'apportera à communier avec les hauts esprits." Ibid.

74 See Souriau, *La Suggestion*, 1–2; the pertinent passage is quoted in Chapter 2, note 36, above. It is worth noting that Souriau was familiar with Puvis's painting and used Puvis's own descriptions of his creative process to formulate a general theory of creativity, which was elaborated in *L'Imagination de l'Artiste* (Paris, 1901). Uses for suggestion are also discussed in educational treatises for primary school children at this time and seem to be part of a more general republican strategy to find a scientific basis for the transformation of youth into good members of the national body.

75 "Dans l'entretien silencieux, puissant et doux des Muses apparues au-dessus de sa pauvre tête, de quoi me consoler et l'oublier tandis qu'il parlera." Michel, "Grand Amphithéâtre," 2.

76 "Les tendances natives de son esprit méditatif et généralisateur, par les lacunes peut-être autant que par les vertus propres de son oeil et de sa main." Ibid.

77 "A fait vivre sur les parois de nos monumens [sic] ses visions et ses rêveries." Ibid.

78 Margaret Werth sets the reception of Puvis's work in the 1890s into the context of more general debates about health and pathology. She argues that many critics in the 1890s saw Puvis as the outstanding example of the healthy, productive man. She discusses the attempts by many of his supporters to prevent his assimilation by mystic or decadent groups. See Werth, "'Le Bonheur de Vivre.'"

79 Paul Desjardins, "Salon de 1887, II: Peinture Décorative," *La République Française*, May 8, 1887, p. 1 For a discussion of Desjardins's attitude toward Puvis in the 1890s see Werth, "'Le Bonheur de Vivre.'"

80 For the most part, these writers were part of a burgeoning neo-Christian movement, which had its aesthetic allegiances to Symbolism. The participant in this phenomenon best known to art historians today is the painter Maurice Denis. The others included Paul Desjardins; Eugène Melchior, Vicomte de Vogüé; and the head of the Salon of the Rose + Croix, Sâr Péladan.

81 The painter Edmond Aman Jean (1860–1936) exhibited regularly with Péladan's Salon de la Rose + Croix, as well as at the Salon. He shared a studio with Seurat in the early 1880s and is said to have assisted Puvis in painting *The Sacred Grove.* See Royal Academy of Arts, *Post-Impressionism: Cross-Currents in European Painting* (London, 1979).

82 "Le matérialisme officiel et la grossièreté de l'analyse auront été de ce monde en même temps que la renaissance d'un certain mysticisme, la résurrection de Jeanne d'Arc et le triomphe définitif de l'art abstrait et synthétique de Puvis de Chavannes." Aman Jean, "Puvis de Chavannes," *L'Art dans les Deux Mondes*, November 29, 1890, pp. 9–11.

83 "Et c'est ainsi qu'après bien des années il a revu avec une intensité si pénétrante de vérité et de mystère les cyprès de collines qui dominent l'Arno; parce qu'il a ce beau don du souvenir que les ans n'effacent pas." Ibid., 10.

84 Ibid., 11.

85 Alfred Paulet, "Au Jour le Jour: L'Oeuvre de Puvis de Chavannes," *Le National*, November 23, 1887, p. 3.

86 "L'art est devenu analytique, plus compréhensible à tous peut-être; mais il s'est menti à lui-même et n'est plus de l'art. Il a suivi la science au lieu de précéder; . . . il oublie qu'il vit d'éternité et qu'il meurt d'analyse" Aman Jean, "Puvis de Chavannes," 9.

87 "Que, si les yeux regardent, c'est le coeur qui voit," "une élite qui traduit les sentiments de la foule avec des moyens qu'elle ne comprend pas. . . . Il est comme ces femmes flétries des baisers de tout le monde, il doit rester mystère ignoré de la foule; rares doivent être les élus pouvant l'aimer et en souffrir." Ibid., 10–11.

88 Aman Jean contrasted Puvis's hemicycle to other paintings decorating the Sorbonne, none of which were compelling. All of them, he said, were created to speak directly to the masses using simple realist depiction and overt narrative. In general, the architecture and decoration of the Sorbonne epitomized the failure of the Republic to inspire spiritual faith and the impossibility that republican civic morality could ever replace Christianity. The architectural layout, like the majority of paintings in the decorative scheme, lacked "contemplative spaces conducive to meditation." Only Puvis's hemicycle offered respite from this dire situation. Indeed, said Aman Jean, the atmosphere of Puvis de Chavannes's mural so dominated the Sorbonne that once it had been seen, the hemicycle would transform the experience of viewing the other murals in the decorative scheme. Looking at the more overtly historical republican iconography that permeated the other murals in the building would only remind viewers of Puvis's work. In Théobald Chartran's mural for the Staircase of Honor, for example, René Théophile Hyacinthe Laennec, the father of French medicine, aids a consumptive patient. However, according to Aman Jean, rather than teaching viewers a lesson about the progress of French medicine, this image of physical suffering would remind them of "the utterly moral pain and Christian resignation of *Poor Fisherman*." Furthermore, the respite that Puvis's Sorbonne mural gave visitors from the rest of the decor in the "pompous palace of the New Sorbonne" would make them dream of *Christian Inspiration*. Aman Jean, "Puvis de Chavannes," 10.

89 Ibid.

90 "Et sera bien à plaindre celui qui, placé sous la fresque, s'adressera à un auditoire qui, la regardant, oubliera de l'entendre; le maître fait chanter les murs, et quand sera plein cet amphithéâtre de trois mille places, combien, venus pour écouter un professeur aux dissertations abstraites, emporteront en eux ce que sans doute ils n'étaient pas venus chercher, et tout surpris, sentiront cet apaisement inconnu que ne donnent pas les savantes paroles!" Ibid.

91 B. Guinaudeau, "La Réaction Idéaliste, XXVI: Puvis de Chavannes," *La Justice*, May 3, 1892, p. 3. Significantly, Puvis always refused to be associated with Sâr Péladan's Salon de la Rose+Croix.

92 "Le corps n'est rien, l'Ame, l'idée est tout," "Plus de matière, n'est-ce pas? Plus d'hommes, plus de femmes, plus de nature! . . . c'est à dire plus de peinture." Ibid.

93 "Quand l'idée d'un tableau me tourmente trop fort. . . . quand je l'ai plastiquement dans l'oeil . . . je le fais," "chez moi, il y a une grande partie, bien difficile à préciser, d'inconscient." Ibid.

94 "Je me suis toujours appliqué, en matérialisant mes rêves, en leur donnant une forme sur la toile, à faire du *possible*, du *vraisemblable*, du *raisonnable*." Ibid.

95 "Est-ce de votre consentement que les catholiques et les néo-chrétiens se réclament de votre oeuvre? Vous savez, sans doute, le jugement qu'ils portent sur vous: que vous êtes un primitif mystique et croyant égaré dans le XIXe siècle.

"Il haussa les épaules et me conduisit devant la reproduction de la fresque du Musée de Lyon. Autour du Rhône et de la Saône, figures allégoriques, sont disposées deux grandes scènes: d'un côté 'L'Inspiration chrétienne', de l'autre 'Vision antique': Si je n'avais peint, me dit-il, que le sujet de gauche on pourrait, à la rigueur, affirmer que j'ai été hanté par le christianisme du moyen-âge; mais, voyons, ce paysage païen, qui manifeste si clairement la joie de vivre sur terre, ne fait-il pas un suffisant contrepoids au panneau dont il est le pendant? Maintenant, si l'on veut bien prendre la peine de regarder mon 'Inspiration chrétienne', est-ce qu'on y trouvera la glorification de l'extase et des macérations? Nullement, voici ce que j'ai fait: un religieux-peintre, quelque Fra Angelico est en train d'achever une décoration murale: loin d'être abîmé devant l'infini, il semble pris d'une fièvre de travail, il a l'air de vouloir s'élancer sur son ouvrage pour y mettre les touches suprêmes: tout son être est en mouvement. Derrière lui, comme le soir approche, un autre religieux commence à allumer des lampes: et puis des jeunes gens arrivent, de jeunes artistes qui s'appuient au seuil de la porte pour prendre une leçon du maître en regardant faire. Je voudrais bien savoir s'il y a autre chose dans tout cela qu'un témoignage en l'honneur de l'activité terrestre. Ces hommes pensent à Dieu, mais d'abord, ils vivent, ils font oeuvre de leurs mains, ils se plaisent à exercer leurs forces physiques et morales: cela c'est ma philosophie à moi et non l'esprit trop contemplatif du moyen-âge." Paul Gsell, "Interview de Puvis de Chavannes," in *Histoire de l'Ecole Française de Paysage*, ed. Georges Lanoe (Nantes, 1905), 375–76 (originally appeared in *La Semaine de Paris*, January 20, 1895).

96 Many aspects of Puvis's paintings prevented them from being described as a total synthesis. Yet the desire to make Puvis's work offer up universal truths was strong. And the description of his paintings as a synthesis came from republican critics as well as from mystic Christians like Aman Jean. However, the works chosen to define Puvis's oeuvre and the truths he was described as offering were quite different in each case. Puvis rejected any interest in the transcendent and sometimes neo-Christian claims that were part and parcel of certain strains of Symbolism, although his use of allegory did have certain things in common with Symbolism. It *was* about the kind of equivocation and undecidability, the play of meaning, and the materialization of that play that characterizes the most interesting moment of Symbolist poetry—the moment of materialization before totalization and transcendence are claimed.

The distinction made by the twentieth-century literary critic Paul de Man between symbol and allegory provides a useful way of understanding what I mean. De Man revises traditional understandings of allegory and symbol in which "allegory appears as dryly rational and dogmatic in its reference to a meaning that it does not itself constitute, whereas the symbol is founded on an intimate unity between the image that rises up before the senses and the supersensory totality that the image suggests . . . a unity between incarnate and ideal beauty." This is Paul de Man's characterization of Gadamer's definition of allegory: "The appeal to the infinity of a totality constitutes the main attraction of the symbol as opposed to allegory, a sign that refers to one specific meaning and thus exhausts its suggestive potentialities once it has been deciphered. 'Symbol and allegory,' writes Gadamer, 'are opposed as art is opposed to non-art, in that the former seems endlessly suggestive in the indefiniteness of its meaning, whereas the latter, as soon as its meaning is reached, has run its full course.'" Rejecting the ultimately transcendent and totalizing pretensions of symbol, de Man proposes an alternative definition of the allegorical mode as admitting, even calling attention to, the disjunction between figure and meaning as providing a space where the materiality of signification—its temporality—is articulated. Symbolism, for de Man, is characterized not by a transcendence of the materiality of language, but rather by a mode of signification that attempts to mystify language's temporality—that is, to mystify its ultimately allegorical nature. Paul de Man, "The Rhetoric of Temporality" in *Blindness and Insight: Essays in the Rhetoric of Contemporary Criticism*, 2 ed. (Minneapolis, 1983), 189.

It is helpful to think of Puvis's redefinition of allegory as somewhat analogous to de Man's. Puvis was interested in rescuing allegory from its transcendent associations. He attempted to do this by always coding the materiality of painting and the contingency of signification that followed from it into his work. The stakes in doing this were particularly high in the end of the nineteenth century. Academic versions of allegory were widely disregarded as bankrupt and mechanical, but allegory was paradoxically still thought of as the appropriate mode for high art. Puvis's rewriting of allegory was an attempt to rejuvenate and reform high art in terms that would reconcile it with the materialist accounts of truth that were being proposed in current science and philosophy. He wanted to provide a new version of allegory grounded in the materiality of signification and the individual response of the viewer that would point forward rather than look back. Although many of his supporters—including Aman Jean, Desjardins, and Vogüé—would attempt to mystify his work in Symbolist terms, what sets Puvis apart from much of Symbolism is that he never rejected allegory for "the Symbol." He never took that leap of "ontological bad faith."

CHAPTER 5. IMAGINING THE MOTHERLAND

Epigraph: "Vous entendez bien: l'Hôtel de Ville! Ce n'est pas là un banal coin de muraille de bâtiment officiel, un lieu quelconque où personne n'ira et qu'il faut recouvrir de sujets coloriés. C'est la maison de tout le monde, le résumé de Paris, un assemblage architectural d'escaliers et de salles que la population doit parcourir, un livre ouvert à tous et dont les pages doivent raconter hier et aujourd'hui, l'histoire des êtres et des choses de notre temps et des temps qui l'ont précédé." Gustave Geffroy, "L'Hôtel de Ville de Paris," February 13, 1885, in *La Vie Artistique* (Paris, 1893), 168–69.

1 These include the decorative scheme for the ceiling of the ceremonial Staircase of Honor, *Victor Hugo Offering His Lyre to the City of Paris* (1894).

2 Jean Mayeur argues that prior to the 1890s "only legitimist reactionaries, the aristocrats, and the priests interested in the Catholic Workers' Circles saw in the popular insurrection a sign of the failure of liberal society that had emerged from the Revolution. The bourgeoisie, Orleanist or republican, did not see in the drama of May 1871 any reasons for doubting its certainties. The Commune seemed a tragic but aberrant parenthesis, and it did not shake people's faith in the liberal social order and in individualism. . . . In the 1890s, on the contrary, the bourgeois classes were affected by 'social remorse.' The indifference of twenty years earlier was replaced by curiosity, interest, pity, and even the desire for reforms to prevent another revolution." Mayeur, *Third Republic*, 147.

3 The French government had given political amnesty to exiled Communards in 1879. For a discussion of the decorative campaign see Daniel Imbert, "L'Hôtel de Ville de Paris: Genèse Républicaine d'un Grand Décor," in *Le Triomphe des Mairies* (Paris, 1986). For an excellent discussion of the relation between Third Republic decorative campaigns and the transformation of the public sphere during this period see Marie Jeannine Aquilino, "Painted Promises: The Politics of Public Art in Late Nineteenth-Century France," *Art Bulletin* 75, no. 4 (1993): 697–712.

4 Puvis's easel paintings, *The Balloon* (1870) and *The Pigeon* (1871), which allegorized France during the siege, were circulated in lithographic form. Puvis's letters from the early 1870s indicate that he had no sympathy whatsoever with the Commune. See Conrad de Mandach, "Lettres de Puvis de Chavannes, 1871–6," *Revue de Paris* (1910): 684–85. In 1891, Puvis was one of several artists who refused to exhibit their work in Berlin. See Boyer d'Agen and Melchior, "Les Peintres à Berlin," *Le Figaro*, February 24, 1891, pp. 1–2.

5 Initially, a commission composed of state-appointed arts administrators, as well as a few municipal councilors, was constituted to oversee the decoration. Although the architect Théodore Ballu's recommendations for an allegorical decorative scheme were adopted in an agreement of 1884 with only slight modifications, this was hardly the end of the story. A prolonged debate arose in reaction to the original report. It focused on two questions: First, should artists be commissioned directly, or should such commissions be the result of an open competition among artists? Second, what kind of subject matter and painterly style was appropriate? The municipal council asked its own commission on art and architecture to issue a new set of recommendations, which was submitted in 1886. Finally, after two years of debate, a third commission composed of members of the state arts administration, the municipal council, and others knowledgeable in matters of art, was formed. The result was a compromise that called for some decorative schemes to be subject to direct command and others to be the result of open competitions. Puvis's commission for the Salon du Zodiaque was an example of the former. In fact, in choosing Puvis to decorate this room, the commission was following Ballu's suggestion in the decorative program of 1884. The controversy over the decorative scheme was largely a matter of the municipal government asserting its independence from the state, which still legally held control over it. In 1884, when Ballu submitted his recommendations, the state promised to contribute 300,000 francs for the decoration of the building. The reaction to Ballu's plan by the municipal council was so hostile that the prefect of the Seine provisionally withdrew the state's funds. The attack on Ballu's plan was launched by municipal council members on the extreme Left, including Abel Hovelaque, Yves Guyot, and Maurice Englehardt, bolstered by the Left moderates Paul Strauss and Louis Vauthier. See Imbert, "L'Hôtel de Ville de Paris."

6 Critics on the Left, especially those with progressive aesthetic tastes, never held out much hope that the Hôtel de Ville would offer anything but the usual fare in public decoration despite its populist pretensions. When the program for the commissions was set, Geffroy complained that the municipal council, despite its radical politics, had given control to a group that would reinforce the aesthetic status quo. It is noteworthy that when the 1886 report was debated, Geffroy came out in favor of the faction that argued for commissions rather than competitions. This he did for aesthetic reasons rather than in favor of antidemocratic principles. When the building was inaugurated in 1892, Geffroy reserved his praise for murals by Puvis de Chavannes and Eugène Carrière. It is tempting to think that he was referring to Puvis in 1888 when he predicted that the building would have very few spaces decorated by artists with "a sense of the decorative" and by certain landscapists who were also "gentle poets." Gustave Geffroy, "L'Hôtel de Ville de Paris," March 2, 1888, in *La Vie Artistique*, 184–85.

Fénéon was even more precise than Geffroy about what he would have liked to see decorating the building—"les apothéotiques couleurs de l'impressionnisme." He was not optimistic that this would come to pass. (In 1892 the Impressionist Claude Monet was rejected as a participant in the project.) Fénéon probably was pleased, in the end, with Puvis's being commissioned to paint the Salon du Zodiaque and later the Staircase of Honor. After all, when discussing the Sorbonne mural in the same essay, he named Puvis as the only artist who could successfully make allegory. Félix Fénéon. "Au Salon de 1887," in *Oeuvres plus que Complètes*, vol. 1. I thank Steven Z. Levine for information about Monet's rejection.

7 "Nous ne voulons pas . . . qu'il soit couvert d'allégories, c'est-à-dire de sujets qui ne correspond plus à l'idée contemporaine de l'art." Quoted in Imbert, "L'Hôtel de Ville de Paris," 67.

8 Ibid., 64.

9 Some images from the Revolutionary period were finally included in the Hôtel de Ville. For example, see J. P. Laurens's *La Voûte d'Acier, 17 Juillet 1789* in the Salon Lobau and E. Detaille's *The Enrollment of the Volunteers in 1792* and *Victory Leading the Armies of the Republic* in the Salon Detaille.

10 "A d'autres la gloire de chanter cette colossale mystification! . . . si Michelet vivait encore, on remplacerait avantageusement un dessin froid, menteur et prétentieux, par quelques alinéas du maître redressant les choses, les ramenant à leur point de départ,—et formant une sorte de catéchisme moral purifié de tous les mensonges historiques, et où les *devoirs* des hommes auraient autant de place que leurs *droits*." L. Wehrlé, "Lettres de Puvis de Chavannes, 1888–1898," 455.

11 The decorative scheme for the building also included works by Paul Baudoüin, Benjamin-Constant, Hippolyte Berteaux, Albert Besnard, Léon Bonnat, Urbain Bourgeois, Georges Callot, Eugène Carrière, Jules Cheret, Gustave Colin, Raphaël Collin, Fernand Cormon, Dagnan-Bouveret, François Flameng, Henri Gervex, Léon Glaize, Ferdinand Humbert, Jean-Paul Laurens, Jules Lefebvre, Henry Lerolle, Léon Lhermitte, Albert Maignan, Luc-Olivier Merson, Paul Millet, Tony Robert-Fleury, and Alfred Roll, among others. Many critics attributed its failure to the clash of painterly styles that resulted from the large number of artists participating. For a general discussion of the decorative scheme see Imbert, "L'Hôtel de Ville de Paris." For a discussion of the Hôtel de Ville as a "Tower of Babylon" see Aquilino, "Painted Promises," 706–8.

12 See *Puvis de Chavannes, 1824–1898* (Paris, 1977), 214–16.

13 "Du plus loin qu'on l'aperçoive, elle vous attire et vous enchante, rien que par ses masses et sa radieuse harmonie. Un ciel très clair; de lointains coteaux violets; une zone de verdure tendre coupée d'une bande de chaume blonde; . . . une rivière bleue qui traverse le paysage en une molle courbe; quelques arbres légers, bordant la rive, et dont les cimes montent vaporeusement vers l'azur; enfin, des personnages enveloppés dans l'ensemble, faisant partie intégrante de cette réalité rêvée." Louis de Fourcaud, "Le Salon de Champ de Mars," *Le Gaulois*, May 11, 1891, p. 1.

14 René Doumic, "Le Salon du Champ de Mars," *Moniteur Universelle*, May 24, 1891, pp. 558–59.

15 Critics who identified the figure as female include Alphonse de Calonne and Gustave Geffroy. Alphonse de Calonne, "Le Salon du Champ de Mars," *Le Soleil*, May 19, 1891, p. 2; Gustave Geffroy, "Salon de 1891," *La Justice*, May 22, 1891, p. 1.

16 Fouquier, "Le Salon"(1884), p. 2.

17 Geffroy, "Salon de 1884."

18 Alfred Ernst, "Le Salon de 1891 Champ de Mars," *Le Siècle*, May 14, 1891, p. 1.

19 Paul Bluysen, "A Travers le Salon du Champs de Mars," *La République Française*, May 14, 1891, p. 2.

20 Georges-Claudius Lavergne, "Beaux-Arts: Salon du Champ de Mars," *L'Univers*, May 21, 1891, p. 1.

21 Calonne, "Le Salon du Champs de Mars," 2; emphasis added.

22 Ibid.

23 Edmond Jacques, "Le Salon II: Au Champ de Mars," *L'Intransigeant*, May 15, 1891, p. 2.

24 Ibid.

25 "Ne suffirait cependant point à nos esprits, si nos yeux n'y trouvaient également leur compte, grâce à un sens incomparable de l'harmonie, de l'accord voluptueux des tons." Alfred Ernst, "Le Salon de 1891 Champ de Mars." *Le Siècle*, May 14, 1891, p. 1.

26 Jacques, "Le Salon II," 2.

27 Ibid.

28 Julia Kristeva has linked this notion of the maternal with the semiotic strategies associated with modernist form, in particular with an emphasis on large areas of saturated color in painting. Kristeva suggests that color exerts "an instinctual pressure linked to external visual objects; the same pressure causing an eroticization of the body proper [that is, the viewer's body] *via* visual perception and gesture." The experience of color taps into those instinctual drives, returning the viewer to a fantasy of the maternal. Thus the erotic pull of color threatens to break down the boundaries and hierarchies normally established by dominant semiotic systems. Kristeva imagines color as a kind of "freedom" and links it to the pre-Oedipal. Her description of the links of color to fantasies of origins is similar in many ways to responses to Puvis's paintings in the 1880s and 1890s. Interestingly, she uses statements by Matisse to support her theorization of the role of color in inciting fantasies of the maternal. Julia Kristeva, "Giotto's Joy," in Kristeva, *Desire in Language: A Semiotic Approach to Literature and Art*, trans. Leon S. Roudiez; ed. Thomas Gora, Alice Jardine, and Leon S. Roudiez (New York, 1980), 219. Matisse was drawing directly on a version of pastoral initiated by Puvis for his own painterly practice. See Werth, "'Le Bonheur de Vivre.'"

29 Roger-Milès, "Salon du Champ de Mars," *Le Soir*, May 14, 1891, supplement, 1.

30 Alphonse Germain, "Puvis de Chavannes et Son Esthétique," *L'Ermitage* 2, no. 3 (1891): 141.

31 William H. Robinson discusses both paintings in "Puvis de Chavannes's *Summer* and the Symbolist Avant-Garde," *Bulletin of the Cleveland Museum of Art* 78, no. 1 (1991): 2–25.

32 Karen Offen, "Depopulation, Nationalism and Feminism in Fin-de-Siècle France," *American Historical Review* 89 (1984): 648–76.

33 The indirect alignment of nation and mother—an association that necessitated the viewer's participation—sets *Summer* apart from more direct allegories of the Republic that also drew on maternal metaphors. Perhaps the most famous of these was Daumier's image of 1848. For a discussion of this work see T. J. Clark, *The Absolute Bourgeois: Artists and Politics in France, 1848–1851* (Princeton, N.J., 1982).

34 For an excellent account of these battles, an account that sets Puvis de Chavannes's work in the 1880s and 1890s into the context of pastoral painting in France at the turn of the century and has implications for a more general understanding of classicism during this period, see Werth, "'Le Bonheur de Vivre.'"

35 René Maizeroy, "Le Salon du Champ de Mars," *Gil Blas*, May 15, 1891, pp. 1–2.

36 "Le morceau capital est *l'Eté*. . . . Ceci vous transporte vraiment dans les temples Serena dont parle Lucrèce, dans les régions supérieures de la nature, de la poésie, et de l'art. C'est un éblouissement doux. Le rêve virgilien, dans sa pureté et sa grandeur rustiques, est ici transporté sur les bords de la Saône . . . ou de la Seine. Une rivière roulant des eaux bleues traverse une prairie au milieu de laquelle se dressent, en architecturale silhouette, de sombres et vigoureux châtaigniers. Un frais rideau de peupliers d'Italie s'agite doucement à la brise d'été, tandis qu'au pied des lauriers sacrés, qui peut-être aussi sont des saules, des femmes d'une beauté antique, que l'on dirait sorties vivantes du ciseau de Phidias, s'essuient au sortir du bain sur l'herbe tendre de la rive. Cependant les moissonneurs, de leurs fourches agiles, chargent de foin le chariot, à la fois antique et moderne, qui a traversé les âges en conservant sa simple structure rustique, chariot auquel se trouve attelée un couple de boeufs calmes et résignés." Charles Frémine, "Le Salon du Champ de Mars," *Le Rappel*, May 15, 1891, p. 2.

37 André Michel, "Les Salons de 1891," *Journal des Débats*, May 14, 1891, p. 2.

38 "Nicolas Poussin . . . écri[t] à M. de Chantelou à propos de *Moise Sauvé des Eaux*: 'J'entends par le *mode*, la raison, la mesure et la forme dont je me sers dans tout ce que je fais et par lesquels je me sens obligé à demeurer dans de justes bornes et à travailler avec une certaine modération et ordre déterminés qui établissent l'ouvrage que je fais dans son être véritable.' Et après quelques mots sur les *ordres* grecs, il ajoutait: 'Je me conduis d'après ces idées: c'est aussi ce qu'on doit observer dans mes ouvrages dans lesquels selon les différents sujets qu'ils traitent, je tâche non seulement de représenter sur les visages des figures les passions différentes et conformes à leurs actions, mais encore d'exciter et de faire naître les mêmes passions dans l'âme de ceux qui voient mes tableaux.'" Ibid.

39 "Si le *symbolisme* n'est en effet qu'une forme renaissante du très ancien désir de noter ou de susciter entre certains états d'âme ou d'imagination et la matière inerte de nos oeuvres, entre notre pensée ou notre rêverie et la nature inanimée, une correspondance mystérieuse et des réactions efficaces, n'a-t-on pas le droit de dire que le paysage classique, tel qu'il fut compris par Poussin en ses admirables *bacchanales*, est l'oeuvre symbolique par excellence et qu'à y regarder d'un peu près il n'y a pas de solution de continuité de Poussin à Puvis de Chavannes, du peintre du *Moise Sauvé des Eaux* et des *Bergers d'Arcadie* à celui de *l'Enfance de Sainte Geneviève*, des *Vendanges de la Terre Promise* et du *Ruth et Boas* à *l'Eté* qui resplendit au Salon du Champ de Mars?" Ibid. Michel is comparing Puvis's work to Poussin's paintings of the seasons—*Vendanges de la Terre Promise*, which represents Autumn, and *Ruth et Boas*, an image of Summer, both in the Louvre.

40 "*L'Eté* de M. Puvis de Chavannes . . . est donc un paysage classique, c'est-à-dire que, fidèle à sa tendance vers les synthèses plastiques, à la recherche, en toutes choses, de l'expression la plus générale et du signe le plus compréhensif, le maître a voulu résumer, dans un ensemble concerté de formes et de couleurs, les caractères essentiels de la chaude saison." Ibid.

41 "C'est l'Eté en soi, absolu, éternel." Ibid. The painter Camille Pissarro proposed a vision of agrarian France at precisely the same moment in his *Two Young Peasant Women*. See Clark, *Farewell to an Idea*, chap. 2, especially 121–27. For a discussion of the idealization of agrarian France between the two world wars see Romy Golan, *Modernity and Nostalgia: Art and Politics in France Between the Wars* (New Haven, 1995).

42 "Par le rythme, l'ordonnance éloquente et simple des lignes, les résonances puissantes et douces des larges tonalités juxtaposées, c'est un admirable morceau d'architecture naturelle et c'est en même temps l'expression la plus intense et comme l'exaltation plastique des ardeurs, des fécondités et des splendeurs de Messidor." Michel, "Les Salons de 1891," 2.

43 "Ce sont de grandes et fortes créatures, vite indiquées, sommairement modelées, surtout conçue en vue de l'ensemble d'attitudes et de carnations en harmonie avec le paysage qui s'étage au-dessus d'elles, et célébrant l'été par la joie saine de leurs corps mouillés et de leurs placides visages." Geffroy, "Salon de 1891," 1.

44 "Et voici, au sommet de cette belle pente cultivée, au milieu de ces champs, au-delà des arbustes légers, sous le ciel profond et lumineux pénétré par l'ardeur du soleil, voici un centenaire impénétrable massif d'arbres, sombre, chenu, opaque, dressé au centre de cette clarté de cette fluidité de l'air. Toute l'ombre de la vallée est amassée là, dans les interstices du feuillage qui sont comme des fentes, des crevasses de rochers, au ras du sol, autour des troncs énormes, trapus, chargés de ramures basses." Ibid.

45 It is tempting to analyze this passage in Freudian terms and read the dark "clefts" and "crevices" as vaginal imagery. The relegation of this aspect of the imagery to one discrete part of the mural could then be read as an attempt to ward off castration anxiety by picturing a pre-Oedipal space throughout the rest of the image. Relevant Freudian texts would include *The Interpretation of Dreams*, "Fetishism," and "The Passing of the Oedipus Complex," all found in Sigmund Freud, *The Standard Edition of the Complete Psychological Works*, trans. James Strachey (London, 1953–1974).

46 "Ça et là, l'activité humaine apparaît. Sur l'eau bleue un bateau passe, une femme assise à l'arrière, un homme debout à l'avant, jetant un filet. Une femme s'abrite avec un enfant à l'ombre de saules. Des travailleurs vont et viennent autour d'un chariot d'herbages. Tout cela disséminé, perdu dans la campagne, les personnages se confondant à demi avec les choses, les êtres vivants teintés des reflets roses et verts de la lumière et du sol. C'est la vie d'un jour qui s'agite et qui défile autour de ce formidable massif d'arbres, si ancien, d'apparence si farouche, si écrasante, si durable, qu'on pourrait le croire sans commencement et sans fin, immuable, éternel." Geffroy, "Salon de 1891."

47 "Il est beau de fixer ainsi le décor dans lequel nous vivons, le décor dans lequel nous promenons notre vain désir de bonheur, le songe mystérieux, sans explication possible, de notre destinée. Les choses sont expressives et parlantes, nous savons quels liens nous unissent à tout ce qui nous entoure, nous savons que nous faisons partie de cet univers qui déroule autour de nous son mirage, et notre sympathie spirituelle et notre joie et notre mélancolie s'en vont vers ces aspects de la matière qui existaient avant nous, qui existeront après nous. C'est la haute raison d'être d'une poésie éloquente et attractive comme la poésie de cet *Eté* de Puvis de Chavannes. L'artiste a su faire parler à notre esprit les nues, les eaux, les champs, les arbres, toute cette nature insensible où nous nous réfugions comme auprès d'une complice et d'une confidente." Ibid.

48 "Ici, au coeur de Paris, dans cet Hôtel de Ville reconstruit sur des ruines, après tant de feu et tant de sang, dans la pleine et visible évolution sociale d'aujourd'hui" "au grand artiste qui traduirait nos tressaillements en images de beauté inquiète" "le vouloir de justice qu'on sent frémir dans les masses nouvelles, l'équité philosophique des éclairés" "inconscience de la nature, éternel décor de tous nos sentiments et de toutes nos passions." Geffroy, "L'Hôtel de Ville" (1892), pp. 195–96.

49 Other examples of those who joined the two include the critics Alphonse Germain and Camille Mauclair, the painter Maurice Denis, and the writer Paul Desjardins.

50 Vogüé, "Devant l'Eté," in *Regards Historiques et Littéraires* (Paris, 1892), 346.

51 "De cette terre maternelle, des hommes sont nés; des êtres anciens et simples, qui ont élevé au degré humain, sans la dénaturer, la vie de ces eaux, de ces champs et de ces bois. Ils travaillent, mais leur travail n'évoque ni l'idée de peine, ni l'idée de gain; c'est un rite, une communion avec la Mère." Ibid.

52 Vogüé's description of primordial memory is much like the one proposed nearly a century later by Pierre Nora. Acknowledging the deep and conservative roots of this definition of memory should make us wary of taking up Nora's formulations with an uncritical eye. Pierre Nora, "Between Memory and History: *Les Lieux de Mémoire*," *Representations* 26 (Spring 1989): 7–25.

53 "Ils disent qu'il y a des fautes de dessin, de la mollesse et de l'indécision dans les contours. C'est bien possible; je n'en sais rien, ne m'étant pas approché. Qu'avaient-ils besoin de s'approcher, avec leur loupe, leur compas, leur trousse d'instruments critiques à déchirer le rêve?" Vogüé, "Devant l'Eté," 345.

54 "Il faut regarder ainsi, de loin, la terre promise de M. Puvis de Chavannes; il faut s'arrêter à trente pas, mieux encore à quarante, oublier le monde ambiant, qui a la folle prétention d'être le monde réel, et laisser lentement pénétrer dans les yeux, descendre dans l'âme, s'insinuer dans tout l'être l'indicible sérénité répandue sur ce tableau." Ibid., 346.

55 "On les aime, ces filles anonymes de la Terre, parce qu'elles sont les formes complaisantes, disponibles, où chacun de nous incarne les idées, les sentiments, les souvenirs qui peuplent pour lui ces campagnes. Elles sont les absentes et les mortes de chacun, celles qui se lèvent des pays où l'on a passé, nous rapportant les parts de vie déjà perdues. Car chacun de nous est par morceaux dans beaucoup de tombes; il restera très peu de chose à mettre dans celle qui portera notre nom, où l'on croira nous enfermer tout entier." Ibid., 349–50.

56 "Il faudrait rester ici le soir. Comme ses figures doivent gagner, comme l'Eté doit être beau, quand la lune monte derrière la forêt! Et la lune y vient sûrement. . . . A sa clarté, ces femmes doivent se mouvoir harmonieusement. Durant le

temps que la nuit libère ces formes immobiles, le site vague deviendrait peut-être le site ressouvenu, les images impersonnelles deviendraient les images appelées. Pourquoi ferme-t-on sitôt?" Ibid., 350.

57 "Si j'étais roi en Bavière, je ferais enlever les cadres inutiles qui dispersent l'attention. . . . Si j'étais roi en Bavière, je ferais graver sur le panneau, autour de *l'Eté*, des poésies harmoniques avec l'oeuvre du peintre, en belles lettres grecques de pourpre, les vers d'Homère . . . en lettres d'azur, les vers de Virgile . . . en lettres d'or, les grands vers calmes de Leconte de Lisle. . . . Si j'étais roi en Bavière, je placerais dans la salle voisine un orchestre invisible, qui jouerait la *Symphonie Pastorale*; et chaque jour, après le conseil, je viendrais oublier ici les sottises que m'auraient contées mes ministres, j'y viendrais oublier tout ce qu'un roi doit souffrir, quand il pense au mal qu'on fait sous lui—Si j'étais reine en Bavière, je crèverais cette toile, pour voir les horizons qu'elle fait pressentir par delà ceux qu'elle montre; je crèverais l'illusion, et je trouverais le mur, le mur qu'on trouve toujours, le mur qui est derrière tout." Ibid., 350–51.

58 "Je crois bien qu'ils s'arrêteraient devant *l'Eté*, comme ils s'arrêtent pour entendre une chanson du pays; leurs poumons respireraient une bouffée d'air natal; ils y retrouveraient ce qu'ils vont chercher le dimanche aux portes de la ville, un peu de communication avec la terre d'où ils furent arrachés. Pour eux aussi, il y a de la paix et de la souvenance dans cette évocation du berceau." Ibid., 352.

59 "Eternelle, indifférente, elle verra se succéder, comme les foins fauchés, ses maîtres d'un jour; elle les nourrira avec la même indulgence, parce qu'ils sont tous ses enfants. . . . Elle leur enseignera, par surcroît, la vérité, la piété; elle leur dira toujours qu'il fallut un Dieu pour la faire si belle. . . . Une station devant *l'Eté*, le matin, c'est le meilleur cordial pour recharger la vie avec soumission." Ibid., 353–54.

60 The position of the queen has strong parallels to the position assigned to Woman in Lacanian psychoanalysis. It would be possible to trace a genealogy of Lacan's gendered description of subjectivity that stretches back to the 1890s and French Symbolism. Steven Levine discusses this Lacanian genealogy with relation to the reception of Monet's work by Symbolist critics; see Levine, *Monet, Narcissus and Self-Reflection*. Werth draws on Vogüé's passage to give an explicitly Lacanian reading of *Summer*. She maps psychoanalytic terms onto the very bodies of the female figures: "In a reading that responds to Vogüé's, I would argue that the Bather-Nymphs represent the Maternal Body as a vessel for the Law of the Father—the idealization of both *la nature maternelle* and *les morts*—but that this conflation of Mother and Father has turned out to be an image of ambivalence and oscillation. The disruption of bodily unity contradicts the pastoral myth of presence, the myth of Culture grounded in Nature. The fantasied Father-Beholder who completes the fictions of family, maternity, and femininity in the image is not securely positioned vis-à-vis the image of idyll." Werth, "'Le Bonheur de Vivre,'" 126–27.

61 Vogüé, "Devant l'Eté," 357.

62 Geffroy, "Salon de 1892," in *La Vie Artistique*, vol. 2 (Paris, 1893), 196.

63 André Michel, "Les Salons de 1892, III," *Journal de Débats*, May 28, 1892, p. 1.

64 "La sérénité de la vie et la bonté résignée de l'humanité, devant le spectacle endeuillé mais bienfaisant de la nature"; "non pas un des maîtres de notre école française, mais le maître, devant qui on s'incline avec respect." L. Roger-Milès, "Le Salon du Champ de Mars," *Le Siècle*, May 6, 1892, supplement. (Also appeared in *Le Soir*, May 6, 1892, supplement.)

65 Clark, *Absolute Bourgeois*, 79–81. The historian Georges Dupreux's characterization of forest workers seems apt here: "As for the workers of the forest, faggot-gatherers, woodcutters, and charcoal-burners, they are recruited by the owners of the forest or the timber-contractors for only a few months of the year: during the summer they look for work as day laborers. They live a life which is both isolated and collective: isolated because they work in the woods, cut off from any contact with the population; and collective because they do the work in teams and eat their meals in common, and because the working group becomes a veritable community. In this sense the proletariat of the forest is not altogether dissimilar to the industrial proletariat." Quoted in ibid., 80.

66 Eugène Richtenberger, "A Travers le Salon," *Le National de 1869*, May 7, 1892, supplement, pp. 1–2.

67 For example, René Doumic described the exchange like this: "une jeune femme donne du pain à un mendiant." Doumic, "Le Salon du Champ de Mars," *Le Moniteur Universel*, May 5, 1892, p. 495.

68 Roger Marx, "Le Salon de 1892: Champ de Mars," *Le Voltaire*, May 7, 1892, p. 1.

69 "La plaine s'étend et la mer, qui ne s'endort jamais, la mer sauvage où ne vont plus les barques." Marcel Fouquier, "Le Salon du Champ de Mars," *Le Dix-Neuvième Siècle*, May 7, 1892, pp. 1–2.

70 "Un père accroupi [qui] fait tendrement chauffer les pieds de son petit qui se pend à son col en un adorable mouvement d'affection, de curiosité et de plaisir." Roger-Milès, "Le Salon du Champ de Mars" (1892).

71 Marx, "Le Salon de 1892," 1.

72 Offen, "Depopulation, Nationalism and Feminism."

73 "Au centre de la composition, on aperçoit une sorte de 'trou' que ne remplissent pas les minces silhouettes des arbres dénudés et d'un charpentier minuscule qui dirige le travail des bûcherons. . . . Il semble qu'il manque là . . . quelque chose, que le panneau se creuse et fuit. . . . Or les lointains n'en sont pas limpides et clairs comme le furent ceux de *l'Eté* . . . c'est un amas de nuages gris et de neige épaisse qui tombent sur la composition et qui l'attristent. Il est évident qu'il faut aux conceptions décoratives de M. Puvis de Chavannes le cadre d'une nature sereine qui s'harmonise avec l'adorable aisance donnée par lui à ses figures." Paul Bluysen, "Le Salon du Champ de Mars," *La République Française*, May 6, 1892, pp. 1–2.

74 Doumic, "Le Salon du Champ de Mars" (1892), p. 495.

75 Bluysen, "Le Salon du Champ de Mars," 1.

76 "On y voit des gens occupés à des besognes divers. Les uns abattent des arbres et pour ce travail, malgré la neige qui recouvre la terre, ils ont le torse nu. Il est vrai qu'il s'agit de nos ancêtres, et que, comme chacun sait, ils étaient autrement solides que nous." "Le Salon au Champ de Mars," *La Lanterne*, May 7, 1892, p. 1.

77 "Ce qu'on ne trouvera pas ici, c'est une somme de réalité qui corresponde à ce mot farouche d'Hiver accepté comme programme. La tristesse de la dure saison est absente, et aussi sa froide et étincelante somptuosité. Cette neige est grise, sans contact avec la pure lumière des gels de décembre—ces personnages et ces groupes classiques: la vieille femme au bâton, les porteurs de fagots, l'homme qui réchauffe son enfant, le vieillard à l'abri, et surtout ces hommes à demi-nus qui abattent un arbre, ne font pas songer à la rigueur du temps, à l'atmosphère hostile, à la course brève de la lumière." Gustave Geffroy, "Salon de 1892," *La Justice*, June 3, 1892, n.p. (reprinted in *La Vie Artistique*, vol. 2 [Paris, 1893], 326–27).

78 "Les bois du lointain, le coteau dressé à l'horizon, donnent à parcourir aux yeux l'étendue coutumière des oeuvres de Puvis de Chavannes. Et c'est, sans doute, cette beauté en profondeur du paysage qui fait paraître, par comparaison, la mise en scène principale des premiers plans insuffisamment hivernale." Ibid., 327.

79 "Un heureux campement, d'une inaltérable sécurité, plutôt qu'ils n'imposent la poésie de l'hiver redoutable." Ibid.

80 "Une telle pensée se trouve ratifiée par ce défilé héroïque de chasseurs qui apparaît au-delà des grands arbres, qui se profile en cavalcade de bas-relief par de si justes mouvements d'hommes et de chevaux. Le rythme grec se retrouve ici, achève de rendre cet hiver passager, d'en faire apercevoir l'apparence conventionnelle." Ibid., 327–28.

81 "Une vision plus âpre de solitude et de silence, de ciel refroidi, de terre désolée—un hiver plus absolu—des personnages moins érigés en statues, davantage confondus avec cette nature dont ils font si étroitement partie—ce sont les désirs sincèrement exprimés devant le panneau décoratif de M. Puvis de Chavannes, malgré l'admiration éprouvée pour l'oeuvre si harmonieusement picturale et intellectuelle de ce grand artiste, ou plutôt à cause de cette admiration même qui n'admet ni les demi-satisfactions, ni les réticences." Ibid., 328.

82 Louis de Meurville, "Le Salon du Champ de Mars," *Gazette de France*, May 14, 1892, p. 2.

83 "des cavaliers qui reviennent de quelque farouche battue; précédés de leur meute et sonnant de l'oliphant à pleine gorge. Puis, aux premiers plans, des bûcherons qui jettent bas un grand arbre et un débris de temple, des miséreux qui s'abritent contre les aiguilles de la bise, qui se réchauffent à la flamme d'un briser." René Maizeroy, "Au Salon de 1892: Au Champ de Mars," *Gil Blas*, May 7, 1892, p. 1.

84 "Si l'hiver est cruel à ceux qui travaillent au dehors, à ceux qui n'ont ni pain ni foyer, il a ses plaisirs pour les riches. Dans le fond, sur la lisière du bois, on voit des chasseurs qui reviennent d'une chasse à courre, les chiens couplés, et les rabatteurs portant suspendu à une branche le cerf tué." Marius Vachon, *Puvis de Chavannes* (Paris, 1895).

85 "De beaux corps bien plastiques, bien galbeux, bien grecs," "ratatinés, assez semblables aux moines étriqués qu'il nous montrait dans sa *Vision chrétienne*." Alfred Paulet, "Le Salon du Champ de Mars," *Le Jour*, May 7, 1892, p. 1. The critic has conflated the titles *Ancient Vision* and *Christian Inspiration* in his discussion, but the tone of the passage makes it clear that he is criticizing the relation of *Winter* to the latter.

86 "Il se dégage de ce tableau une telle majesté, une telle noblesse, qu'il est impossible de n'y plus songer après qu'on l'a vu. Ces grands arbres, qui montent droits et parallèles, semblent les tuyaux d'un organe calme, délicieusement reposant, chante doucement dans votre cerveau, évoquant des rêves d'art primitif, pieux et consolants. . . . Avez-vous remarqué, lorsque la neige vient de tomber, ce silence impressionnant qui se fait immédiatement? C'est d'une chanson très grande, presque religieuse . . . la nature semble tirer son drap sur ses épaules et s'endormir en priant. . . . La France peut être fière d'un tel artiste à une époque où tout semble crouler dans la matérialité la plus dégradante. Chavannes est un symbole. Il faut aller à lui, parce que c'est un poète; il faut aller à lui parce qu'on anoblit; il faut aller à lui parce qu'il élève les coeurs et qu'à défaut d'autre chose, c'est déjà une grande consolation." G. Goetschy, "Au Champ de Mars," *Le Matin*, May 6, 1892, pp. 1–2.

87 A similar interpretation was given by Maizeroy, who described the painting as full of "solennité paisible, presque sacrée, élève et trouble l'âme comme certaines psalmodies d'orgue."

88 "C'est partout l'impression du froid, de la tristesse. Voici bien l'hiver, tueur de pauvres gens! Et certes, nul motif ne fut plus accessible et, partant, nul ne saurait être mieux en situation dans une maison commune; mais le haut, le rare mérite de l'oeuvre vient, à n'en point douter, de la conformité du sujet au génie, ou plus exactement de ce que la maîtrise de M. Puvis de Chavannes atteint son degré suprême dans l'expression de pareils symboles. . . . sa vision le port plutôt aux généralisations, aux synthèses, à l'évocation, dans leur rythme éternel, de ces spectacles de temps, de lieu, de sujets imprécis, qui sont l'histoire même de l'humanité; parmi ces spectacles, à mesure que le paysage prend, dans son oeuvre, une place considérable, sa préférence ira aux images de calme, de paix, de recueillement, qui rassérénent l'âme et lui ouvrent l'infini de la méditation et du rêve. Quels programmes conviennent à M. Puvis de Chavannes, on le pressent désormais, et voici, pour l'indiquer, par surcroît, sa palette éprise des modulations mineurs, de nuances dont les atténuations (rigoureusement subordonnées au cadre de pierre gris attendu) semblent annoncer l'architecture sévère des monuments élevés pour exalter le devoir civique et social." Roger Marx, "Le Salon de 1892: Champ de Mars," *Le Voltaire*, May 7, 1892, p. 1.

89 "A la fois très classique et tout à fait en dehors des formules banales enseignées dans les écoles." André Michel, "Les Salons de 1892, III," *Journal de Débats*, May 28, 1892, p. 1.

90 Ibid., 2.

91 "L'art de Puvis de Chavannes est de l'art français, sans alliage étranger, et c'est de l'art classique, au meilleur sens du mot.—Toutes les qualités de composition, d'éloquence, pourrait-on dire, et de pondération chère à notre génie s'y retrouvent avec ce goût de la grandeur que nous avons toujours aimée aussi à nos grandes époques. . . . par-dessus la tête des italianisants et des ultramontains, il donne la main aux vieux maîtres fondateurs de la tradition française—française et non latine ou romaine,—à ceux qui inventèrent *l'opus francigenum*." Ibid.

92 It is worth noting that Michel's analysis of Puvis was not pitched against anti-Semitism.

93 Aman Jean's article on Puvis's Sorbonne mural discussed in the previous chapter stands as an example of this. I might also point to Maurice Denis's enthusiasm for Puvis and to the fact that Puvis's student Alexandre Séon exhibited in the Salon de Rose+Croix. Puvis was invited to do so but refused.

94 "De toutes les erreurs qui se sont implantées chez nous depuis la Renaissance, la plus funeste a été de croire et de laisser dire que l'art du moyen âge n'était que confusion, mystère et alchimie. . . . M. Joséphin Péladan . . . continue de se propager que tout ce vieux monde . . . fut un composé de sorciers, de somnambules et de mystiques hallucinés. . . . ils avaient l'esprit clair, je vous assure, et leur idéalisme charmant allait sans le moindre ésotérisme, comme on dit si souvent aujourd'hui; ils mêlaient même à leurs grandes figures beaucoup de petits tableaux de genre où se reconnaît une verve populaire, une bonhomie familière pleine de saveur. . . . Et . . . c'est *l'Hiver* de Puvis de Chavannes qui nous a induits en ces digressions." Michel, "Les Salons de 1892," 2.

95 "Ce n'est pas par la subtilité des symboles, par la rareté des attributs ou l'ingéniosité des allusions littéraires que l'oeuvre plastique pourra nous toucher. Elle ne doit être ni une vague abstraction, ni un rébus ou une énigme, encore moins une scène de comédie. Il s'agit de réunir dans l'action la plus simple et l'unité décorative la mieux équilibrée les caractères principaux de la froide saison. Un enfant pourrait en donner le scénario: en hiver, on a froid; il neige; on coupe le bois; on chasse. N'allons pas chercher plus loin." Ibid., 1.

96 "Toutes les lignes, toutes les formes, le concert atténué de toutes les notes de couleur se résolvent dans une harmonie totale et dans un rythme général qui ne laisse à l'oeil ni à l'esprit aucune indécision et nous pénètrent, en même temps que de la beauté et de la majesté de l'éternelle nature, du sentiment de mélancolie et de pitié qui envahit le coeur aux temps durs de l'hiver." Ibid.

CONCLUSION

Epigraph: "l'idée fusa, à droite, à gauche, au centre, à l'Institut, au Napolitain, au café de Versailles, hanté des peintres déjà colons de Montparnasse et de Plaisance, dans les grands journaux et dans les petites revues, d'un banquet à Puvis de Chavannes." Gustave Kahn, "Et le Cher Baudelaire au Grand Coeur Douloureux!" *Silhouettes Littéraires* (Paris, 1925), 113.

1 The exhibition was held at the Durand-Ruel galleries in the end of 1894.

2 *La Plume*, no. 138 (special number devoted to Puvis de Chavannes), January 15, 1895, pp. 27–61. This issue of *La Plume* contained a biography of Puvis, an account of the banquet, including the texts of the speeches, essays on Puvis's life and works, and samples of poetry from the *Album des Poètes*, which was presented to Puvis and included poems dedicated to him—many addressing particular paintings—by more than a hundred writers, including Stéphane Mallarmé, Paul Verlaine, Gustave Kahn, Emile Verhaeren, Paul Fort, Alfred Jarry, Camille Mauclair, and Joachim Gasquet, just to name a few.

3 The banquet was organized by the sculptor Auguste Rodin. For a list of guests (there were hundreds of them) see *La Plume* (special number devoted to Puvis de Chavannes), 52–53. Among those who attended the banquet were various state officials, critics, writers, and artists including (just to name a small selection): Arsène Alexandre, Edmond Aman Jean, Edouard Aynard, Frederic Bartholdi, S. Bing, Eugène Boudin, Ferdinand Brunetière, Carolus-Duran, Pierre Carrier-Belleuse, Eugène Carrière, Cazin, Félicien Chaumpsaur, Jules Chéret, Henri Edmond Cross, Paul Durand-Ruel, Durand-Tahier, Léon Duvauchel, Charles Ephrussi, Henri de Fantin-Latour, Jules Ferry, Paul Gauguin, Gustave Geffroy, Henri Gervex, René Ghil, Jules Huret, Firmin Javel, Gustave Kahn, Gustave Larroumet, Jules Lemaître, René Maizeroy, Roger Marx, Charles Maurras, Charles Meissonnier, Catulle Mendès, Constantin Meunier, André Michel, Emile Michelet, Octave Mirbeau, Claude Monet, Dr. Louis Monod, Mathias Morhardt, Antonin Proust, Raffaelli, Ary Renan, Auguste Renoir, Edouard Rod, Auguste Rodin, Roger-Ballu, Roger-Milès, Félicien Rops, Edouard Schuré, Gabriel Séailles, Paul Signac, Jules Simon, Thiébault-Sisson, Vicomte E.-M. de Vogüé, and Emile Zola.

4 "Puvis était le grand peintre qui nous divisait le moins." Kahn, "Et le Cher Baudelaire," 112.

5 Fénéon noted the "summarizing drawing style" as well as the ordering of bodies, "some seated at right angles, others stretched out horizontally, others standing rigidly, as though by a modernizing Puvis." Félix Fénéon, "Les Impressionistes en 1886," in *Oeuvres* (Paris, 1948), 81 (originally published in *La Vogue*, 1886).

6 On Neoimpressionism and anarchism see John G. Hutton, *Neo-Impressionism and the Search for Solid Ground: Art, Science and Anarchism in Fin de Siècle France* (Baton Rouge, 1994); Eugenia W. Herbert, *The Artist and Social Reform: France and Belgium, 1885–1898* (New Haven, 1961). See also Ward, *Pissarro*.

7 See Wattenmaker, *Puvis de Chavannes and the Modern Tradition*.

8 See Werth, "Engendering Imaginary Modernism."

9 Léonce Bénédite, "L'Exposition des Oeuvres de M. Puvis de Chavannes," *L'Artiste* (1888): 33–37.

10 Judith Gautier, "Exposition des Oeuvres de Puvis de Chavannes," *Le Rappel*, November 20, 1887, p. 3. Indeed, this notion was encouraged by the catalogue for the exhibition, which began with a description of the "agitation" and "noise" of daily life that melted away when one entered into the "peace" and "calm" of the exhibition. The catalogue was written by Roger-Ballu. See "Chronique," *La France*, December 1, 1887, for the opening lines of the preface.

11 Furetières, "Paris Vivant, l'Exposition Puvis de Chavannes," *Le Soleil*, November 29, 1887, p. 2.

12 Henri Matisse, "Notes of a Painter," in *Matisse on Art*, ed. Jack D. Flam (New York, 1908), 38. "Ce que je rêve, c'est d'un art d'équilibre, de pureté, de tranquillise, . . . qui soit, pour tout travailleur cérébral . . . un lénifiant, un calmant cérébral, quelque chose d'analogue a un bon fauteuil qui le délasse de ses fatigues physiques." Matisse, "Notes d'un Peintre," in *Ecrits et Propos sur l'Art*, ed. Dominique Fourcade (Paris, 1972), 50.

13 Kahn, "Cher Baudelaire," 117. Kahn gave the young poets' point of view: "Even corrected by the poem, the speech promised to Brunetière still offended us. Perhaps we should not attend the banquet. But it was necessary to consider that Puvis was certainly completely innocent in this business. We attended en masse."

14 "L'unité du moi dans une diversité d'états d'âme successifs . . . de le rendre à la volupté vagabonde du rêve." Brunetière, "Le Symbolisme Contemporain," 685.

15 "Je n'ai pas accepté en dernier lieu, de parler au banquet Chavannes, pour bien des raisons. . . . Il eût été bon, pourtant, qu'une voix revendiquât Puvis de Chavannes au-dessus des Instituts, dont, par la malchance fâcheuse, ce banquet va être la fête! Ironie des choses!" Octave Mirbeau, *Correspondance avec Auguste Rodin*, ed. Pierre Michel and Jean-François Nivet (Tusson, Charente, 1988), 139: letter, ca. January 12, 1895.

16 "Vous n'avez point vu l'énigme dans le bleu, ni cherché de mystère dans le rouge." Brunetière, speech given at the banquet for Puvis de Chavannes, in *La Plume* (special issue), 49.

17 Brunetière, "Le Symbolisme Contemporain," 685.

18 "Si la couleur et la forme, en raison même du pouvoir de séduction qu'elles exercent sur nos sens, ont quelque chose de trop matériel parfois, vous les avez spiritualisées. En subordonnant la signification de la forme aux exigences de la pensée, vous l'avez simplifiée." Brunetière, speech, 49.

19 "Vous avez demandé à la nature le secret des harmonies enchanteresses qu'elle compose avec des éléments quelquefois si grossiers, vous vous en êtes rendu pleinement maître, et quand vous l'avez été, vous l'avez réduite au rôle d'interprète de l'idéal que vous trouviez en vous." Ibid.

20 "La nature ne vous a fourni qu'une matière ou qu'un prétexte." "Le pouvoir d'évoquer des visions . . . qui purifient les yeux des hommes." Ibid. Brunetière specifically mentioned *Ludus pro Patria*, Amiens; *The Sacred Grove Dear to the Arts and Muses*, Lyons; *Inter Artes et Naturam*, Rouen; and the Sorbonne mural.

21 "Vous avez rendu l'art à la dignité de sa fonction ou de sa mission sociale." Ibid.

22 "Le peintre comme le poète, a vraiment charge d'âmes." Ibid.

23 "Polissait son discours (ordre, pureté, majesté) et ciselait des pointes contre les impressionnistes. Respect de l'art . . . Beauté classique . . . unité. . . . Il disait son fait au modernisme." Kahn, "Cher Baudelaire," 115–16.

24 Maître! Nous célébrons votre gloire, et la nôtre.
Car, poètes fervents qui vous fêtent ici,
Nous avons, en ce jour, notre victoire aussi;
Le triomphe de Dieu fait honneur à l'apôtre.
Et tous viennent, avec des palmes dans la main,
Ceux d'autrefois, ceux d'aujourd'hui, ceux de demain,
Hugo, Gautier, du haut de leurs apothéoses
Et le cher Baudelaire au grand coeur douloureux,
Et De Lisle, et Banville, éclair des cieux heureux
Et nous de qui les fronts surchargés d'ans moroses
Se relèvent encore pour aimer ou prier,
Et la Jeunesse à tout cet antique laurier
Mêlant ses lauriers roses! (Catulle Mendès, in *La Plume,* special issue, p. 50)

25 Max Nordau, *Degeneration* (originally published in German, 1892; English-language edition, New York, 1895; reprint, Lincoln, Nebr., 1993), 11, 27. Nordau was a physician practicing in Paris and a follower of Caesar Lombroso, to whom the book was dedicated. See the introduction by George L. Mosse.

26 "Il n'est pas une idée nouvelle, une pensée noble qui ait trouvé grâce devant le pion qui férule à la *Revue des Deux Mondes.*" *La Plume* (special edition), 48.

27 "On peut dire qu'il n'y a pas un mot de ce discours contre lequel ne proteste de toute son énergie le grand enseignement de Puvis de Chavannes." Mathias Morhardt, "Le Banquet Puvis de Chavannes," *Mercure de France,* August 1, 1935, p. 528.

28 "Je connais peu d'hommes aussi réfractaires aux jouissances de l'art que les hommes de lettres. On compte ceux qui sont capable de les éprouver, et le compte en est vite réglé. . . . Non seulement ils ne le comprennent pas, mais ils vont jusqu'à en nier le caractère intellectuel et la puissance éducatrices. La plupart, ils le considèrent comme une perversion de l'intelligence, par conséquent comme un danger social. Pour eux, ce n'est qu'une des formes—et non la moins haïssable—de la basse sensualité, du vice et du crime." "Comme par miracle, échappé à cette loi de proscription." Octave Mirbeau, "Le Peintre de la Vie," *Le Gaulois,* June 26, 1897, p. 1 (reprinted in *Combats Esthétiques,* vol. 2, pp. 196–99).

29 "Une fois de plus l'art et la politique s'y affrontaient. Mais surtout, l'antagonisme qui divisait les admirateurs de Puvis de Chavannes en deux groupes irréductiblement ennemis dominait, de toute sa violence, l'unanimité de l'hommage qu'on rendait au maître illustre." Morhardt, "Banquet," 499.

30 An article in the conservative *Observateur Française* described the controversy that arose when excerpts from Brunetière's essay, which was to appear in the *Revue des Deux Mondes,* were published in *Figaro:* "M. Brunetière y a simplement constaté qu'un indéniable mouvement de réprobation s'était manifesté dans le monde pensant, depuis quelques années, à l'égard des doctrines matérialistes qui avaient été l'aliment intellectuel des lettrés, des politiques et des sociologues. . . . Là dessus *tolle* général, de la part surtout des publicistes politiques qui, relevant de l'ancienne école avec laquelle M. Brunetière a fait scission, ont applaudi, si nous pouvons ainsi parler, à la *matérialisation* de la politique, c'est-à-dire à ces abominables lois jacobines qui ont introduit par exemple le divorce dans nos codes, l'esprit antireligieux dans nos moeurs administratives, l'athéisme et le mensonge historique dans notre enseignement public. Le *Temps,* les *Républiques,* grande et petite, les journaux officieux même dont les directeurs sont à Mazas, enfin, chose plus surprenante, le *Journal des Débats* ont donné le concert. Que vaut leur argumentation? Elle se résume, en somme, à travestir la pensée de M. Brunetière et à l'accuser de méconnaître systématiquement les bienfaits de la science. M. Brunetière n'a rien conçu, rien imaginé de pareil." X.Z., "Sur un Controverse," *Observateur Français,* January 10, 1895, p. 1.

Often articles about Puvis were published side by side with responses to Brunetière's views on science. For example, in *Le Matin,* an article by Geffroy on Puvis appeared in the same issue as an article by Yves Guyot entitled "Où Est la Foi?" In it he described Brunetière's recent visit to the Vatican, where he was received by the pope, and aligned him with such neo-Christians as Vogüé and Desjardins, saying that devotion to the church was incompatible with liberty of thought. See also "La Banqueroute de la Science," *Dix-Neuvième Siècle,* January 15, 1895, p. 1; Bernard Lazare, "Le 'Banqueroute de la Science'" (and letters to the editor), *Echo de Paris,* January 12, 1895, p. 2; "Le Banqueroute," *Le Figaro,* January 3, 1895, p. 1.

31 André Michel, "Puvis de Chavannes," *Journal des Débats,* January 14, 1895, p. 1. The republican government's point of view was also given voice at the banquet in both a speech by the director of fine arts, M. Leygues, and (indirectly) in a speech by Jules Simon. In the state's view, Puvis's paintings were explicit signs of the glory of the French nation. M.

Leygues, for example, ended his very general and laudatory speech by declaring that Puvis had "held up the name of France and made *la patrie* more glorious and greater." "Discours de M. Leygues," *La Plume* (special issue), 47.

32 "La génération actuelle, en dépit de toutes les accusations portées contre elle, sait comprendre les vertus sociales et les admirer." Marius Vachon, "Puvis de Chavannes," *La Nouvelle Revue* (1895): 483. Vachon also wrote a biography of Puvis to coincide with the banquet. See Vachon, *Puvis de Chavannes* (Paris, 1895). Given that Vachon had conducted surveys for the arts administrations in the 1880s and continued to do so in the 1890s under the personal sponsorship of Méline, it seems safe to assume that his position would have been compatible with those promoted by the state. On Vachon see D. Silverman, *Art Nouveau*, 55.

33 "Une telle vie et une telle oeuvre protestent contre le pessimisme du temps. A travers cet oeuvre, j'ai voulu chercher à la fois l'artiste et l'ouvrier, dans la certitude de montrer en l'un et l'autre un beau type, qui sera la preuve vivante de la puissance de travail et de la volonté, au service d'une grande intelligence et d'un idéal supérieur." Vachon, "Puvis de Chavannes," 484.

34 "A fait entrer, comme forme, l'individu dans le groupe, et le groupe dans la collectivité." Ibid., 495.

35 "Le peintre aura soin de donner exclusivement à cet individu la couleur nécessaire pour le caractériser au point de vue de l'influence de l'être et du milieu sur sa physionomie." Ibid., 496.

36 "On a observé scientifiquement que le rouge produit dans le cerveau une vibration intense de chaleur," "les couleurs tendres, légères, lumineuses . . . le violet, qui, à l'opinion des savants, constitue actuellement l'étape la plus élevée du développement du sens visuel." Ibid. Scientists, Symbolist poets and avant-garde painters shared an interest in the physiology of the aesthetic. See Charles Henry, "L'Esthétique des Formes," *La Revue Blanche* 7, no. 34 (1894): 118–29, and the following series of articles. The interest of painters such as Seurat and the Nabis in Henry's theories is well known.

37 Wyzewa: "Tous les critiques d'art ont été unanimes, une fois de plus, à exalter le génie de celui qu'ils appellent 'le plus magnifique artiste de notre temps.' . . . Il m'a paru que notre culte pour l'art de M. de Chavannes était un phénomène psychologique tout à fait anormal, sans aucun rapport avec notre admiration pour le talent de tel ou tel autre peintre. . . . Une soif nous a pris de rêve, d'émotion et de poésie. Saturés d'une lumière trop vive et trop crue, nous avons aspiré au brouillard. Et c'est alors que nous nous sommes passionnément attachés à l'art poétique et brumeux de M. de Chavannes. . . . L'art de M. de Chavannes a ainsi été pour nous comme une guérison; nous nous sommes attachés à lui comme des malades à un traitement nouveau. Mais encore ne faut-il pas que le traitement, à son tour, devienne une maladie." Téodor de Wyzewa, "Une Exposition d'Oeuvres de Puvis de Chavannes," 1894, reprinted in *Peintres de Jadis et d'Aujourd'hui* (Paris, 1903), 364–70.

Kahn: "Puvis devint incontestable, national. Il n'y eut plus de monuments que pour lui." Kahn, "Cher Baudelaire," 113.

Maurras: "Je ne fais qu'y sentir, avec une volupté que je ne sais dire, un sentiment, un goût, une entente de l'art qui me donnent l'idée même de la perfection, d'une perfection fraternelle où je reconnais l'image que s'en fire depuis des siècles, les hommes de notre sang." Charles Maurras, "Le Goût de Puvis de Chavannes," *Gazette de France*, January 8, 1895, p. 2.

Herold: "S'il est un mot qui, aujourd'hui, semble exprimer une idée noble et pure, c'est le mot *patrie*; les gouvernements savent jouer de ce mot avec une adresse singulière, et des hommes qui détestent, et très sincèrement, les tyrannies, se laissent pourtant tyranniser, sans protester, au nom de la patrie. Qui oserait s'avouer non patriote?" A.-Ferdinand Herold, "Quelques Notes sur la Patrie et le Patriotisme," *Entretiens Politiques et Littéraires* 6, no. 37 (1893): 156.

38 Morhardt, "Banquet," 517.

39 Maurras's definitions of subjectivity and creativity were developed in a Symbolist context—in particular, through his association with Jean Moréas and the Ecole Romane, a group within the literary avant-garde that battled for control of the Symbolist movement. On Maurras see Michael Curtis, *Three Against the Third Republic: Sorel, Barrès, and Maurras* (Princeton, N.J., 1959).

40 See Eugen Joseph Weber, *Action Française: Royalism and Reaction in Twentieth-Century France* (Stanford, Calif., 1962).

41 Alain Pagès, *Emile Zola: Un Intellectuel dans l'Affaire Dreyfus* (Paris, 1991), 10.

42 In 1898, *Le Cri de Paris* retrospectively told the story. After Luce's arrest his friends started a petition, demanding that his "professor," M. Charles, sign his name at the top. Refusing to do so, Charles proposed this: "Go see Puvis. If he signs, I'll sign; I want to protect myself." At Puvis's studio Luce's supporters had more luck: "Brought up-to-date, the illustrious painter took a pen and added a long paragraph to the petition, saying with an exquisite, delicate smile: 'With pleasure, my friends, because it's a good cause.' Then after a time: 'Ah! Good L. is anarchistic, eh? . . . Well, well!' And, as if speaking to himself: 'After all, aren't we all a little anarchistic?'" "Puvis et M. Charle," *Le Cri de Paris*, November 6, 1898, p. 5. Although this story is perhaps somewhat apoc-

ryphal in its details, it does suggest that Puvis's signature at the head of a petition supporting an artist suspected of anarchist ties might have been taken as an alignment with the younger generation of artists and poets falling prey to government censorship for just that reason. His question "Aren't we all a little anarchistic?" could suggest solidarity with an anarchist worldview. Given the political slant of *Le Cri de Paris,* this story seems to claim Puvis for the causes on the Left. But it also seems to signal the ridiculousness of calling Luce an anarchist. We might imagine Puvis to imply that "if he was an anarchist, then so am I." Above all, it suggests the fluidity of the term *anarchist* at that moment, the recklessness with which it was bandied about, and its capacity to encompass figures as diverse as Octave Mirbeau, Félix Valloton, and sometimes Camille Pissarro. For a brilliant analysis of Pissarro's relationship to anarchism in the 1890s see Clark, *Farewell to an Idea*, chap. 2.

INDEX

Page numbers in bold indicate illustrations.

PHOTO CREDITS

Alinari/Art Resource, NY (fig. 41); Photograph © 1997, The Art Institute of Chicago. All Rights Reserved (fig. 50); Photograph © reproduced with the permission of The Barnes Foundation. All Rights Reserved (fig. 53); Photograph by Antoine Darnaud (fig. 51); © Charles Dufrêne (figs. 11, 22–23, 30); © Cleveland Museum of Art (fig. 46); Giraudon Bridgeman (fig. 31); Erich Lessing/Art Resource, NY (figs. 1, 2, 4); © Françoise Masson (fig. 42); © Photothèque des Musées de la Ville de Paris/Bridgeman Art Library (figs. 43, 44); © Photothèque des Musées de la Ville de Paris. Photograph by P. Pierrain (figs. 12–13, 47); Photograph © 2001 Board of Trustees, National Gallery of Art, Washington, D.C. (fig. 3); Photographie Bulloz (fig. 20); from A. Brown Price, *Pierre Puvis de Chavannes*, Amsterdam: Van Gogh Museum, 1994. Photograph by E. Bernard (frontispiece); © 1989 Trustees of Princeton University. Photograph by Clem Fiori (fig. 15); Réunion des Musées Nationaux/Art Resource, NY (figs. 36, 39); from P. Richer, *Etudes cliniques sur la grande hystérie ou hystéro-épilepsie*, Paris: Delahaye et Lecrosnier, 1885 (fig. 18); Photograph by Jennifer L. Shaw (figs. 5, 8–10, 16–17, 26, 32–34, 48–49); © Studio Basset (fig. 24); © 2002 Succession H. Matisse, Paris/Artist Rights Society (ARS), New York (fig. 52); from L. Trepsat, *Nouvelle Iconographie de la Salpêtrière*, vol. 17. Paris: Lecrosnier et Babe, 1904 (fig. 19)